This Book Comes With Lots of
FREE Online Resources

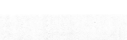

Nolo's award-winning website has a page dedicated just to this book. Here you can:

KEEP UP TO DATE. When there are important changes to the information in this book, we'll post updates.

GET DISCOUNTS ON NOLO PRODUCTS. Get discounts on hundreds of books, forms, and software.

READ BLOGS. Get the latest info from Nolo authors' blogs.

LISTEN TO PODCASTS. Listen to authors discuss timely issues on topics that interest you.

WATCH VIDEOS. Get a quick introduction to a legal topic with our short videos.

And that's not all.
Nolo.com contains thousands of articles on everyday legal and business issues, plus a plain-English law dictionary, all written by Nolo experts and available for free. You'll also find more useful **books, software, online apps, downloadable forms,** plus a **lawyer directory.**

Get updates and more at
www.nolo.com/back-of-book/SOA.html

23rd Edition

Social Security, Medicare & Government Pensions

Get the Most Out of Your Retirement & Medical Benefits

Attorney Joseph L. Matthews

TWENTY-THIRD EDITION

Editor

Production

Proofreader

Index

Printing

FEBRUARY 2018

BETH LAURENCE

SUSAN PUTNEY

SUSAN CARLSON GREENE

THÉRÈSE SHERE

BANG PRINTING

ISSN: 2163-6419 (print)
ISSN: 2325-3800 (online)

ISBN: 978-1-4133-2472-3 (pbk)
ISBN: 978-1-4133-2473-0 (epub ebook)

This book covers only United States law, unless it specifically states otherwise.

Please note

We believe accurate, plain-English legal information should help you solve many of your own legal problems. But this text is not a substitute for personalized advice from a knowledgeable lawyer. If you want the help of a trained professional—and we'll always point out situations in which we think that's a good idea—consult an attorney licensed to practice in your state.

Acknowledgments

Many thanks to Barbara Kate Repa for her considerable and thoughtful input to the content and structure of this book, and for her thorough editorial work on various drafts of the manuscript.

Later editions owe a large measure of thanks to Spencer Sherman, whose ideas for improvements to the book were extremely helpful, and to Ilona Bray, who guided several incarnations into existence with clarity and graciousness. And thanks to Marcia Stewart and Cathy Caputo, who brought fresh eyes, intelligence, and enthusiasm to the major revisions needed for recent editions of the book. Also, a large measure of credit to Stan Jacobsen, whose thorough ongoing research helps keep this book current and comprehensive.

Special thanks go to the National Council of Senior Citizens in Washington, DC, for many helpful suggestions on the original edition of the book, and to Bruce Campbell, Karen Fuller, and Sue Schwab of the Health Care Financing Administration office in San Francisco for their assistance in sorting out the many state variations in Medicaid.

Special thanks also to the Health Insurance Counseling and Advocacy Program and Legal Assistance for Seniors office in Oakland, California, as much for their example in tirelessly serving the interests of low-income seniors as for their suggestions for improving this book.

Finally, for the most recent editions, a large measure of gratitude goes to Beth Laurence, who not only did assiduous work as an editor but also brought her considerable knowledge and experience to bear on the materials in the book pertaining to disability benefits, and improved them considerably.

About the Author

Joseph L. Matthews has been an attorney since 1971. In the early years of his career, he taught at the law school of the University of California at Berkeley (Boalt Hall). Mr. Matthews is the author of *Long-Term Care: How to Plan & Pay for It, How to Win Your Personal Injury Claim*, and *The Lawsuit Survival Guide: A Client's Companion to Litigation*, all published by Nolo.

Table of Contents

Your Social Security, Medicare & Government Pensions Companion

A re you approaching retirement, or are you disabled? Do you help support someone who is?

If so, you may be facing a series of problems for which you are unprepared: getting the most retirement and pension income and obtaining the broadest medical coverage you can afford. People in their retirement years may have access to a wide variety of programs to help with financial support and medical care. But many people are unaware of the extent of such programs, or are unable to wade through the programs' rules and regulations, and so do not receive all the benefits they could.

For people who are or soon will be on fixed incomes, an unnecessary loss of benefits can cause critical problems. This book is intended to help you get all the benefits to which you are entitled: Social Security (both retirement and disability based), Supplemental Security Income, veterans benefits, and civil service benefits.

Most people want the broadest possible medical coverage they can afford, because a serious medical problem can cost a fortune. Almost everyone is aware that Medicare is available, but few people understand how it works and what it does and does not cover. This book carefully, completely, and in plain language explains Medicare rules and regulations. It also explains how the holes in Medicare can be filled by medigap private insurance, Medicare Advantage health plans, Medicaid, and veterans benefits.

Locating Chapters That Fit Your Needs

Each chapter in this book explains a different benefit program or set of laws designed to protect the rights of older Americans. It explains how each particular program works, and how it may relate to the other programs discussed in the book. Not all of these benefits will apply to you. But, even if you don't think you are eligible for a particular benefit, take a look at the general requirements discussed in that chapter. You may be surprised to find that a program, or some part of it, applies to you in ways you had not previously realized. Pay special attention to explanations of how your income, or your participation in one benefit program, might affect your rights in another program.

> **TIP**
>
> **You have earned these benefits.** A key word in this book is "entitled." Almost all of the benefits discussed here are paid to you because you worked for them, paying contributions into the system throughout your working life. If you are an older American facing retirement and a fixed income, you need all the financial support these programs are supposed to provide. And you are entitled to it.

> **RESOURCE**
>
> **Private pensions and 401(k) deferred benefit plans** are far more complex than can be covered in a book of this breadth. We recommend that you consult *IRAs, 401(k)s & Other Retirement Plans: Strategies for Taking Your Money Out*, by Twila Slesnick and John C. Suttle (Nolo).

Depending on your age and stage of life, there are a number of major issues you should consider as you first scan through the book.

If You Are 60 to 62 and Not Yet Retired

- Find out how soon (at what age) you will become eligible for Social Security retirement, dependents, or survivors benefits. (See "Timing Your Retirement Benefits Claim" in Chapter 2.)
- Learn how much your Social Security retirement benefits will be reduced if you retire early or increased if you retire later. (See "Timing Your Retirement Benefits Claim" and "The Amount of Your Retirement Check" in Chapter 2.)
- Explore when would be the best time to claim your benefits, and which benefits to claim. (See Chapter 6.)
- Find out how much income you can earn without affecting your Social Security benefits if you claim them before full retirement age. (See "Working After Claiming Early Retirement Benefits" in Chapter 2.)
- See whether you can claim civil service retirement benefits if you have ever worked for the federal, state, or local government or any public agency or institution—such as a school system, library, or public health facility. (See Chapter 10.)

- Check the rules of your private pension plan—if you worked for any private company that had a pension plan, or if you belonged to any union—including whether your pension will be affected by your Social Security benefits. (Private pension plans are outside the scope of this book.)

This Book Provides Ongoing Help to Caregivers

People in their 60s must make initial decisions about Social Security, Medicare, and other benefit programs. But over the years, people will also have to make new decisions, concerning how they receive their Medicare coverage, choose medigap insurance or prescription drug plans, qualify for long-term care insurance benefits, and determine eligibility for Medicaid and other programs for people with low incomes. This book serves as a guide for caregivers, such as adult children, who may not have been involved in original choices about these matters, but who now must help loved ones make ongoing decisions over time.

If You Are Within Six Months of Your 65th Birthday

- If you have not already claimed retirement benefits, obtain a current estimate of the benefits you could receive from your civil service retirement system, the private pension plan of any company where you've worked for at least three years, Social Security, and the Department of Veterans Affairs if you are a veteran. (See Chapters 10 and 11.)
- Be ready to claim your Medicare coverage as soon as you become eligible. (See Chapter 12.)
- Look into ways to supplement your Medicare coverage, including medigap insurance, a Medicare Advantage plan, and a Medicare drug coverage plan. (See Chapters 12, 14, and 15.)
- If you have low income and few assets, check into your eligibility to receive assistance with medical bills from Medicaid. (See Chapter 16.)

If You Are 65 or Older

- If you have a low income and few assets, see whether you can get financial assistance from the Supplemental Security Income (SSI) program. (See Chapter 7.)
- Arrange for your access to medical treatment, after reading about the Medicare rules as well as those of a Medicare Advantage or medigap insurance plan. (See Chapters 13, 14, 15, and 16.)
- If you have low income and few assets other than your home, see whether you are eligible for Medicaid or for expanded Medicare coverage for prescription drugs. (See "Part D Prescription Drug Coverage" in Chapter 12; and Chapter 16.)
- If you were in the military, see whether you can claim financial or medical benefits from the Department of Veterans Affairs (VA). (See Chapter 11.)

If You Are Within Six Months of Your 66th Birthday

If you have not already claimed Social Security retirement benefits, obtain a current estimate of the benefits you could receive when you reach full retirement age, which is now 66. (See Chapter 1.)

If You Can Work Very Little or Not at All
Because of a Physical or Mental Condition

- Look into whether you might qualify for Social Security disability benefits. (See Chapter 3.)
- If you have low income and few assets, see whether you might qualify for Supplemental Security Income (SSI). (See Chapter 7.)
- If you were in the armed forces and your physical condition is in any way related to your time in the service, investigate the qualification rules for veterans disability benefits and medical care. (See Chapter 11.)

If You Are a Spouse, Minor Child, Surviving Spouse or Child, or Former Spouse of a Worker Who Is Retirement Age

- Learn whether you're eligible for Social Security or civil service survivors or dependents benefits. (See Chapters 4 and 5.)
- Obtain an estimate of your own retirement benefits, and compare them to estimates of survivors or dependents benefits.
- Check the rules of the pension plan of any company or government entity for which your spouse worked for more than three years. (See Chapter 10 for government pensions.)
- If you or your spouse were in the military, look into whether you are entitled to any veterans benefits. (See Chapter 11.)

If You Are Age 60 or Older and Are Considering Getting Married

- Find out what effect marriage would have on your right and your intended spouse's right to collect Social Security retirement, survivors, and dependents or disability benefits, and on the amount of those benefits. (See "The Amount of Your Retirement Check" in Chapter 2; and Chapters 4 and 5.)
- Determine what effect marriage would have on your and your intended's eligibility for Supplemental Security Income (SSI) and Medicaid. (See Chapters 7 and 16.)

A Note for Same-Sex Spouses

Two United States Supreme Court cases—one ordering the payment of federal benefits to same-sex married couples, the second upholding the constitutional right to same-sex marriage—have made clear that same-sex spouses are entitled to federal benefits such as Social Security dependents and survivors payments, veterans spousal benefits, and Medicare, on exactly the same terms as for other spouses. These benefits may also be available retroactively to same-sex married couples who filed for Social Security benefits before June 26, 2015, the date of the same-sex marriage decision. For rules concerning particular benefits for spouses, refer to the chapters in the book that explain those benefits.

Living Together: Unofficial Marriages and Benefit Programs

Your eligibility for certain benefits and the amount of those benefits may depend on your marital status. Although Social Security and other programs provide a number of benefits to the spouse of a worker, they do not provide for people who live together without being married even if they are registered domestic partners or have entered into a civil union under their state's laws.

On the other hand, your eligibility for some benefits may depend on the combined amount of income and assets of you and your spouse. If you are not married, your partner's income and assets won't be considered, so you are more likely to be eligible for benefits.

Many people who live together believe they have a common law marriage —a legally recognized marriage—even though they never went through a formal ceremony, took out a marriage license, or filed a marriage certificate.

In fact, common law marriages are recognized only in Alabama, Colorado, the District of Columbia, Iowa, Kansas, Montana, Oklahoma, Rhode Island, South Carolina, Texas, and Utah. In Georgia, Idaho, Ohio, and Pennsylvania, common law marriages are recognized only if they were formed before a certain date. If you do not live in one of these states and meet your state's particular requirements, you do not have a common law marriage.

If you do live in one of these states, you will be considered to have a common law marriage only if you and another person intend to be considered as married. You can show this in a number of ways—including living together as husband and wife for several years, using the same last name, referring to yourselves as married, having children together and giving them the family name you share, and owning property together. You can even write out an agreement that says you regard yourselves as being in a common law marriage. However, there is no one thing you can count on to absolutely prove the existence of your common law marriage. And nothing guarantees that Social Security or other programs will consider you married when making a decision about your benefits.

Finally, if either you or the person with whom you live is still lawfully married to someone else, there can be no common law marriage.

Online Help on Social Security, Medicare, and Other Government Programs

The Internet has greatly increased public access to information about government programs. But not all this information is created equal. Plenty of information on the Web is helpful, but there is also a lot of confusing or misleading material. The government's own websites—like Social Security's www.ssa.gov and Medicare's www.medicare.gov—contain a huge amount of material, but the sites themselves can be hard to navigate.

This book will point you to some of the most useful Internet tools and information from government websites covering retirement, pension, and medical benefits programs. If you find information on your own from nongovernment Web sources, make sure to confirm its accuracy on an official site before you use it to make a decision.

Get Updates to This Book and More on Nolo.com

When there are important changes to the information in this book, we'll post updates online, on a page dedicated to this book:

www.nolo.com/back-of-book/SOA.html

You'll find other useful information there, too, including author blogs, podcasts, and videos.

Social Security: The Basics

S
ocial Security is the general term that describes a number of related programs—retirement, disability, dependents, and survivors benefits. These programs operate together to provide workers and their families with some monthly income when their normal flow of income shrinks because of the retirement, disability, or death of the person who earned that income.

The Social Security system was initially intended to provide financial security for older Americans. It was meant to help compensate for limited job opportunities available to older people in our society. And it was intended to help bridge the financial gaps created by the disappearance of the multigenerational family household—a breakup caused in large measure by the need for American workers to move around the country to find decent employment.

Unfortunately, this goal of providing financial security is today increasingly remote. The combination of rapidly rising living costs, stagnation of benefit amounts, and penalties for older people who continue to work has made the amount of support offered by Social Security less adequate with each passing year. This shrinking of the Social Security safety net makes it that much more important that you get the maximum benefits to which you are entitled.

This chapter explains how Social Security programs operate in general. It is helpful to know how the whole system works before determining whether you qualify for a particular benefit program and how much your benefits will be. Once you understand the basic premises of Social Security, you will be better equipped to get the fullest benefits possible from all Social Security programs for which you might qualify. (See Chapters 2, 3, 5, and 6.)

History of Social Security

Public images of our society generally render invisible many millions of economically hard-pressed older Americans. The older person with little income and assets is left out of the standard media pictures of two-car, two-kid suburbanites and of wealthy retired couples in gated luxury communities. Modern Western capitalism produces expendable workers. And the most vulnerable, such as people older than 65, are the most easily expended.

In what is commonly thought to be the most advanced of modern societies, the United States, there is a shockingly large economic gap between most working people and the wealthy few. The richest 1% of U.S. households control over 42% of the nation's financial wealth, with the richest 10% controlling over 85% of that wealth. On the other end, the lower 80%—that is, the vast majority of us—control less than 10% of the nation's financial wealth, with the bottom 40% having less than 1%.

During periods of extreme economic retrenching, the number of people cast off by the economy spills over the normal barriers of invisibility. And with so many people during these crises sharing their complaints about economic injustice, it is sometimes difficult to keep them all under control. One such period of extreme economic dislocation was the Depression of the 1930s. Many millions of people were displaced—not only from job, home, and family, but from any hope for a place in the economy.

The Beginning of Social Security

Faced with the crisis of the Depression and with the possibility of massive social upheaval, Franklin Roosevelt and Congress decided to act. Roosevelt pushed through a number of programs of national financial assistance—one of which was a system of retirement benefits called Social Security, enacted into law in 1935.

When benefits began, Social Security retirement cushioned slightly the crushing effects of the Depression. But retirement benefits were set at levels that were never enough to guarantee a standard of living above the poverty line. In 1939, Social Security benefits were extended to a retired worker's spouse and minor children; in 1956, to severely disabled workers. These extensions helped cover more people in need, but neither new program deviated from the basic premise of Social Security: Provide just enough to keep starvation from the door, but not enough to guarantee a decent standard of living.

Benefits Now Provide Diminished Security

The economic position of many older Americans is increasingly precarious. People are living longer, their private pensions are disappearing, and their Social Security benefits—despite cost-of-living increases in most years—are not keeping up with their true living expenses.

The Social Security system is facing pressure to lower benefits even more. Due to longer life spans, an overall population increase, and the bubble of Baby Boomers beginning to reach retirement age, there is a steady increase in the number of people collecting Social Security benefits. If the system continues as is, the total benefits that retirees, dependents, and survivors collect will eventually surpass the amount of taxes paid into the system by younger workers. If the system is not altered, at some point—although experts disagree widely about exactly when—the system will no longer be able to pay the full benefits currently promised.

"Saving" Social Security

Clearly, the Social Security system requires some adjustment to ensure its continued health. But most discussion about this subject from recent political campaigners is nothing more than ideological hot air, giving the false impression that the system is about to collapse. There are simple ways to fix the Social Security system, but they are ignored by politicians who want nothing less than to end all public pensions and other support systems and force all retirement savings into the stock market. There, people's savings would be bled by the financial institutions and other corporate profiteers that run Wall Street—a happy prospect for the people who bankroll presidential candidates, but a disaster for working Americans. Instead, simple adjustments to the system—none raising the basic Social Security tax rate—could address its financial problems without introducing investment risk or siphoning off funds to Wall Street.

Remove cap on earnings subject to Social Security (FICA) tax. At present, the Social Security system does not tax earned income over $128,400 per year (the amount goes up slightly most years).

This makes it a regressive tax (a tax that takes a larger percentage of the income of low-income people than of high-income people). For example, someone earning $30,000 per year pays about 6.2% of their income in FICA tax while someone earning $200,000 pays only 2.9% of their total income. The Congressional Research Service has found that removing this cap on taxed income, *by itself,* would keep the Social Security retirement system solvent for the next 75 years. So far, however, national politicians and their high-income supporters have resisted this change.

Setoff against early benefits for nonearned income. Under current rules, people may claim Social Security retirement or dependents benefits as early as age 62 and survivors benefits as early as age 60. During any year before full retirement age, if someone collects any of these Social Security benefits but continues working, the benefits are reduced by income the beneficiary earns over a certain amount. The rule does not apply, however, to someone who has income from sources other than current work—such as investments, real estate, trusts, and so on. This rule penalizes those who must continue to work in order to survive, at the same time permitting others to collect their full benefit amount despite any amount—no matter how enormous—of nonearned income. If the same rule were applied to nonearned income, the system could save significantly without taking anything away from those who most need benefits.

Delay full retirement age. The original standard age for full Social Security retirement benefits was 65. That age has been raised for people born in 1938 or later, saving a great deal of money for Social Security. The age at which most people stop working continues to rise, so there is no reason why the full retirement age for collecting Social Security benefits should not also rise again to parallel this changing reality.

Slight reduction in benefits for high-income recipients. This limit on benefits could happen in one of two ways. There could be a yearly reduction in retirement benefits to people who continue to have a high income from work or investments. Or, there could be progressive price-indexing, by which initial retirement benefit levels are slightly reduced for upper-income claimants.

Any one of the adjustments discussed above would make a significant contribution to the long-term stability of Social Security. Several of them together could put the system on sound financial footing for many decades to come.

What You Can Do

In response to this deteriorating situation, anyone facing retirement should take two important steps.

First, understand the rules regarding Social Security benefits. (These are described in Chapters 1 through 5.) That will enable you to plan wisely for your retirement years, including answering the basic questions of when to claim your benefits and how much you can work after claiming them.

And second, become aware and active concerning proposed moves by Congress regarding the Social Security and Medicare programs. Local senior centers and national seniors organizations such as the Alliance for Retired Americans in Washington, DC (www.retiredamericans.org) are good sources of current information.

If you are even beginning to think about your retirement, it is not too early to begin trying to safeguard it.

Social Security Defined

Social Security is a series of connected programs, each with its own set of rules and payment schedules. All of the programs have one thing in common: Benefits are paid—to a retired or disabled worker, or to the worker's dependent or surviving family—based on the worker's average wages, salary, or self-employment income from work covered by Social Security.

The amount of benefits to which you are entitled under any Social Security program is not related to your need. Instead, it is based on the income you have earned through years of working. In most jobs, both you and your employer will have paid Social Security taxes on the amounts you earned. Since 1951, Social Security taxes have also been paid on reported self-employment income.

Social Security keeps a record of your earnings over your working lifetime and pays benefits based upon the average amount you earned. However, the only income considered is that on which Social Security tax was paid. Income such as interest or dividends, or income from the sale of a business or investments, and unreported income is not counted in calculating Social Security benefits.

Four basic categories of Social Security benefits are paid based upon this record of your earnings: retirement, disability, dependents, and survivors benefits.

Retirement Benefits

You may choose to begin receiving Social Security retirement benefits as early as age 62. But the amount of your benefits permanently increases for each year you wait, until age 70. The amount of your retirement benefits will be between 20% of your average income (if your income is high) and 50% (if your income is low). For a 66-year-old single person first claiming retirement benefits in 2018, the average monthly benefit is about $1,400; $2,340 for a couple. The highest earners first claiming their benefits in 2018 (at full retirement age) would receive about $2,788 per month; $4,180 for a couple (receiving benefits on one spouse's earnings record). These benefits usually increase yearly with the cost of living. (See Chapter 2 for a full description of retirement benefits.)

Disability Benefits

If you are younger than full retirement age but have met the work requirements and are considered disabled under the Social Security program's medical guidelines, you can receive disability benefits. The amount of these benefits will be roughly equal to what your retirement benefits would be. (See Chapter 3 for a full discussion of disability benefits.)

Dependents Benefits

If you are married to a retired or disabled worker who qualifies for Social Security retirement or disability benefits, you and your minor or disabled children may be entitled to benefits based on your spouse's earning record. This is true whether or not you actually depend on your spouse for your support.

Married recipients should determine whether they will receive a greater sum from the combination of one Social Security benefit and one dependent benefit or from two Social Security retirement benefits (assuming both partners are entitled to one). A spouse may be awarded retirement or dependent benefits, but not both. (See Chapter 4 for a full discussion of dependents benefits.)

TIP
Note for same-sex spouses. Same-sex spouses are entitled to Social Security dependents and survivors benefits on the same terms as other spouses.

Survivors Benefits

If you are the surviving spouse of a worker who qualified for Social Security retirement or disability benefits, you and your minor or disabled children may be entitled to benefits based on your deceased spouse's earnings record. (See Chapter 5 for a full discussion of survivors benefits.)

TIP
You can choose the program from which to claim benefits. You may meet the eligibility rules for more than one type of Social Security benefit. For example, you might be technically eligible for both retirement and disability, or you might be entitled to benefits based on your own retirement as well as on that of your retired spouse. You can collect which-ever one of these benefits is higher, but not both.

Eligibility for Benefits

The specific requirements vary for qualifying to receive retirement, disability, dependents, and survivors benefits. The requirements also vary depending on the age of the person filing the claim and, if you are claiming as a dependent or survivor, on the age of the worker.

However, there is a general requirement that everyone must meet to receive one of these Social Security benefits. The worker on whose earnings record the benefit is to be paid must have worked in "covered employment" for a sufficient number of years by the time he or she claims retirement benefits, becomes disabled, or dies.

Earning Work Credits

All work on which Social Security taxes are reported is considered covered employment. About 95% of all American workers—around 175 million people—work in covered employment, including self-employment. For each year you work in covered employment, you receive up to four Social Security work credits, depending on the amount of money you have earned. Once you have enough work credits, you can qualify for Social Security benefits.

The amount of work credits you need in order to qualify for specific programs is discussed in Chapter 2 (retirement benefits), Chapter 3 (disability benefits), Chapter 4 (dependents benefits), and Chapter 5 (survivors benefits).

The Social Security Administration keeps track of your work record through the Social Security taxes paid by your employer and by you through FICA taxes.

The self-employed—that is, people who take a draw from a self-owned or partnership business, or who receive pay from others without taxes being withheld—earn Social Security credits by reporting income and paying tax for the net profit from that income on IRS Schedule SE. Income that is not reported will not be recorded on your earnings record. Although many people fail to report income to avoid paying taxes, a long-term consequence is that the unreported income will not count toward qualifying for Social Security retirement or other benefits, and will reduce the amount of benefits for those who do qualify.

The Importance of Names and Numbers

The Social Security system does everything—records your earnings, credits your taxes, determines and pays your benefits—according to your Social Security number. On every form you fill out or correspondence you have with the Social Security Administration, you must include your Social Security number. You should also use your name exactly as it appears on your Social Security card. This will make it easier for Social Security to track the correct records.

If you have used more than one name on work documents, indicate all names you have used on correspondence with the Social Security Administration. As long as you have used the same Social Security number, your records should reflect all of your earnings.

If you have changed your name and want to ensure that all your future earnings will be properly credited to your Social Security record, you can protect yourself by filling out an *Application for Social Security Card*. This form allows you to register your new name and match it with your existing Social Security number. You will be sent a new Social Security card with your new name, but the same number.

To complete this form, you must bring to your local Social Security office the originals or certified copies of documents that reflect both your old and new names. If your name has changed because you married or remarried, bring your marriage certificate.

If your name change is due to divorce, bring the final order of divorce, which includes reference to the return of your former name.

If you have any questions, particularly concerning the type of documents you may bring to show your old and new names, call Social Security at 800-772-1213.

Coverage for Specific Workers

There are special Social Security rules for coverage of some workers in certain sorts of employment.

Federal Government Workers

If you were hired as an employee of the federal government on or after January 1, 1984, all your work for the government since then has been covered by Social Security.

If you worked for the federal government before 1984, your work both before and after January 1, 1984 has been covered by the separate federal Civil Service Retirement System. (See Chapter 10 for a full description of civil service retirement benefits.)

State and Local Government Workers

Many state and local government workers are not covered by Social Security. State government employees are usually covered by their own pension or retirement systems, and local government employees have their own public agency retirement system, or PARS.

However, some state and local government employees are covered by Social Security instead of—or in addition to—a state or PARS pension system. If so, these governments and their workers pay at least some Social Security taxes. And workers under these plans are entitled to Social Security benefits if they meet the other regular requirements.

If you are a government employee and aren't sure whether you are covered by Social Security, check with the personnel office at your workplace. And remember, even if your employment at a state or local agency does not entitle you to Social Security benefits, any other work you have done during your lifetime may qualify you, if you paid Social Security taxes.

Workers for Nonprofit Organizations

Since 1984, all employment for charitable, educational, or other nonprofit organizations is covered by Social Security. (Some churches and religious organizations, however, are exempt from this rule.) Before that time, nonprofit organizations were permitted to remain outside the Social Security system, and many chose to do so. Because people who worked for such organizations were left out of any retirement plan, the Social Security system now permits some of them to qualify for benefits with about half of the normal number of years of work credit. If you reached age 55 before January 1, 1984, and you worked for such a nonprofit organization, you and your family can qualify for Social Security benefits with a reduced number of work credits.

Members of the Military

Whether your military service was considered by Social Security to be "covered employment" depends on when you served and whether you were on active or inactive duty. From 1957 on, all service personnel on active duty have paid Social Security taxes, and so all active service from that date is covered employment. Since 1988, periods of active service, such as reserve training, while on inactive duty have also been covered.

Household Workers

Household work—cleaning, cooking, gardening, child care, minor home repair work—has been covered by Social Security since 1951; work before that date is not credited on a worker's earnings record.

A major problem for household workers is that most employers do not report their employees' earnings to the Internal Revenue Service (IRS) and do not pay Social Security taxes on those earnings. Of course, a lot of domestic workers do not want their earnings reported. They are paid so little that they prefer to receive the full amount, often in cash, without any taxes withheld.

One result of this nonreporting, however, is that the earnings do not get credited to the worker's Social Security record. So when the worker or worker's family later seeks Social Security benefits, they may have trouble qualifying and, if qualified, may have lower benefit amounts.

If you want your earnings from household work reported to Social Security, you have several options. If you work for different employers and make less than $1,000 per year from any one of them, you can report that income yourself as self-employment income and pay 15.3% self-employment tax on it in addition to income tax. Paying self-employment tax, on federal income tax Form 1040, Schedule SE, credits the earnings to your Social Security earnings record.

If you work for any one employer who pays you a total of $1,900 or more over the course of a year, you can ask that employer to withhold Social Security taxes from your pay, report your income to Social Security, and pay the employer's share of the Social Security tax on that income, as the law requires. (See "Employer's Duty to Report Earnings of Household Workers," below.)

Farmworkers

Farm and ranch work is covered by the Social Security system. If you do crop or animal farmwork, your employer must report your earnings and pay Social Security taxes on them. The employer must also withhold your share of Social Security taxes from your paycheck if you earn $150 or more from that employer in one year, or if the employer pays $2,500 or more to all farm laborers, regardless of how much you earn individually. Any amounts you are paid in housing or food do not have to be reported by the employer.

Farmworkers have long faced problems with employers who do not pay their share of the Social Security tax. To make sure your farmwork is counted toward your Social Security record, check your pay stub to see if Social Security taxes—labeled FICA—are being withheld. Also ask the person who handles payroll to give you paperwork indicating that Social Security taxes are being paid on your earnings. If your employer is not paying Social Security taxes on your earnings, or you get the runaround and you are unsure what the employer is doing, ask your local Social Security office to find out for you.

If you are worried about your employer's finding out that you are checking on this, ask the Social Security field representative to make a confidential inquiry. Social Security can request all the employer's wage records without letting the employer know which employee in particular has brought the matter to its attention.

Employer's Duty to Report Earnings of Household Workers

If an employer hires a household worker—cleaner, cook, gardener, child sitter, home care aide—who is not employed by and paid through an agency, and the employer pays that worker a total of $1,900 or more during the year, the employer is required by law to report those payments and pay Social Security taxes on them. This rule exempts any worker who was younger than 18 during any part of the year.

An individual employer can report these taxes on his or her own federal income tax return Form 1040, and pay the Social Security tax obligation along with the personal income taxes. To file and pay these taxes, the employer will need the name of the employee as it appears on his or her Social Security card, the employee's Social Security number, and the amount of wages paid.

Earning Work Credits

To receive any kind of Social Security benefit—retirement, disability, dependents, or survivors—the person on whose work record the benefit is to be calculated must have accumulated enough work credits. The number of work credits you need to reach the qualifying mark—what Social Security calls insured status—varies depending on the particular benefit you are claiming and the age at which you claim it.

You can earn up to four work credits each year, but no more than four, regardless of how much you earn. Before 1978, work credits were measured in quarter-year periods: January through March, April through June, July through September, and October through December. You had to earn a specific minimum amount of income to gain a work credit for that quarter:

- Before 1978, you received one credit for each quarter in which you were paid $50 or more in wages in covered employment, or each quarter in which you earned and reported $100 or more from self-employment.

- Beginning in 1978, the rules were changed to make it easier to earn credits. From 1978 on, you receive one credit, up to four credits per year, if you earn at least a certain amount in covered employment, regardless of the quarter in which you earn it. That means that if you earn all your money during one part of the year and nothing during other parts of the year, you can still accumulate the full four credits. The amount needed to earn one credit increases yearly. In 1978, when the new system was started, it was $250; in 2018, it is $1,320.

EXAMPLE 1: In 1975, Ulis was paid $580 between January and March, nothing between April and July when he could not work because of a back injury, $340 in August, and $600 in cash from self-employment in October and November. For the year 1975, Ulis earned three credits: one credit for the first quarter, in which he was paid more than the $50 minimum; nothing in the second quarter, so he got no credit; one credit in the third quarter, because he earned well over the $50 minimum even though he worked only one month; and one credit for the last quarter, because in 1975 self-employment income was covered by Social Security.

EXAMPLE 2: Eve was paid $800 in January 1978, but did not earn anything the rest of the year. Based on the earnings test in effect in 1978, she got three credits for the year—one for each $250 in earnings—based on her earnings for January alone.

EXAMPLE 3: Rebecca was paid $500 a month in 2018 at her part-time job, for total earnings for the year of $6,000. Because her earnings of $6,000 divided by $1,320 (the amount needed to earn one credit in 2018) is more than 4, she received the maximum four credits for 2018.

Determining Your Benefit Amount

If you are eligible for a Social Security benefit, the amount of that benefit is determined by a formula based on the average of your yearly reported earnings in covered employment since you began working. Social Security adjusts your earnings records every year that you have Social Security–taxed earnings. This is true even after you begin collecting benefits.

How Your Earnings Average Is Computed

Social Security computes the average of your yearly earnings, but places a yearly limit on the amount you can be credited with, no matter how much you actually earned that year. These yearly income credit limits are shown in the following table, "Yearly Dollar Limit on Earnings Credits."

CAUTION

Only employment-related income counts, and you must have paid Social Security taxes on that income. Other income that you may have earned, such as interest, dividends, capital gains, rents, and royalties, will not be considered in calculating your Social Security benefits.

Benefit Formula

Based on a worker's earnings record, the Social Security Administration computes what is called the worker's Primary Insurance Amount, or PIA. This is the amount a worker will receive if he or she claims retirement benefits at full retirement age, which is 66 for everyone born in 1943 through 1954. The full retirement age is 67 for those born in 1960 or later. The exact formula applied to each worker's earnings record depends on the year the worker was born.

Yearly Dollar Limit on Earnings Credits

1951–1954	$ 3,600	1992	$ 55,500
1955–1958	4,200	1993	57,600
1959–1965	4,800	1994	60,600
1966–1967	6,600	1995	61,200
1968–1971	7,800	1996	62,700
1972	9,000	1997	65,400
1973	10,800	1998	68,400
1974	13,200	1999	72,600
1975	14,100	2000	76,200
1976	15,300	2001	80,400
1977	16,500	2002	84,900
1978	17,700	2003	87,000
1979	22,900	2004	87,900
1980	25,900	2005	90,000
1981	29,700	2006	94,200
1982	32,400	2007	97,500
1983	35,700	2008	102,000
1984	37,800	2009–2011	106,800
1985	39,600	2012	110,100
1986	42,000	2013	113,700
1987	43,000	2014	117,000
1988	45,000	2015	118,500
1989	48,000	2016	118,500
1990	50,400	2017	127,200
1991	53,400	2018	128,400

CAUTION

There is no "minimum" Social Security benefit amount. If your average earnings were quite low, your check will also be low.

Social Security benefits for a disabled worker (as described in Chapter 3), or for a worker's dependents (as described in Chapter 4) or survivors (as described in Chapter 5), are based on a percentage of the worker's PIA. Social Security will give you an estimate of your future retirement or disability benefits, or those of a worker on whose earnings record you will receive dependents or survivors benefits.

Veterans May Receive Extra Earnings Credit

If you're a veteran of the U.S. Armed Forces, you may be eligible for extra earnings credit, including:

- an extra $300 per quarter for active duty from 1957 through 1977, and
- $100 of credit for each $300 of active duty basic pay, up to a maximum credit of $1,200 per year for active duty from 1978 through 2001. No extra credit is given if you enlisted after September 7, 1980 and did not complete at least 24 months' active duty or your full tour. Notice that no extra credit is given for active duty after 2001.

Don't be alarmed if you don't see your extra credits reflected on your Social Security Statement. These will be added to your record when you actually apply for benefits, at which time you'll have to provide proof of your military service. Active duty earnings from 1968 on should be included in the benefit estimates on your statement, although the extra credit amounts will not show up in the statement's year-to-year list of your earnings.

Taxes on Your Benefits

A certain amount of Social Security benefits may be taxable, depending on your total income. In determining whether you owe any income tax on your benefits, the Internal Revenue Service looks at what it calls your combined income. This consists of your adjusted gross income, as reported in your tax return, plus any nontaxable interest income, plus one-half of your Social Security benefits. If your combined income as an individual is between $25,000 and $34,000 (or, for a couple filing jointly, between $32,000 and $44,000), you may have to pay income taxes on 50% of your Social Security benefits. If your combined income is more than $34,000 ($44,000 for a couple filing jointly), you may owe income taxes on up to 85% of your benefits.

The way to calculate any income taxes you may owe on your Social Security benefits is explained in the instruction booklet that accompanies the Form 1040 federal tax return. The IRS also publishes a free information booklet explaining numerous tax rules pertaining to older people. It is called *Tax Guide for Seniors*, Publication 554. To get the booklet, call the IRS at 800-829-3676 or download it from the website www.irs.gov.

Taxes paid on Social Security benefits go back into the Social Security Trust Fund, not the general fund.

Unpaid Student Debt May Reduce Benefits

More and more people still have student loan debt when they become eligible to collect Social Security benefits. You should be aware that if you still have federally guaranteed student debt when you begin receiving retirement, disability, dependents or survivors benefits, the Social Security Administration may reduce the amount of your benefit until the debt is paid off. The size of the benefit reduction depends on the amount of your remaining debt and the amount you are supposed to be paying off monthly. There is also a $15 per month processing fee for this "service." The average benefit reduction is about $150 per month.

Note: If you are collecting Social Security disability benefits and your disability might be considered "total and permanent" by special Social Security rules, your entire remaining student debt might be discharged (wiped off the books). For discussion of this discharge of debt, see Chapter 3.

Your Social Security Earnings Record

The Social Security Administration keeps a running account of your earnings record and the work credits it reflects. (It tracks these by use of your Social Security number.) Based on those figures, Social Security can give you an estimate of what your retirement benefits would be if you took them at age 62, full retirement age, or age 70. It can also estimate benefits for your dependents or survivors, or your disability benefits, should you need them.

It makes good sense to find out what your Social Security retirement benefits will be several years before you actually consider claiming them. You're probably curious, and finding out can help you plan for the future. And because so much is riding on your official earnings record, it is important to check the accuracy of that record every few years. You want to make sure that all your covered earnings are credited to you.

To check your earnings record and estimate of benefits, go to the Social Security Administration's website at http://ssa.gov/mystatement.

A Social Security Statement is supposed to be mailed yearly to everyone age 60 and older who is not currently receiving Social Security benefits *and* who has not signed up to receive a benefit statement online through the Social Security Administration website. If you have not received a Social Security Statement, or if you have a question about your earnings record, call Social Security at 800-772-1213.

U.S. Citizens' Rights to Receive Benefits While Living Abroad

If you are a U.S. citizen living in another country, you are entitled to the same Social Security benefits—to the extent you have earned them through work in the United States—as if you lived in the United States. However, your retirement benefits may be reduced if you also receive a pension in the other country. (See "Reductions for Government or Foreign Pensions" in Chapter 2.)

If you are married to someone who is not a U.S. citizen, and you both live outside the United States, your spouse is not entitled to Social Security dependents or survivors benefits based on your work record. (Your spouse might still be entitled to Social Security retirement benefits based on his or her own work performed while living in the United States; see the following section, "Receiving Benefits as a Noncitizen.")

If you live in one of a few particular countries, there are restrictions on the sending of your Social Security benefits. If you live in Cuba or North Korea, a law passed during the days of Cold War anti-Communist policy forbids the Social Security system from sending your benefits there. Instead, you would have to have the benefits sent to a bank in the United States or in some third country, and then transfer the money on your own. If you live in Vietnam or Cambodia, or in one of the Central Asian former Soviet republics, you may be able to receive Social Security payments there, but only if you make special arrangements with Social Security and the U.S. embassy in that country.

Receiving Benefits as a Noncitizen

It is increasingly common for people who are not U.S. citizens to live and work here for long periods of time. This section explains your rights to collect Social Security benefits if you are not a U.S. citizen, whether you're living in the United States now or have since left to live in another country.

Noncitizens Living in the United States

Noncitizens living in the United States are entitled to all the Social Security benefits that they or their spouse or parents have earned—under the same rules as U.S. citizens—if they are lawfully in the United States. For example, you might benefit from this if you:

- were not a U.S. citizen during some or all of the time you or your family member worked in the United States, but have since become a U.S. citizen, or

- are not a U.S. citizen, but are a lawful permanent U.S. resident or have another immigration status permitting you to be lawfully present in the United States.

Non-U.S. Citizens Living Abroad

Many non-U.S. citizens live and work for a time in the United States, paying Social Security taxes and earning enough work credits to qualify for benefits for themselves and their families. However, many of these people ultimately leave the United States. Their ability to collect earned Social Security benefits after departing depends in large part on whether the United States has entered into agreements with their home countries. If you've formerly worked in the United States, you need to look at three things to figure out your eligibility for benefits, including:

- your country of citizenship
- the country where you're living when you request Social Security benefits, and
- the type of benefit you're requesting.

To find out what your rights are to collect Social Security benefits based on your country of citizenship, your country of residence, and the type of Social Security benefit you're entitled to receive, see the Social Security Administration's official online publication "Your Payments While You Are Outside the United States," available at www.socialsecurity.gov/pubs/10137.html. ●

Social Security Retirement Benefits

Many people look forward to retirement as a time of contentedness and quiet, a new time for old friendships, a period of calm sufficiency. They imagine they will be able to do things they always wanted to do but never had time for. While this may prove to be a true picture for some people, others find a far different reality. Reduced financial resources make it tough to cope with a high-priced world. In a society that has forgotten how to revere and support its elders, retirement often becomes another difficult siege in the old battle for survival.

The reality for many Americans is that after what they had hoped would be retirement age—usually anticipated as age 65—they must continue working to make ends meet. Often, they end up doing so at lower-paying work than they had before retiring.

The Social Security retirement benefit program, as well as private pension and other retirement plans, help with some of the financial strain of retirement years. But Social Security retirement benefits alone are not sufficient for most people to live at anything near the standard of living they had during their working years.

These problems bring into question both the age at which you retire and whether you'll continue to work after beginning to collect Social Security. Under Social Security rules, retirement does not necessarily mean you have reached a specific age, or that you have stopped working altogether. It merely refers to the time you claim and start collecting Social Security retirement benefits. If you claim benefits before you reach your full retirement age, but continue to work, the amount of your benefits will be reduced if you earn more than a specific amount of income. (See "Timing Your Retirement Benefits Claim," below.) Once you reach your full retirement age, however, you will collect the full amount of your retirement benefits no matter how much you continue to earn.

This chapter explains how Social Security figures your eligibility for retirement benefits, when you may and when you should claim the benefits, and what the rules are regarding earnings after you have begun to claim your retirement benefits.

Work Credits Required

To be eligible for Social Security retirement benefits, officially referred to by Social Security as being "fully insured," you must have earned at least 40 work credits over all your working years. See Chapter 1 to review how work credits are earned.

Checking Your Earnings Record

Even if you have not worked for many years, and you did not make much money in the few years you did work, check your earnings record. You may be surprised to find that you have quite a few credits from years gone by, since the rules for getting work credits were pretty easy to comply with before 1978.

To check your earnings record, go to the Social Security Administration website at http://ssa.gov/myaccount.

If you find that you do not have enough work credits to be eligible for retirement benefits now, you may be able to work part time for a while and earn enough new credits to become eligible. You've got a high incentive for doing this, because once you qualify for retirement benefits, you are eligible to receive them for the rest of your life. That could mean a lot of money over the years to come.

> EXAMPLE: After graduating from college in 1970, Millie immediately got a good-paying job at a large insurance company. After several years there, she married and stopped working outside the home. Her husband was quite a bit older and had earlier made money in business for himself, and he supported them both on his investments. After his death in 1980, Millie was able to live carefully on these investments. By the time she was in her 50s, however, Millie found that her assets were dwindling and the monthly income they produced no longer went very far.
>
> When Millie turned 60, she asked Social Security whether she was eligible for survivors benefits (see Chapter 5) based on her husband's work record. But because he had made almost all his money from his

investments rather than from work, Millie found that she was not entitled to any survivors benefits based on her husband's work record.

But Millie also checked her own Social Security work record and found that she had 36 work credits from her time at the insurance company many years before. With 36 credits, she needed only four more to be eligible for her own retirement benefits (born in 1949, she needed a total of 40 credits). She was able to get a part-time job at a local restaurant—the pay was low, but the work allowed her to earn her four additional work credits within a year, qualifying her for Social Security retirement benefits. Even though these benefits were not that much, when added to her income from savings and investments, they made Millie's life much more comfortable.

Timing Your Retirement Benefits Claim

Two factors determine the amount of your retirement benefits. The first is your earnings record: how much you have earned over your working life. The higher your earnings, the higher your benefits.

The second is the age at which you claim your retirement benefits. You are allowed to claim benefits as early as age 62 up to age 70, but the earlier you claim them, the lower the benefits will permanently be. This section explains how the timing of your claim affects the amount of your retirement benefits.

If You Claim Benefits Before Full Retirement Age

You're allowed to claim retirement benefits as soon as you turn 62, but if you claim benefits before your "full retirement age," your monthly payment will forever be considerably less than if you wait until full retirement age. Nonetheless, out of financial need or other calculation, about 60% of all people eligible for retirement benefits claim them before they reach full retirement age. Also, if you claim benefits before your full retirement age but continue to work, your benefits may be significantly reduced if your earnings are over certain yearly limits. (See "Working After Claiming Early Retirement Benefits," below, for these limits.)

The amount by which your benefits would be permanently reduced if you claimed them early depends on the year of your birth and the time between when you claim benefits and when you reach your full retirement age. If you were born in 1937 or earlier, the reduction is about 0.555% per month, or 6.7% per year, up to a total reduction of 20% if you claim benefits three years early. And, remember, the reduction in monthly benefits is permanent. Benefits do not increase to the full amount when you reach your full retirement age.

Full retirement age is going up gradually, from 65 to 67, for people born after 1937. For these people, early (and reduced) retirement benefits will still be available at exactly age 62. As you'll notice on the "Benefit Reductions for Early Retirement" table below, those born in 1960 or later who retire at 62 will see their benefits shrink by as much as 30%.

Your Break-Even Point

Of course, claiming retirement benefits at less than full retirement age means you will collect benefits for a longer time. But the permanent reduction in the amount of your monthly benefits means that if you live past a certain age—in your early 80s, depending on whether you are a man or a woman and when you were born—you will wind up collecting less in total lifetime benefits than if you had waited until full retirement age. This point in life is referred to by Social Security as the "break-even age." See Chapter 6 to learn more about the break-even point.

The following two tables, "Benefit Reductions for Early Retirement" and "Retirement Benefits at Age 62," illustrate the effect of claiming early benefits. The first table shows how much a monthly retirement benefit is reduced for each month it is claimed before full retirement age. The second table assumes a retirement benefit for the worker at full retirement age of $1,000; this table shows exactly how much claiming benefits at age 62 would reduce the retired worker's monthly amounts, plus the overall percentage reduction in benefits.

Benefit Reductions for Early Retirement

Year Born	Full Retirement Age	Monthly Reduction
1938	65 + 2 months	0.548%
1939	65 + 4 months	0.541%
1940	65 + 6 months	0.535%
1941	65 + 8 months	0.530%
1942	65 + 10 months	0.525%
1943–54	66	0.520%
1955	66 + 2 months	0.516%
1956	66 + 4 months	0.512%
1957	66 + 6 months	0.509%
1958	66 + 8 months	0.505%
1959	66 + 10 months	0.502%
1960	67 and later	0.500%

Retirement Benefits at Age 62

(based on a $1,000 retirement benefit at full retirement age)

Year of Birth*	Normal (or full) retirement age	Retirement Benefit	
		Amount	Percent Reduction
1937 or earlier	65	$800	20.00%
1938	65 + 2 months	790	20.83%
1939	65 + 4 months	783	21.67%
1940	65 + 6 months	775	22.50%
1941	65 + 8 months	766	23.33%
1942	65 + 10 months	758	24.17%
1943–54	66	750	25.00%
1955	66 + 2 months	741	25.83%
1956	66 + 4 months	733	26.67%
1957	66 + 6 months	725	27.50%
1958	66 + 8 months	716	28.33%
1959	66 + 10 months	708	29.17%
1960 and later	67	700	30.00%

* If you are born on January 1, use the prior year of birth.

TIP

What if you must retire for health reasons? Some people are forced to stop working before full retirement age because of ill health. If you are under full retirement age and in that position, consider applying for Social Security disability benefits rather than early retirement. The reason is that disability benefits are calculated by the same formula as full retirement benefits, but the amount does not depend solely on the age at which you qualify for them. And the "disability freeze," a benefit calculation rule by which Social Security ignores your low-earning years that were caused by your disabling condition, can actually increase your disability and retirement benefits. Be warned, however, that proving you're incapable of doing any sort of work can be a long and difficult process.

TIP

Widows and widowers can switch from retirement to survivors benefits. Financial straits force many widow(er)s to claim their retirement benefits at or before full retirement age, even though they would become eligible for a higher monthly retirement amount if they waited longer. Although claiming early retirement benefits permanently reduces their retirement benefits based on their own earnings record, Social Security rules permit widow(er)s who have previously claimed early retirement to switch to survivors benefits at full retirement age. And, for many people, these full survivors benefits are higher than their own reduced retirement benefits. (See Chapter 5 for a full description of survivors benefits.)

The same rules apply to widows as to widowers, although the disparity in earnings between men and women means this ability to switch benefits is used mostly by women.

Full Retirement Age

For a long time, Social Security considered 65 to be full or normal retirement age. Benefit amounts were calculated on the assumption that most workers would stop working full time and would claim retirement benefits upon reaching age 65.

Now that people are generally living longer, the Social Security rules for what is considered full retirement age are changing. Age 65 is still considered full retirement age for anyone born before 1938. However, full retirement age gradually increases from age 65 to 67 for people born in 1938 or later. For people born between 1943 and 1954, full retirement age is 66.

In addition, to give incentive for people to delay making their retirement claims, Social Security offers higher benefits for people who wait to make their claims until after reaching full retirement age.

Full Retirement Age for Those Born After 1937	
Year Born	**Full Retirement Age**
1938	65 years + 2 months
1939	65 years + 4 months
1940	65 years + 6 months
1941	65 years + 8 months
1942	65 years + 10 months
1943–1954	66 years
1955	66 years + 2 months
1956	66 years + 4 months
1957	66 years + 6 months
1958	66 years + 8 months
1959	66 years + 10 months
1960 or later	67 years

If You Claim Benefits After Full Retirement Age

If you wait until after your full retirement age to claim Social Security retirement benefits, your benefit amounts will be permanently higher. Your benefit amount is increased by a certain percentage each year you wait up to age 70. Also, if you increase your retirement benefits by delaying your benefits claim until after full retirement age, after you die, your spouse's survivors benefits (see Chapter 5) will also be correspondingly higher. This is a particularly good strategy if, financially, you do not need your retirement benefits at full retirement age and you are in good health, expecting to live well past age 70, which means you are likely to collect your higher benefits for many years.

After age 70, there is no longer any increase and no reason to delay claiming benefits. This is true even if you keep working after you reach full retirement age, because reductions in Social Security benefits due to earned income end when you reach full retirement age. The amount of the yearly percentage increase in benefits depends on when you were born.

Increase per Year in Benefits for Delayed Retirement	
Year Born	Percentage Increase
1927–1928	4.0
1929–1930	4.5
1931–1932	5.0
1933–1934	5.5
1935–1936	6.0
1937–1938	6.5
1939–1940	7.0
1941–1942	7.5
1943 or later	8.0

TIP

Everyone can claim some or all Medicare coverage at age 65.
Even if you do not claim Social Security retirement benefits when you turn
65, you are eligible for Medicare benefits and may want to sign up for some
or all of them. (Enrolling in Medicare does not affect your current or future
retirement benefits.) (See Chapter 12 for more information.)

Reversing a Suspension of Benefits

What happens if you delayed collecting retirement benefits when you
reached full retirement age, but at some point before age 70, your
financial or health circumstances change and you need those benefits
right away? You may file papers with Social Security "undoing"
your suspension of benefits and begin collecting them. And once
you begin collecting them, an eligible spouse (and/or ex-spouse) and
child can begin collecting dependents benefits as well. However, the
benefits will include only those amounts you (and your dependents, if
any) are entitled to beginning with the month you file your request to
undo the suspension. Benefits you might have collected during those
suspended months may not be collected retroactively.

The Amount of Your Retirement Check

Your Social Security retirement benefits depend on how much you
earned in covered employment over all your working years. Social
Security calculates your benefits based on the amounts in your
highest-earning 35 years. Then it applies a set of formulas to these
earnings; the exact figures depend on the year you were born.

Social Security's calculations are complex and the results are
less than bountiful. For example, the average retirement benefit for
someone who reaches full retirement age in 2018 is about $1,400 per
month. The maximum retirement benefit for someone first claiming
benefits in 2018 is about $2,788 per month. Once you claim your
benefits, there is a small cost-of-living increase most years.

Dependents Benefits Do Not Affect Amount of Retirement Benefits

The amount of your retirement benefits is not affected by the fact that your spouse (and/or ex-spouse), or child(ren) are receiving benefits. This is true whether your spouse collects retirement benefits based on his or her work record or collects dependents benefits based on your work record. There is a limit on how much all your dependents may collect based on your work record (see Chapter 4), but this does not affect the amount you personally receive in retirement benefits.

Under Social Security's benefit calculation system, the lower your average lifetime earnings, the higher a percentage of those earnings you'll receive in benefits. If your earnings have averaged in the middle range—the equivalent of around $30,000 to $40,000 in today's dollars—you can expect full retirement benefits of about 40% of your average earnings for the last few years before you reach full retirement age.

If your average earnings have been on the low side—under $30,000 a year in current dollars—then your benefits will be about 50% of your earnings in the years just before you claim retirement benefits.

If your earnings have always been at or near the maximum credited earnings for each year (see Chapter 1), then your retirement benefits may be about 20% of your earnings in the year in which you retire.

But these figures are just rough averages. To get a much more accurate estimate of what your retirement benefits will be, you can either phone Social Security at 800-772-1213 or use the online benefits estimator on the Social Security Administration website, at www.ssa.gov/estimator. This tool will provide you with an estimate of what your monthly retirement benefits would be if you claim benefits at age 62, at full retirement age, or at age 70. The actual amount you will receive in retirement benefits will depend on what your actual earnings are in the years between getting this estimate and claiming those benefits. So, the closer you are to actually claiming your retirement benefits, the more accurate this estimate will be.

Increases for Cost of Living

Whatever the amount of your Social Security retirement benefit, you will usually receive an automatic cost-of-living increase on January 1 of each year. This increase is tied to the rise in the Consumer Price Index: the cost of basic goods and services. In the late 1970s, this Consumer Price Index rose more than 10% each year, causing Social Security benefits to rise more than 10% per year. In the 1980s, however, the yearly cost-of-living increase began to drop. In some years, there is no cost-of-living increase at all. For 2018, the cost-of-living increase is 2.0%.

Increases If You Keep Working After
Claiming Retirement Benefits

As explained above, the amount of your Social Security retirement benefits depends on your average qualifying income over your highest 35 years of lifetime earnings. But can your benefit amount go up if you continue to earn and pay Social Security taxes after you claim retirement benefits? The answer is yes. If, after you claim benefits, your earnings in any year raise your earnings average over your highest 35 years, Social Security will raise your retirement benefit amount accordingly. This is true whether you claimed benefits early, at full retirement age, or after full retirement age.

Reductions for Government or Foreign Pensions

Many people have earned retirement benefits from work covered by Social Security and also public employee retirement system benefits from government jobs not covered by Social Security. Similarly, some people have earned Social Security retirement benefits from work in the United States and also a pension from work in another country.

Social Security artificially boosts the retirement benefits of people who have many years of non–Social Security earnings—to make sure people have at least a minimum amount. But because of a law called the Windfall Elimination Provision, this artificial benefits raise is eliminated for people who have either public employee system or foreign retirement benefits.

Those Affected

If your age and work history fit certain categories, your Social Security check will be reduced by 10% to 35% because of this windfall. You may be affected by this reduction if you:

- first became eligible for a government pension in 1986 or later, and
- worked fewer than 30 years at jobs covered by Social Security.

Those Not Affected

The windfall reduction does not affect you if you:

- only worked for an employer not covered by Social Security before 1957
- only earned a government pension based solely on work for the railroad, or
- were a federal government employee hired on January 1, 1984 or after.

 CAUTION

Government pensioners seeking spouse's benefits may face limits. Another rule limits benefits to people who collect both Social Security benefits as the spouses of retired or deceased workers and public employment pensions based on their own work records. (See "Government Pension Offset" in Chapters 4 and 5 for details.)

Working After Claiming Early Retirement Benefits

Because Social Security retirement benefits plus savings and other investments are often not enough to live on comfortably, many people keep working for at least a few years after they claim Social Security retirement benefits. Other people keep their jobs or take new ones to stay active and involved in the world of work. If you keep working at a high enough salary, you may increase your lifetime earnings average, thereby slightly increasing your benefits for the years to come.

If you claim early retirement benefits and continue to work, be aware that the money you earn over a certain amount each year may reduce your Social Security retirement benefits (until you reach full retirement age). Such a reduction in benefits applies only to that year. It has no permanent effect on the amount of benefits you'll receive in future years.

Limits on Earned Income If Claiming Early Benefits

Until you reach full retirement age, Social Security will subtract money from your retirement check if you exceed a certain amount of earned income for the year. For the year 2018, this limit on earned income is $17,040 ($1,420 per month). The amount goes up each year. If you are collecting Social Security retirement benefits before full retirement age, your benefits are reduced by $1 for every $2 in any month you earn over the limit. Once you reach full retirement age, there is no limit on the amount of money you may earn and still receive your full Social Security retirement benefit.

EXAMPLE: Henry is considering claiming early retirement benefits this year, at age 64. Social Security calculates that if he does so, he'll receive $866 a month (which is about 13% less than if he waited until his full retirement age of 66). But Henry also intends to continue working part time, with an income that will be about $5,000 over the yearly limit on earned income. If he does claim the early benefits and makes that part-time income, Henry would lose one dollar out of two from the $5,000 he earns over the limit, which means $2,500 for the year, or $208 per month. Therefore, his $866 per month retirement benefit amount would be reduced to $658. So, by claiming early retirement and continuing to earn over the limit, Henry incurs a double penalty: His retirement benefits are permanently reduced by 13%, and he loses an additional amount every month (until he reaches full retirement age) to the extent he earns over the income limit.

The amounts of early retirement benefits you lose as a setoff against your earnings are not necessarily all gone forever. When you reach full retirement age, Social Security will recalculate upward the amount of your benefits to take into account the amounts you lost because of the earned income rule. The lost amounts will be made up only partially, however, a little bit each year. It will take up to 15 years to completely recoup your lost benefits. And remember, none of this readjustment will change the permanent percentage reduction in your benefits that was calculated when you claimed early retirement benefits (look again at the chart "Benefit Reductions for Early Retirement" earlier in this chapter).

Change in How You Report Earnings

The Social Security Administration bases its benefit calculations on earnings reported on W-2 forms and self-employment tax payments. Most individual benefit recipients are not required to send in an estimate of earnings.

But the Social Security Administration does request earnings estimates from some beneficiaries: those with substantial self-employment income or whose reported earnings have varied widely from month to month, including people who work on commission. Toward the end of each year, Social Security sends those people a form asking for an earnings estimate for the following year. The agency uses the information to calculate benefits for the first months of the following year. It will then adjust the amounts, if necessary, after it receives actual W-2 or self-employment tax information in the current year.

Once a beneficiary reaches full retirement age, his or her income will no longer be checked. Because there is no Social Security limit on how much a person can earn after reaching full retirement age, there is nothing to report.

TIP

You can collect retirement benefits plus unemployment benefits. As this chapter explains, you may continue to work even after you begin claiming your Social Security retirement benefits. If you are working and you lose your job, you may collect unemployment benefits (assuming you otherwise qualify for them) even though you are also collecting your Social Security retirement benefits.

Only "Earned Income" Affects Your Benefits

The rule that reduces your early retirement benefits based on income over a certain yearly amount applies only to what Social Security considers "earned income." Basically, earned income means money you receive during the year for work you currently do. This rule favors the well-to-do who have significant income from sources other than current work.

Earned income does *not* include:

- interest on savings or investments
- capital gains (profits from the sale of stock, property, or other assets)
- IRA or 401(k) withdrawals
- insurance cash-ins
- rental income, or
- private pensions.

Also, money you receive from certain types of sources based on work you performed before you claimed retirement benefits—known as "special sources"—is not counted as earned income. These exempted amounts include:

- bonuses
- accumulated vacation pay or sick leave compensation
- private retirement fund payments
- deferred compensation
- accumulated commissions, and
- payments to the self-employed, for work performed before claiming retirement benefits, received more than one year after claiming benefits.

Special Rule as You Approach Full Retirement Age

If you are already receiving your retirement benefits, a special higher earnings limit applies in the 12 months while you're approaching full retirement age. If you will reach full retirement age in 2018, you may earn up to $3,780 per month without losing any of your benefits. For every $3 you earn over that amount in any month, you will lose $1 in Social Security benefits. Beginning in the month you reach full retirement age, you become eligible to earn any amount without penalty.

If you are self-employed, you may receive full benefits for any month during this first year in which you did not perform what Social Security considers substantial services. The usual test for substantial services is whether you worked in your business more than 45 hours during the month (or between 15 and 45 hours in a highly skilled occupation).

Social Security Disability Benefits

Over eight million disabled workers and their families receive Social Security disability benefits. Many of these people developed their severe injuries or illnesses when they were not old enough to collect retirement benefits. Social Security disability benefits provided an answer.

If you find it very difficult to work because of a physical or emotional condition that is not likely to resolve itself within a year—and you are short of retirement age—read this chapter carefully. If you have enough work credits for your age, you may be eligible for monthly disability benefits. And if you are eligible to receive disability benefits, your spouse and minor or disabled children may also be eligible to collect benefits. (See Chapter 4 for more information about dependents benefits.)

Who Is Eligible

Social Security disability benefits are paid to workers and their families only when workers have enough work credits to qualify. Work credits for disability benefits are calculated in the same way as for retirement benefits, although the number of credits required to qualify for the disability program depends on a person's age. A person can earn up to four work credits per year, and anyone who works part time, even at a very low-paying job, easily accumulates them. (See Chapter 1 for a discussion of how work credits are earned.)

RESOURCE

This chapter will introduce you to Social Security disability benefits. To learn more about disability benefits, including how to convince the Social Security Administration that a particular disability makes you unable to work, read *Nolo's Guide to Social Security Disability: Getting & Keeping Your Benefits*, by David A. Morton III, M.D. (Nolo). It includes details on whether you might qualify for benefits, how to apply, how to keep existing benefits, and how to work while you're still receiving benefits.

Work Credits Required

The number of work credits you'll need to qualify for disability benefits depends on your age when you become disabled.

The "Work Credits Required to Qualify for Disability Benefits" chart below provides a quick reference to see how many work credits you need to qualify for disability benefits.

There are also rules that make it easier for younger workers and people who become blind to qualify for disability benefits. (See "Young Workers" and "Blind Workers," below.)

Work Credits Required to Qualify for Disability Benefits	
If you became disabled at age:	You need this many work credits:
21 to 24	6
24 to 31	6-18
31 to 42	20
44	22
46	24
48	26
50	28
52	30
54	32
56	34
58	36
60	38
62 or older	40

Help From the Americans with Disabilities Act

A federal law, the Americans with Disabilities Act, or ADA, prohibits employment discrimination on the basis of a worker's disability. The ADA is intended to help people with disabilities who want to work but are frustrated by noncooperative employers.

In general, the ADA prohibits employers from discriminating against disabled people when hiring, promoting, and making other job decisions. It also requires employers to maintain a workplace that doesn't have substantial physical barriers to people with disabilities. Under the ADA, employers must make reasonable accommodations for qualified workers with disabilities, unless that would cause the employers undue hardship.

Unfortunately, the ADA is full of vague language. Disability rights advocates, lawyers, employers, and courts are still wrangling over precisely what terms like "reasonable accommodations" and "undue hardship" mean. And given the current antiregulation climate in government, it is not clear how strenuously the government or the courts will enforce the law. All in all, it is difficult to say how effective the law will be in the coming years in assisting people to keep working despite their disabilities.

For information about how the ADA is being enforced and where you can go for help in seeking its protection, contact the Office on the Americans with Disabilities Act in the Civil Rights Division of the U.S. Department of Justice at 800-514-0301 (voice) or 800-514-0383 (TDD). The Justice Department also has an ADA website at www.ada.gov. For help and referrals from an activist disabled citizens action group, contact the Center for Independent Living in Berkeley, California, at 510-841-4776 or 510-848-3101 (TTY), or see its website at www.cilberkeley.org.

Requirement of Recent Work

You must have earned at least 20 of the required work credits within the ten years just before you became disabled, unless you qualify under one of the special rules for young or blind disabled workers.

> EXAMPLE: Monica worked for ten years before she had children, earning 40 work credits during that time. After her children were in high school, she went back to work. That was in 2013, and, at the end of 2017, she became disabled with a back injury.
>
> Although she had more than the 40 total credits required for disability benefits, she could not collect them because she had only worked four years—earning 16 credits—within the ten previous years (2008 through 2018). She would need to work long enough to earn four more credits before she could qualify for disability benefits. In 2018, that means she would need to earn $5,280 during the year (four credits at $1,320 per credit) before she could qualify.

Young Workers

If you were disabled between the ages of 24 and 31, you need only half of the work credits you could have earned between age 21 and the time you became disabled. And if you were disabled before age 24, you would need only six credits in the three-year period immediately before you became disabled. These special rules exist because workers who become disabled at a young age obviously do not have the opportunity to acquire many work credits.

> EXAMPLE: Boris became disabled at age 29. There were eight years between when he was age 21 and the time he became disabled. During those years he could have earned 32 work credits: four per year. Under the special rule for young workers, however, Boris needs only half, or 16 credits, to qualify for disability benefits.

Blind Workers

If you are disabled by blindness, you must have the same number of work credits as anyone else your age. However, you need not have earned your work credits within the years immediately preceding your disability, as required for other workers. Your work credits can be from any time.

For purposes of Social Security disability benefits, being blind generally means having no better than 20/200 vision in your better eye with glasses or other corrective lenses, or having a visual field of 20 degrees or less (or a combination of the two). (See "What Is a Disability?" below, for more information on blindness as a disability.)

Disabled Widows and Widowers

If you are a widow or widower age 50 or older and disabled, you may receive disability benefits even though you do not have enough work credits to qualify. The amount of these benefits depends entirely upon your deceased spouse's average earnings and work record. Because they are based on your spouse's work record, you will lose eligibility for these benefits if you remarry before age 50.

You must meet a number of qualifications:

- You must be disabled as defined by Social Security rules. (See "What Is a Disability?" below, for more on these rules.)
- Your spouse, at death, must have been fully insured—meaning he or she had enough work credits to qualify for disability benefits based on his or her age.
- Your disability must have started no later than seven years after your spouse's death.
- If you already receive Social Security benefits as a surviving widow or widower with children, your disability must have begun no later than seven years after your child or children became adults, causing those benefits to end. (See Chapter 5.)
- If you divorced before your former spouse died, you will be eligible for these benefits only if the two of you were married for ten years or more.

Getting Married Does *Not* Affect Disability Benefits Based on Your Own Work Record

If you collect Social Security disability insurance (SSDI) benefits based on your own work history and earnings record, neither your right to collect those benefits nor the benefit amount would be affected if you get married. Your spouse's prior, current, or future earnings or assets are not considered by Social Security when you apply for or collect disability benefits based on your own work record.

Note: This is *not* the case, however, if you are a widow or widower collecting disability benefits based on your prior spouse's work record (see "Disabled Widows and Widowers," above) or for Supplemental Security Income (SSI) benefits based on disability, for which total household income and assets are considered (see Chapter 7).

If you are collecting SSDI benefits based on your own work record, marriage might actually have a positive effect. If you get married and become entitled to Social Security dependents' benefits (see Chapter 4) or survivors benefits (see Chapter 5) based on your spouse's retirement or disability, and those benefits would be higher than your own disability benefits, then you can collect the higher amount (but not both). Also, your spouse might be entitled to Social Security dependents or survivors benefits based on your eligibility for Social Security disability benefits; if so, these benefits for your spouse would not cause any reduction in your own benefits.

What Is a Disability?

To receive Social Security disability benefits, you must have a physical or mental disability that both:

- is expected to last (or has lasted) at least one year, or to result in death, and
- prevents you from doing any "substantial gainful work."

Of course, several of the terms within these definitions are subject to different interpretations. This section explains some guidelines developed by Social Security and the courts regarding qualifications for disability.

Conditions That May Qualify

Social Security keeps a list of common conditions it considers disabling. (See "Listed Impairments," below.) And the medical community has a tendency to treat more seriously the things it can easily name. But every person's physical and mental state is different, and the human mind and body can be very complex. So you may well have a condition that prevents you from working but is difficult to get doctors to name and describe. Don't let that discourage you from filing for disability benefits.

The only absolute rule regarding disability is that your impairment must be "medically determined," meaning that it can be discovered and verified by doctors. It does not have to be a simple condition that can be immediately given a name, however.

If you are considering making a claim for disability benefits, examine the requirement that the disability must prevent you from performing substantial gainful work, as described below. Discuss the matter thoroughly with your doctor or doctors.

Listed Impairments

To simplify the process of determining whether a disability makes a person eligible for benefits, Social Security has developed a list of common serious conditions that it considers disabling if your condition meets the criteria in the listing. If you prove, through medical records and doctors' reports, that you have one of the listed conditions—paralysis of both an arm and a leg, for example—Social Security will likely consider you eligible for benefits without making you prove that you cannot perform substantial gainful work. If you have one of the listed conditions, Social Security will simply assume that you cannot do full-time work.

The more common serious conditions that Social Security normally considers disabling are listed below. Every person's disability claim is considered individually, however, and having a condition on this list does not automatically qualify you for disability benefits. You must have evidence that your condition meets the requirements of the "listing." If you do, your application for disability benefits is likely to be approved unless you have been working since you became disabled. If you have been working, Social Security will determine whether this work disqualifies you from getting disability or whether it can be considered an "unsuccessful work attempt."

A select few of the conditions Social Security lists as being disabilities include the following, simplified for our discussion:

- a disease of the heart, lung, or blood vessels resulting in a serious loss of heart or lung reserves as shown by X-ray, electrocardiogram, or other tests—and, in spite of medical treatment, causing breathlessness, pain, or fatigue
- severe arthritis causing recurrent inflammation, pain, stiffness, and deformity in major joints so that the ability to get about or use the hands is severely limited
- mental illness resulting in marked limiting of activities and interests, deterioration in personal habits, and/or seriously impaired ability to get along with other people, such that it prevents substantial gainful employment
- damage to the brain, or brain abnormality, resulting in severe loss of judgment, intellect, orientation, or memory
- cancer that is progressive and has not been controlled or cured (though some cancers qualify at any stage)
- Acquired Immune Deficiency Syndrome (AIDS) or its related secondary diseases, causing an inability to perform substantial gainful employment
- a disease of the digestive system that results in severe malnutrition, weakness, and anemia
- loss of major function of both arms, both legs, or a leg and an arm
- serious loss of function of the kidneys, and
- total inability to speak.

The full listings are found in the Code of Federal Regulations (C.F.R.) Title 20, Part 404, Subpart P, Appendix 1. You can also find the listings on the Social Security website at www.ssa.gov.

Must Be Expected to Last One Year

No matter how seriously disabling a condition or an injury is, it will not make you eligible for disability benefits unless it has lasted, or is expected to last, one year. The disability will also qualify if it is expected to cause death.

TIP

Apply for benefits upon diagnosis. Even though the disability must be expected to last at least a year, you do not have to wait for a year to apply for benefits. As soon as the condition is disabling and a doctor can predict that it is expected to last a year, you may qualify. (The application process is described in Chapter 8.)

EXAMPLE: Ladonna fell down some stairs and dislocated her hip. She was placed in a body cast and was told by her doctor to stay in bed for three to four weeks. The cast would stay on for four months. After that, Ladonna would need a cane for another two or three months. In six to nine months, she would be walking normally again, although a little bit more cautiously. She would be off work for a total of seven or eight months.

Despite the seriousness of her injury and her total inability to work while she recovered, Ladonna will probably not qualify for Social Security disability benefits. The reason is that her disability is not expected to last for a year. However, she might qualify for her company's disability benefits, if the company provides them, or for unemployment or state disability compensation through her state's employment or disability office.

If, after you begin receiving benefits, it turns out that your disability does not actually last a year, Social Security cannot ask for its money back. You are not penalized for recovering sooner than expected, as long as the original expectation that the disability would last a year was expressed in writing by your doctor and accepted by the Social Security review process (and there was no fraud involved). You do have the obligation to tell Social Security if you return to work.

> **EXAMPLE:** Ravi had a stroke, leaving most of his left side paralyzed. He was unable to walk on his own, was unable to speak clearly, and needed help with most simple daily life tasks. He began physical and speech therapy, but his doctors predicted that he was unlikely to recover full use of his left arm and leg. He applied for disability benefits, and after waiting three months to see if Ravi's condition was likely to improve, Ravi was found eligible for disability benefits because his condition was totally disabling and it was not expected that within a year he would recover sufficiently to return to work. However, through hard work, Ravi recovered both his speech and enough of the use of his arm and leg to return to work in ten months.
>
> Although his disability did not last the required year, Ravi was able to keep the disability payments he had already received because the doctors had expected that his condition would be totally disabling for at least a year and the Social Security disability review process had accepted that prognosis.

No Substantial Gainful Activity

To be eligible for Social Security disability benefits, you must be unable to perform any substantial gainful activity—generally considered to be any work from which you earn $1,180 (in 2018) per month or more.

In determining whether your condition prevents you from doing substantial gainful activity, Social Security will first consider whether it prevents you from doing the job you had when you became disabled, or the last job you had before becoming disabled. If your disability prevents you from performing your usual job, Social Security will next decide whether you are able to do any other kind of substantial gainful work— that is, any job in which you could earn $1,180 per month or more.

For some applicants, as part of this determination, Social Security considers your education, training, and work experience (vocational factors). For example, a highly trained professional, whose work does not require any physical exertion but which is highly compensated, may still be able to earn $1,180 a month despite a certain physical disability. However, someone whose entire working life has been in lower-skilled, lower-paying work that requires considerable physical labor might have a harder time earning $1,180 per month with exactly the same physical disability.

Age is also taken into consideration. Social Security realizes that it won't be committing to as great an outlay of money when it grants disability benefits to people nearing retirement age as it does to younger workers (older workers were on the brink of collecting retirement benefits anyway). For this reason, and because it is more difficult for older workers to find new employment or to retrain for other kinds of work, Social Security approves the disability claims of those over 50 more readily than those of younger workers.

In determining whether you can switch to a less demanding job, Social Security will assess whether you are able to perform any kind of work for pay existing anywhere in the economy, whether or not there are actually any such jobs available close to where you live. However, it is up to Social Security to prove that there is gainful employment you can perform, unless you fit into its grid of medical-vocational guidelines that specify when you are disabled.

Special Rules for Blindness

If your vision in your better eye is no better than 20/200 with correction, or if your peripheral field of vision is limited to 20 degrees or less, you are considered blind under Social Security disability rules. (There are a few other ways to qualify for disability for blindness as well.) Assuming that your work credits add up to the required amount for your age, you (and your family) can receive disability benefits.

Some blind persons are able to continue working, at least part time, while simultaneously collecting benefits. If you are blind you can earn up to $1,970 per month—the amount increases from year to year—before your job is considered substantial gainful work that would disqualify you from benefits.

Applying Protects Your Retirement Benefits

If you are legally blind and earning too much money to qualify for disability benefits, but also earning significantly less than before your blindness, you may want to apply for disability benefits. Even though you won't receive cash benefits, Social Security can put what is called a "disability freeze" on your earnings record to protect your overall average.

The amount of your retirement benefits, or of your disability benefits if you later qualify, is determined by your average income over the years. (See "Determining Your Benefit Amount" in Chapter 1 for further explanation.) If, because of your disability, you are now making considerably less than you were before, these lower earnings will pull your lifetime average income lower, resulting in a lower ultimate Social Security payment. This special disability freeze provision for blindness permits you to work without having your lower income figured into your lifetime average earnings.

If you are over 55 and blind, you can qualify for disability benefits even if you're still doing substantially gainful work. The key is to show that you are unable to perform work requiring skills or abilities comparable to those required by the work you did before you turned 55 or before you became blind, whichever was later. This level of performance is measured by whether you work at the kind of job you previously had and you earn more than $1,970 every month. If you earn that much occasionally but not every month, you can still qualify for benefits. Disability checks will be withheld, however, for any month in which you do perform substantial gainful work—that is, earn over $1,970.

Examples of Disability Determinations

The following examples help illustrate Social Security's reasoning in applying its guidelines and making disability determinations.

Unsuitability for Other Work

EXAMPLE: Arnold has been a longshoreman for most of his life. At age 58, his back has been getting progressively worse. His doctor told him that he could no longer do longshore work. The doctor also said that sitting for any length of time will aggravate the condition. Arnold applies for disability.

Because there is no question that Arnold's condition will last more than a year, Social Security will next ask whether it prevents Arnold from performing substantial gainful activity. Arnold's back prevents him not only from doing his regular job or other physical labor, but also from sitting for long periods of time. Unless Social Security can describe a job that requires neither heavy physical labor nor sitting, Arnold would probably get disability payments. Because Arnold has done physical labor all his life, he may not have the training, work experience, or education to do many other jobs. Considering his age and the difficulty finding any type of work for which he could be retrained, it is likely that Social Security would find him eligible for disability benefits.

Two Conditions Combined

EXAMPLE: Ernestine has been a music teacher for many years. She is now 60 years old and is losing her hearing. She has also developed phlebitis, which makes it difficult for her to walk very far or to stand for long periods of time. She has to elevate her legs for a while every few hours. When her hearing loss makes it impossible for her to continue teaching music, she applies for disability benefits.

The combination of her two conditions may make her unable to maintain any gainful employment. She would have to find a job that required neither good hearing nor standing, and permitted her to put her legs up for a half hour several times a day. Because such jobs are scarce, Social Security would very likely find Ernestine eligible for disability, particularly in light of her age.

Mild Disability

EXAMPLE: Rebecca is 52 and has an aortic aneurysm. Despite medication, she has intermittent fatigue and shortness of breath, especially at her job as a waitress. Her doctor says that her work is too physically demanding and stressful for her heart. Rebecca applies for disability benefits.

Although Rebecca's condition—aortic aneurysm—is on Social Security's listing of impairments, she is not automatically eligible for disability benefits. Her condition has to meet the criteria in the cardiovascular listing; in this case, an aneurysm must be dissecting (that is, separating from the wall of the artery).

If Rebecca's aneurysm is not dissecting, Social Security would assess her limitations to see if she could do some type of less demanding work. Even if Social Security found she could only do sedentary work, Social Security would probably find that she has job skills, such as dealing with the public and taking orders, that could be used at a desk job (called "transferable skills"). She would probably not be found disabled.

Amount of Disability Benefit Payments

Like other Social Security benefits, the amount of your actual disability check is determined by your age and your personal earnings record: your average earnings for all the years you have been working, not just the salary you were making most recently.

Disability benefits are also available for disabled workers' families (spouses and minor or disabled children). The maximum amount for worker and family combined is either 85% of what the disabled worker was earning before becoming disabled, or 150% of what the worker's individual benefit is, whichever is lower.

EXAMPLE: Manu was making $3,200 a month when he became disabled at age 56. At that time, Manu's Social Security earnings record gives him an individual disability benefit of $900 a month. Manu's wife and teenage daughter are also eligible to collect dependents benefits. Their benefits would be the lower of 85% of Manu's $3,200 monthly salary, which comes out to $2,720, or 150% of what Manu's individual disability benefit

($900) would be, which comes out to $1,350. Manu's wife and daughter together would receive $1,350 a month, the lower of the two amounts.

Estimating Benefit Amounts

There is no simple formula for what your actual disability payments will be. Although some books and magazines print tidy charts matching age and income with disability benefit amounts, more often than not these charts mislead people, causing them to overestimate their benefits. The charts all base their figures on your current earnings and assume that you have had a consistent earning pattern during your entire working life. Most people, however, do not have such a perfect curve of earnings, so the estimates the charts give you are bound to be wrong.

You can get a general idea of disability benefits amounts by considering average payment and maximum amounts for 2018:

- Overall average monthly payment for disabled individual: $1,200
- Overall average monthly payment for disabled individual plus spouse and children: $2,050, and
- Maximum monthly payment for disabled individual: $2,788.

In addition, it can be helpful to look at averages based on income levels.

Estimated Disability Benefits for 2018

Average Annual Lifetime Income in Current Dollars	Monthly Benefits
$10,000 to $20,000	$550 to $825 (individual)
	$935 to $1,150 (couple or parent and child)
$20,000 to $30,000	$770 to $1,100 (individual)
	$1,210 to $1,650 (couple or parent and child)
$30,000 to $40,000	$1,100 to $1,980 (individual)
	$1,350 to $2,530 (couple or parent and child)
$40,000 and up	$1,500 to $2,600 (individual)
	$1,800 to $3,000 (couple or parent and child)

TIP

Check your eligibility for supplemental benefits. If you receive only a small disability benefit, and you have savings or other cash assets of less than $2,000 ($3,000 for couples), you may be eligible for Supplemental Security Income benefits (SSI) in addition to your Social Security disability benefits. (See Chapter 7 regarding SSI.)

Relying on general estimates of disability benefits makes little sense, however, because you can get a very accurate estimate, based on your exact earnings record, directly from Social Security. You can get this estimate when you apply for benefits or by going to http://ssa.gov/myaccount.

Cost-of-Living Increases

Monthly disability benefit amounts are based entirely on your personal earnings record, with no consideration given to the minimum amount you need to survive. Whatever your monthly amount, however, there is usually a yearly cost-of-living increase based on the rise in the Consumer Price Index; in recent years, the increase has been only 1% to 4%, and in some years, there is no cost-of-living increase at all.

CAUTION

Don't expect to start receiving disability benefits right away. Applying for disability benefits and proving your disability can be a slow, sometimes difficult business. You need to organize your paperwork, have the cooperation of your doctors, and be patient and persistent. What to expect in the application process and how best to prepare for it are discussed in Chapter 8.

Student Debt and Disability Benefits

Many people who qualify for Social Security disability benefits still owe money on their federally guaranteed student loan. If you are in this situation, the Social Security Administration may deduct an amount from your monthly disability benefits payment to pay off this debt. The average amount of this reduction is about $150 per month. The exact amount depends on the amount of your debt and the scheduled monthly payment terms.

Discharge of Debts for Permanent Disability

If you have what is considered "total and permanent disability" (TPD), you may apply to have the entire remaining amount of your student debt wiped off the books ("discharged"). In general, a disability is considered total and permanent if it renders you unable to work and the condition is expected to last more than five years (as opposed to the one-year qualifying requirement for collecting Social Security disability benefits). Those who qualify for TPD status include:

- veterans who are completely unemployable due to a service-connected disability, as determined by the U.S. Department of Veterans Affairs (VA)
- someone already receiving SSDI or SSI benefits based on disability (see Chapter 7), whose next scheduled disability review is five years or more from the date of the most recent Social Security disability determination (or from the date of the original approval), or
- someone who is unable to engage in any substantial gainful activity by reason of a physical or mental impairment that can be expected to result in death, has lasted for a continuous period of at least five years, or is expected to last for a continuous period of at least five years, as certified by the treating physician.

The discharge applies only to the Federal Direct Loan Program, Perkins Loans, the Federal Family Education Loan (FFEL) Program, and TEACH grants. Other loan programs and private loans have their own discharge rules.

To learn more about qualifying for this TPD discharge of debt, and about the process for applying, visit the special TPD web page of the Office of Federal Student aid, U.S. Department of Education, at www.disabilitydischarge.com.

Collecting Additional Benefits

Because disability payments are often not enough to live on, it is important for you to collect all the other benefits to which you may be entitled. You may even want to try to supplement your income by working to the extent you can.

Disability and Earned Income

Your benefit check will not be reduced if you earn a small amount of income while collecting Social Security disability benefits. However, if you regularly earn enough income for your work to qualify as gainful employment, you might not be considered disabled any longer and your benefits could be cut off entirely.

Social Security usually permits you to earn up to about $1,180 a month—$1,970 if you are blind—before you will be considered to be performing substantial gainful work. Also, in deciding how much you are earning, Social Security is supposed to deduct from your income the amounts of any disability-related work expenses, including medical devices or equipment such as a wheelchair, attendant care, drugs, or services required for you to be able to work. It will be up to you to prove the necessity and cost of such expenses.

The $1,180 per month amount is not fixed. You cannot simply keep your income just below this level and expect that your disability benefits will automatically continue. Both your physical condition and the amount of your work will be reviewed periodically. (See "Continuing Eligibility Review," below, regarding periodic reviews.) This review will take into account the amount and regularity of your income, your work duties, the number of hours you work, and, if you are self-employed, the extent to which you run or manage your own business.

If you are working long hours or have significant work responsibility, particularly if you are in business for yourself, Social Security will look hard, during its review of your disability status, at whether the $1,180 income limit is a true measure of your work. If, for example, family members are suddenly earning quite a bit more than they used to from the business, Social Security may suspect that you are doing the work and simply paying them instead. Or, if you are not getting paid much but you are working long hours for a business in which you have an ownership interest, they may look more closely at whether you are still disabled.

Other Social Security Benefits

You are not permitted to collect more than one Social Security benefit—retirement, dependents, survivors, or disability—at a time. If you are eligible for more than one monthly benefit based either on your own work record or on that of a spouse or parent, you will receive the higher of the two benefit amounts to which you are entitled, but not both. Supplemental Security Income (SSI) is an exception; you may collect SSI in addition to any other Social Security benefit. (See Chapter 7 for more on SSI.)

Other Disability Benefits

You are permitted to collect Social Security disability benefits and, at the same time, private disability payments from an insurance policy or coverage from your employer. You may also receive veterans (VA) disability coverage at the same time as Social Security disability benefits. (See Chapter 11 for a full discussion of VA benefits.)

Workers' Compensation

You may collect workers' compensation benefits—payments for injuries suffered during the course of employment—at the same time as Social Security disability benefits. Workers' compensation benefits are paid only until you recover, or until your injuries are determined to be permanent, at which time you receive a lump sum compensation payment.

While you are receiving monthly workers' compensation payments, the total of your disability and workers' compensation payments generally cannot be greater than 80% of what your average wages were before you became disabled. If they are, your disability benefits or workers' comp benefits will be reduced so that the total of both benefits is 80% of your earnings before you became disabled. If you are still receiving Social Security disability benefits when your workers' compensation coverage runs out, you can again start receiving the full amount of your Social Security benefits.

> EXAMPLE: Maxine became disabled with a back condition while working as a gardener and earning $1,400 a month. Her Social Security disability benefits were $560 a month, and, because her disability was related to her job, she also received workers' compensation benefits of $625 a month. The total of the two benefits was more than 80% of her prior salary (the combined benefits of $560 and $625 total $1,185, and 80% of $1,400 is $1,120), so her disability benefits were reduced by the extra $65, down to $495 a month.
>
> If Maxine was still disabled when her workers' compensation benefits ended, her Social Security disability benefits would go back up to $560 a month (plus whatever cost-of-living increases had been granted in the meantime).

Medicare

After you have been entitled to disability benefits for 24 months—and those months need not be consecutive—you become eligible for Medicare coverage. This is true even if you are not age 65, which is otherwise the standard age to qualify for Medicare. Medicare hospitalization coverage (Part A) is free. However, you must pay a monthly premium if you want to be covered by Medicare Part B medical insurance or by Part D for prescription drug costs. (See Chapter 12 for a full discussion of Medicare.)

Medicaid and SSI

If you have few or no assets—or your disability and the resulting medical costs deplete your assets and hamper your ability to earn income—you may qualify for Medicaid coverage. Medicaid is a program of government medical coverage available to people based on their low income and assets, excluding their home. You may be eligible for Medicaid coverage as soon as you qualify under its rules, without the 24-month wait Medicare requires. And even when you do qualify for Medicare, Medicaid can continue to pay medical bills that Medicare won't. (See Chapter 16 for a full discussion of Medicaid.)

If you qualify for Medicaid assistance, you may also qualify for cash payments from the SSI program, on top of your Social Security disability benefits. Like Medicaid, SSI is intended to assist people with low income and assets. (See Chapter 7 for more on SSI.)

Protecting Your Medicaid Eligibility

If your disability was caused by an accident that was someone else's fault, you may have a chunk of money coming to you as the result of an insurance claim or a lawsuit. Receiving that money, however, might disqualify you from Medicaid and eligibility for other benefits, which would mean you'd have to spend it all on future medical bills, with nothing left for other living expenses.

Federal law and the laws of many states address this problem by allowing you to set up a "special needs trust." This permits you to accept accident compensation without losing your Medicaid and other benefit eligibility. With such a trust, instead of the accident compensation going to you in a lump sum, it is held for you by a bank or similar institution and is used to pay only certain types of bills—usually medical and basic living expenses. If your situation requires a special needs trust, consult an experienced estate planning lawyer for help.

In many states, a cheaper and easier alternative to special needs trusts is now available. The Achieving a Better Life Experience (ABLE) Act allows for the creation of ABLE savings accounts, special bank accounts for individuals with disabilities. Funds in the accounts don't count as assets for the purpose of Medicaid (or SSI, up to $100,000).

Continuing Eligibility Review

Eligibility for disability benefits is not necessarily permanent. Depending on the nature and severity of your condition, and on whether doctors expect it to improve, Social Security will periodically review your condition to determine whether you still qualify for benefits.

When Your Eligibility Will Be Reviewed

If, when you apply for disability benefits, your doctors and Social Security's medical experts expect that your condition will improve, your medical eligibility will be reviewed six to 18 months after you are approved for benefits. If improvement in your condition is theoretically possible but not predicted by the doctors, Social Security will review your eligibility approximately every three years. If your condition is not expected to improve after you apply, Social Security will review your case every five to seven years.

If at any point after you are receiving disability benefits, you earn a steady or frequent monthly income of close to $1,180 (in 2018) a month, Social Security may also call you in for a work review. The agency will determine whether you are actually able to perform substantial gainful employment for more than $1,180 per month. Social Security will also check to see whether you are arranging to be paid less than $1,180 per month by having someone close to you receive money for your work, or whether you are being paid in some way other than cash wages or salary.

If you are in a trial work period, however, your benefits will not be terminated if you are doing work over the limit (see below).

The Review Process

The first step in a review of your eligibility for disability benefits is a letter from Social Security. The notice will either include forms for you to fill out, instruct you to call Social Security, or will summon you to a local office for an interview. The subject of the interview will be your medical condition and any work you are doing. You should bring with you the names and addresses of the doctors, hospitals, and other medical providers you have seen since your original eligibility was established, or since your last review. You should also bring with you information about any income you are currently earning, if any—including where you work, how much you earn, and the person to contact at your place of employment.

The local Social Security office service worker will ask you about your condition and work, and will then refer your file to Disability

Determination Services (DDS), the state agency that reviews all disability claims.

The DDS will obtain your current medical and employment records and may ask that you undergo a medical consultation or examination. The DDS will make a determination about your continued eligibility based on the medical records and reports and on your earned income. Unless your condition has substantially improved, or you have regularly been earning more than $1,180 per month, or you are found to be doing substantial gainful employment despite being paid less than $1,180 a month, your benefits will continue.

If your eligibility is terminated, you have a right to appeal that decision. (See Chapter 9 for a full discussion of the appeal process.) And if you lose your eligibility, benefits can continue for an adjustment period of up to three months while you look for work and wait for a paycheck.

Returning to Work

Most disabled people would rather work than not, and many try to find ways of working despite their disabling conditions. Social Security provides various forms of encouragement for people to return to work. For example, it ensures that people will continue to receive their disability benefits during time they spend testing the workday waters. And if, after returning to work, a person later finds that his or her disability makes the work too difficult, the person's disability benefits can be restarted quickly and easily.

Trial Work Period

Within any five-year period, you may try out some kind of work—and keep any income you earn—for up to nine months while still receiving full disability benefits. (Your medical condition must still qualify you as disabled during this trial period.) You may try one job for a month or two and, if it doesn't work out, attempt the same or another job sometime later—up to a total of nine months within any five-year period. These nine months do not have to be consecutive.

Any month in which you make more than $850 is considered one of the nine trial work months (so you could be doing trial work without even knowing it). If you are self-employed, any month in which you work 80 hours or more is considered a trial work month.

After you have worked for nine trial work months, your trial work period is over, and Social Security will assess whether you've been doing substantial gainful activity during this time. Generally, if you made over $1,180 on average, your disability benefits will be discontinued.

Extended Eligibility for Benefits

After you have worked for nine months—the trial work period—during a five-year span, Social Security gives you another 36-month period of eligibility during which you can continue to work without necessarily losing your eligibility for benefits. During this time, you will receive your full disability benefits for any month you do not have "substantial" earnings. Again, earnings of $1,180 per month are considered "substantial"; the amount is $1,970 if you are blind. You do not need to file a new application for benefits or go through any eligibility review.

The first time that you make substantial earnings during this "extended period of eligibility" (EPE), a grace period starts, during which you can receive your full benefits and keep the income you make from work. The grace period lasts three months.

Quick Restart of Benefits

What if you've finished your trial work period and EPE, your benefits have been stopped because you're working enough to bring in "substantial" earnings, but you again find yourself unable to work? In such a situation, Social Security makes it easy to restart your benefits. For five years after your disability benefits stop, called the "expedited reinstatement" period, you may get an immediate restart of benefits if you again are unable to work, so long as your inability to work is caused by the same disabling condition as before.

You need not file a new application for benefits, although you do need to file a simple form requesting the resumption of benefits. Social Security will again review your condition to determine whether you are disabled. However, your benefits should be restarted on the first of the month following your request, without waiting for the review to be completed.

> EXAMPLE: Roberta qualified for Social Security disability benefits because of a congenital back condition that worsened so much in her 30s that she could no longer work. After several years, however, a new surgical technique was developed that greatly improved Roberta's condition. Roberta returned to work part time and soon earned a "substantial" income. That meant she no longer qualified for disability benefits. Her back remained strong enough for her to work for two years, but then it began to deteriorate again. Within another six months, she found she could no longer work. Because Roberta's original disability was the same disability that caused her to stop working again within 60 months after she had returned to work, she regained her disability benefits within a month, simply by applying for reinstatement.

Continuing Medicare Coverage

If you became eligible for Medicare coverage because you qualified for disability benefits, you do not immediately lose that Medicare coverage once you return to work. After you return to "substantial" work for more than nine months, and therefore your disability benefits stop, your Medicare coverage continues for another 93 months. This is the period between the end of your grace period and the end of your expedited reinstatement period. During that time, your Medicare Part A coverage is free; you must pay the same premium for Medicare Part B as other Medicare beneficiaries.

Social Security Dependents Benefits

A retired or disabled worker with a family obviously needs more money than someone living alone—especially given that Social Security benefits currently average only about $1,300 per month. The situation is particularly acute when the retired or disabled worker was the family's primary breadwinner. Congress woke up to this reality in 1939, four years after it passed the original Social Security retirement law. It began providing dependents benefits to the spouse and minor children of a retired or disabled worker.

Who Is Eligible

Certain family members of a retired or disabled worker are eligible for monthly dependents benefits if the worker has enough work credits to qualify for, and has claimed and actually begun collecting, his or her own retirement or disability benefits. If a worker delays claiming retirement benefits until after reaching full retirement age, his or her dependent(s) must also wait to collect dependents benefits until the worker begins collecting. A qualifying divorced spouse may not need to wait until the ex-spouse worker actually claims retirement benefits (see "Effect of Marriage and Divorce," below).

The amount of benefits paid to dependents is determined by the worker's earnings record and, for a spouse, the age at which the spouse claims the benefit.

You don't have to actually depend on the worker for support in order to claim dependents benefits.

Individuals Who Qualify

To be entitled to benefits, you need to fit one of the following categories:
- a spouse age 62 or older
- a divorced spouse age 62 or older, with certain conditions (see "Effect of Marriage and Divorce," below)

- a spouse younger than 62 who is caring for the worker's child who is younger than 16 or became disabled before age 22
- unmarried children younger than 18 (although the mother's or father's benefit ends when the child turns 16, the child continues to receive benefits until age 18)
- unmarried children up to age 19 and still in high school
- unmarried children of any age if they were severely disabled before they reached age 22, for as long as they remain disabled (disability is defined by Social Security in the same way as for Supplementary Security Income benefits; see Chapter 7)
- unmarried stepchildren up to age 18 (19 if still in high school) if living with and under the care of the retired or disabled worker, or
- grandchildren of the worker, if they live with and are under the actual care of the worker and the parents are deceased or disabled, or if the grandparent has adopted them.

Effect of Marriage and Divorce

Couples come in many forms: companions who are not married; couples who are divorced; people who were divorced but have married again. Each status has some ramifications regarding dependents benefits.

Divorced Spouses

You are eligible for dependents benefits if both you and your former spouse have reached age 62 and your marriage lasted ten years, and you have been divorced two years. This two-year waiting period does not apply if your former spouse was already entitled to retirement benefits before the divorce.

You can collect benefits as soon as your former spouse is eligible for retirement benefits at age 62. He or she does not actually have to be collecting those benefits for you to collect your dependents benefits.

Remarried

If you are collecting dependents benefits on your former spouse's work record and then marry someone else, you lose your right to continue those benefits. However, you may be eligible to collect dependents benefits based on your new spouse's work record.

If you divorce again, you can collect benefits again on your first former spouse's record, or on your second spouse's record if you were married for ten years the second time as well.

Try to Stretch the Marriage to Ten Years

If you are in the process of getting a divorce and you have been married almost ten years, try to have your spouse agree—or stall the legal paperwork long enough—that the divorce will not become final until after ten years. This is the amount of time you must have been married to get dependents benefits.

Under Social Security rules, the marriage is considered in effect until the divorce legally becomes final, even if you and your spouse have already been living apart, you have separated your property, and one of you has begun paying spousal or child support.

If you anticipate that your spouse might object to the delay, you might remind him or her that your dependents benefits have no effect on the amount he or she may collect in retirement benefits. Nor would your benefits affect the amount of dependents benefits a new spouse could collect in addition to yours.

Whether your former spouse remarries does not affect your eligibility. Nor does your collecting dependents benefits through your former spouse affect his or her new spouse's right to collect benefits. And there is no reduction in either of your benefits because two spouses are collecting them.

Dependents Benefits for Same-Sex Spouses

The United States Supreme Court has made clear that same-sex spouses are entitled to federal Social Security dependents benefits on the same terms as other spouses. This is true regardless of whether the couple lives in the state where the marriage was performed.

Foreign marriages. A spouse in a same-sex couple who was married outside the United States but now lawfully lives in the United States might be entitled to dependents benefits based on the other spouse's work record in the United States, depending on the status of that marriage in the country where it was performed. Even if you have doubts about your right to dependents benefits as a same-sex spouse, the Social Security Administration encourages you to apply for them so that the agency can determine whether you are eligible.

Retroactivity. These benefits may be retroactive. The Department of Justice and the Social Security Administration have decided in several cases that the right to spousal benefits for a same-sex spouse may apply to someone who applied for such benefits before the Supreme Court's same-sex marriage decision on June 26, 2015. If you were married and applied for spousal benefits before that date but were denied those benefits (because you lived in a state that did not recognize your marriage), reapply to Social Security specifically requesting retroactive benefits back to the date you first applied.

Unmarried

For the most part, Social Security laws do not recognize the relationship between two adults who are not officially married. There are two exceptions.

First, if one person in an unmarried couple adopts the minor child of the other person, that child becomes eligible for dependents benefits based on the adoptive parent's work record. The other person in the couple does not, however, become eligible for Social Security benefits.

Second, if you live in a state that recognizes common law marriage and you qualify under that state's rules for such marriages, you may also qualify for dependents benefits. The states that recognize common law marriages are Alabama, Colorado, the District of Columbia, Iowa, Kansas, Montana, Oklahoma, Pennsylvania, Rhode Island, South Carolina, Texas, and Utah. Georgia, Idaho, and Pennsylvania recognize common law marriages that were formed before certain dates.

The qualifying rules for a common law marriage vary somewhat from state to state, but all require that you have lived together and have represented yourselves as married by such things as using the same name and owning property together.

Calculating Dependents Benefits

The amount of benefits available to a retired or disabled worker and his or her dependents is calculated based on the total number of people in the immediate family. Social Security figures that the economies of scale permit two to live more cheaply than one, three to live more cheaply than two, and so on. Therefore, the amount by which benefits increase with each additional dependent is smaller and smaller for each person added. (But don't worry, claiming dependents benefits won't reduce the primary worker's retirement or disability benefits.)

One Dependent

The basic Social Security benefit for one dependent, whether the dependent is a spouse, divorced spouse, or qualifying child, is 50% of the worker's retirement or disability benefit amount. If a divorced spouse and a new spouse both receive dependents benefits, each receives 50%.

The actual amount of your dependents benefit is based on the earnings record and timing of the retirement benefit claim of the worker on whom you are a dependent. Even if the worker has claimed retirement benefits at less than his or her full retirement age, dependents benefits will be based upon what the worker would have received at full retirement age.

Some workers delay claiming retirement benefits until after full retirement age, up to age 70, in order to receive higher benefits. If so, the worker's retirement benefits will be higher, but the dependent's benefits will not. Dependents benefits are based on what the worker would have received if he or she had claimed retirement benefits at full retirement age, not on the worker's higher delayed benefit amount. However, if you are the worker's spouse, the amount of your dependents benefits depends on your age when you first claim the benefits. The amount of a spouse's dependents benefits is permanently lower if he or she claims them between age 62 and his or her full retirement age. At each of the ages listed below, a dependent whose full retirement age is 66 receives a benefit as follows:

Dependent Spouse's Age	Percent of Worker's Benefit
62	35.0%
63	37.5%
64	41.7%
65	45.8%
Full Retirement Age	50.0%

The best way to find out the amount of retirement or disability benefits that you and your dependents are likely to receive is to review your official Social Security Statement (discussed in Chapter 1).

T P

Dependent eligible for Medicare at age 65. At age 65, a spouse may be eligible for Medicare coverage based on the worker's earnings record, even if he or she does not have enough Medicare earnings to qualify on his or her own. In order for a spouse to qualify for Medicare on the worker's record, the worker must be at least age 62 and personally have sufficient work credits to qualify for Social Security benefits.

Family Benefits

If your family includes more than one dependent—a spouse and one or more children, or no spouse but two or more children—the benefits paid to the worker and the dependents will be calculated according to the "family benefit amount." This amount is less than the total would be if the worker's benefits and individual dependents benefits were paid separately without a family limit.

The maximum family benefit is 150% to 180% of a retired worker's benefits—the precise amount depends on a complicated Social Security formula—or 150% of a disabled worker's benefits. The retired or disabled worker collects 100% of his or her benefits, and the remaining 50% to 80% is divided equally among the dependents. This maximum family benefit does not apply to spouses who collect retirement benefits based on their own work record.

EXAMPLE: Chiang-Fa is retired. Alone, he would be entitled to $900 per month in retirement benefits. He and his wife Yoka have a 17-year-old daughter. With no daughter, Yoka would be entitled to a $450-per-month dependents benefit—50% of Chiang-Fa's $900 retirement benefit.

However, because his daughter is also eligible, the three of them together are limited to a maximum family benefit of 180% of Chiang-Fa's benefit, or $1,620. That amount would be divided as follows: Chiang-Fa, $900; Yoka and the daughter, each $360. Once the daughter reaches age 18, however, she is no longer eligible for dependents benefits, and Yoka would begin to get a full 50% dependents benefit of $450 per month.

If Yoka is entitled to her own benefit (on her own work record), that could lower the portion of Yoka's benefit that counts toward the family maximum and raise the daughter's amount.

Eligibility for More Than One Benefit

Many people are not only eligible for their own Social Security retirement or disability benefits, but also for dependents benefits based on their spouses' work records. As with other Social Security benefits, you are not permitted to double up and collect both at the same time.

If your own earnings record is low and your spouse's earnings record high, you may be entitled to higher monthly benefits as a dependent than you would be by collecting your own retirement or disability benefits. What you are permitted to do in this situation depends on the year you were born, due to the Bipartisan Budget Act of 2015:

- If you turned age 62 before 2016, you can choose *either* to claim dependents benefits when your spouse claims retirement or disability benefits, *or* you can claim your own retirement benefits and then switch to higher dependents benefits when your spouse later claims retirement or disability benefits. This choice is explained in more detail in Chapter 6.
- If you turned 62 in 2016 or later, you have no choice about claiming one benefit or another. If at any time you claim either your own retirement benefits or dependents benefits, Social Security will "deem" you to have applied for both. You will then collect whichever of the two benefits is higher, but you cannot claim one while putting off the other to allow it to grow.

Working While Receiving Benefits

Before full retirement age, a dependent's benefit will be reduced by $1 for every $2 of income earned over the yearly maximum. Once a dependent reaches full retirement age, benefits are not reduced, regardless of how much the dependent is earning. (See Chapter 2 for a full explanation of benefit reductions.)

If several dependents are receiving a combined family benefit amount, one dependent's earnings do not affect the amount the other family members receive.

EXAMPLE: Grace and Omar and their teenage son receive a combined family retirement and dependents benefit of $1,650 a month. Grace and the son's portions of the family benefit are $350 each. Grace is offered a job for a year as a substitute teacher at a salary that is $6,000 over the yearly earnings limit for her age of 63 years old.

Since Grace's benefit amount is reduced $1 for every $2 she earns over the limit, her benefit would be reduced by half ($1 out of $2) of $6,000. That means a reduction of $3,000, or $250 per month. Since her own part of the family benefit is $350, that benefit would be reduced to $100 per month. The rest of the family's benefits—Omar's $950 per month and the son's $350—would not be affected.

Perils of Claiming Early: Reduced Benefits

If you claim retirement benefits before full retirement age, your retirement benefits are reduced by between 0.5% and 0.55% per month before full retirement age, depending on the year you were born. (See Chapter 2 for details.) And if you later switch to dependents benefits, those benefits, too, will be reduced by the same amount as your retirement benefits were reduced.

EXAMPLE: Clare became eligible for retirement benefits of $500 per month at age 65. She decided to claim early retirement benefits at age 62—her full retirement amount of $500 less 20%, for a monthly sum of $400. When her husband turned 65, he applied for retirement benefits and received $1,200 per month. Clare switched from her own retirement claim to dependents benefits, which ordinarily would have been $600, or 50% of her husband's monthly amount. But because Clare had already taken 20% reduced retirement benefits at age 62, her dependents benefits were now reduced by 20%. She ended up getting $480 per month, instead of the $600 per month she would have received had she waited.

Government Pension Offset

Most people who work for a federal, state, or local government or for a public agency are now fully covered by the Social Security system, and are also eligible to receive benefits under their agency's public retirement system. But millions of people of retirement age worked for a branch of government—federal, state, or local—or for a public agency, such as a school district, and earned a retirement pension under the Civil Service Retirement System (CSRS) or a similar pension system that paid no Social Security taxes. (See Chapter 10 for more information about the CSRS.) These people may be subject to a reduction in Social Security dependents benefits called the "government pension offset."

The government pension offset applies if you receive Social Security dependents or survivors benefits and also receive a retirement pension based on your own work record from the CSRS or another Civil Service pension system that did not contribute to Social Security. If you receive this type of pension, your Social Security dependents or survivors benefits are reduced dollar for dollar by two-thirds of the amount of your Civil Service pension.

The government pension offset does not apply, however, to people who are eligible to receive retirement benefits under the Federal Employees Retirement System (FERS), state or local Public Employees Retirement System (PERS), or any other public employment retirement system that does pay Social Security taxes.

In particular, the government pension offset does not apply to:

- federal employees who pay Social Security taxes on their earnings
- federal Civil Service Offset employees (employees who had at least five years of federal employment under the CSRS, then left federal employment but were rehired after December 31, 1983 following a break of a year or more)
- federal employees who switched from the CSRS to the FERS before July 1, 1988

- federal employees who switched from the CSRS to the FERS after June 30, 1988 and worked for at least five years under FERS
- people whose retirement benefit is based on work for a state or local government or public agency whose pension system paid Social Security taxes at the time they retired (and who retired before July 1, 2004), or
- people who retired on or after July 1, 2004, and whose retirement benefit is based on work for a state or local government or public agency whose pension system paid Social Security taxes during the last five years of employment.

If you are entitled to benefits under any CSRS pension, you should consider this government pension offset when calculating the amount of your combined CSRS retirement pension and Social Security dependents or survivors benefits. This rule may also affect which pension benefit you choose to collect.

EXAMPLE: Gina and her husband both worked for the government under the Civil Service Retirement System (CSRS). Her husband also worked in the private sector, paying Social Security taxes on his earnings. Gina is entitled to $500 per month in Social Security dependents benefits, based on her husband's private sector work record. She is also entitled to a CSRS pension of $400 per month (her own retirement pension) and a $250 per month CSRS dependents benefit based on her husband's work under the CSRS.

If Gina claims her own CSRS retirement pension, her Social Security dependents benefits would be reduced by two-thirds of her $400 pension (meaning the amount deducted from her Social Security benefit would be $266). If, instead, she claims her CSRS pension dependents benefits but not her own CSRS retirement pension, her Social Security dependents benefits are not affected. So, she is better off collecting her smaller CSRS dependents benefits ($250) plus her full Social Security dependents benefits ($500), for a total of $750 per month, than she would be collecting her own larger CSRS retirement benefit ($400) with her reduced Social Security dependents benefit amount ($500 – $266 offset = $234), for a total of only $634 a month.

TIP

Private employer pensions are not affected. The pension offset rule does not apply to pensions paid by private, as opposed to Civil Service Retirement System, employers. As far as Social Security is concerned, you are entitled to your full Social Security dependents benefits as well as your private pension benefits. However, your private pension plan may require that your pension benefits be reduced by the amount you receive from Social Security.

Social Security Survivors Benefits

T he Social Security laws recognize that a worker's family may need financial support after the worker dies. Even if the surviving spouse has always worked, the loss of the deceased spouse's income will almost surely be an economic blow to the family. And if the surviving spouse did not work, or earned much less than the deceased spouse, the loss of the deceased worker's income can be financially devastating. Recognizing the family financial burden brought on by the loss of the primary earner, Social Security provides for what are called survivors benefits to be paid to the spouse and children of an eligible worker who has died.

Work Credits Required for Eligibility

Surviving family members of a deceased worker are entitled to survivors benefits only if the worker earned enough work credits before dying. Work credits are accumulated based on earnings from employment covered by Social Security. The required number of work credits depends on the worker's age at death. (See Chapter 1 for more on work credits.)

Number of Work Credits Required

The number of work credits on the worker's Social Security record needed for survivors to collect benefits is listed in the "Credits Required on Deceased's Work Record" chart, below.

Credits Earned Just Before Death

Even if the deceased worker did not have enough work credits according to the chart below, benefits may still be paid to the surviving spouse and children if the worker had at least one and one-half years of work in covered employment in the three years immediately before dying.

Credits Required on Deceased's Work Record	
If the worker died or became disabled at age:	Work credits needed:
28 or younger	6
30	8
32	10
34	12
36	14
38	16
40	18
42	20
44	22
46	24
48	26
50	28
52	30
54	32
56	34
58	36
60	38
62	40

Who Is Eligible

Provided the deceased worker had enough work credits, here's who can claim survivors benefits:

- a surviving spouse age 60 or older
- a divorced surviving spouse age 60 or older, if the marriage lasted at least ten years
- a surviving spouse younger than 60, if he or she is caring for the worker's child who is younger than 16 or disabled; this benefit, sometimes called the mother's benefit or father's benefit, may also be paid to a surviving divorced spouse

Survivors Benefits for Same-Sex Spouses

The U.S. Supreme Court has made clear that a same-sex surviving spouse is entitled to federal Social Security survivors benefits on the same terms as any other surviving spouse. This is true regardless of the state in which the same-sex couple lived, if the marriage was lawful in the state where it was performed.

Foreign marriages. The surviving spouse of a same-sex couple who was married outside the United States but who now lawfully lives in the United States might be entitled to survivors benefits based on the deceased spouse's work record in the United States The right to benefits in this situation depends on the status of that marriage in the country where it was performed. Even if you have doubts about your right to survivors benefits as a same-sex surviving spouse, the Social Security Administration encourages you to apply so that they can determine whether you are eligible.

Retroactivity. These benefits may be retroactive. The Department of Justice and Social Security Administration have decided in several cases that the right to spousal benefits for a same-sex spouse may apply to someone who applied for such benefits before the Supreme Court's same-sex marriage decision on June 26, 2015. If you were married, widowed, and applied for survivors benefits before that date but were denied those benefits (because you lived in a state that did not recognize your marriage), reapply to Social Security specifically requesting retroactive benefits back to the date you first applied.

- a surviving spouse age 50 or older who becomes disabled within seven years of the worker's death or within seven years after mother's benefits or father's benefits end; if you were divorced, you can collect these disabled survivors benefits only if your marriage lasted at least ten years
- unmarried children younger than 18; benefits may continue to age 19 if the child is still a full-time high school student

- unmarried children of any age who were severely disabled before age 22 and are still disabled, or
- one or both parents of the worker who are at least age 62 and who were dependent on the worker for at least one-half of their financial support. If an unmarried dependent parent remarries after the worker's death, the parent loses the survivors benefits.

Length of Marriage Rule

To collect benefits as a surviving spouse, you must have been married for at least the nine months before the worker's death. However, there are some exceptions to this rule. If you are the biological parent of a child with the worker, or you adopted the worker's child or adopted a child with the worker before the child was 18, the nine-month rule does not apply.

The rule is also waived if you were previously married to the same person and your first marriage lasted more than nine months. And the nine-month rule does not apply if the worker's death was the result of an accident, as opposed to illness, or occurred while he or she was on active military duty. There are a few other rare exceptions as well.

Effect of Remarrying

One of the assumptions behind survivors benefits for spouses is that the majority of surviving spouses are women and that women are financially dependent on their husbands. Although things are changing, the fact that there are still fewer women than men in the workforce and that women still make less than 80 cents for every dollar men earn in wages in comparable jobs means this assumption isn't entirely out of date.

Another assumption is that if a surviving spouse—usually a woman—remarries, her need for survivors benefits will end, because there is a new spouse upon whom to depend financially. So a series of qualifying Social Security rules apply to collecting survivors benefits after remarriage:

- A widow or widower who remarries before age 60 loses the right to collect survivors benefits through the deceased spouse, even if he or she still cares for the former spouse's children. The children, however, remain eligible for benefits. (At age 62, the remarried spouse may be eligible for dependents benefits based on the new spouse's record.)
- If the widow or widower is over the age of 50 and disabled, getting remarried won't affect his or her benefits.
- A widow or widower who remarries after reaching age 60 does not lose survivors benefits from the deceased former spouse. However, he or she may want to transfer—at age 62 or later—to dependents benefits based on the new spouse's earnings record if that benefit would be higher than the survivors benefits.
- If you were divorced from your now-deceased former spouse, and the two of you had been married for at least ten years, you are eligible for survivors benefits even if you remarried before age 60 but are again widowed or divorced. After age 60, you may remarry without losing your survivors benefits.
- If you were divorced from your now-deceased spouse, you are over the age of 50, and you are disabled, getting remarried won't affect your benefits.

EXAMPLE: Akiko and Yosh were divorced ten years ago, after being married for 25 years. Three years ago, Yosh died. Akiko has a new sweetheart, Ben. They have been together for the past year and are now considering marriage. But Akiko is concerned about the effect their marriage would have on her right to collect Social Security survivors benefits. Akiko is 59, and next year she would be eligible for survivors benefits based on Yosh's work record because their marriage had lasted more than the required ten years.

If Akiko waits one more year, she and Ben can marry and she will still be able to collect survivors benefits based on Yosh's record. If she marries before reaching age 60, she will lose those benefits.

Amount of Survivors Benefits

Like all other Social Security benefits, the dollar amounts of survivors benefits are determined by the deceased worker's earnings record. In addition, the amount of the survivors benefit depends on whether and when the worker had claimed retirement benefits. If the worker had claimed Social Security retirement benefits before death, the amount of survivors benefits is equivalent to what the deceased worker was receiving. That is, if the worker claimed reduced retirement benefits before full retirement age, survivors benefits will be similarly reduced. On the other hand, if the worker waited until after full retirement age to claim benefits, and therefore got a higher benefit amount, the survivors benefits will be similarly higher. If the worker died before claiming retirement benefits, Social Security determines what the worker's retirement benefit would have been and bases the survivors benefits on that amount.

Percentage of Benefits Awarded

Exactly what percentage of the deceased worker's retirement benefit will be awarded to a survivor depends on whether you are the spouse or child of the deceased worker. Also, if you're a surviving spouse, the amount goes up or down depending on the age between 60 and "full benefits age" at which you first claim benefits. Full benefits age is set by Social Security based on the year of your birth; it parallels the full retirement age set for workers.

As with retirement benefits, the full benefits age will be going up in the coming years. The changes are shown on the following chart.

As with retirement benefits, the age at which a person may collect full survivors benefits is currently 66—but this will change for some people. For people born in 1940 or after, the survivors full benefits age is gradually rising, finally reaching age 67 for those who were born in 1962 or after.

Surviving Spouse at Full Benefits Age

A surviving spouse who waits until the age at which he or she becomes eligible for full benefits to claim benefits will receive 100% of what the deceased worker's full retirement benefit would have been if the deceased worker died before claiming those benefits or if the worker claimed the benefits at full retirement age. If the deceased worker had claimed retirement benefits early or deferred payments until after full retirement age, the amount of the survivors benefits will be based on the level of benefits the worker was actually receiving (reduced for an early claim, increased for a delayed claim).

Full Benefits Age for Widow(er)s	
Birth Date	**Full Benefits Age**
1/1/40 or earlier	65 years
1/2/40–1/1/41	65 + 2 months
1/2/41–1/1/42	65 + 4 months
1/2/42–1/1/43	65 + 6 months
1/2/43–1/1/44	65 + 8 months
1/2/44–1/1/45	65 + 10 months
1/2/45–1/1/57	66 years
1/2/57–1/1/58	66 + 2 months
1/2/58–1/1/59	66 + 4 months
1/2/59–1/1/60	66 + 6 months
1/2/60–1/1/61	66 + 8 months
1/2/61–1/1/62	66 + 10 months
1/2/62 and later	67 years

Surviving Spouse Under Full Benefits Age

A surviving spouse at age 60 will receive 71.5% of what the worker would have been receiving (reduced if the worker claimed early benefits, enhanced if the worker delayed the claim until after full retirement age). Each year a surviving spouse delays claiming benefits after age 60, those benefits will rise 4.1% to 5.7% per year, depending on the year of birth, until the survivor reaches full benefits age. (See the "Full Benefits Age for Widow(er)s" chart, above.) A widow or widower who waits until full retirement age to collect survivors benefits will receive 100% of what the worker would have been receiving.

Delaying benefits may be a good idea for survivors who are under full retirement age and who are still working. (See "Working While Receiving Benefits," below, for more information.)

Surviving Spouse Caring for Child

A surviving spouse who is caring for the worker's child, if that child is younger than 16 or disabled, is eligible for benefits regardless of the surviving spouse's age. The amount of benefits will be 75% of what the worker's retirement benefits would have been.

Minor or Disabled Child

A surviving minor or disabled child receives 75% of what the worker's retirement benefits would have been. This is over and above what the parent receives. This amount is, however, subject to the per-family maximum discussed in "Surviving Spouse and Children Together," below.

Dependent Parent

A surviving parent who was dependent on his or her deceased son or daughter for at least half of his or her financial support may be eligible for 82.5% of what the deceased worker's retirement benefit would have been. If there are two surviving dependent parents, they each get 75%.

Surviving Spouse and Children Together

A surviving spouse and children together are not entitled to the full amount each would get alone. A maximum is placed on the total amount that one family can receive.

The family benefit limit is 150% to 180% of what the deceased worker's retirement benefits would have been. The benefits are divided equally among the surviving spouse and children.

Estimating Benefit Amounts

You can get a general idea of survivors benefit amounts by looking at these recent average figures:

- overall average monthly benefit for surviving spouse: $1,336, and
- overall average monthly benefit for surviving spouse with two children: $2,771.

In addition, it can be helpful to look at averages based on income levels.

Low Income

The survivor of a worker who had relatively low income most of his or her working life—less than $30,000 per year in current dollars—will receive monthly benefits between $600 and $1,000. If both a surviving spouse and a minor child will be receiving benefits, the total for the two would be between about $1,000 and $1,500.

Moderate Income

The survivor of a worker who had a moderate annual income—around $30,000 to $40,000 in current terms—will receive between $1,000 and $1,500 per month. A surviving spouse and child would receive a total between about $1,500 and $2,000.

High Income

The survivor of a worker who averaged relatively high earnings—$40,000 per year or more in current dollars—can expect between $1,400 and $2,600 per month. The high earner's surviving spouse and child together would receive between $1,600 and $3,900.

Getting an Official Estimate

While a worker is alive, he or she can get a very accurate personal estimate of what his or her family members' survivors benefits are likely to be, directly from Social Security.

Eligibility for More Than One Benefit

Many surviving spouses are eligible for their own Social Security retirement or disability benefits, and also for benefits based on their spouses' work records. However, you are permitted to collect only one type of benefit. If your own earnings record is low and your deceased spouse's earnings record was high, you may be entitled to higher benefits as a surviving spouse than as a retired or disabled worker.

Even if you will ultimately be eligible for a higher retirement benefit after you turn age 62, you can claim survivors benefits as soon as you are eligible at age 60, and then switch to your own retirement benefits whenever they become higher than your survivors benefits. Claiming survivors benefits before you reach full retirement age does not reduce your own retirement benefit.

It also works in reverse: You can claim reduced early retirement benefits—between age 62 and full retirement age—on your own work record, and then switch to full survivors benefits at any later age if those benefits would be higher. Options for claiming one benefit and later switching to another, and the best time to do so, are explained in Chapter 6.

> EXAMPLE: Francesca would be eligible for full retirement benefits of $600 per month at age 65, based on her own work record; at age 62, she is eligible for reduced retirement benefits of $480 per month. At age 65, she would also be eligible for a full survivors benefit of $800 per month based on her deceased husband's work record; at age 62, she is eligible for a reduced survivors benefit of $660 per month.
>
> Francesca has two choices at age 62: She can claim her early retirement amount of $480 per month and then switch to full survivors benefits of $800 per month at age 65. Or she can claim her reduced survivors benefits of $660 per month at age 62 and collect that amount, plus cost-of-living increases, for the rest of her life. (She would not want to switch to full retirement benefits at age 65, because in her case they would be only $600 per month, less than her reduced survivors benefits.)

Francesca has to decide whether she can get along well enough with the $480-per-month retirement benefits she would receive for three years until she switched to her $800 survivors benefits. If she can manage, then waiting would be better in the long run. Waiting makes particularly good sense if she will also be working during those three years, because her benefits might be reduced because of her earnings.

One-Time Payment for Funeral or Burial Expenses

In addition to the monthly survivors benefits to which family members may be entitled, a family may also receive a one-time-only payment—currently $255—intended to defray funeral or burial expenses. A surviving spouse can claim the money if the couple was not divorced or legally separated at the time of death.

A divorced widow or widower can still collect the $255 if there is no surviving spouse and if he or she qualifies for the regular survivors benefits. Also, if there is no qualifying spouse, the sum may be paid to the surviving minor children, divided equally among them. You must file a claim for the death benefit at your local Social Security office within two years of the worker's death.

Working While Receiving Benefits

Many surviving spouses find that despite their survivors benefits, they also have to work to make ends meet. How much a surviving spouse earns, however, can affect the amount of benefits he or she receives.

The benefit for a surviving spouse who is less than full retirement age will be reduced by $1 for every $2 of income earned over the yearly maximum. Once a surviving spouse reaches full retirement age, there is no reduction in benefits, regardless of how much is earned. (See Chapter 2 for details.)

If a widow or widower and children are receiving a combined family benefit amount, the parent's earnings do not affect or lower the amount the children receive.

EXAMPLE: Manjusha and her teenage son receive a combined family survivors benefit of $1,500 a month, or $750 each. Manjusha is taking a job at a salary that is $6,000 over the yearly earnings limit.

Since Manjusha is 62, her benefit amount is reduced $1 for every $2 she earns over the limit. Her benefits would be reduced by half of $6,000, for a total reduction of $3,000, or $250 per month. Since Manjusha's part of the family benefit is $750, that benefit would be reduced to $500 per month. Her son's $750 would not be affected.

Government Pension Offset

If you worked enough years for a local, state, or federal government or public agency, you may be entitled to retirement benefits from that agency's pension system. You may also be entitled to Social Security survivors benefits based on your deceased spouse's work record. Most people don't have any problem collecting the full amount of both benefits. But people whose government agency work was more than 20 years ago may find themselves subject to a reduction in their survivors benefits. If your government agency work was under the Civil Service Retirement System (CSRS) or another pension system that did not pay into the Social Security system, collecting your own retirement pension may cause you to lose a substantial portion of your Social Security survivors benefits.

This government pension offset rule for Social Security survivors benefits is the same as for Social Security dependents benefits. (For more information, see "Government Pension Offset" in Chapter 4.)

This rule will not only affect how much your combined government pension and dependents benefits are, but it may also cause you to choose to collect your own Social Security retirement benefits, if you are eligible for them, rather than Social Security survivors benefits. The combination of your CSRS pension and your own Social Security retirement benefits may total a higher amount than your survivors benefits reduced by two-thirds of the amount of your pension.

EXAMPLE 1: Marta worked for a state government for a number of years, earning a CSRS pension of $690 per month. She is also entitled to a Social Security survivors benefit of $1,400 per month based on her late husband's work in the private sector, for which he and his employers paid Social Security taxes. Because of the public pension offset rule, however, Marta may not collect the full amount of both benefits. Her Social Security survivors benefit will be reduced by two-thirds of the amount of her CSRS pension. So, she collects her $690 per month retirement benefit plus a $940 per month survivors benefit ($1,400 − $460 offset [which is two-thirds of $690] = $940).

EXAMPLE 2: Alice is entitled to $500 per month in Social Security survivors benefits based on her deceased husband's nongovernment work record, for which he and his employer paid Social Security taxes. She is also entitled to both a CSRS pension of $400 per month and a $250 per month benefit as a widow based on her husband's public employee retirement record. Ordinarily, she would choose to claim her own CSRS pension rather than the lower public employee widow's benefit.

But her Social Security survivors benefits would be reduced by two-thirds of her CSRS pension ($400); if she claims CSRS pension dependents benefits, her Social Security amounts will not be reduced at all. She is better off collecting both her smaller CSRS pension dependents benefits ($250) and her full Social Security dependents benefits ($500) rather than her larger CSRS pension retirement benefit ($400) and the reduced Social Security amount which would result ($500 − $267 offset = $233).

The pension offset rule does not apply to pensions paid by private, nongovernmental employers. However, the rules of a few private pension plans provide that your pension benefits will be reduced by what you receive from Social Security.

When to Claim Social Security Benefits, and Which One to Claim

A s explained in Chapters 1 through 5, the age at which you claim Social Security retirement, dependents, or survivors benefits affects the monthly amount you receive—earlier claims (up to age 70) mean lower monthly benefits. In some situations, an early claim will also reduce how much you will receive if you later switch to a different benefit. Also, when you claim your benefits can affect how much your survivors collect. Altogether, the difference between filing a claim before or after full retirement age can be many thousands of dollars over your and your family's lifetime.

So, how do you choose the best time to claim a Social Security benefit? And which benefit should it be? There is no simple answer, but several factors may help you make a decision that best fits your personal situation. This chapter discusses the factors that apply to everyone, and then explains how specific situations—which depend on your family situation and work history—may present you with certain options.

Considerations for All Beneficiaries

You may claim your Social Security retirement or dependents benefits as early as age 62, or survivors benefits as early as age 60 (and sooner if you are disabled or caring for the deceased worker's child who is under age 16 or disabled; see Chapter 5). But the monthly amount you receive—for your lifetime—is reduced for every month before you reach full retirement age (66, for people born 1943–1954) that you claim these benefits. (See Chapter 2 to learn about full retirement age.) On the other hand, you can increase your retirement benefit amount for every year past full retirement age (up to age 70) that you wait to claim benefits. Also, by delaying retirement benefits, you increase the amount your surviving spouse can collect.

Your Lifetime Total: The Break-Even Point

Based on the way the Social Security system calculates benefits, if you claim benefits early but you live past a certain age—called your "break-even point"—you will wind up collecting less in total lifetime benefits than if you had waited to claim them at full retirement age. Similarly, if you wait until full retirement age to claim benefits, or delay them further, but do not live past your break-even point, you will have collected less in total lifetime benefits than if you had claimed benefits early.

Here's how these break-even points work.

Early claim break-even point. For people who claim benefits at age 62, their break-even point is between 75 and 76 years old (the exact point depends on your earnings record and the year you were born). That means, if you claim early benefits but live past that age, your total lifetime benefits will be less than if you had waited until full retirement age to claim them. The longer you live past the break-even point, the more you lose by having claimed early benefits. (Remember, though, that you might want to claim early benefits despite this, for other reasons discussed in this chapter.) Because average life expectancy for people age 62 is about 18 years for men and 21 years for women, most people will lose money over their lifetime if they claim benefits at age 62.

Delayed claim break-even point. For most people who delay claiming retirement benefits until age 70, their break-even point is about age 79. For people who live past that age and delayed benefits until age 70, total lifetime benefits will be more than if they had claimed them at full retirement age.

Your personal break-even point. Your personal break-even point may differ slightly from the figures above. Your actual break-even point will depend on a combination of factors, including your earnings record and when you were born. However, the figures above will give you a very close estimate. To get more specific information about your personal break-even point, you can call Social Security at 800-772-1213 and ask them to do the calculations for you, or go to the Social Security website's page "When To Start Receiving Retirement Benefits" at https://www.ssa.gov/pubs/EN-05-10147.pdf.

Factors to Consider

Many people jump at the chance to begin collecting benefits as early as possible, regardless of their break-even point. For some, claiming early benefits is a necessary, or at least sensible, financial choice. But for others, it may be a poor decision that can cost them many thousands of dollars over a lifetime. Before you decide whether to claim early benefits or to delay your claim, consider the following factors.

You Can Undo an Early Claim

Some people claim early benefits because they need the money immediately, but then their work situation changes. If, after claiming early benefits, you find new work, switch jobs, or get a pay raise, your new income could reduce your need for early benefits, or even wipe out those benefits entirely because of the earned income offset rule. (For more about this rule see "Continuing to Earn Before Full Retirement Age," below.)

If you find yourself in this situation, you're not stuck with the decision you made to claim early benefits. You have the following two options.

Suspend benefits. You can ask Social Security to suspend your benefits. This means your benefits will stop until you notify Social Security that you want your benefits to resume. While your benefits are suspended, your lifetime benefits will not suffer the monthly percentage reductions that would have occurred if you had continued to collect early benefits. When you resume collecting your benefits, Social Security will recalculate them, with a reduction based only on those months you actually collected early benefits.

Withdraw claim, repay benefits. Another option is to withdraw your benefit claim. You may withdraw your application within 12 months after first becoming eligible for benefits, if you repay all the benefits you have received so far. This removes all early claim reductions from Social Security's calculation of your benefit amounts, meaning you will be able to claim your full benefit at full retirement age, or a greater amount if you delay your claim even further. To learn more about how to withdraw a claim, and what you will have to repay, see Social Security's online information "Retirement Planner: If You Change Your Mind" at www.ssa.gov/planners/retire/withdrawal.html.

Immediate Financial Need

You may be in a financial situation that leaves you no real choice—you need your Social Security benefits now, even though your monthly benefits will be lower than if you wait, and your total lifetime benefits will probably be lower. For many people in these difficult economic times, the extra income of even a substantially reduced Social Security benefit is what allows them to afford the bare essentials of daily life.

Even if you do not need your Social Security benefit to meet essential daily expenses, you may want to collect a reduced benefit early in order to have a little extra money to make yourself or your family more comfortable. Having the extra money to use now—to do things you might not otherwise be able to afford—may be worth the chance that you will collect less in benefits over your entire lifetime. For example, you might want to use the extra money to do some traveling that you could not otherwise afford or might not be physically able to do later. Or, you might want to use the money to offer financial help to your children or grandchildren at a time when they could really use it. If there is any reason why you feel that using the money now is important to you, you may want to claim benefits early even though in a purely financial sense it may not be the best decision.

Continuing to Earn Before Full Retirement Age

Even if you could really use your retirement benefits before you reach full retirement age, it may not make sense to claim them now if you are going to keep working and earning more than a very small income. As explained in Chapters 2, 4, and 5, a Social Security penalty takes $1 from your retirement, dependents, or survivors benefits for every $2 in income you earn (until you reach full retirement age) over a low, yearly limit. If you will be earning only a slight amount over the yearly limit, it may still make sense to claim early benefits if you immediately need the amount that would be left over after this offset deduction. But if you will be working and earning a substantial amount over the yearly limit, claiming your benefits early would be a double mistake: Your immediate benefits would be substantially reduced if not wiped out altogether by the $1-out-of-$2 earnings offset rule; and your lifetime benefits would be permanently lower because you claimed them early.

Life Expectancy

If a health condition makes it likely you will not have a long life (meaning not live past your mid-70s), then claiming early retirement benefits makes sense. You will get to use or save the money, even though it's a reduced amount, for however many years you live. If, instead, you wait until full retirement age to claim benefits, but die within a few years of receiving them, you will have received less in total lifetime benefits even though your monthly benefit amount will have been greater than if you had claimed early benefits.

If, on the other hand, you have no life-threatening medical conditions, your health is generally good, and you have a family history of relatively long life, you may want to delay claiming retirement benefits at least until, and perhaps even later than, full retirement age. With a long life expectancy (likely to live past your mid-70s), you are more likely to collect greater total lifetime benefits by delaying your benefits claim.

Availability of Other Benefits

Your eligibility for Social Security dependents (see Chapter 4) or survivors (see Chapter 5) benefits may allow you to delay claiming your own retirement benefits past full retirement age, making those retirement benefits higher than if you claim them earlier. Claiming early survivors benefits may be a good idea even if those benefit amounts are lower than your early retirement benefits. That's because in the long run, the yearly increase in your unclaimed retirement benefits can make up the difference between lower dependents or survivors benefits you claim now and what your present retirement benefits would be. The scenarios for claiming one benefit while delaying another are discussed in the following sections.

Considerations for Specific Situations

In addition to the factors that apply to everyone (discussed above), if you qualify for more than one type of Social Security benefit, you may want to delay claiming one benefit while you collect another type instead. How this works depends on your prior and current marital status and the benefit amounts available to you.

Dependent Children Can Change the Equation

Any decision about when to claim retirement benefits might be a bit different if you have a minor or disabled child who is eligible for dependents benefits (which would pay the child an additional 50% of your retirement benefits). Dependents benefits payable to a minor child last only until the child turns 18, so if your child is already close to that age, the extra benefits wouldn't last long and probably won't affect your decision one way or the other. If, on the other hand, you have a much younger child, the total benefits your child could collect until age 18 might make it worth claiming your retirement benefits earlier than you otherwise would.

Unmarried, Divorced, or Widowed

If you have never been married, or if you were married but are now divorced or widowed, the best time to claim benefits depends on which benefits you are eligible for, and whether you have dependents yourself.

With No Benefits From Anyone Else's Work Record

If you are not eligible for dependents or survivors benefits based on the work record of a prior spouse, you probably only need to consider the factors discussed in the previous sections—your immediate financial need, continuing work, and life expectancy—in deciding when to claim your retirement benefits.

With Other Benefits From a Former Spouse's Work Record

If you were married previously, you may be eligible for dependents or survivors benefits based on your former spouse's work record. (Remember, though, that if you are divorced, you must have been married for at least ten years to be eligible for dependents or survivors benefits. A divorced spouse may be able to claim dependents benefits as soon as the former spouse reaches full retirement age, whether or not he or she actually claims retirement benefits then; see Chapter 4.) If either your dependents or survivors benefits are higher than your own retirement benefits, you can claim those instead of your own benefits. Whether and when to consider such benefit claims also depend on the following rules.

Dependents benefits. If you claim reduced dependents benefits before you reach full retirement age and then switch to your own retirement benefits later, which is permitted only for those who turned 62 before 2016, the early dependents claim will also cause your retirement benefits to be reduced by the same percentage.

Survivors benefits. A wrinkle in the Social Security laws allows you to claim early retirement or survivors benefits and then switch to the other of these two benefits without the early claim reducing the new benefit amount. It can work in either of two ways:

- You can claim survivors benefits as early as age 60 (or earlier if you're disabled or caring for the deceased worker's child who is under age 16 or disabled; see Chapter 5). If you claim survivors benefits before full retirement age, your early claim reduces those survivors benefits but does not affect your own retirement benefits. Your retirement benefit will continue to grow (until you reach age 70) while you are collecting survivors benefits. At any point, you can switch to your own retirement benefits. Given this rule, even if your survivors benefits are slightly smaller than your retirement benefits, you might want to claim those smaller benefits for several years while your retirement amount grows.
- You can claim your own retirement benefits before you reach full retirement age even if your survivors benefits would be

larger. Why? Because your early retirement benefits claim will not affect your later survivors benefits, which can grow if you delay claiming them. So, you can first take your reduced retirement benefits without affecting your survivors benefits. When you switch to the survivors benefits later, they will be higher for the rest of your life.

Married Couples

The rules for married couples allow for some manipulations that can mean higher lifetime benefits for one or both spouses.

If Only One Spouse Is Eligible for Retirement Benefits

Although their numbers are shrinking rapidly, there are still many married women who did not do enough paid work outside the home during their lifetime to have earned Social Security retirement benefits. (This happens with men, too, of course; but the number of men in this situation is so small that the discussion here will assume a no-retirement-benefit wife/retirement-benefit husband example.)

The wife in this circumstance is eligible for dependents benefits only when her husband claims retirement benefits, and survivors benefits when the husband dies. If she claims dependents or survivors benefits before her full retirement age, she gets a reduced benefit.

The husband, in this case, is eligible only for his own retirement benefits. He would have no dependents benefits based on his wife's work record, and no survivors benefits if she died before him.

In addition to reductions in benefits if the husband makes a claim before reaching full retirement age, a married couple with only one retirement benefit is faced with two Social Security rules that make for a difficult choice:

- If the husband delays his retirement benefits claim until after full retirement age (up to age 70), both his retirement benefits and the wife's survivors benefits (if she outlives him) will go up.
- The wife cannot claim dependents benefits (the spousal benefit) until the husband claims his retirement benefits.

Early Retirement or Dependents Claim Reduces the Other Benefit But Doesn't Affect Your Spouse or Child's Dependents Benefits

You are eligible for a reduced retirement benefit at age 62. If you claim retirement benefits at any time before you reach full retirement age, that early claim permanently reduces those benefits by 0.52% per month (up to full retirement age). The same is true for dependents benefits: if you claim dependents benefits between age 62 and full retirement age, those benefits are permanently reduced by 0.52% per month.

Many people don't realize, though, that claiming either early retirement or early dependents benefits also permanently reduces that other benefit for you. You cannot claim early retirement benefits and then switch to full dependents benefits, or claim early dependents benefits and then switch to full retirement benefits. As soon as you claim one early, the other one is also reduced by the same percentage.

Note, however, that your claiming early retirement benefits does not reduce the amount of your spouse's or child's dependents benefit amount. Nor does your early retirement benefits claim affect the amount of your survivors benefits based on your spouse's work record.

Both Spouses Eligible for Their Own Retirement Benefits

In most couples now reaching retirement age, both husband and wife have earned Social Security retirement benefits. That means that each one is also entitled to dependents (and, eventually, survivors) benefits based on the other spouse's work record. At any time after each one reaches age 62, he or she can claim retirement benefits. As soon as one claims retirement benefits, the other (once reaching age 62) can claim dependents benefits (the spousal benefit). And when one spouse dies, the other can claim survivors benefits, as early as age 60 (or earlier if disabled, or if caring for the deceased spouse's minor or disabled child).

All this operates, though, under one basic principle: You can claim only one benefit (the higher), not both. For some people, however, there may be some options that allow switching from one benefit to another, resulting in higher lifetime total benefits. There are time limits on each of these options that will determine whether you can make use of them:

- **Claim lower dependents benefits at full retirement age, allowing retirement benefits to grow (only for people who turned 62 before 2016).** At full retirement age, a spouse may be eligible for either full retirement benefits (based on his or her own work record) or full dependents benefits (if the other spouse has claimed his or her retirement benefits at full retirement age). But for those born before 1954, that might not be the only option. If you turned 62 in 2015 or earlier, you have a choice: 1) You can simply claim your retirement or your dependents benefits, which is higher; 2) If the amount of your dependents benefits is not too much lower than your retirement benefits would be, it might make good financial sense for you to file what's sometimes called a "restricted application" that claims only dependents benefits, which allows your retirement benefits to grow. You can later switch to your own retirement benefits, which will be 8% higher—and will remain so for the rest of your life—for each year you delayed past full retirement age (up to age 70).

  Reminder: This "restricted application" is permitted only for people who turned 62 by the end of 2015. If you were born later, any claim for one benefit is also "deemed" to be a claim for the other benefit at the same time (and you will be paid whichever benefit is higher at that time).

- **Claim early retirement or dependents benefits, then switch to survivors benefits.** At age 62, a spouse may be reluctant to claim reduced retirement or dependents benefits because those reductions are permanent. Plus, an early claim of either of those benefits permanently reduces the other one, too. But the same is not true for survivors benefits; claiming your own early retirement or dependents benefits (while your spouse is living) does not affect the amount of your survivors benefits you can collect (after your spouse has died). (Though if your spouse claims early retirement benefits, your eventual survivors benefit will be reduced.) So, if you have a considerably older spouse who has a higher earnings record, or your higher-earning spouse is in poor health, you might want to claim your early retirement or dependents benefits (whichever is higher), relying on the fact that you will be able to switch to full survivors benefits in the not-too-distant future.

Worker With Minor Child

A worker approaching full retirement age may want to delay claiming his or her retirement benefits for a year or more, up to age 70, to get the benefit of a permanently higher retirement benefit amount, and also a higher amount for his or her surviving spouse. But if the worker has a minor child, the child would be eligible for dependents benefits as soon as the worker claims retirement benefits. This presents a conflict: Either wait to claim and therefore get higher delayed retirement benefits but no dependents benefits for the child, or get dependents benefits now for the minor child but lose out on the higher delayed retirement benefits. ●

Supplemental Security Income

Over eight million people receive some Supplemental Security Income, or SSI, benefits. SSI is a program jointly operated by the federal and state governments and administered by the Social Security Administration. SSI is intended to guarantee a minimum level of income to financially hard-pressed older, blind, and/or disabled people.

SSI eligibility is based on your age or disability and on financial need as determined by both your income and your assets. SSI benefits do not depend on how long you have worked, or on how much you have paid into the Social Security system.

You must be quite financially needy to qualify for SSI payments. Indeed, your income and assets must be so low that many people with no income other than their Social Security retirement benefits are not eligible for SSI. Others whose Social Security retirement benefit is very low may receive a small SSI payment.

Nevertheless, if after reviewing the rules explained in this chapter, you think you may be close to meeting the requirements for SSI eligibility, it will be worth your while to apply for it. If you qualify for SSI, you may also be eligible for Medicaid (discussed in Chapter 16) and food stamps, as well as free rehabilitation and home care programs, should you need them.

Who Is Eligible

You must meet four basic requirements to be eligible for SSI cash benefits:

- You must be 65 or older, or blind or disabled.
- If you're a new applicant for SSI benefits, you must be a citizen of the United States, or meet strict requirements for longtime residency, military service, or political asylum or refugee status. Some legal permanent residents of the United States may be eligible for SSI benefits if they are blind or disabled.
- Your monthly income must be less than a certain minimum amount established by the state in which you live.
- Your assets must be worth less than $2,000, or $3,000 for a couple, although certain items are exempted from this amount, including your car and home.

TIP

The rules for each of these requirements are more complicated than they first appear. But the complications almost always make it easier for you to qualify for SSI benefits than you might imagine. Generally speaking, you are permitted to have more income and assets than the initial figures indicate (more on this below).

Blind or Disabled

If you are younger than 65, you can qualify for SSI payments if you are blind or disabled.

Basically, you are considered blind if your vision is no better than 20/200, or your field of vision is limited to 20 degrees or less, even with corrective lenses. (There are a few other ways to qualify as well.)

You are considered disabled if you have a physical or mental impairment that prevents you from doing any substantial work and that is expected to last at least 12 months, or to result in death. This definition of disabled is the same as the test used for Social Security disability insurance benefits. But unlike the Social Security disability program, which looks only at the income you currently earn in order to determine whether you are doing substantial work, SSI looks at income from all sources, and measures that income in a more complicated way.

Citizens or Longtime Residents

SSI benefits are generally available only to U.S. citizens and longtime legal residents. Noncitizens must fall within one of the narrow categories described below.

The restrictions hit some of the country's neediest people the hardest. These are people, often elderly, who have lawfully immigrated to this country to join their children or siblings, only to be met here by joblessness and poverty.

As a noncitizen of the United States, you qualify for federal SSI benefits only if one of the following applies:

- You have a legal right to live in the United States and you were already receiving SSI benefits on August 22, 1996.
- You were legally living in the United States on August 22, 1996, and you are now blind or disabled.
- You are a lawful permanent resident of the United States (a green card holder) and you or your spouse have worked for at least ten years in this country, having paid at least the minimum Social Security taxes to qualify for 40 quarters of work credits (see Chapter 1 for more information about work credits).
- You are a veteran (honorably discharged) or active duty member of the U.S. Armed Forces, or the spouse or child of one.
- You have been granted political asylum or refugee status; however, your benefits in this situation will last for only seven years after you have been admitted to the country.

 RESOURCE

For a more detailed discussion of immigrants' eligibility for SSI: See the National Immigration Law Center website at www.nilc.org or contact their Los Angeles office at 213-639-3900.

State Benefits May Be Available

Nondisabled noncitizens who were in the United States but not receiving SSI benefits as of August 22, 1996 are generally not eligible for federal SSI benefits. However, if you fall into this category but you have now reached age 65, your state might provide you with state supplement benefits as well as food stamps. You may also be eligible if you arrived in the United States after August 22, 1996 but your immigration sponsor has since died or become disabled. If you are in one of these categories, apply for both federal and state SSI assistance; you may be entitled to state benefits even if you are denied federal SSI.

Income Limits

To figure out whether your income is low enough to qualify for SSI, you first need to understand that there may actually be two SSI payments:

- the basic federal SSI payment, and
- a supplemental SSI payment in some states. Most states pay an additional amount over and above the federal benefit, and some of these states pay it alone if you qualify for it, even if you do not qualify for the federal payment.

Not all your income is counted when deciding whether you qualify for SSI. In fact, more than half of your earned income—wages and self-employment income—is not counted. And even though you may have income over the allowable maximum for federal SSI payments, you might still qualify for your state's supplemental payment. A few states set a higher income limit than the federal SSI program does, making it easier to qualify for those states' supplemental payment than for the federal one. (See "Benefit Amounts," below.)

The federal SSI limit on *counted* income is $750 per month for an individual (this means a total monthly earned income of $1,585), or $1,125 per month for a couple. The exact figure varies from state to state. In many states, however, you might qualify for the state's SSI supplemental payment—as well as Medicaid, food stamps, and other assistance—even if your counted income was too high to qualify for federal SSI.

Income That Is Counted

In general, half of any income you earn in wages or self-employment plus any money you receive from investments, pensions, annuities, royalties, gifts, rents, or interest on savings is counted toward the SSI limits. Social Security benefits are also considered counted income. In addition, if you receive free housing from friends or relatives, SSI may attribute some value to that housing. (See "Reductions to Benefits," below, regarding these limits on outside support.)

Income That Is Not Counted

Some specific amounts of money and support are not counted in determining whether you need SSI benefits.

SSI will not count:

- the first $20 per month you receive from any source—except other public assistance based on need, such as General Assistance
- the first $65 per month of your earned income—wages or self-employment
- one-half of all your earned income over $65 a month
- irregular or infrequent earned income—such as from a one-time-only job—if such income is not more than $10 a month
- irregular or infrequent unearned income—such as a gift or dividend on an investment—up to $20 per month
- food stamps, energy assistance, or housing assistance from a federal housing program run by a state or local government agency
- some work-related expenses for blind or disabled people that are paid for through public assistance
- some other types of one-time payments, such as tax refunds, reimbursement for financial losses such as insurance payments for medical bills, or compensation for injury to you or your property, or
- up to $100,000 in a special "Achieving a Better Life Experience" (ABLE) bank account.

Differences in Local Rules

Keeping in mind that different income limits apply in various states, one general suggestion applies to everyone: If you are age 65, blind, or disabled, and you are living on a small fixed income, and you have relatively few assets, apply for SSI benefits. The local Social Security or social welfare office may consider certain income differently than you do, and you may be pleasantly surprised to gain some help from SSI.

> **EXAMPLE:** Carmela receives Social Security survivors benefits of $310 a month and a $40-per-month private pension payment, for a total of $350 in regular unearned income. She also receives a quarterly dividend check; the most recent was $15.
>
> The dividend check would not be counted at all, because it is infrequent income less than $20. The first $20 of income from any source is not counted, so the $350 total of unearned income would be reduced to $330 of countable income.
>
> Carmela also earns $210 a month doing part-time work. Since the first $65 a month of earned income is not counted, her earned income amount would be reduced to $145; and since one-half of all earned income over $65 a month is not counted, half of $80 ($145 – $65) would not be considered for SSI purposes.
>
> This leaves Carmela with $105 countable earned income to be added to the $330 countable unearned income for the month, for a total of $435 countable income. Since this amount is under the basic SSI qualifying limit of $750 per month, Carmela would be eligible for the basic federal SSI payment. Because Carmela lives in New York where there is a state supplemental benefit, she may be eligible for that amount as well. (See "States With Federally Administered Supplements," below.)

Asset Limits

In addition to the limits on your income, SSI rules limit the amount of assets and other resources you may have and still qualify. The general limit is $2,000 in assets for an individual, $3,000 for a married couple living together. But as with the rules regarding income, people are actually allowed more assets than these figures seem to indicate.

Assets That Are Counted

The assets or resources that are counted by SSI include money in the bank, investments of any kind, real estate other than a primary residence, and personal property and household goods over certain limits.

SSI also counts any money or property in which you have an interest, even if you are not the sole owner. If you have a joint bank account with someone, or hold any property in joint tenancy with someone else, SSI will consider that you own the entire account or property, because you have access to all of it. If you have only a partial interest in some property—for example, an ownership interest in a family home along with other family members—SSI will determine how much your individual ownership portion is worth and count that as an asset.

Assets That Are Not Counted

You are allowed to have more property of value than the $2,000 and $3,000 limits first seem to indicate. Several important categories of assets are not counted in determining your eligibility for SSI benefits. They include:

- your home and the land it sits on, regardless of value, as long as you live in it
- one automobile, regardless of market value
- your personal property and household goods—such as clothing, furniture, appliances, tools, sporting goods, and hobby or craft material—up to a total current value of $2,000; the value is not judged by what the articles cost new, but by what you could sell them for now, less the amounts you still owe on them
- wedding and engagement rings, regardless of value
- property needed for medical reasons, such as wheelchairs, hospital beds, and prosthetics
- property essential to "self-support"—such as tools and machines used in your trade—up to a value of $6,000
- life insurance policies with a total face value of $1,500 or less per person, and term life insurance policies with no cash surrender value, and
- burial spaces for you and your spouse, plus a specially earmarked fund of up to $1,500 for funeral and burial expenses.

EXAMPLE: Rose and Peter are living on Peter's Social Security retirement benefits and on Rose's pension. They qualify under SSI income limits, and have the following assets: their home; a five-year-old car; $1,500 in savings; stocks worth $500; kitchen appliances worth about $300; a TV worth about $100; a stereo worth perhaps $150; Peter's carpentry tools, worth about $500; and Rose's jewelry, which, aside from her wedding band, is worth about $200.

Despite the fact that Rose and Peter's house is now worth $120,000, it is not counted as an asset. The value of their car is not counted at all. Their personal property and household goods add up to about $1,350, but none of it will be counted because this is within the permissible amounts for personal property.

Their total counted assets would be their savings and stocks worth about $2,000. Since the SSI limit on resources is $3,000 for a couple, Rose and Peter would qualify for SSI benefits.

Periodic Review of SSI Eligibility

Social Security periodically reviews your SSI eligibility and the amount of SSI you receive. These reviews take place at least once every three years, although there may be a brief review of your finances annually. When you receive a notice of review, you will have to produce the same kinds of information as you did for the original application: your income, assets, living arrangements, and, if claiming based on a disability, updated medical information. Often, most of this process can be handled by mail or telephone, although you may have to make a trip to the Social Security office for an interview.

Selling or Spending Assets

Even if your countable assets appear to be over the limit, it may still be possible for you to qualify to receive some SSI benefits. You may begin to receive SSI payments if you sell or spend enough property to come under the limits within a certain time period. That time period begins when you apply for benefits and runs six months for real estate and three months for personal property and liquid assets.

However, the sale or transfer must be a real one. Simply transferring title on the property to someone else while you keep control or use of it is not enough; neither is selling something for a small token amount.

> **EXAMPLE:** Mariana applies for SSI benefits when she has more than $5,000 in the bank. She is told that she will not be immediately eligible for benefits unless that amount is reduced to $2,000 within the next three months. Mariana had always planned to be buried near her deceased husband, but never got around to making the arrangements. She now buys a burial space for $2,000 in the same cemetery as her husband. Then she puts $1,000 in a special account to cover her funeral expenses. Since funeral and burial amounts are not counted as assets under SSI rules, and her assets are now down to $2,000 (within three months of her application for SSI), she will begin receiving benefits as of the date she applied.

Benefit Amounts

Because supplement payments vary from state to state, the amount of your SSI check will vary depending on where you live, as well as on the amount of your countable income. The basic federal SSI payment for 2018 is $750 a month for an individual and $1,125 a month for a couple. These figures usually go up on January 1 each year; the amount of increase depends on the rise in the federal Consumer Price Index.

States With Federally Administered Supplements

A number of states pay supplements to the basic federal SSI amount. In some of these states, the supplement is added on directly to the federal SSI payment. This means that a person needs to apply only once, to Social Security, to receive both the basic amount and the supplement. Both amounts are included in one payment, which is administered by Social Security.

SSI May Get You Medicaid

If you are found eligible for SSI benefits, most states will also give you free health coverage through the Medicaid program (called Medi-Cal in California). You don't need to qualify for Medicare to get Medicaid. For an explanation of what Medicaid offers, see Chapter 16.

Your enrollment is automatic in many states, including Alabama, Arizona, Arkansas, California, Colorado, Delaware, District of Columbia, Florida, Georgia, Indiana, Iowa, Kentucky, Louisiana, Maine, Maryland, Massachusetts, Michigan, Mississippi, Montana, New Jersey, New Mexico, New York, North Carolina, Pennsylvania, Rhode Island, South Carolina, South Dakota, Tennessee, Texas, Vermont, Washington, West Virginia, Wisconsin, and Wyoming.

In other states, you must separately apply for Medicaid after being granted SSI. This usually involves submitting an application to a state social services or welfare office. Some states will automatically enroll you based on your SSI grant. Others have slightly more restrictive eligibility standards and will separately evaluate your Medicaid application.

The states that automatically enroll you after you apply for Medicaid are Alaska, Idaho, Kansas, Nebraska, Nevada, Oregon, and Utah. The states that make an independent decision about whether you are eligible for Medicaid are Connecticut, Hawaii, Illinois, Indiana, Minnesota, Missouri, New Hampshire, North Dakota, Ohio, Oklahoma, and Virginia.

The supplement amount differs for a single individual, a couple, or a person who is blind. Also, the amount may be affected if the person receiving SSI lives in the home of a family friend, in congregate living arrangements, or in a nursing facility.

States in which SSI recipients receive a federally administered supplement include:

California	Iowa	Pennsylvania
District of Columbia	Nevada	Rhode Island
Hawaii	New Jersey	Vermont

In addition, Delaware and Montana have federally administered supplements that are available only to people who live in protective care arrangements (Delaware administers the state supplement for all others). Social Security administers the supplement for some SSI recipients in Iowa and Michigan.

States With Their Own Supplements

Most other states provide some kind of supplement to the basic federal SSI payment, but the kinds of supplements and rules for qualifying are administered entirely by the states. You must apply for these state supplements separately, at the social welfare agency in the county where you live.

Your supplement payments might range from a few dollars to a few hundred dollars above the basic federal SSI payment, or include noncash assistance with food, housing, transportation, and/or medical care. The amounts change frequently, based on the willingness of state legislatures to provide for SSI recipients in their state budgets.

Reductions to Benefits

Your maximum SSI benefit amount will be reduced by income you make over allowable countable limits, as dictated by a number of specific rules.

Limit on Earned Income

Your benefits are reduced by one dollar for every two dollars more than $65 per month that you earn in wages or self-employment.

> EXAMPLE: Ronda has a part-time job at which she earns $280 a month. She is entitled to the basic federal SSI benefit of $750 per month, but that amount is reduced by $107.50 because of her earnings. (The total of $107.50 is arrived at by taking the amount of her earned income over $65 ($215) and dividing it in half—$1 out of every $2 over the limit.) Her monthly income would then be her earnings of $280 plus her SSI benefit of $642.50, for a total of $922.50.

Limit on Unearned Income

Your benefits are reduced dollar for dollar by the amount of any *unearned* income you receive over $20 a month. This unearned income includes Social Security benefits, pensions, annuities, interest on savings, dividends, or any money from investments or property you own.

> EXAMPLE: Carl lives alone in a home he owns. His only income is his Social Security retirement check of $330 per month. From Carl's $330 Social Security check, $20 is excluded, making his total countable unearned income $310. Since he has no earned income, his total countable income would be the same: $310. In the state in which Carl lives, the basic SSI payment is $800 per month. From this, Carl's total countable income of $310 is subtracted, leaving $490 as Carl's monthly SSI payment.

Limit on Outside Support

Your basic SSI payment may be reduced up to one-third if you live in a relative's or friend's home without paying rent and/or you receive regular, substantial support in the form of food, clothing, and personal items.

> EXAMPLE: Adam lives in his daughter's house without paying rent. His daughter also provides Adam all of his meals. Adam's only income is his $370 per month Social Security check. The basic monthly SSI benefit of $750 in Adam's state would be reduced by one-third because Adam receives both regular food and free lodging from his daughter. This would leave an SSI amount of $500. In determining Adam's countable income, SSI does not count $20 of his $370 Social Security check, leaving a total countable amount of $350. This $350 is subtracted from his reduced SSI benefit, leaving an actual monthly SSI payment to Adam of $150, in addition to his Social Security benefit.

Limit on Working Couples

A final example shows how SSI amounts are figured for a couple, and how SSI payments change when one person takes a job.

> EXAMPLE: Beverly marries Carl and together they collect a monthly Social Security check of $455. In figuring Carl and Beverly's SSI payment, $20 would be exempted from the $455 Social Security check, for a total countable income of $435 a month. That $435 would be subtracted from the basic SSI benefit for a couple, which in Carl and Beverly's state is $1,200, leaving a monthly SSI payment of $765.
>
> When Beverly takes a part-time job paying $100 a month, their SSI payment changes. Beverly and Carl's countable unearned income is still the same, $435 a month—their Social Security check minus $20. But now they have an earned income of $100 a month. The first $65 of this $100 is not counted under SSI rules. Of the remaining $35 of earned income, only one half of it, or $17.50, is considered counted income. Only $17.50 is added to the $435 of counted unearned income, making a total countable income of $452.50 a month.
>
> The basic SSI benefit for a couple in Carl and Beverly's state is $1,200 a month. The $452.50 countable income would be subtracted from this amount, leaving a monthly SSI payment to Carl and Beverly of $747.50. Their monthly income would be their Social Security check of $455, plus their part-time income of $100, plus their SSI check of $747.50. ●

Applying for Benefits

Once you get an accurate estimate of how much your Social Security benefits will be and decide when it is best to begin receiving them, applying for those benefits is usually fairly simple. Most people will already have all the documents needed and can complete their application in one or two trips to a local Social Security office. This chapter discusses the application process and explains how to organize the required documents relating to your income and assets.

Retirement, Dependents, and Survivors Benefits

The application processes for retirement benefits, dependents benefits, and survivors benefits all involve the same basic documents and procedures. The hardest part is figuring out the best time to claim benefits. For this, you must understand the relationship between your age and the amount you will receive.

When to Claim Benefits

You may be eligible for different types of benefits at different times in your life—for example, survivors benefits at age 60, based on your deceased spouse's work record, and retirement benefits at age 62, based on your own work record. And you are eligible for increased benefits for every month you wait to claim them up to age 70.

As a result, your decision about which benefits to claim and when to claim them should be based on how much each benefit would be, measured against the earnings limit for your age, if you intend to continue working. (For earnings limits and reductions, see Chapter 2; for reductions for working dependents, see Chapter 4; for reductions for working survivors, see Chapter 5; and for options about choosing between benefits and deciding when to claim them, see Chapter 6.)

To see what each type of benefit would be at different ages, take a look at your Social Security Statement. Social Security used to send it to you each year, but you can now view it online (see Chapter 1 for details). You should examine your statement about six months before you might claim any benefit. This will give you plenty of time to decide what's best for you, and to get the process started if you choose to file soon for a benefit.

How and Where to File Your Claim

All Social Security claims for benefits can be filed at local Social Security offices. In addition, retirement, dependents, survivors, and disability benefits may be initiated by phone or through the Internet (see "Begin your application process online," below). Even online applications often require a visit to a local office to complete, however.

Most sizable cities have at least one local Social Security office, and in major urban areas there are usually several. To find the address and telephone number of the nearest office, check your telephone directory under the listing for U.S. Government, Social Security Administration, or sometimes under U.S. Government, Department of Health and Human Services, Social Security Administration. The SSA website also has listings of local offices, at www.ssa.gov. Click "MENU," then click "Contact Us." Look for the link "Find an office." If you're still having trouble finding a local office, call the SSA at 800-772-1213.

The following subsections describe how to get personal assistance with and local information about filing your claim.

Help on the Internet

The Social Security Administration now offers a good deal of information and some of its application processes online at www.ssa.gov. Some of the information can be hard to locate, but Social Security is making good progress in helping people to apply for many Social Security benefits online.

You can also find a lot of information to help you with a disability claim at www.disabilitysecrets.com.

COMPUTER

Begin your application process online. Social Security allows people to use its website to file many types of claims for benefits, which may save one or more trips to a Social Security office.

You may file an online application—or at least begin the process—for:

- retirement benefits
- survivors benefits
- disability benefits
- spouse's (dependents) benefits
- Supplemental Security Income (SSI)—in some circumstances
- Medicare Part A and Part B, and
- extra help with Medicare Part D.

To learn more about what Social Security permits you to do over the Internet, see its Web page "What You Can Do Online" at www.ssa.gov/onlineservices.

Help in Person

A Social Security worker in your local office is usually the best source of information and assistance for filing your claim. Face-to-face conversation is almost always more productive than discussions over the phone or via email messaging. And when you're ready to file your application, handing it to a real person is more secure than sending it by mail.

Most offices permit you to phone in advance and make an appointment to speak to someone personally—a good idea, because you may face long lines if you show up unannounced.

Whenever you consult with someone in a Social Security office, write down the person's name and keep it with your other Social Security papers. That way, when you next contact the office, you can ask to speak with the same person, or you can refer to that person if a question arises about what occurred during your previous visit.

When filing papers, make sure the office gives you some proof that you filed—for example, bring along your personal copy and ask them to stamp it "received" with the date, as they would for their daily mail.

Help Over the Telephone

Social Security offers advice and help over its toll-free phone line at 800-772-1213. The phone lines are open between 7 a.m. and 7 p.m. Eastern time Monday through Friday. It's busiest at the beginning of the month and early in each week, so choose your time to call accordingly.

You can accomplish a great deal over the phone. The Social Security workers can answer your general questions about benefits and rules and tell you how to fill out or submit a particular form. They may also be able to start your claim process for retirement and dependents benefits. However, that process cannot be completed over the phone. Before your claim can actually be processed, you'll have to sign a written application and bring certain original documents to Social Security (see "Documents You'll Need," below).

For Early Retirement, Sign Up Three Months Before Your Birthday

If you will need to actually receive a Social Security benefit payment as soon as you reach the youngest eligibility age, file your claim three months before the birthday on which you will become eligible. This will give Social Security time to process your claim so that you will receive benefits as soon as you become eligible. If you file a claim for early retirement later, you cannot get benefits retroactively for the months during which you were eligible but before you applied. (If you file after full retirement age, on the other hand, you can receive six months of retroactive benefits.)

What about Medicare? At age 65, anyone eligible for Social Security benefits is also eligible for Medicare coverage (explained in Chapter 13). Even if you are not going to claim Social Security benefits at age 65—because your benefit amount will be higher if you wait—you should sign up for Medicare coverage three months before your 65th birthday. There is no reason to delay signing up for Medicare, and waiting until after your 65th birthday will delay coverage. If you have current health care coverage through your employer when you turn 65, you may want to sign up for Part A only. (See Chapter 12 for more information.)

Getting the Best Results: Preparation, Patience, Perseverance

Social Security offices are usually understaffed. Although individual Social Security workers are often helpful, polite, and well versed in the various regulations that govern Social Security programs, the maze of rules, when added to normal human fallibility, inevitably makes for delays, misunderstandings, and mistakes.

It's up to you to help yourself. The best way to begin the Social Security application process is to use this book to understand the workings of whichever benefit program you will apply for.

The next most important thing is to keep your papers organized. During the benefit application process, you may mail papers and forms to your local Social Security office. However, it is best to deliver important papers—any original document or certified copy—in person. That way, the papers not only will be sure to get to the local office but also will go directly into your file. This will cut some time off the process and will help to avoid the adventures that sometimes befall papers that go into Social Security's incoming mail stacks.

Keep copies of any form or document you submit to Social Security. If the local Social Security office asks to see the original or a certified copy, it will usually make a copy on the spot and return the original to you. It's best to keep a copy in your files in case the original gets lost.

Documents You'll Need

Whether you file for a Social Security benefit in person at a local Social Security office or do all or some of it online through the Social Security website, you'll need to have certain personal papers or information. What you need will depend upon the type of benefit you're applying for, as explained below.

Most documents required by Social Security must be originals or certified copies. However, if you want to apply for benefits right away but do not yet have all your documents together, file your claim anyway—either by phone, on the Internet, or by going to your local Social Security office. The Social Security workers will advise you about how to get the documents you need, and, in the meantime, the application process can begin.

CAUTION
Make sure all your papers can be traced to you. On any copy of a document you bring or send to Social Security, write your name as it appears on your benefit application and your Social Security number. Also include the name and Social Security number of the person on whose work record you are claiming benefits. If you bring or send an original document, clip a piece of paper to it with those names and numbers.

When you apply for any type of benefit, bring with you the number of your account at a bank, a credit union, or another financial institution. Social Security will arrange to have your monthly benefit payment sent directly to your account—a process called direct deposit. Direct deposit is now used for all Social Security and SSI beneficiaries. It saves money for the Social Security Administration and also avoids the problem of lost or stolen checks.

Retirement Benefits

You may need some or all of the following documents or information to apply for retirement benefits:

- your Social Security number. You do not need your actual Social Security card.
- your birth certificate. If you do not have a birth certificate, bring any other evidence of the date of your birth: baptism record, military papers, immigration papers, driver's license, or passport.
- your military discharge papers, if you served in the military, and
- your most recent W-2 tax form or federal self-employment tax return.

Dependents Benefits

You may need some or all of the following documents or information to apply for dependents benefits:

- marriage certificate, if you are applying for benefits based on your spouse's work record, and
- birth certificate of any children claiming benefits. If you do not have a birth certificate, bring any other evidence of the date of your child's birth: baptism record, immigration papers, or passport.

Survivors Benefits

You may need some or all of the following documents or information to apply for survivors benefits:

- Social Security number of the deceased person on whose work record you are claiming benefits, and your own Social Security number
- divorce papers, if you are applying as a divorced spouse
- death certificate of your deceased spouse
- your birth certificate and those of your children who are claiming benefits. If a birth certificate is not available, bring any other evidence of date of birth: baptism record, military papers, immigration papers, or passport.
- if your spouse died within the past two years, the most recent W-2 tax form or federal self-employment tax return of your deceased spouse, and
- if applying as a surviving dependent parent who was receiving support from your son or daughter who died, a recent tax return from your deceased child showing you as a dependent, or proof of expenditures by your deceased child showing how much support was given to you, as well as your own most recent tax returns.

If You Retire From Your Own Business

If you are self-employed and are claiming retirement benefits before your full retirement age, Social Security may require some extra information from you. They'll want to see evidence that you are really giving up full-time work and not merely shifting your pay (in name only) to someone else.

The reason for this concern is the rule that retirement benefits will be reduced if you are less than full retirement age and earn income over certain limits for your age. (See Chapter 2 for these limits.) Some people with their own businesses try to get around this rule by continuing to work and paying a relative instead of themselves, or by continuing to run the business but being paid only for reduced work time.

Social Security is likely to ask for information regarding your continuing involvement with your own business if any of the following are true:

- You maintain ownership of the business.
- Other family members are involved in the business and a relative is assuming most of your previous duties.
- You continue to work for the business at lower pay.
- You control the amount you work and how much you are paid, such that you could manipulate either one.
- Your relatives now receive the salary you previously earned.

Social Security may ask for such documents as the business's pay and personnel records, personal and business tax returns, stock transfer agreements, and business expense records. Try to contact your local Social Security office several months in advance, so that you'll learn what documents Social Security wants and have time to gather the documents.

If Social Security determines that you provide services to the business that exceed the amount you are paid—based on the time you spend, the level of your responsibility, and the value of services you provide—the agency may attach a dollar value to those services. If this dollar value exceeds the amount of earned income permitted for your age, your benefits may be reduced.

At the Social Security Office

When submitting your application at your local Social Security office, you will be interviewed by a case worker. If you haven't already submitted your claim application form online or over the telephone, the worker will help you fill out the form. The worker will open a file for you, which from then on will contain all of the documents pertaining to your application.

Write down the name of the worker who talks with you, and his or her direct telephone line if available, so that you can speak with the same person if you need to call in to provide or receive further information. The Social Security worker will make copies of the documents you have brought and will explain what other information is needed to process your application.

If additional documents are needed, ask whether you may mail in copies instead of bringing originals in person.

When you first apply, do not expect to be told precisely how much your benefits will be. Exact benefit amounts are based upon the computerized records kept at the Social Security Administration's national records center. Your precise benefit amount will be calculated there.

Applications take six to eight weeks to be processed, but when you receive your first payment, it will include benefits back to the date you first applied, or to the date on which you are first eligible, whichever is later (except in the case of disability benefits).

Withdrawing a Benefits Application

It may happen that after you have turned in your application for retirement, dependents, or survivors benefits, your work situation changes, altering significantly the amount of benefits to which you are entitled. This might, for example, occur if you are offered a new position, a new job, or an increased salary, or you are not laid off from a job you expected to lose, or you are called back to work after a temporary job loss, or you simply change your mind and decide to continue working full time.

In any of these situations, if the income you earn at your continued work significantly exceeds the earnings limit for your age, it may eat up your benefits. If so, your decision to claim benefits may prove to be a bad one, because you will receive little or no benefit payments while you continue to work, and your benefit amount will be permanently lower than if you had waited to file your claim at a later age.

You may withdraw your application within 12 months after first becoming eligible for benefits if you repay all the benefits you have received so far. To do so, you may go to Social Security's official online publication "Retirement Planner: If You Change Your Mind" at www.ssa.gov/planners/retire/withdrawal.html, which explains the procedure and also the amounts you will have to repay. You can also make an appointment at a local Social Security office to discuss with a Social Security worker the process and consequences of withdrawing your application.

Disability Benefits

Eligibility for disability benefits depends upon your physical or mental condition, and your inability to work because of that condition. (See Chapter 3 for a more detailed account of the eligibility requirements.) Because it involves these qualifying standards, the application requires much more time and effort than other Social Security benefit applications do. You must get and keep your papers organized, and be thorough and persistent in your contacts both with doctors and with Social Security personnel.

RESOURCE
Proving that your particular medical condition renders you unable to work may not be easy. This book provides an introduction, but for more information and specialized advice concerning particular physical and mental conditions, see *Nolo's Guide to Social Security Disability: Getting & Keeping Your Benefits,* by David A. Morton II, M.D. (No o).

When to File Your Claim

You will not be paid any disability benefits until you have been disabled for five full months. This waiting period begins with the first full month after the date your disability began. That date is usually the date you stopped working because of your physical or mental condition.

However, disability claims take at least two to six months for an initial decision. You do not need to wait for six months of disability to elapse before filing your claim. Don't even wait to gather all the necessary information and doctors' reports. File the claim as soon as your medical condition forces you off work and the doctors expect that it will prevent you from working for a year or more. You can complete the gathering of necessary documents while the claim is being processed, with the help of your local Social Security office.

Fast Claims for Severe Medical Conditions

The Social Security Administration has created a streamlined disability benefits claims process for people with certain severe medical conditions. For these people, the Social Security Administration will process benefit claims within a few days of completing the application. There are over 200 conditions for which this fast application process, called "Compassionate Allowance," applies. To see the list of conditions and to get more information, go to the Social Security website: www.ssa.gov/compassionateallowances.

Documents You'll Need

When you file an application for Social Security disability benefits, whether online or in person at a local Social Security office, you may need some or all of the following documents or information:

- your Social Security number and proof of age (such as a birth certificate) for yourself and any person eligible for dependents benefits
- names, addresses, and phone numbers of doctors, hospitals, clinics, and other health service institutions that have diagnosed your medical condition and have given estimates of the length of time it is expected to keep you disabled, plus the approximate dates of your treatment. Although you are not required to produce medical records of your disability—Social Security can request them directly from doctors and hospitals—you might speed up the process if you bring copies of medical records you already have.
- a list of where you have worked in the past 15 years and a description of the kinds of work you did
- a copy of the past year's W-2 forms, or your last federal income tax return if you are self-employed
- the dates of any military service
- information concerning any other type of disability payment you are receiving
- if your spouse is applying based on your work record, the dates of any prior marriages. A certified copy of the divorce papers will provide this information.
- if you are applying as a disabled widow or widower, your spouse's Social Security number and a copy of the death certificate, and
- if you are applying as a disabled surviving divorced husband or wife, proof that your marriage lasted ten years. Marriage and divorce papers will serve this purpose.

If you are physically unable to get to a Social Security office in person, or you are unable to complete the forms or meet other filing requirements, your application can be completed by your spouse, a parent, another relative, a friend, or your legal guardian. And once the initial claim has been filed, a service worker in the local Social Security office can assist you by having the Social Security office directly request necessary documents.

How Your Eligibility Is Determined

Applications for disability benefits go through several stages. Initially, you will fill out an application at a local Social Security office or online and provide documents regarding your age and employment. After that, however, the process becomes more complicated, as Social Security determines whether your physical condition is actually disabling according to its standards.

Disability Determination Services

When your application has been completed and the local Social Security office has checked to see that you meet all the general requirements regarding work credits for your age (see Chapter 3 for the work credit requirements), it will forward your claim to a Disability Determination Services (DDS) office in your state. The DDS office will use your medical records and employment history to decide whether you are disabled under the rules of the Social Security law.

The decision at DDS is made by a doctor and a disability evaluation specialist. They examine all medical records you have provided with your application and may request more information from you, your doctors, and your employers.

Based on these records, the doctor and the specialist determine whether your disability is expected to last more than one year and whether it is severe enough to interfere with your ability to perform any work you have done over the past 15 years. If so, they then determine whether it is also so severe that you cannot perform any substantial gainful work. (See "No Substantial Gainful Activity" in Chapter 3 for more on how Social Security determines this.)

If your existing medical records show your condition limits you from performing substantial gainful work, you will be found eligible for benefits. If not, those evaluating you may request further medical records and/or refer you for a consultative physical examination.

Enlisting the Help of Your Doctor

Your medical records will be the biggest factor in the state DDS office's determination of your eligibility for disability benefits. Therefore, what your doctor puts in your records can be all-important.

If possible, discuss the matter with your doctor before you file your application for disability benefits. Inform your doctor that you intend to apply, and ask him or her to make specific notations in your medical records of how your physical activities—particularly work-related activities, such as walking, sitting, lifting, carrying—are limited or how your emotional condition affects your ability to regularly perform work. Ask also for your doctor to make a note of when your disability reached a point that it interfered with your ability to work.

Do not ask the doctor to give an opinion about whether you are disabled according to Social Security guidelines. Doctors will readily describe a specific medical condition, but many are unwilling to give an opinion about your ability to do any work at all. And, in any event, the DDS evaluation team would not accept your doctor's opinion on this ultimate question of eligibility. Instead, it will base its determination on its own evaluation of your symptoms and limitations that appear in your medical records.

In determining the nature and extent of your disability, the DDS will rely almost exclusively on the medical opinions of medical doctors, as opposed to physical therapists, chiropractors, and other nonphysician healers. This reflects an institutional bias against nontraditional medical treatment. But it also reflects the fact that physicians have diagnostic tools—such as laboratory tests, X-rays, and other technological and intrusive procedures—that are not available to nonphysician healers.

Medical Examinations

In some cases, the DDS evaluators may not feel that they can come to a conclusion about your disability based on your existing medical records. They may request further reports from doctors who have examined or treated you. And they may request that you undergo a medical evaluation or test, called a consultative examination.

Social Security pays the cost of the additional reports, examinations, or tests. If you must travel outside your immediate area to get to this examination, Social Security can pay for the cost of that travel, if you request it.

This extra examination or testing is often done by a physician who has already examined or treated you. This is particularly true if one of your doctors is a specialist in the area of medicine that deals directly with your disability. In other words, if you have seen an orthopedic surgeon for your back problem, Social Security is likely to have that same doctor perform the consultative examination. However, if you have not been treated by a specialist in the field— for example, if only your internist or general practitioner has treated you for a particular medical problem—Social Security may send you to another doctor for this examination.

Consultative examinations are limited to specific issues the DDS needs to clarify regarding your ability to work. The exam often involves certain kinds of tests—a range of motion test, for example, if your disability involves restricted movement—that your doctor has not recently performed and that give DDS specific information on the extent of your disability.

The DDS will set up the examination and send the doctor a written request for the information needed and any specific tests it wants performed. The doctor will not conduct a general examination and will not prescribe any treatment for you. On occasion, a representative from DDS will attend the examination to record specific test results. The doctor will send a report to DDS describing the results of the examination, but he or she will not take part in the final decision about whether you are eligible for disability benefits.

Even though you may not like the idea of going through another medical examination, especially if it is by a doctor you do not know, you must cooperate with the DDS to successfully process your disability claim.

Vocational Rehabilitative Services

When you apply for disability benefits, you may be referred to your state's vocational rehabilitation agency for a determination of whether any of its services might be of help to you. These free services can include job counseling, job retraining and placement, and specialized medical assistance. The services can also train you to use devices—such as a modified computer keyboard—that may enable you to work despite your disability.

Supplemental Security Income (SSI)

You may file a claim for SSI benefits at your local Social Security office at the same time you file for retirement, disability, dependents, or survivors benefits. (See Chapter 7 for a full discussion of the SSI program.) However, SSI is not automatically included in these other applications, so you must tell the Social Security worker that you wish to file for SSI benefits as well.

If you believe you might be close to the qualifying income and asset limits for SSI benefits, go ahead and apply. If your state offers a separate state-administered supplementary payment in addition to the basic federal SSI payment, you will have to apply for that supplement at your local county social welfare office.

The process of applying for SSI benefits is very similar to applying for Social Security benefits. You will need to provide the same general documents. (See "Retirement, Dependents, and Survivors Benefits," above, for instructions.) However, unlike Social Security benefit applications, SSI benefit applications also require that you show records of your income and assets.

Proof of Income and Assets

Regardless of whether you are applying for SSI payments as disabled or over age 65, you must also bring information regarding your income and assets. This includes:

- information about where you live: for homeowners, a copy of your mortgage papers or tax bill; for renters, a copy of your rental agreement or lease and the name and address of the landlord
- documents indicating your current earned income, such as pay stubs and income tax returns
- papers showing all your financial assets, such as bankbooks, insurance policies, stock certificates, car registration, burial fund records, and
- information about your spouse's income and assets, if the two of you live together.

Even if you do not have all these papers available, go to your local Social Security office and file your application for SSI as soon as you think you may qualify for assistance. The Social Security workers can tell you how to get whatever papers and records are necessary, and in some instances will get copies of the required records for you.

Proof of Age If 65 or Older

If you are age 65 or older, bring your Social Security number and proof of your age, such as a birth certificate. If you do not have a birth certificate, bring any other evidence of the date of your birth: baptism record, military papers, immigration papers, driver's license, or passport. If you are already receiving any kind of Social Security benefit, you do not have to bring proof of your age.

Proof of Blindness or Disability

The process for proving that you are blind or disabled for purposes of SSI benefits is the same as the disability determination process when qualifying for Social Security disability benefits. (See Chapter 3 for the medical eligibility requirements.) The information you need to gather and the process of applying for disability benefits is discussed in "Disability Benefits," above.

Proof of Citizenship or Qualifying Legal Residence

For a reminder of what immigration status you must hold in order to qualify for SSI, see Chapter 7.

If you are a U.S. citizen, you'll need to prove your citizenship by showing copies of your birth certificate, baptismal records, U.S. passport, or naturalization papers.

If you are a noncitizen, bring proof of your qualifications under one of the categories listed in Chapter 7.

For proof of work for ten years, bring your legal resident alien card ("green card") and Social Security numbers for yourself and your spouse. The Social Security or local welfare office will use the numbers to check your reported Social Security taxes.

If you seek to qualify as a veteran of the U.S. Armed Forces, bring evidence of honorable discharge from the military. You will also need a copy of your marriage certificate if you are seeking SSI as the spouse of a veteran.

Finding Out What Happens to Your Claim

You will not find out from your local Social Security office whether your claim for benefits has been approved; that word has to come from the Social Security Administration in Washington, DC.

Notification of Eligibility

Social Security will notify you in writing whether your claim has been approved, how much your benefits will be, and when you will get your first check.

From the time the application is filed, a retirement, dependents, or survivors claim usually takes from four to eight weeks. A disability claim can take up to six months. For all retirement, dependents, or survivors claims, you will receive benefits dating back to the date you first applied, or first became eligible if you applied before you reached an age of eligibility. The timing of Social Security disability payments is discussed below.

SSI benefits based on age usually begin four to eight weeks after you complete the necessary paperwork. If your claim is based on a disability that has not already been established for Social Security disability payments, it may take three to six months. When you do finally get your money, however, it will cover the period from the month after you filed your claim.

If you were unable to work for more than five months before applying for Social Security disability benefits, you might be eligible for back benefits. If Social Security determines that your disability actually began more than five months before your application, based on when you actually stopped work, it can grant up to 12 months of back benefits.

If your claim for any Social Security or SSI benefit is denied, the written notice of denial will state the reasons why. You have a right to appeal a denial of your claim. Your appeal must be submitted within 60 days from the date you receive written notice of the denial or other decision. (See Chapter 9 for appeal procedures.)

When You Need Money in a Hurry

It is possible to get some SSI payments even before your claim is finally approved. If you appear to be eligible for SSI and you need immediate cash to meet a financial emergency, the Social Security office can issue you an advance payment. The amount of this emergency payment will be deducted from your first regular SSI check.

Similarly, if you have already qualified for Social Security disability benefits and you appear financially eligible for SSI, you may be approved for and begin receiving SSI benefits immediately.

If you are financially eligible and appear to meet the disability requirements, but your disability application has not yet been approved by Social Security, you may receive SSI payments while your claim is being reviewed by the disability office. These are called presumptive disability payments, and they don't need to be repaid.

Methods of Receiving Payment

All new beneficiaries are expected to receive their Social Security and SSI benefits by direct deposit into their bank accounts or with a Direct Express debit card. It is possible, however, for a representative payee to receive payments on your behalf. You must indicate on the application if you want one of these options. You may change your method of payment after you begin to receive benefits.

Direct Deposit

Direct deposit has a number of advantages: You do not have to wait for your check to arrive in the mail, nor do you have to travel to your bank to make the deposit. And you do not have to worry about your check's being lost or stolen.

When you first sign up for benefits at your local Social Security office, workers there will ask for the name and address of your bank branch and the number of the account where you want the funds deposited. The bank where you have your account can help you fill out the form to request direct deposit.

If you change banks—or want to close one account and open another—you must fill out a new direct deposit form. The bank where you open your new account will assist you with the form. But do not close your old account until you see that your benefit has appeared in your new one. If your benefit continues to be deposited in the old account, contact your local Social Security office.

Debit Card

Some Social Security recipients don't want to receive their payments by direct deposit, either temporarily or for the long term. For example, you may not want to pay the bank charge to maintain an account. Or, you may be moving and temporarily will not have a local bank account. If, for any reason, you do not want to receive your benefit payment by direct deposit, you may arrange with your local Social Security office to receive your payments via a Direct Express debit card.

Substitute Payee

If you are unable to handle your own banking and check writing, you may have a family member, close friend, or legal representative receive the benefit payments on your behalf. That person should spend the money according to your wishes or directions. This may be done informally, by simply adding the other person as a joint account holder on the bank account where Social Security deposits your check. The bank can make this arrangement for you.

If you feel more comfortable with some oversight on how that person spends your benefits, you can have this other person officially appointed by Social Security as a substitute, or representative, payee. That person would then personally receive the benefit payments on your behalf.

Anyone proposing to be your representative payee must bring to the local Social Security office medical proof—for example, a letter from your doctor—that you are unable to care for yourself. The representative payee must sign a sworn affidavit at the Social Security office stating that he or she will use the Social Security check for your benefit. The Social Security office will then verify your medical condition and the identity of the representative payee.

If a person has already been appointed by a court to serve as legal guardian or conservator, proof of that court appointment is all that is required to be appointed representative payee. But people who are named to act in powers of attorney do not automatically qualify as representative payees; they must still apply for representative payee status at the local Social Security office.

The rules require that a representative payee deposit and keep the money belonging to the person entitled to Social Security in a separate bank account and periodically file an accounting with Social Security to show how the money has been spent to care for the beneficiary. The representative payee should keep all bills and receipts in a systematic and organized way so they can be produced easily. ●

Appealing a Social Security Decision

No matter how certain you feel that you deserve Social Security benefits, the agency may have other ideas and deny your claim. Sometimes this is a mere mistake and can be corrected. More often, the decision was a matter of judgment, as with disability claims, where questions about medical conditions, ability to work, or income levels (in SSI cases) are subjective and susceptible to different interpretations.

But if your application for benefits is initially denied, or is granted but you are awarded less than you had hoped, that need not be the end of the matter. Virtually all decisions of the Social Security Administration may be appealed, and many appeals are successful. If a new benefit has been denied or an existing benefit reduced or ended, you may appeal the decision as long as you follow some fairly simple rules and are willing to think creatively about how to present your case in a more convincing way. You'll need to put yourself into the shoes of the Social Security workers who first denied your claim, try to understand their reasoning, and then provide convincing evidence so that the next person who sees your file won't view your claim in exactly the same way.

This chapter explains the four possible levels of appeal following any Social Security decision. In most states, the first level is called reconsideration; it is an informal review that takes place in the local Social Security or Disability Determination Services (DDS) office where your claim was filed. (Technically, this isn't really an "appeal," because it doesn't go to a higher authority—but it's a step that you must take, nonetheless.)

The second level is a hearing before an administrative law judge (an ALJ); this is an independent review of what the local Social Security office has decided, made by someone outside the local office. The third level is an appeal to Social Security's national Appeals Council in Falls Church, Virginia. And the final level is filing a lawsuit in federal court.

RESOURCE

Get extra advice regarding disability appeals. More than 90% of all Social Security appeals involve claims for disability benefits (including SSI). Most of these appeals revolve around whether the claimant's physical or mental condition actually prevents gainful employment. Proving this requires careful presentation of medical information as well as completing certain special forms. This book will give you an introduction to this process, but for more information and specialized advice for various physical and mental conditions, see *Nolo's Guide to Social Security Disability: Getting & Keeping Your Benefits*, by David A. Morton III, M.D. (Nolo), and www.disabilitysecrets.com.

CAUTION

Beware of the time limit for filing appeals. The same time limit applies to each step of the appeals process. From the date on the written notice of Social Security's decision—whether denying or granting a benefit—you have 60 days within which to file a written notice that you are appealing that decision to the next stage in the process. If you receive the notice by mail, you have an additional five days within which to file your notice of appeal.

Reconsideration of Decision

When a claim for any type of Social Security benefit—retirement, disability, dependents, or survivors—is denied, or an existing benefit is ended, or you receive an amount you feel is less than that to which you are entitled, in most states, the first step to appeal that decision is to request reconsideration.

As part of an experiment to streamline appeals, some states have eliminated the reconsideration review for disability appeals; in these states, when you appeal a disability denial, the first level of appeal is a hearing in front of an ALJ. Social Security may end this experiment in the future, but at the time of printing, the states without a reconsideration step for disability appeals were:

Alabama	Colorado	New Hampshire
Alaska	Louisiana	New York
California (L.A. North and L.A. West Branches only)	Michigan	Pennsylvania
	Missouri	

If the negative decision involved a denial of Social Security benefits, follow the procedures discussed below. Some special procedures to follow when appealing denial of an SSI claim are discussed in "Requesting Reconsideration of SSI Decision," below.

Is an Appeal Worth the Effort?

The first question that may occur to you when considering an appeal is whether it is worth the effort.

Let's start with some encouraging numbers: A substantial percentage of decisions are changed on appeal. Almost half of all disability appeals, which are by far the most common, are favorably changed in the appeal process.

And appealing a Social Security claim need not be terribly difficult. If you properly organized and prepared your original claim, most of your work for the appeal has already been done. In many situations, the appeal will require little more from you than explaining once more why the information you already presented should qualify you for a benefit. In other cases, it will simply involve presenting one or two additional pieces of information that better explain your situation to Social Security personnel.

A negative Social Security decision may affect your rights for many years. Because it is so important, and because the appeal process is relatively simple, it is almost always worth the effort to appeal.

Requesting Reconsideration of Decision on Initial Benefits Claim

To start the appeal process, you file a written request for review of the decision, called a *Request for Reconsideration* (SSA-561-U2). The form is available online from Social Security's website at www.ssa. gov/forms/ssa-561.pdf. You can also obtain a copy at your local Social Security office or by calling Social Security at 800-772-1213. If you were denied Social Security or SSI disability benefits for medical reasons, you can file a request for reconsideration online. A sample of the form follows.

The form comes in duplicate: a top copy for the Claims Folder (the Social Security office's copy) and a bottom Claimant's Copy (for you). You fill in only the top part of the form. The information requested is straightforward: name, address, Social Security number, and type of claim—retirement, disability, dependents, or survivors.

The appeals process is explained in the sections below. Social Security also provides information about the appeals process on its website at www.ssa.gov/pubs/EN-05-10041.pdf. More specific information about filing an appeal of the denial of a claim for disability benefits is also available online from Social Security at www.ssa.gov/disability/appeal.

Completing the Request for Reconsideration Form

The first few lines of the *Request for Reconsideration* form are fairly simple. On the top left, fill in your own name, exactly as it appears on your Social Security card.

On the top right is the box for the Social Security claim number. Copy that number from the written denial of your claim that you received from Social Security.

Form **SSA-561-U2** (12-2016) uf (12-2016)
Prior Edition May Be Used Until Exhausted
Social Security Administration

Page 1 of 4
OMB No. 0960-0622

REQUEST FOR RECONSIDERATION

NAME OF CLAIMANT: CLAIMANT SSN: CLAIM NUMBER: *(If different than SSN)*

ISSUE BEING APPEALED: *(Specify if retirement, disability, hospital or medical, SSI, SVB, overpayment, etc.)*

I do not agree with the Social Security Administration's (SSA) determination and request reconsideration.
My reasons are:

SUPPLEMENTAL SECURITY INCOME (SSI) OR SPECIAL VETERANS BENEFITS (SVB) RECONSIDERATION ONLY
THREE WAYS TO APPEAL

I want to appeal your determination about my claim for **SSI** or **SVB**. I have read about the three ways to appeal. I have checked the box below:

☐ **CASE REVIEW - You can pick this kind of appeal in all cases**. You can give us more facts to add to your file. Then we will decide your case again. You do not meet with the person who decides your case.

☐ **INFORMAL CONFERENCE - You can pick this kind of appeal in all SSI cases except for medical issues. In SVB cases, you can pick this kind of appeal only if we are stopping or lowering your SVB payment.** You will meet with a person who will decide your case. You can tell that person why you think you are right. You can give us more facts to help prove you are right. You can bring other people to help explain your case.

☐ **FORMAL CONFERENCE - You can pick this kind of appeal only if we are stopping or lowering your SSI or SVB payment.** This meeting is like an informal conference, but we can also get people to come in and help prove you are right. We can do this even if they do not want to help you. You can question these people at your meeting.

CONTACT INFORMATION

CLAIMANT SIGNATURE - *OPTIONAL:*   NAME OF CLAIMANT'S REPRESENTATIVE: *(If any)*

MAILING ADDRESS: MAILING ADDRESS:

CITY: STATE: ZIP CODE: CITY: STATE: ZIP CODE:

TELEPHONE NUMBER: *(Include area code)*   DATE: TELEPHONE NUMBER: *(Include area code)*   DATE:

TO BE COMPLETED BY SOCIAL SECURITY ADMINISTRATION

1. HAS INITIAL DETERMINATION BEEN MADE? ☐ Yes ☐ No

2. IS THIS REQUEST FILED TIMELY? ☐ Yes ☐ No

(If "NO", attach claimant's explanation for delay. Refer to GN 03102.125)

SOCIAL SECURITY OFFICE ADDRESS AND DATE APPEAL RECEIVED:

FIELD OFFICE DEVELOPMENT (GN 03102.300)
☐ NO FURTHER DEVELOPMENT REQUIRED
☐ REQUIRED DEVELOPMENT ATTACHED
☐ REQUIRED DEVELOPMENT PENDING, WILL FORWARD OR ADVISE STATUS WITHIN 30 DAYS

SSI CASES ONLY - GOLDBERG KELLY (GK) (SI 02301.310) RECIPIENT APPEALED AN ADVERSE ACTION:
☐ WITHIN 10 DAYS AFTER RECEIVING THE ADVANCE NOTICE;
☐ AFTER THE 10-DAY PERIOD AND GOOD CAUSE EXISTS FOR EXTENDING THE TIME LIMIT
☐ PAYMENT CONTINUATION APPLIES AND INPUT MADE TO SYSTEM

NOTE: Take or mail the **completed original** to your local Social Security office, the Veterans Affairs Regional Office in Manila, or any U.S. Foreign Service post and keep a copy for your records.

The most important part of the form comes on the lines following the words: "I do not agree with the Social Security Administration's (SSA) determination and request reconsideration. My reasons are: ...." On those lines, state briefly and simply why you think you were unfairly denied your benefits.

You need not go into great detail, because your entire file will be examined—including any additional materials you want to submit. Your statement should simply identify the problem, such as: "The decision that I am not disabled was based on insufficient evidence about my condition. I am submitting an additional letter from my doctor about my condition." Or: "The DDS evaluation of my disability did not take into account my inability to sit for prolonged periods."

Along with your completed *Request for Reconsideration* form, you may submit a form called a *Disability Report—Appeal* (SSA-3441-BK) to explain any changes in your condition since you filed your original claim for benefits. Instructions for completing this form can be found in *Nolo's Guide to Social Security Disability: Getting & Keeping Your Benefits*, by David A. Morton III, M.D. (Nolo). In addition, you can submit a letter describing in more detail why you think Social Security's decision was incorrect.

You should also submit any other relevant materials to your file, such as recent medical records or a letter from a doctor or an employer about your ability to work. Such new material may be crucial to winning your reconsideration request—government workers have a tendency to believe that their agency was right the first time, unless you give them something new and different to change their minds.

This additional information does not have to be submitted by the 65th day after the written decision. But if you are planning to submit it after your *Request for Reconsideration*, indicate this on the form. (Use the space where you explain your disagreement with the decisions.)

Be sure to include your Social Security number and your claim number, in addition to your full name and the date, on all material you send in. And keep a copy for your records.

The Importance of Reviewing Your File

Sometimes a Social Security or SSI claim is denied because a document or another piece of information that should be in your file is not there. Or perhaps some misinformation has gotten into your file without your knowledge. This happens most often on the question of medical condition, where an incomplete medical record is in your file, or the report from the DDS examination includes a mistake based on a misunderstanding with the doctor who did the examination.

The only way for you to find out if such mistakes exist is to look at your file, which should contain all documents related to your claim. After you file your *Request for Reconsideration*, call your local Social Security office to set up an appointment to see your file.

If you find a mistake in the file, write a letter to Social Security explaining the situation. Send the letter to your local Social Security office, asking that it be made part of your file for reconsideration. And, as always, keep a copy of the letter.

The Reconsideration Process

Your claim will be reconsidered by someone in the Social Security or DDS office other than the person who made the decision on it the first time around. He or she will consider everything that was in your file when the decision was made, plus anything you have submitted to the office since the original decision.

Generally, you do not appear in person at this review; you do not have the right to speak face to face with the person making the decision, although you can request a chance to do so. The person doing the review may request more information and may ask you to come in for an informal interview.

You will receive a written notice of the decision made on your request for reconsideration—usually within 30 days (except for disability claims). If 30 days go by with no word, contact the local Social Security office and ask about the delay. Reconsideration of a disability claim often takes two to three months, particularly if new medical information has been provided during the course of the appeal.

Once you receive your written decision, you can, if the decision is negative, file a request for an administrative hearing if you want one. (See the discussion of administrative hearings, below, for more information.) You must file your request within 65 days of the date on the written decision.

Continuing Your Benefits During an Appeal

In some circumstances, you can continue to receive Social Security disability benefits and SSI benefits while Social Security is deciding your appeal. You can request this in either of the following situations:

- You have been collecting Social Security disability benefits and you are now appealing Social Security's decision to end your benefits because it has determined that your condition has improved.
- You have been collecting SSI benefits and Social Security has decided that you are no longer eligible, or that you are eligible for lower benefits.

If you want your benefits to continue during the appeal process, you must make the request to your local Social Security office within ten days of the date you receive a written notice ending or reducing your benefits.

CAUTION

Continued benefits may not be for keeps. If you continue to collect benefits while appealing Social Security's decision to end those benefits, and Social Security denies your appeal, you may have to pay back the benefits you received during the appeal process.

Requesting Reconsideration of SSI Decision

If you request a reconsideration of a decision regarding a claim for SSI benefits, you'll be asked to choose among three possible procedures listed on the *Request for Reconsideration* form. Which one you choose depends upon how and why you were denied:

- If Social Security denied your claim for SSI because it says that you are not disabled, you are entitled only to what is called a "case review." This means that you can add more documentation to your file, which will then be reviewed again. You will not, however, be permitted to meet face to face with the Social Security representatives deciding your claim.

- If your claim for SSI benefits was denied for nonmedical reasons—such as your immigration status, or your income and asset levels—you may request a case review or an "informal conference." This permits you to speak with the person reviewing your claim and to show additional documents. You can also bring along anyone you want to help support your argument.

- If you have been receiving SSI benefits but Social Security decides to end or reduce them, you can request a "formal conference." This is actually an informal meeting at which you can present whatever written materials you want, have people come to the meeting and give information, and also explain your situation in your own words. It is only formal in the sense that the Social Security office can issue a legal summons for people to show up and answer questions if they refuse to come voluntarily. If you want Social Security to force someone to appear, you must notify your local office several weeks before the hearing date.

Informal Hearings at Social Security

You might have an opportunity to meet with the Social Security representative who is reviewing your file during the initial reconsideration of your retirement, disability, dependents, or survivors claim. Or, you might meet with him or her during the informal or formal conference regarding an SSI claim. These meetings are very informal. You will be given the chance to explain, in your own words and in person, why you believe the decision denying or ending your benefits was wrong.

There are several things to bear in mind during one of these meetings:

• Focus on addressing whatever reason Social Security gave (in the notice denying or ending your benefits) to justify its decision. Perhaps it was your physical condition, changes in your condition, your income, or your work hours. Be strong and direct in explaining why its reasoning was wrong. Don't dilute your argument by telling your whole life story or explaining your whole medical history.

• If, along with your appeal, you submitted material that was not in your original file, ask whether the representative has had a chance to read it. If so, explain how the new material shows that the original decision was incorrect. If not, give the representative copies of these new materials and ask that he or she read them before you continue with the meeting.

• There is no need to go over all the documents in your file except to point out what you believe are errors, or to focus on something in a document that you believe is important but that seemed to have been ignored in the original decision.

• The Social Security representative will ask you questions to focus in on what Social Security considers important. Do not dismiss or ignore any question. Try to answer all questions clearly and directly. If there is other information—from your doctor or employer, for example—that you believe might help answer the question, tell the representative and either direct the representative to an existing document in your file, or ask that you be allowed to provide the information before the representative makes a decision.

> ## Informal Hearings at Social Security (continued)
>
> - Be calm and polite. Social Security representatives understand that the denying or ending of benefits is an emotional matter for you, but they did not make the initial decision, and they are human, so you will not do yourself any good by taking out your frustration on them.

Administrative Hearing

If Social Security denies your claim again after reconsidering it, you may request a formal administrative hearing. The hearing will be held in front of an administrative law judge. The people in the office that denied your claim won't take part in the judge's decision. That means you have a good chance of having the denial of your claim reversed at this hearing, even if you have no new information to present.

Requesting a Hearing

As with other steps in the appeal process, you must file a request for this hearing with your local Social Security office within 65 days of the date on the written notice of the decision after reconsideration.

Your request must be filed on a form called *Request for Hearing by Administrative Law Judge* (HA-501-U5), reproduced below.

Along with your completed *Request for Hearing* form, you will need to submit a form called a *Disability Report—Appeal* (SSA-3441-BK) to update your disability information. This is the same form you may have used in filing for reconsideration of your original claim. Complete instructions for completing this form can be found in *Nolo's Guide to Social Security Disability: Getting & Keeping Your Benefits*, by David A. Morton III, M.D. (Nolo).

SEE AN EXPERT

Consider getting assistance with hearing preparation from an outside professional, such as a lawyer or another counselor specializing in Social Security matters. This is particularly true if the issue is whether your physical or emotional condition qualifies you as disabled, because you'll need to gather and present evidence that's convincing enough to sway a judge's subjective determination. Your best chance of reversing Social Security's decision comes at the administrative hearing, and so you will want to be as well prepared as possible at this stage.

Completing the Request for Hearing by Administrative Law Judge Form

The first three sections of the form are straightforward. Section 4 of the *Request for Hearing by Administrative Law Judge* form asks for you to state the reasons you disagree with the determination made on your claim. State your reasons here simply and briefly, for example: "The decision that I am not disabled was based on incorrect statements about the number of hours I regularly work. I am submitting letters from my coworkers explaining that I actually work fewer hours than stated in the decision ending my benefits." Or: "The DDS evaluation of my disability did not take into account my inability to travel to and from work without assistance."

Section 5 includes two boxes to indicate whether you have additional evidence to submit. You should always check the first box—the one that says you do have additional evidence. This will allow you to submit a new written statement to the judge, as well as any letters or documents that were not already in your file. If it turns out that you do not have any additional letters or documents to submit, at the hearing you can inform the judge that you have no new written materials but would like an opportunity to speak.

After you and your representative have organized your papers and spoken with your doctor, your employer, or another person who can provide additional or clarifying information about your claim, you, or you and your representative, should write a detailed statement summarizing and arguing your claim. Send that statement to your local Social Security office to be placed in your file, and also send it directly to the administrative law judge who will hear your claim. Do this at least two weeks before your hearing date so that the administrative law judge will have a chance to read the statement before the hearing. If you do not prepare it in advance, bring it with you to the hearing and present it there.

In Section 6 on the hearing request form, you must indicate whether you want to attend the hearing in person. If you don't, the judge will make a decision based on the papers in your file. It is almost always to your advantage to be present at the hearing. Your presence puts a human face on your claim and shows the judge that you are truly concerned about the outcome. It also allows the judge to ask you questions that might not get answered if you were not there.

If you check "I wish to appear at a hearing" in Section 6 but later decide not to attend the hearing, you must notify the hearing judge's office beforehand. If, on the other hand, you checked the box saying that you do not want to attend the hearing but later decide you do, contact the hearing judge's office as soon as you can. The hearing will probably have to be rescheduled to a later date. That is because hearings with the claimant present are usually scheduled at different times and places than a hearing consisting solely of a review of the file.

Section 8 asks for your representative's name and address. If you do not have a lawyer or other representative by the time limit for filing your request for hearing, file the request without naming anyone. If later you obtain a representative, you can supply that information then.

CAUTION

Timing may be important. To make sure that all your evidence gets in your file and to the administrative law judge in time for your hearing, you must submit all new evidence—letters, documents, records that were not previously given to Social Security—within ten days of filing your request for a hearing. So, even if you are ready to file a request for an administrative hearing immediately after you receive written notice of the reconsideration decision, it is a good idea to wait until you have gathered whatever additional information you want the hearing judge to see. This may delay slightly the date of your hearing, but it will allow you to make sure all your evidence will be considered there.

Preparing for the Hearing

During the time between filing your request for a hearing and the hearing date, you should take several steps.

First, discuss your claim with the attorney or representative who will assist or represent you at the hearing. (See "Lawyers and Other Assistance," below, for suggestions on obtaining legal representation.) It is particularly important to make sure that your representative understands what you believe to be the most important part of your claim and that he or she has thoroughly reviewed any documents that you believe support your position.

Second, examine your file, either at your local Social Security office or at the hearing office. This allows you to see that all the papers you have given to Social Security have found their way into your file. It also allows you to review all of the positive and negative information that Social Security has collected, such as a report on your disability from a DDS examination. Call your local Social Security office to see when and where you can examine your file, or if a CD containing your file can be sent to you.

SOCIAL SECURITY ADMINISTRATION	Form Approved
OFFICE OF DISABILITY ADJUDICATION AND REVIEW	OMB No. 0960-0269

REQUEST FOR HEARING BY ADMINISTRATIVE LAW JUDGE

See Privacy Act Notice

(Take or mail the completed original to your local Social Security office, the Veterans Affairs Regional Office in Manila or any U.S. Foreign Service post and keep a copy for your records)

1. Claimant Name	2. Claimant SSN	3. Claim Number, if different

4. I REQUEST A HEARING BEFORE AN ADMINISTRATIVE LAW JUDGE. I disagree with the determination because:

An Administrative Law Judge of the Social Security Administration's Office of Disability Adjudication and Review or the Department of Health and Human Services will be appointed to conduct the hearing or other proceedings in your case. You will receive notice of the time and place of a hearing at least 20 days before the date set for a hearing.

5. I have additional evidence to submit. ☐ Yes ☐ No

Name and source of additional evidence, if not included.

Submit your evidence to the hearing office within 10 days. Your servicing Social Security office will provide the hearing office's address. Attach an additional sheet if you need more space.

6. Do not complete if the appeal is a Medicare issue. Otherwise, check one of the blocks

☐ I wish to appear at a hearing.

☐ I do not wish to appear at a hearing and I request that a decision be made based on the evidence in my case. (Complete Waiver Form HA-4608)

Representation: You have a right to be represented at the hearing. If you are not represented, your Social Security office will give you a list of legal referral and service organizations. If you are represented, complete and submit form SSA-1696 (Appointment of Representative) unless you are appealing a Medicare issue.

7. CLAIMANT SIGNATURE (OPTIONAL)	DATE	8. NAME OF REPRESENTATIVE (if any)	DATE
RESIDENCE ADDRESS		ADDRESS	

CITY	STATE	ZIP CODE	CITY	STATE	ZIP CODE

TELEPHONE NUMBER	FAX NUMBER	TELEPHONE NUMBER	FAX NUMBER

TO BE COMPLETED BY SOCIAL SECURITY ADMINISTRATION- ACKNOWLEDGMENT OF REQUEST FOR HEARING

9. Request received on _____ by: _____

(Date) (Print Name) (Title)

_____ (Address) (Servicing FO Code) (PC Code)

10. Was the request for hearing received within 65 days of the reconsidered determination? ☐ Yes ☐ No
   If no, attach claimant's explanation for delay and supporting documents if any.

11. If claimant is not represented, was a list of legal referral service organizations provided? ☐ Yes ☐ No	15. Check all claim types that apply:

11. If claimant is not represented, was a list of legal referral service organizations provided? ☐ Yes ☐ No

12. Interpreter needed ☐ Yes ☐ No

Language (including sign language):

13. Check one: ☐ Initial Entitlement Case
☐ Disability Cessation Case or ☐ Other Postentitlement Case

14. HO COPY SENT TO: _____ HO on _____
☐ Claims Folder (CF) Attached: ☐ Title (T) II; ☐ T XVI;
☐ T VIII; ☐ T XVIII; ☐ T II CF held in FO ☐ Electronic Folder
☐ CF requested ☐ T II; ☐ T XVI; ☐ T VIII; ☐ T XVIII
(Copy of email or phone report attached)

16. CF COPY SENT TO: _____ HO on _____
☐ CF Attached: ☐ Title (T) II; ☐ T XVI; ☐ T XVIII
☐ Other Attached:

15. Check all claim types that apply:
☐ Retirement and Survivors Insurance Only (RSI)
☐ Title II Disability - Worker or child only (DIWC)
☐ Title II Disability - Widow(er) only (DIWW)
☐ Title XVI (SSI) Aged only (SSIA)
☐ Title XVI Blind only (SSIB)
☐ Title XVI Disability only (SSID)
☐ Title XVI/Title II Concurrent Aged Claim (SSAC)
☐ Title XVI/Title II Concurrent Blind (SSBC)
☐ Title XVI/Title II Concurrent Disability (SSDC)
☐ Title XVIII Hospital/Supplementary Insurance (HI/SMI)
☐ Title VIII Only Special Veterans Benefits (SVB)
☐ Title VIII/Title XVI (SVB/SSI)
☐ Other - Specify:

Form HA-501-U5 (01-2015) ef (01-2015)
Use 08-2012 Edition Until Stock is Exhausted

TAKE OR SEND ORIGINAL TO SSA AND RETAIN A COPY FOR YOUR RECORDS

Finally, ask for letters or records from your medical providers or employers establishing your claim and responding to the reasons expressed by the Social Security office or DDS examiners for rejecting your claim. Submit copies to your local Social Security office and directly to the administrative law judge, while keeping the original and at least one more copy.

The Hearing

After you file the request for hearing, you will be notified by mail of the hearing date and place. You'll receive this notice 75 days before the hearing.

If you cannot attend on that date, contact the office of the administrative law judge and arrange for a new date. Act quickly: Most offices of administrative law judges are reasonable about rescheduling, but if you wait until the last week to request a change, and you do not have a medical or another valid emergency, the judge could refuse to postpone your hearing. In that case, the judge would hold the hearing without you.

The hearing itself is conducted in a style less rigid than in a traditional courtroom but a bit more formal than a hearing at the local Social Security office. An administrative law judge presides, and everything said or done is recorded. You may be represented or assisted at the hearing by a friend or relative or by a lawyer or another advocate. (See "Lawyers and Other Assistance," below, for more information about getting legal or other help.)

You need to submit any new evidence, or at least notify the hearing office that you will be bringing new evidence to the hearing, at least five days before the hearing. If you don't, and you don't have a valid reason such as illness or an unavoidable circumstance, the judge does not have to consider the evidence. It's important to submit new, updated medical evidence, such as any recent test results or doctor's notes from recent appointments—the judge will want to see medical evidence from the last 30-60 days if possible.

You may present the testimony of any witnesses you would like to have help prove your claim. This testimony is informal. The person simply gives information regarding your employment or medical condition to the judge and answers any questions from the judge. The judge will give you an opportunity to explain your claim in your own words, and may also ask you some questions.

The administrative law judge who presides at your hearing is a lawyer who works for the Social Security Administration. He or she must not have taken part in the original claim decision or in reconsidering your claim. The judge will follow certain rules of procedure and may ask you questions about your claim that are not easy to answer. In general, however, the judges try to be as helpful as possible. If you are not sure how to present certain information to the judge, explain the problem and the judge should help you get the information into the official record of the case.

The judge will issue a written decision on your appeal, usually within four to six weeks of the hearing. You will receive a copy of this decision in the mail. If your claim has been denied, you will have 65 days from the date on the written notice of the denial to file a further appeal. If your claim has been approved, you may be entitled to receive benefits dating all the way back to the time you filed your original claim or even earlier.

Appeal to the National Appeals Council

If your appeal has been denied after an administrative hearing, your next step is to file a written appeal with the Social Security Administration Appeals Council. You must file this within 65 days from the date on the written notice of the administrative law judge's decision.

Completing the Form

The form you'll need at this stage of the appeals process is called *Request for Review of Hearing Decision/Order* (HA-520-U5).

SOCIAL SECURITY ADMINISTRATION		Form Approved OMB No. 0960-0277
REQUEST FOR REVIEW OF HEARING DECISION/ORDER (**Do not** use this form for objecting to a *recommended* ALJ decision.) (Either mail the signed original form to the Appeals Council at the address shown below, or take or mail the signed original to your local Social Security office, the Department of Veterans Affairs Regional Office in Manila, or any U.S. Foreign Service Post and keep a copy for your records.)		**See Privacy Act Notice**

1. CLAIMANT NAME	2. CLAIMANT SSN	3. CLAIM NUMBER (If different than SSN)

4. I request that the Appeals Council review the Administrative Law Judge's action on the above claim because:

☐ Please grant me an extension of time to submit evidence or argument.

ADDITIONAL EVIDENCE

If you have additional evidence that relates to the period on or before the date of the hearing decision, you must inform the Appeals Council about it or submit it. If you have a representative, then your representative must help you obtain the evidence unless the evidence falls under an exception. You may also submit any other additional evidence to the Appeals Council. If you need additional time to submit evidence or legal argument, you must request an extension of time in writing now. This will ensure that the Appeals Council has the opportunity to consider the additional evidence before taking its action. If you submit neither evidence nor legal argument now or within any extension of time the Appeals Council grants, the Appeals Council will take its action based on the evidence currently in your file.

IMPORTANT: WRITE YOUR SOCIAL SECURITY NUMBER ON ANY LETTER OR MATERIAL YOU SEND US. IF YOU RECEIVED A BARCODE FROM US, THE BARCODE SHOULD ACCOMPANY THIS DOCUMENT AND ANY OTHER MATERIAL YOU SUBMIT TO US.

SIGNATURE BLOCKS: You should complete No. 5 and your representative (if any) should complete No. 6. If you are represented and your representative is not available to complete this form, you should also print his or her name, address, etc. in No. 6.

I declare under penalty of perjury that I have examined all the information on this form, and on any accompanying statements or forms, and it is true and correct to the best of my knowledge.

5. CLAIMANT'S SIGNATURE	DATE	6. REPRESENTATIVE'S SIGNATURE	DATE
PRINT NAME		PRINT NAME ☐ ATTORNEY	☐ NON-ATTORNEY
ADDRESS CITY, STATE, ZIP		ADDRESS CITY, STATE, ZIP	
TELEPHONE NUMBER	FAX NUMBER	TELEPHONE NUMBER	FAX NUMBER

THE SOCIAL SECURITY ADMINISTRATION STAFF WILL COMPLETE THIS PART
7. Request received for the Social Security Administration on _____ by: _____
(Date)   (Print Name)

(Title)	(Address)	(Servicing FO Code)	(PC Code)

8. Is the request for review received within 65 days of the ALJ's Decision/Dismissal? ☐ Yes ☐ No

9. If "No" checked:	☐ (1) attach claimant's explanation for delay; and ☐ (2) attach copy of appointment notice, letter or other pertinent material or information in the Social Security Office.

10. Check one:	11. Check all claim types that apply:
☐ Initial Entitlement ☐ Termination or other	☐ Retirement or survivors (RSI) ☐ Disability-Worker (DIWC) ☐ Disability-Widow(er) (DIWW) ☐ Disability-Child (DIWC) ☐ SSI Aged (SSIA) ☐ SSI Blind (SSIB) ☐ SSI Disability (SSID) ☐ Title VIII Only (SVB) ☐ Title VIII/Title XVI (SVB/SSI) ☐ Other - Specify:
APPEALS COUNCIL OFFICE OF DISABILITY ADJUDICATION AND REVIEW, SSA 5107 Leesburg Pike FALLS CHURCH, VA 22041 - 3255	

Form HA-520-U5 (01-2016) UF (01-2016)
Destroy Prior Editions

TAKE OR SEND ORIGINAL TO SSA AND RETAIN A COPY FOR YOUR RECORDS

The form is fairly straightforward, asking only that you give a brief explanation of why you think the administrative law judge's decision was wrong. If there's more to say than will fit onto this form, attach a separate piece of paper with the explanation. Also submit any documents that the judge did not consider but that you believe are important to your claim.

On Question 10 of the form, you'll be asked to check either "Initial Entitlement" or "Termination or other." Initial Entitlement means you were denied after your first attempt to obtain a particular benefit. Termination or other refers to when you were already receiving a benefit but Social Security decided to end it or to reduce the amount you receive.

Also notice the explanation in the middle of the form under the heading Additional Evidence. Any documents you wish to submit to the Appeals Council that are not already in your file must be either attached to the form or sent directly to the Appeals Council within 15 days after filing your request for review.

 SEE AN EXPERT

If you are not yet represented by a lawyer who specializes in Social Security matters, hire one now. The Appeals Council usually reverses an administrative law judge's decision only when a technical argument can be made as to why the administrative law judge made a legal mistake. Simply arguing to the Appeals Council that the judge was wrong in deciding your case will not be enough.

Appeal Procedure

Unfortunately, your appeal to the Appeals Council is not likely to meet with much success. The Appeals Council usually reviews a case based on the written documents in your file only. It very rarely accepts a case for a hearing, and when it does, the council meets only in Falls Church, Virginia. If you want to appear at the hearing, you have to go or send a representative to the hearing.

More often, if the Appeals Council believes there is some merit to the appeal, it sends the case back to the administrative law judge with the direction that the judge hold a new hearing and reconsider something the Appeals Council points out in its written decision.

Although the success rate of having claims denials overturned by the Appeals Council is very low, filing an appeal may be important. You are required to file this appeal before you can move on to the next step, which is filing a lawsuit in federal court.

Lawsuit in Federal Court

If your claim has been denied and you have unsuccessfully exhausted all the Social Security Administration appeals procedures, you are entitled to bring a lawsuit against the Social Security Administration in federal district court. You must file the initial papers of this lawsuit within 60 days after the Appeals Council's decision is mailed.

A federal court lawsuit is a complicated, time-consuming, and expensive procedure. However, it may be worth it. When you add up the total amount of benefits you might receive in your lifetime if your claim is approved, there may be a lot of money at stake. If the amount seems worth the time and effort to you, then you should at least investigate the possibility of filing a lawsuit. Consult with attorneys who specialize in Social Security appeals.

Whether or not you had legal assistance at some earlier stage of the appeal process, you certainly need expert legal assistance to file a lawsuit in federal court. Your odds of winning there depend almost entirely on convincing a court that the administrative law judge who heard your appeal made a mistake in interpreting the Social Security law. Simply asking a court to take another look at the facts of your case is almost never enough to win a federal lawsuit.

The main things to weigh in deciding whether to file a lawsuit are your chances of winning (as explained to you by an attorney specializing in such cases), the money it will cost you to fight the legal battle, and the amount of money in benefits that you stand to gain. If you balance all these things and it still seems like a good idea to go ahead with the lawsuit, then consider hiring an attorney to help you proceed.

Lawyers and Other Assistance

Under Social Security rules, you have a right to be represented at every stage of the appeal process by someone who understands the Social Security rules. This person may be a lawyer who specializes in Social Security matters, a nonlawyer from one of the many organizations that help people with Social Security claims, or a family member or friend who may be better than you are at organizing documents, writing letters, or speaking.

Deciding Whether You Need Assistance

It is not usually necessary to get assistance in preparing or presenting your appeal at the reconsideration stage. After reconsideration, however, and particularly if your appeal involves medical issues, it is often wise to seek assistance. This assistance can take several forms: talking over your appeal with a knowledgeable friend or relative; having a person who specializes in Social Security problems go over your papers with you, make suggestions, and assist you at hearings; or having a lawyer or another specialist prepare and present the appeal on your behalf.

Deciding whether to hire a lawyer or to seek an experienced nonlawyer representative depends on several things, such as:

- the complexities of your case. The more complicated the issues—particularly those involving a physical or emotional condition as it relates to qualification for disability benefits—the more likely that you need expert help.
- how much money is at stake. For example, if your appeal is only about whether your disability began in March or April, it is probably not worth hiring an attorney to represent you. On the other hand, if your benefits have been reduced significantly or denied entirely, it may well be worth it to hire an attorney.
- how comfortable you feel handling the matter yourself. Particularly in the reconsideration stage of the appeal process, many people feel confident obtaining their own records and

documents and discussing their claim with a local Social
Security office worker. However, many other people are
uncomfortable about explaining things convincingly, and so
would like assistance even at this early stage. And most people
become uncomfortable at the prospect of an administrative
hearing, because they have never been through such a procedure
before. If so, it is a good idea at least to get some advice, and
perhaps representation, before this stage of the appeal process.

What a Representative Can Do to Help

If you decide to have someone represent you during the course of your
appeal—either a lawyer or another specialist—he or she can handle as
much or as little of the process as you want. A representative can:

- look at and copy information from your Social Security file
- file a request for reconsideration, hearing, or Appeals Council
  review, and schedule or reschedule hearings
- provide Social Security with information on your behalf
- accompany you, or appear instead of you, and speak on your behalf
  at any interview, conference, or hearing, and
- receive copies of any written decisions or other notices sent by
  Social Security.

Where to Find Assistance

Whether you should seek assistance from a lawyer or another
specialist depends on whether one or the other is easily available to
you, and with whom you are most comfortable. If you reach the
stage of considering going to federal court, however, you should
consult with an attorney who is experienced in similar cases.

CAUTION

Appointment of a representative must be in writing. Once a
person has agreed to become your representative for the appeal, you must

provide his or her name to Social Security on a form entitled *Appointment of Representative* (SSA-1696). If the representative is not a lawyer, he or she also has to sign the form, agreeing to serve as your representative. If your representative is a lawyer, he or she needs only to be named on the form. The form is available online (www.ssa.gov) or at your local Social Security office, which is also where the completed form is to be filed.

Hiring Specialists Other Than Lawyers

The first place to inquire about assistance with your Social Security appeal may be Social Security itself. Every written notice denying a claim is accompanied by a written list of local community groups and legal services organizations—such as disability rights groups, legal aid offices, and senior counseling services—that either assist with appeals or refer claimants to appeal representatives.

The fact that you find someone through one of these groups or organizations does not guarantee that you will want that person to represent you; that will depend on how well you and the person communicate and whether you feel confident in his or her advice. But finding someone to assist or represent you through one of these organizations at least assures you that the person has experience in Social Security appeals and has backing from a legitimate organization.

Senior centers are good resources, too. Many have regularly scheduled sessions during which trained advocates offer advice on Social Security problems. Whether or not a particular senior center has such a program, it can usually refer you to a Social Security advocacy group whose members are trained to assist in Social Security matters. You can usually make use of these referrals if you have a disability claim, even if you are not a senior citizen.

Each state has its own agency or department handling problems of older people, including Social Security disputes. They are referred to, variously, as the office, department, bureau, division, agency, commission, council, administration, or center on aging. In most cases, this state agency will be able to refer you to some place near your home that offers assistance in preparing and presenting Social

Security appeals. Call your state's agency and explain what you are looking for.

Other sources of assistance with Social Security matters are religious and social groups, business and fraternal associations, and unions. If you belong to such a group, it may have a referral service that can put you in touch with Social Security advocates.

Although many nonlawyer assistants and representatives provide free services, most charge a fee (although the amount is limited by Social Security rules—see below). The time to ask about fees is before you hire someone to assist or represent you. Get any fee agreement in writing.

Hiring Lawyers

If your income is low, a lawyer may be available to assist or represent you through a "legal services" organization that has specialists in Social Security appeals. These are nonprofit organizations that seek funding from outside sources in order to serve low-income people. The first place to look for legal services offices is on the list of references provided by Social Security along with its notice denying your claim. You can also find legal services offices—sometimes listed as Legal Aid—online or in the white pages of your telephone directory.

Beware, however, that in the steady campaign by the federal government over the past 20 years to slash public services for low-income people, many legal services offices have suffered staff cutbacks or have been eliminated altogether. So, it may not be easy to find a legal aid lawyer who can help you with your appeal.

You may also find an attorney in private practice. Be aware, though, that most private lawyers know very little about Social Security; you need to find one who specializes in Social Security claims. For directories of lawyers who specialize in Social Security issues, see www.disabilitysecrets.com or www.nolo.com.

Your local county bar association will also have a reference list of lawyers who specialize in Social Security appeals. And while, in general, these bar association referral lists do not always include the best lawyers, in Social Security appeal matters, they usually do have the best people. That is because very few lawyers specialize in Social

Security appeals, and the few who are expert in the field usually list themselves with the bar association.

Normally, lawyers cost a lot of money. However, Social Security rules strictly limit the amount of money a lawyer or anyone else can charge for a Social Security appeal, which may explain why so few lawyers specialize in the field.

Legal Limits on Lawyers' Fees

Whether your representative is a lawyer or another specialist, Social Security rules limit the fees your representative may charge. And not only are fees limited, but they must be approved by Social Security in each individual case.

Fee Agreements

Most lawyers and some nonlawyers can charge a fee only if, with their help, you are approved for benefits. If you win your appeal at any stage of the process, you will be entitled to benefits from the date you first applied for them (or for Social Security disability, the date you became disabled)—referred to as past-due benefits. The lawyers take their fees as a percentage of your past-due benefits. Social Security rules say that a lawyer or another representative can take as a fee 25% of your past-due benefits, or $6,000—whichever is less. If the lawyer pursues a lawsuit for you in federal court, these limits do not apply.

Fee Petitions

In some situations, lawyers are allowed to ask Social Security if they can charge more than the $6,000 cap. Social Security has the power to limit how much you are made to pay, however. If you agree to hire a lawyer under such a fee-for-service arrangement, the lawyer can't collect from you until after he or she has submitted a kind of bill called a "fee petition" to Social Security for approval.

The petition is filed when the appeal is finished, and lists in detail each service the lawyer provided for your appeal and the amount of time the lawyer spent on each such service. The lawyer must provide you with a copy of the petition. If you disagree with any of the information on the petition, you must notify your local Social Security office within 20 days of the date you receive it.

Social Security will examine the petition and determine a reasonable fee for the lawyer's services. Social Security will send you a written notice of the amount it has approved under the fee petition. The lawyer or other representative cannot charge you any more than the fee Social Security decides on, except for out-of-pocket expenses incurred during your appeal (such as costs for photocopying, phone calls, postage, and transportation to and from your hearings).

Get It in Writing

If you come to a fee arrangement with your lawyer or other representative, the representative must put it in writing, you both must sign it, and the representative must submit it to Social Security for approval. This can be done at any time before your claim is approved.

Federal Civil Service Retirement Benefits

More than three million people are employed by federal government agencies and departments; millions more have previously been employed there. And although the salaries of these government jobs are not always as high as those in the private sector, a comprehensive retirement system is one of the benefits that makes federal government employment attractive.

This chapter discusses the two different federal retirement systems—the Civil Service Retirement System and the Federal Employees Retirement System—and explains the benefits available under each.

Employees of State and Local Governments

Each state and many local governments have their own retirement systems for their employees. It isn't possible here to discuss the rules of all these plans, but most of them work very much like the federal government's Civil Service Retirement System (CSRS), described in this chapter.

The amount of pension funds to which an employee may be entitled is not based on total payroll contributions, as with the Social Security system, but on the highest average salary the employee reached and the number of years of employment. The age at which the employee can claim retirement benefits also depends on the number of years of employment.

As of July 1, 1991, employees of state or local governments who are not covered by an employer pension plan are covered by Social Security. These are usually part-time, temporary, or probationary workers.

To find out what retirement plan covers your work, contact your personnel or retirement plan office, or the pension office of your public employees' union, if you belong to one.

On request, the pension office should provide you with an estimate of how much your pension benefits would be if you claimed those benefits at the various retirement ages permitted by the plan.

RESOURCE

For information about nongovernment, personal retirement plans. See *IRAs, 401(k)s & Other Retirement Plans: Strategies for Taking Your Money Out,* by Twila Slesnick and John C. Suttle (Nolo).

Federal Retirement Spousal Benefits for Same-Sex Spouses

The United States Supreme Court and the Department of Justice have made clear that same-sex spouses are entitled to federal spousal benefits on the same terms as other spouses. This is true regardless of the state where the marriage was performed.

Foreign marriages. A spouse in a same-sex couple who was married outside the United States but now lawfully lives in the United States might be entitled to spousal benefits based on the other spouse's federal employment record, depending on the status of that marriage in the country where it was performed. Even if you have doubts about your right to federal spousal benefits as a same-sex spouse, the federal retirement system encourages you to apply for them so that it can determine whether you are eligible.

Retroactivity. The Department of Justice has decided that the right to spousal benefits for a same-sex spouse may apply to someone who applied for such benefits before the Supreme Court's same-sex marriage decision on June 26, 2015. If you were married and you applied for federal spousal benefits before that date but were denied those benefits (because you lived in a state that did not recognize your marriage), reapply to the federal retirement system specifically requesting retroactive benefits back to the date you first applied.

Two Retirement Systems: CSRS and FERS

There are two entirely separate retirement systems for federal workers, depending on the date the worker was first hired. Until 1984, all federal government workers were part of the Civil Service Retirement System, or CSRS. Workers covered by the CSRS do not receive Social Security benefits for their government employment; the CSRS provides the only benefits those workers will receive for their years of federal government employment.

All federal workers hired on or after January 1, 1984 were made part of a different plan called the Federal Employees Retirement System, or FERS. Workers hired by the federal government on or after January 1, 1984 are also covered by Social Security, which means that work for the government simultaneously builds toward both FERS and Social Security benefits.

Employees who were already working for the federal government on January 1, 1984 were given a choice. They could either remain in the CSRS or switch over to the FERS. For those who switched, their years of employment under the CSRS were credited to the FERS.

The rules for both systems are quite similar, and both are administered by the federal government's Office of Personnel Management (OPM). Both the CSRS and the FERS are funded by a combination of automatic payroll deductions from federal employees and by contributions made by the employing agencies.

Under both systems, an employee can receive benefits if disabled, take early retirement, provide for a survivor, take a lump sum retirement amount instead of monthly benefits, and participate in a special savings program called the Thrift Savings Plan.

CSRS Retirees May Face Pension Offset

People who earned a retirement pension under the Civil Service Retirement System (CSRS) or a similar pension system that paid no Social Security taxes may be subject to a reduction in certain Social Security dependents benefits called the "government pension offset." This applies if you receive Social Security dependents or survivors benefits and also receive a retirement pension based on your own work record from the CSRS. The government pension offset does not apply to people whose own retirement benefit is under the Federal Employees Retirement System (FERS). (For a full explanation of the government pension offset, see Chapter 4.)

However, eligibility and benefit amounts are determined in a very different way than under the Social Security system. In particular, benefits are based on the highest average salary for any three years of employment, but do not depend on the total amount contributed in payroll deductions. And although benefits may be paid to retirees and to survivors, they are not increased if the retiree has dependents.

Retirement Benefits

Both CSRS and FERS retirement benefits are easy to qualify for and can be paid out in any one of several ways. Both programs also permit retirement benefits to be structured to provide for a survivor after the retired worker has died. And both offer a special savings plan that provides tax benefits and, in the case of the FERS, includes contributions by the government.

If You've Left Federal Work, Then Returned

Some people may be entitled to retirement benefits under the CSRS and FERS: those who worked for the federal government before 1984, when CSRS was their only option, and then left but rejoined after 1984.

If you worked for the federal government for at least five years but left that job before 1984, you may return to the CSRS if you started a new job with the federal government after January 1, 1984. If you do not choose to reenter the CSRS, you will work under the FERS, and you may qualify for retirement benefits under both the CSRS and the FERS once you have more than five years of employment under each system.

If you left federal employment for at least a year and you choose to reenter CSRS, you will also be covered by Social Security, as are FERS employees. Once you collect both Social Security benefits and CSRS retirement, your CSRS payment will be reduced by the amount of your Social Security benefits attributable to your federal employment.

This prevents double payment, since most CSRS recipients do not receive Social Security benefits from their federal employment, and the amount of CSRS benefits is calculated as if there were no additional retirement money from Social Security.

Who Is Eligible

If you have worked at least five years for the federal government as a civilian employee, you can qualify for a pension, referred to as a retirement annuity. In addition, you can get retirement credit for any years of military service after 1956 if you pay a premium based on the amount of your military pay. However, you cannot get credit for military service if you are collecting a military retirement pension. You can also get credit, after paying a small premium, for time you spent in the Peace Corps.

There are two types of retirement annuities under the CSRS and FERS: an immediate annuity and a deferred annuity.

Minimum Retirement Age (MRA) by Year of Birth	
The following chart tells you when you reach your MRA, depending on the year you were born.	
Birth Year	**MRA**
Before 1948	55
1948	55 + 2 months
1949	55 + 4 months
1950	55 + 6 months
1951	55 + 8 months
1952	55 + 10 months
1953–64	56
1965	56 + 2 months
1966	56 + 4 months
1967	56 + 6 months
1968	56 + 8 months
1969	56 + 10 months
1970 and after	57

Immediate Annuity

You can retire at age 62 and immediately begin receiving an annuity if you worked for the federal government a total of five years. The years do not have to be consecutive, nor do they have to be for the same federal agency or department. Any combination of jobs totaling five years of work will qualify you.

If you have 20 years of service with the federal government, you can claim your immediate annuity at age 60.

With 30 years of service, a CSRS-covered worker can retire with a pension at age 55. A worker covered by FERS with 30 years of service can retire with a pension at what is called the minimum retirement age (MRA). Your MRA depends on the year you were born. For people born before 1948, it is 55. For those born in 1948 and after, see the chart above.

If You Are Laid Off Before Becoming Eligible for Your Pension

CSRS and FERS rules allow some long-term workers to collect an immediate annuity if they are laid off from their jobs before reaching the normal eligibility age.

Under CSRS, a worker who has been employed for at least one year in the two years immediately before being laid off, and who is age 50 with 20 years of service or any age with 25 years of service, may be eligible for an immediate annuity.

Under FERS, the eligibility for this immediate annuity is the same, except that you need not have been employed within the past two years.

The amount of the immediate annuity is reduced from its full amount by 2% per year for every year you are under age 55 when claiming this immediate annuity.

There are two circumstances in which you may not be entitled to an immediate annuity after losing your job. The first is if you have been fired for cause: misconduct, delinquency, or poor job performance. The second is if you have been offered another job in the same agency, in the same geographic area, which is not more than two grades or pay levels below the current job, but you refuse to take it.

TIP

Special rules apply to law enforcement personnel, firefighters, and air traffic controllers. Recognizing the high stress of these jobs, the CSRS system has set early retirement years and lower requirements for years of service for these jobs. If you have been a law enforcement officer or firefighter under the CSRS, you can claim retirement benefits at age 50 with 20 years of service. If you have been an air traffic controller, you may be able to retire at age 50 with 20 years of employment, or at any age once you have 25 years of service.

Deferred Annuity

If you end your federal employment before retirement age, you have a choice of leaving your payroll contributions in the CSRS or FERS, or withdrawing them in a lump sum when you leave employment. If you leave the contributions in the system when you end your federal job, you can claim a retirement annuity at age 62. If you leave the money in the retirement system but later decide you want it without waiting for retirement, you can collect it in a lump sum at any time before you reach age 62.

If you switch jobs, then depending on the amount of your salary and your years of service with the government, it may be to your benefit to leave your money in the retirement system. The amount of your federal retirement annuity would be based on your length of service and the highest levels of pay you received. (See "Calculating Benefits," below, for more information.)

If you have worked for a long time and have reached a relatively high salary, you will be eligible for a large pension when you reach age 62. That pension will probably amount to much more money than the lump sum you could withdraw when leaving your federal job.

EXAMPLE 1: Kazuo worked for the federal government from 1965 through 1992. In 1984, he decided to remain in the CSRS rather than switch to the FERS. By the time he left his government job, he had contributed over $10,000 to the CSRS retirement fund. Kazuo moved to another job outside the government, and did not immediately need the money in his retirement fund, so he left his contributions in the CSRS.

When Kazuo turns 62, he could collect a deferred annuity, which would then add to his monthly income from his job, or to Social Security retirement benefits if he had qualified for them by working long enough in the private sector both before and after his government job.

EXAMPLE 2: Angela worked for the federal government from 1980 through 2000. In 1984, she switched her pension coverage from the CSRS to the FERS. By the time she left her job, she had contributed almost $28,000 to the retirement fund. When Angela left the federal government, she did not immediately need the money in her retirement fund, so she left her contributions in the FERS.

When she turns 62, she can collect her FERS deferred annuity, in addition to whatever she is making on a nonfederal job, or to Social Security retirement benefits that she also earned from her years of FERS-covered government employment.

Before deciding which course of action to take, find out from the OPM exactly how much your lump sum withdrawal would be, and get an estimate of what your annuity would be at age 62. Of course, your decision will also depend on how badly you need the cash immediately upon leaving your federal job.

Calculating Benefits

Two factors are used to figure the amount of your federal CSRS or FERS retirement annuity.

The first factor is the number of years you have been employed by the federal government and contributing to the retirement fund. This can include years of military service if you also have at least five years of civilian service (unless you are receiving a military retirement pension).

The second factor is your "high-three average salary"—meaning your average salary for the three consecutive years in which you had your highest earnings. For example, if in three successive years you reached $55,000, $55,000, and $58,000, you would add these together and divide the total by three. (The total would be $168,000, which divided by three equals a high-three average of $56,000.)

Both CSRS and FERS base the retirement annuity on the high-three average, but each computes the resulting benefit differently.

TIP

You'll get a cost-of-living increase. Both CSRS and FERS benefits are increased annually to keep pace with the rising cost of living. As with Social Security benefits, these cost-of-living increases are tied to the rise in the Consumer Price Index, a yearly indicator of the cost of goods and services. In some years, however, there will be no cost-of-living increase if there is no increase in the Consumer Price Index.

COMPUTER

You can get benefit estimates online. The Office of Personnel Management (OPM), which operates the CSRS and FERS systems, now offers a website with a calculator that will estimate your federal civil service retirement benefits. Go to www.opm.gov and click "Calculators" (under "Retirement"). The calculator can estimate what your normal, early, or disability retirement benefits are likely to be. However, the accuracy of the estimate depends greatly on how near you are to claiming your benefits—the nearer you are, the more accurate the estimate.

CSRS Benefits

Once your high-three average pay is calculated, CSRS computes your pension benefits by adding:

- 1.5% of your high-three average pay, multiplied by your first five years of service, plus
- 1.75% of your high-three average pay, multiplied by the number of your years of employment over five, up to ten, plus
- 2% of your high-three average pay, multiplied by the number of years of service over ten.

EXAMPLE: John put in 25 years working for a federal government agency. His highest three consecutive years of pay were $28,000, $30,000, and $32,000. That makes his high-three average pay $30,000. After 25 years, John's retirement pension would be figured like this:

- 1.5% of the $30,000 average is $450; that $450 is multiplied by the first five years of service, for a total for the first five years of service of $2,250; plus

- 1.75% of the $30,000 average is $525; that $525 is multiplied by the second five years of service, for a total for the second five years of $2,625; plus

- 2% of the $30,000 is $600; that $600 is multiplied by the remaining 15 years of service, for a total for the last 15 years of service of $9,000.

Together, the three parts of John's pension would add up to a yearly benefit of $13,875.

CSRS Benefits and Social Security

If your federal employment is covered by CSRS, it is not also covered by the Social Security system. However, most people who worked for the federal government under CSRS have also worked, or will work, at some other jobs during their lifetimes. If that other work is covered by Social Security and you have enough work credits to qualify for Social Security retirement benefits, you can collect both your retirement benefits and your CSRS annuity.

If you receive a CSRS pension and also Social Security dependents or survivors benefits based on your spouse's work record—rather than Social Security retirement benefits based on your own work record—those benefits will be severely reduced. This is known as the pension offset rule. (See Chapters 4 and 5 for further discussion of the offset rule.) If you are receiving a CSRS annuity as the survivor of a CSRS worker, this rule does not apply.

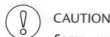

CAUTION

Some workers will receive separate CSRS and FERS benefits.
If you had years of service under the CSRS, left that job, and later returned
to work for the federal government under the FERS, you will receive two
separate annuities, one using your high-three earnings under CSRS and
the other your high-three earnings under FERS.

FERS Benefits

FERS has several different types of retirement benefits: full benefits,
reduced early retirement benefits, deferred benefits for people who
left their federal jobs before retiring, and a supplement for longtime
employees.

Full retirement annuity. Full FERS pension benefits are figured
by taking 1% of the high-three average and multiplying it by the
number of your years of service.

> EXAMPLE: Elvira worked 25 years for the federal government, switching
> to FERS in 1984. Her highest three consecutive years of pay were $38,000,
> $40,000, and $42,000. That makes her high-three average pay $40,000.
> Elvira's retirement pension would be figured like this: 1% of $40,000 =
> $400; $400 x 25 (years of service) = $10,000, which would be her yearly
> pension annuity. And under FERS, Elvira would also collect Social
> Security retirement benefits as soon as she reaches an eligible age.

Reduced benefits for early retirement. If you have accumulated
enough years of service under the FERS, you can take early retirement with lower benefits. With ten years of service, you can take
early retirement at the minimum retirement age (MRA). (See chart
above.) Your benefits will be reduced from the full retirement amount
by 5% for each year under age 62 at which you claim retirement.

Deferred benefits if you leave. If you leave your federal job after at
least five years of service but before reaching retirement status, you
can claim retirement benefits when you reach a certain retirement
age, which depends on your years of service. With five years of
service, you can claim retirement benefits at age 62. With ten years

or more, you can claim retirement at the minimum retirement age, currently 55, but the benefit will be reduced by 5% per year for every year earlier than age 62 at which you claim benefits.

TIP

Reduced benefits may make financial sense. Although your deferred retirement benefits will be reduced 5% for every year under age 62 at which you claim them, it may still be to your advantage to claim as early as age 55. Since you are not adding any more years of service and your high-three salary remains the same, the base amount of your benefit will be the same whenever you take it.

Annuity supplement for long-term employees. A special supplement to the retirement annuity is available at age 55 to people with 30 years' service and at age 60 with 20 years' service. The supplemental amount is based on total earnings and years of service and is figured using a complex set of calculations. To determine how much your annuity supplement would be, contact the OPM office at the agency where you work.

CAUTION

Your supplement may be reduced by your earnings. Unlike the standard FERS annuity, if you are under age 62, your annuity supplement is reduced by $1 for every $2 over a certain yearly amount in earnings from other employment after you retire from federal government work. This earnings limit rule works the same as the earnings limit for Social Security benefits. (For more information, see "Working After Claiming Early Retirement Benefits" in Chapter 2.)

Survivors Benefits

Unlike Social Security retirement benefits, the surviving spouse or another survivor of a federal CSRS retiree does not necessarily receive survivors benefits after the retiree dies. To plan ahead for this, the federal worker is given several choices at retirement.

The retiring worker can choose to:
- take a full retirement annuity—if so, no benefits will be paid to any survivors after the retiree dies
- elect a full survivor benefit for a current spouse, in which case the retiree's own annuity will be less
- elect to have survivor benefits paid to someone other than a current spouse (which would also reduce the retiree's own annuity), or
- choose to provide a reduced survivor benefit, which means his or her own annuity will be lower than a full retirement annuity but higher than if a full survivor annuity were provided.

Annuity Without Survivor Benefits

At retirement, a CSRS or FERS employee can choose to take full retirement benefits without any provision for survivors. This makes particular sense if the retiree is unmarried and has no one else depending on him or her for financial support. It also makes good sense if the retiree, or retiree and spouse, have extremely limited income and immediately need the full retirement annuity to get by. Finally, it is a wise choice if the retired worker is married but his or her spouse is not likely to outlive the worker.

A worker who is married at retirement must specifically choose this no-survivor-benefit option by filing a form with the Office of Personnel Management (OPM). The worker's spouse must sign and notarize this form, which acknowledges that the retiree has given up the right to a survivor annuity. If the spouse's whereabouts are unknown, or the spouse is unable to understand the waiver and knowingly sign the form, a petition can be filed with the OPM to waive the requirement of a written consent form.

Annuity With Full Spousal Survivor Benefits

If you are married when you retire from federal employment, and you and your spouse do not waive your right to a survivor annuity, your retirement annuity will be reduced slightly to provide a lifetime annuity for your spouse if you die first.

This full survivor annuity can also be provided for a former spouse, although if the worker has remarried, the current spouse must consent. A survivor benefit ends when the surviving spouse dies, or when the surviving spouse remarries before age 55. After age 55, the surviving spouse is free to remarry without losing the survivor annuity.

The amount of full survivor annuity is slightly different for CSRS and FERS employees.

CSRS full survivor benefits. A CSRS retirement annuity is reduced, to provide full survivor benefits, by 2.5% of the first $3,600 per year, plus 10% of any amount over $3,600. The surviving spouse's annuity will be 55% of the full retirement annuity—that is, 55% of the amount before the 2.5% and 10% reductions are taken. And the 55% will include any yearly cost-of-living raises the retiree has received since the pension began.

> EXAMPLE: Ethel is eligible to receive a pension of $9,250 a year. She provides a full survivor benefit for Dante, her husband, so her own retirement annuity is reduced.
>
> The first $3,600 is reduced by 2.5%, which means Ethel receives $3,510 of that first $3,600. The remaining $5,650 is reduced by 10%, leaving $5,085. Ethel's total pension is $8,595 a year instead of $9,250, a reduction of $655 a year. For that reduction, Dante is entitled (if Ethel dies) to a surviving spouse's pension of 55% of the original $9,250, which works out to $5,087.50 a year.

FERS full survivor benefits. A FERS full retirement pension is reduced by 10% to provide an annuity for the surviving spouse. The surviving spouse's annuity will be 50% of the retiree's full pension amount—that is, 50% of the amount before the 10% reduction.

A retiring FERS worker can also choose a 5% reduction in his or her annuity, which will provide for a 25% annuity for a survivor. The survivor annuity will include any yearly cost-of-living raises the retiree receives after the pension begins.

EXAMPLE: Rigoberto is eligible to receive a pension of $12,000 a year. He provides for a full survivor benefit for Doris, his wife, reducing his own retirement annuity by 10%, or $1,200. So instead of $12,000 per year, Rigoberto receives $10,800—$12,000 minus the $1,200 reduction. In exchange for that reduction, Doris will be entitled, upon Rigoberto's death, to receive a surviving spouse's pension of 50% of the original $12,000, which works out to $6,000 a year.

Survivor Annuity to Other Than Spouse

Both the CSRS and FERS provide for a 55% survivor annuity that can be paid to a person other than a current spouse. The amount your own retirement annuity is reduced to pay for this annuity depends on the difference in age between you and the named beneficiary.

If the beneficiary you name is older than you or no more than five years younger than you, your annuity will be reduced by 10%. Your annuity is reduced 5% for every additional five years the beneficiary is younger than you—reduced 15% if five to ten years younger, 20% if ten to 15 years younger, and so on.

If the person you name as beneficiary dies before you do, you can have your own annuity restored to the full amount for the rest of your life by simply notifying the OPM. Once you have chosen to name a beneficiary, however, you cannot change your mind and restore yourself to a full pension as long as that person lives.

Reduced Survivor Benefits

Both CSRS and FERS rules allow a retiring employee to divide up his or her annuity, taking the full amount of one part and using the rest to set up a survivor annuity. You can split up your annuity into survivor and nonsurvivor parts in any proportions you want.

For example, if you are entitled to a $10,000-per-year annuity, you can choose to keep $5,000 as fully your own and direct that the other $5,000 be allotted to and reduced for a survivor benefit. That second $5,000 would be reduced by the normal survivor percentages—2.5% of the first $3,600, and 10% of the remaining $1,400—leaving you $4,770 plus the untouched $5,000. This arrangement would provide a survivor with 55% of the $5,000 you assigned to the survivor annuity, which amounts to a yearly benefit of $2,750 after your death.

Deciding Whether to Reduce Your Annuity

No obvious answer exists regarding whether to take a reduced pension to provide for another person. Each retiree and spouse, or other person who would be named as beneficiary, must decide for him- or herself. It will help to consider the following:

Age. If your spouse or other potential beneficiary is considerably younger than you are and likely to outlive you by many years, taking a reduced pension now probably makes good sense. The 55% pension could go for many years to your beneficiary. On the other hand, if your beneficiary is considerably older than you are, there may be little advantage to reducing your own immediate pension.

Health. If you are in poor health and may not survive for many years, then it is probably more important to provide a survivor annuity. Conversely, if your beneficiary is in poor health and not likely to survive you, it is probably better to take your full pension.

Income. If your spouse or other beneficiary has or will have a substantial retirement pension or other income of his or her own, there is less need to reduce your own pension to protect your beneficiary. On the other hand, if your beneficiary is working now and earning a salary that will enable you to afford taking a reduced pension, that will permit your beneficiary to count on a survivor annuity after you are gone.

Thrift Savings Plan

In addition to the annuity pension plan to which both the employee and the employer contribute, the federal employee has the opportunity to build up tax-deferred retirement savings through the Thrift Savings Plan (TSP). The TSP is similar to 401(k) savings plans made available to some employees in the private sector.

Contributions to TSP Account

The TSP for a CSRS worker is funded solely by the worker; it is a savings account of the worker's own money, which defers tax liability until retirement. For FERS employees, the government also contributes to TSP accounts, so that the TSP is both a tax-deferring savings plan and an additional pension.

CSRS contributions. CSRS-covered workers may put up to 5% of their before-tax wages into a TSP savings account. They pay no income tax on the income, or on interest earned, if they leave the money in the account until retiring from federal service with a CSRS annuity.

FERS contributions. The government automatically contributes an amount equal to 1% of an employee's pay into a TSP account for the employee. A worker who is covered by FERS may also put up to 10% of his or her pretax wages into the TSP savings account. If so, the government will match some of the amounts an employee puts in, in addition to its automatic 1% contribution.

The government matches dollar for dollar the first 3% of wages that an employee puts in the TSP account, and matches 50 cents per dollar for the next 2% of pay the employee puts in the TSP account. If the employee leaves the money in the account until retiring from federal service, he or she won't owe any tax on the money put into the account or on the interest earned until the money is withdrawn at retirement.

Withdrawal From TSP Account

When an employee retires from federal service with either a deferred or immediate annuity, the employee may take out his or her TSP money in a lump sum or in payments of equal amounts over time. The employee will owe income tax when the amounts are withdrawn. But a person who is no longer working full time is likely to be in a lower individual income tax bracket and so will owe less in taxes.

The retiring employee also has the option to transfer the money to an Individual Retirement Account (IRA), which continues the money's tax-deferred status. The retiring employee may also use the

TSP account funds to purchase an annuity, which is a plan that pays a set amount for life to the retired worker. Some annuities also permit additional payments to the spouse of a retired worker after the worker dies.

An employee who leaves federal service and withdraws the TSP money before being eligible for a retirement annuity will owe a 10% penalty tax on the money in the account. However, the employee has the option of transferring, or rolling over, the money in the TSP account to a nongovernment Individual Retirement Account (IRA), which will maintain the same tax-exempt status and avoids the tax penalty. The normal limit on yearly contributions to an IRA account does not apply to this one-time transfer of TSP funds.

CAUTION

There is a time limit for withdrawing your funds from your TSP account. If you leave your retirement money in your TSP account after you stop working for the federal government, you are required to start withdrawing your money by April 1 of the year following either:

- the year you turn age 70½, if you are at that time no longer employed by the federal government, or
- if you continue in federal employment after age 70½, whatever year you end that employment.

Disability Benefits to Federal Workers

Both the CSRS and FERS provide benefits for employees who become disabled while working for the government.

Who Is Eligible

If you have worked for the federal government for five years or more under CSRS, you may be eligible for benefits if you become disabled before you reach retirement age. If you are covered by FERS, you need to have been employed for only 18 months.

Definition of Disability

Under both CSRS and FERS rules, you are considered disabled if, because of disease or injury, you are unable to perform your job. In deciding whether a worker is disabled, the OPM determines if all of the following are true:

- The employee can perform useful and efficient service in the specific job.
- Every reasonable effort to preserve the person's employment, such as making physical modifications to the jobsite, has failed.
- There is no other vacant position in the same government agency and geographic area and at the same civil service grade or class as the current job that the employee could perform.

It is somewhat easier to qualify for federal civil service disability than for Social Security disability benefits. Under federal civil service rules, you don't have to be so disabled that you are unable to do any sort of paid work. Instead, you can qualify for disability benefits merely because you are unable to work in the same government agency where you already work, doing a vacant job there, at the level you had attained when you became disabled. It doesn't matter that you might be able to work at some other job at a different level or outside the government agency.

Proof of disability depends on information from two separate but equally important sources. First, your physician must write a letter to the OPM fully describing your disability and the date it began, and explain why he or she believes you are unable to perform your job effectively. You can assist your doctor by carefully explaining what your job entails and why your disability prevents you from performing it.

The second source of information is your supervisor at work. He or she must give the OPM a written statement explaining your duties at work, how your disability impairs your job performance, and whether any other job of comparable rank and pay is available to you. You can help yourself and your supervisor by pointing out the specific ways in which your disability interferes with your job and by noting when your disability began to make efficient work impossible.

Review of Disability Status

Your disability does not have to be permanent for you to receive federal employees' disability benefits. But the government, at its expense, will periodically require that you be examined by a physician to determine whether or not you continue to be disabled.

As with your original claim for disability benefits, it will be helpful if your own physician can write a letter detailing the specific ways in which your condition continues to be disabling. The letter will assist the government's doctor—who will probably only see you once, for a brief examination—in understanding why you are still disabled. The best approach is to have your own doctor write to the government doctor directly, so that the explanation of your condition and its limitations will already be in his or her file when you undergo your examination.

If your disability is found to be permanent, or if you reach age 60 without recovering from the disability, you will receive permanent disability retirement benefits. You will not be subjected to any further government examinations, and you will receive your disability benefits for life unless you are later considered to have recovered.

You are officially considered recovered if:

- You voluntarily take any new job with the federal government.
- Your yearly earnings at jobs or self-employment outside the federal government reach 80% of the current pay for your previous government job.
- A medical examination determines you are physically able to perform your job.

If any of these types of recovery occur, your disability payments will end either:

- on the date you begin reemployment with the government
- six months from the end of the year in which you earn 80% of your prior salary, or
- one year from the date of the medical exam that determined you had physically recovered.

Amount of Benefits

The amount of disability benefits is figured differently by the CSRS and the FERS.

CSRS Disability Benefit Amounts

CSRS disability benefits are the lower of either:

- 40% of your high-three average pay (defined in "Calculating Benefits," above), or
- a portion of the regular pension you would have received if you had worked until age 60. This pension figure is computed by adding together your years of service plus the number of years remaining until you reach age 60. Depending on this total, your high-three average salary is multiplied by a certain percentage—slightly more than 16% for ten years total; slightly over 26% for 15 years; slightly over 36% for 20 years; 40% for 22 years or more—to arrive at the disability benefits figure.

EXAMPLE 1: Henry went on disability at age 55, after ten years of employment during which he had reached a high-three average pay of $34,000; 40% of his high-three pay would be $14,400. Using the alternate method of computation, the number of years remaining until he reached age 60 is five, which would be added to his number of years of employment for a total of 15 years. At 15 years, the high-three average salary is multiplied by just over 26%, for a total of $8,925. Since Henry is entitled only to the lower of the two computations, he would receive $8,925 per year in benefits.

EXAMPLE 2: Alice went on disability at age 50, with 15 years of service. Her high-three average salary was $38,000. She had ten years until she reached age 60, which were added to her 15 years of service for a total of 25 years. Because this is more than 22 years, her yearly disability benefit would be 40% of her high-three average salary—which is the same figure as the alternate method of computing benefits—amounting to $15,200.

FERS Disability Benefit Amounts

Benefit amounts under FERS change over time. In the first year after disability, the disabled worker receives 60% of the high-three average pay, reduced by any Social Security disability benefits he or she may be receiving.

From the second year of FERS disability until age 62, the worker receives 40% of the high-three salary, minus 60% of any Social Security disability benefits. These benefits are increased yearly, based on a cost-of-living formula that is 1% lower than the rise in the Consumer Price Index.

At age 62, FERS computes what the disabled worker's retirement annuity would have been had he or she worked until reaching age 62. A benefit figure is determined by taking 1% of the total number of years of employment plus the number of years on disability up to age 62, and multiplying that by the worker's high-three average salary plus all cost-of-living increases since going on disability. That figure will be the yearly disability benefits for the remainder of the worker's lifetime.

Payments to Surviving Family Members

In addition to their retirement pension programs, the CSRS and FERS provide some financial support for the family of a federal worker who dies while still employed by the government.

Who Is Eligible

If a federal worker covered by either CSRS or FERS dies while still employed by the government, the surviving spouse and minor children can receive survivor benefits if the worker had been employed by the government for at least 18 months.

Benefits for Spouse

For the surviving spouse to collect benefits, either the couple must have been married at least a year when the worker died, or the surviving spouse must be the parent of the worker's child. The survivor benefit is paid to the surviving spouse regardless of the spouse's age.

A surviving spouse who also works for the federal government can collect both survivor benefits and his or her own retirement pension.

Benefits for Children

The children of a deceased federal worker also receive benefits until each reaches 18 years of age or gets married. If the child is a full-time high school or college student, benefits can continue until age 22. If a child becomes disabled before reaching age 18, the survivor benefits may continue for as long as the child is incapable of full self-support.

A child of an unmarried deceased worker also qualifies for a survivor annuity. If the unmarried worker was the father, the worker must have acknowledged the child or a court must have established paternity. A stepchild may also qualify for benefits if he or she lived with the worker in a parent-child relationship.

Amount of Benefits

The amount of survivor benefits depends on whether the deceased employee was covered by CSRS or FERS.

CSRS Benefits

If a CSRS-covered worker dies while still employed by the government, his or her surviving spouse and qualifying children will each receive an annuity.

Spouse. The surviving spouse's CSRS annuity is 55% of the retirement annuity that the worker earned before dying. The survivor is guaranteed a minimum benefit of 55% of whichever is less, either:

- 40% of the worker's high-three average pay, or
- the amount the worker's retirement annuity would have been at age 60.

A surviving spouse loses the annuity if he or she remarries before age 55; after age 55, the annuity continues regardless of remarriage. If the second marriage ends before the surviving spouse turns 55, he or she can have the survivor annuity reinstated.

Children. The amount payable to the surviving children of a CSRS-covered worker depends on whether the other parent is still alive. Each qualifying child receives an annuity based on the following computations:

- if there is a surviving parent who was the spouse of the deceased employee, 60% of the worker's high-three average pay, divided by the number of qualified children, or approximately $350 per month (the figure goes up slightly most years, adjusted for inflation), whichever is less, or
- if there is no surviving parent, 75% of the high-three average pay, divided by the number of qualified children, or approximately $400 per month, whichever is less.

FERS Benefits

FERS benefits payable to a qualified surviving child are the same as for CSRS-covered employees, discussed just above. However, they are reduced by any Social Security survivors benefits the child receives. (See Chapter 5 regarding survivors benefits.)

The amount of FERS benefits a surviving spouse may receive depends on the number of years the deceased worker was employed. If the worker was employed for more than 18 months but less than ten years, the surviving spouse is entitled to a lump sum payment. That payment is approximately $22,000 (the figure goes up most years, adjusted for inflation), plus either 50% of the worker's yearly pay at the time of death, or 50% of the worker's high-three average, whichever is higher.

If the worker was employed for more than ten years, the surviving spouse also gets an annuity equal to 50% of what the employee's retirement annuity would have been.

These spouse's survivors benefits are not reduced by any Social Security survivors benefits.

Applying for CSRS or FERS Benefits

Decisions about both CSRS and FERS benefit claims are made by the federal government's Office of Personnel Management (OPM). You must file a written application for specific benefits. You may apply at the personnel office within the agency at which you work. If you no longer work for the agency, you may file your application at any OPM office.

You can get general information about benefits, application forms, the application process, and appeals from decisions of the OPM by telephone from the OPM's Retirement Information Office. Recorded information is available 24 hours a day at 202-606-0400. For additional help, call 888-767-6738 (toll-free) or visit www.opm.gov/retirement-services.

To obtain information about the benefits available to you based on your personal employment record, go in person to your agency's personnel office or put your request in writing and send it to:

U.S. Office of Personnel Management
Employee Services and Records Center
Boyers, PA 16017

This is the office where employee records are maintained, and most questions can be answered by the staff there. If there is some complicated question they cannot answer, they will forward your inquiry to the Washington office of the OPM, which will respond. ●

Veterans Benefits

I n addition to the pensions and benefits that arise from both public and private civilian employment, many older Americans may be eligible for certain benefits based on their military service.

The Department of Veterans Affairs (VA) operates a number of programs providing financial, medical, and other assistance to veterans. Eligibility may depend on financial need or time of service.

For older veterans, three major benefit programs are of particular value: disability compensation, veterans pensions, and, perhaps most significant, free or low-cost medical care through VA hospitals and medical facilities. This chapter explains some of these benefits.

Types of Military Service Required

Veterans benefits are available only to people who performed active service in a uniformed branch of the military: Army, Navy, Marine Corps, Air Force, Coast Guard, Women's Army Auxiliary Corps (WAAC), or Women's Air Service Pilots (WASP).

Active service is defined as either active duty or active duty for training.

Active Duty

Active duty means full-time service in one of the uniformed branches of the military forces mentioned above. It also includes full-time duty in the Commissioned Officer Corps of the Public Health Service or National Oceanic and Atmospheric Administration (NOAA), formerly Coast and Geodetic Survey. And, under some circumstances, full-time members of the Merchant Marine who served during wartime and wartime members of the Flying Tigers may also qualify.

Any length of active duty can qualify a veteran for benefits, with the exception of pensions for financially needy veterans, which require at least 90 days of active duty service. (See "Pension Benefits for Financially Needy Disabled Veterans," below, for more on need-based pensions.)

Active Duty for Training

Generally, membership in the National Guard or Reserve Corps does not qualify a person for veterans benefits. However, if a person in the Guard or Reserves is called up for full-time duty in the armed forces, this period of service is called active duty for training. A person who is injured or becomes ill during that period of active duty for training may be eligible for veterans disability benefits if the injury or illness leads to a disability.

Compensation for Service-Connected Disability

The VA administers a system of benefits for veterans who have a disability that can be connected in any way to a period of service. More lenient than civil disability benefit programs, a veteran can receive assistance even if he or she is only partially disabled, and almost regardless of the cause, as long as it occurred while performing some duty related to service. And if your injury or illness first arose during a period of wartime, the rules for compensation are even easier to meet.

Who Is Eligible

Compensation is available for veterans who have a "service-connected disability." Service connected means that they were wounded, injured, or became ill—or aggravated an existing condition—while on active duty, or training for active duty, in the armed forces.

If your condition arose while you were on active duty during peacetime, your disability must have resulted directly from military duties. In reality, though, this requirement rules out only injuries sustained while on leave, for example, or while AWOL or committing some militarily punishable offense. Virtually all other activities—including playing for the base softball team, eating in the mess, traveling to and from training, and going on authorized leave—are considered part of military duties.

The rules are even more lenient if the condition or injury occurred during time of war or national emergency, as officially designated and listed below. In such cases, you can be compensated even though the injury or illness was completely unrelated to military duties, such as while on furlough or leave. These official periods of war or national emergency include:

- **World War II.** December 7, 1941 through December 31, 1946
- **Korean War.** June 27, 1950 through January 31, 1955
- **Vietnam War.** August 5, 1964 through May 7, 1975, and
- **Persian Gulf War.** August 2, 1990 through a date yet to be set by Congress or Presidential Proclamation.

Note that the periods of time considered part of the Second World War and the Korean War are longer than the time spans normally attributed to those conflicts.

Amount of Benefits

The amount of disability compensation to which you are entitled depends on the seriousness of the disability. When you apply for disability compensation, your medical records are reviewed and VA personnel will examine you to assess your disability.

Your disability is given a rating, based on the extent to which it interferes with the average person's ability to earn a living. This rating is expressed in percent of disability—0% to 100% disabled, in increments of 10%.

Unfortunately, this rating system does not normally take into account the real effect of your disability on the work you do. Rather, it applies arbitrary percentages—20% or 30% for the loss of a finger or toe, for example—to the theoretical average person's ability to earn a living. Obviously, the loss of a finger affects a piano player much more than it affects an opera singer. But the VA usually applies its fixed schedule of disabilities to common injuries and diseases.

Disabilities From Agent Orange, Radiation, and Gulf War Syndrome

Because of the military use of chemicals and radioactive materials, many veterans have fallen ill with serious, disabling diseases years after their service ended. These veterans used to have no way to prove their disease was caused by exposure during military service. After sustained pressure from veterans groups, the VA has finally admitted that certain exposure does indeed cause specific diseases. As a result, if a veteran was exposed to Agent Orange or radiation and later is disabled by certain diseases, the disability is *presumed* to be service connected. To a limited extent, the same can be said of "Gulf War Syndrome."

Vietnam and Agent Orange: If you served in Vietnam and have become disabled by one of the following diseases, you are presumed to have contracted the disease through exposure to Agent Orange and may be eligible for service-connected disability benefits. Diseases include prostate cancer, Hodgkin's disease, multiple myeloma, respiratory cancers (lung, bronchus, larynx, trachea), non-Hodgkin's lymphoma, chloracne, porphyria cutanea tarda, soft-tissue sarcoma, and acute/subacute peripheral neuropathy.

Radiation exposure: If your work in the military exposed you extensively to ionizing radiation, you may be eligible for service-connected disability benefits if you have become disabled by most types of leukemia or lymphoma, most types of cancer, brain or central nervous system tumors, thyroid disease, or multiple myeloma.

Gulf War Syndrome: Almost immediately after serving in the Gulf War, many veterans complained about illnesses—joint pain, rash, fatigue, memory loss, intestinal problems—that they did not have before service in the Gulf. The cause(s) of these illnesses have not been definitively diagnosed, and the government initially went to great lengths to deny that they were caused by military service—even suggesting that they were not really illnesses at all. Slowly and grudgingly, the government changed its tune. If a veteran has a

**Disabilities From Agent Orange, Radiation,
and Gulf War Syndrome (continued)**

chronic qualifying disability, that illness may now be presumed to be connected to Gulf service. And if the illness results in a persistent disability, the veteran may be eligible for service-connected disability compensation. For information about Gulf War–related illness and compensation, a veteran may call a special Gulf War Veterans Information Hotline at 800-PGW-VETS.

However, if your disability does not match any of the simple descriptions in the VA's rating system, when rating your individual disability, the VA may consider the effect of your condition on the work you are able to do.

Benefits range from about $130 per month for a 10% disability to about $2,900 per month for total or 100% disability. If you have at least a 30% disability rating, your dependents are also eligible for some minimal benefits.

Eligible dependents include your spouse and your children up to age 18, or age 22 if a full-time student, or of any age if disabled. The total amount received depends on the number of dependents and on your disability rating—the higher the rating, the higher the benefits. The additional amounts for dependents range from $45 to $160 per month for a spouse and $30 to $100 per month for each child.

Changes to Your Rating

Although most service-connected disabilities show up during or soon after military service, some conditions may not appear, or not become disabling, until years after you get out of the service. Regardless of when a condition actually becomes disabling, if it can be traced to injury or illness that occurred while you were in the service, it can be compensated.

EXAMPLE: Claudio's knee was bashed while serving as a cook at a training camp during the Vietnam War. The knee healed well and Claudio had no serious trouble with it during the war or the years immediately following it. However, as he got older, his knee got steadily worse. His doctor diagnosed Claudio with a serious arthritic condition in the knee, a result of the wartime injury.

Because Claudio's knee condition resulted from his wartime service, he was entitled to claim disability benefits when the knee began to interfere with his normal activities, even though he made no such claim before he was discharged from the service.

Sometimes, a disability that rated low when it first appeared will grow progressively worse in later years. In such a case, a veteran can claim disability benefits even if he or she was previously rated by the VA as not disabled. Or the veteran can apply for an upgrading of an already-existing disability rating if the condition has worsened over time.

EXAMPLE: Ernie was an M.P. in Kuwait during the Persian Gulf War. While on leave, Ernie picked up a lung infection. The scarring from it, over the years, occasionally gave him minor respiratory difficulty. A few years after his discharge, Ernie applied for a service-connected disability. Although he picked up his illness while on leave, he was eligible for benefits because he had been on active duty during wartime. He was given a 10% disability rating for his labored breathing.

As he got older, Ernie experienced more breathing difficulties, to the point that even mild exertion made his breathing painful and dangerously difficult. His doctor said that poorer circulation with age was making Ernie's lung condition worse. Since his doctor verified that his condition had worsened, Ernie could apply for an upgrading of his disability rating. The new disability rating was 40%, which meant not only that Ernie's own benefits would be higher, but that his wife was also eligible for some benefits as a qualifying dependent. (See "Amount of Benefits," above, regarding dependents benefits.)

Pension Benefits for Financially Needy Disabled Veterans

A small monthly cash benefit is available to a financially needy wartime veteran who is 100% disabled from causes that are not service-connected. Unfortunately, the amount is usually extremely low, only enough to bring the veteran's total income from all sources to just above the poverty line.

To qualify for this small cash benefit, the veteran must have had 90 days or more of active duty, with at least one day during a period of war. (See "Compensation for Service-Connected Disability," above, for the list of recognized periods of war.) However, there is no requirement of service in or near actual combat.

A totally disabled veteran who meets the service requirements is granted an amount that will bring his or her total annual income—including income from private pensions, Social Security, and SSI—up to minimum levels established by Congress. Those minimum levels, however, are extremely low: about $1,000 per month from all sources for a veteran with no dependents, about $1,350 per month for a veteran with one dependent—a spouse, or a child under age 18, or disabled—and slightly higher for each additional dependent.

Some veterans are entitled to a larger benefit if they live in nursing homes, are unable to leave their houses, or are in regular need of aid and attendance. Veterans with out-of-pocket medical expenses are also entitled to a larger benefit.

Limits on Assets

The pension described in this section is not for veterans with savings or other assets that could be used or cashed in for living expenses. (Fortunately, these potential living expense assets exclude the value of a home the veteran lives in.) Even disabled veterans with little or no income will not qualify for the pension benefits if they have assets over $80,000, depending on the cost of living where the veteran lives and the amount of ongoing medical expenses that the veteran pays out of pocket.

Survivors Benefits

Several VA programs provide benefits to a veteran's surviving spouse, and in some instances to surviving children.

The VA's Definition of Eligible Marriage

To collect benefits as the surviving spouse of a veteran, you must have been married to the veteran for at least one year and be married at the time of his or her death.

If you were divorced from the veteran, you cannot claim survivors benefits. Even if you were still married when the veteran died, you lose survivors benefits if you later marry someone else.

If you remarried after the veteran's death but that later marriage has ended, you may again be eligible for survivors benefits through your first spouse's record.

Dependency and Indemnity Compensation

A benefit known as Dependency and Indemnity Compensation (DIC) is paid to the surviving spouse of an armed forces member who died either while in service or from a service-connected disability after discharge. However, if the veteran was dishonorably discharged, no benefits will be paid to the survivor.

The amount of the DIC benefit depends on when the veteran died, and on whether he or she had a service-connected disability at the time of death:

- For the surviving spouses of veterans who died on or after January 1, 1993, the basic monthly DIC benefit is $1,280; an additional $271 per month is paid if the veteran had a 100% disability rating from a service-connected disability during the eight years immediately before his or her death. Additional amounts can be paid if the veteran has a minor child or the surviving spouse is in a care facility or housebound.

- For the surviving spouses of veterans who died before 1993, the benefit amounts depend on the veteran's military rank.

For a complete listing of DIC benefit amounts, see the Department of Veterans Affairs website at www.benefits.va.gov/compensation.

VA Benefits for Same-Sex Spouses

The United States Supreme Court has now made clear that same-sex spouses are entitled to federal spousal benefits, including VA benefits, on the same terms as other spouses. This is true regardless of whether the couple lives in the state where the marriage was performed.

Foreign marriages. A spouse in a same-sex couple who was married outside the United States but now lawfully lives in the United States might be entitled to VA benefits based on the other spouse's military record, depending on the status of that marriage in the country where it was performed. Even if you have doubts about your right to VA spousal benefits as a same-sex spouse, the VA encourages you to apply for them so that they can determine whether you are eligible.

Retroactivity. The Department of Justice has decided that the right to spousal benefits for a same-sex spouse may belong to those who applied for such benefits before the Supreme Court's same-sex marriage decision on June 26, 2015. If you were married and applied for VA spousal benefits before that date but were denied those benefits (because you lived in a state that did not recognize your marriage), reapply to the VA specifically requesting retroactive benefits back to the date you first applied.

Wartime Service Pension

The surviving spouse of a veteran may claim a monthly pension, regardless of whether death was connected to service, if that veteran would have been eligible for a wartime service pension. This survivor pension, like the veteran's wartime pension, requires that the survivor have a low income, taking into account money from any other pensions or Social Security benefits the surviving spouse receives.

A veteran's surviving children may also collect a survivors wartime pension after the veteran's death.

The amount of a survivors pension depends on the survivor's income and whether or not the survivor also has dependent children, is housebound, or requires "aid and attendance" (see below). Maximum pensions are between about $700 and $1,300 per month, but these amounts are usually reduced based on the survivor's income.

Aid and Attendance

The Aid and Attendance (A&A) benefit is a special additional program to assist veterans and survivors who are eligible for DIC benefits and who are either living in a nursing facility or are housebound. If a survivor is in a nursing facility, an A&A benefit can add about $300 per month to whatever DIC benefit he or she is already receiving; for a housebound survivor, the benefit is usually slightly less. The amount of the benefit depends on whether the survivor has additional sources of income, and on the survivor's medical expenses.

TRICARE Medical Coverage for Military Retirees and Dependents

A comprehensive and generous system of medical coverage, completely separate from veterans benefits, is available for retired military service members, their spouses, and their children younger than 21. This system is known as TRICARE and is administered by the Department of Defense. People with TRICARE coverage who become eligible for Medicare must be enrolled in both programs. For details on TRICARE eligibility, benefits, and the coordination of TRICARE and Medicare, visit the TRICARE website at www.tricare.mil.

Medical Treatment

One of the most important benefits available to veterans is free or low-cost medical care. The VA operates more than 150 hospitals throughout the country. In addition, a great number of outpatient clinics provide health care for veterans. Also, specialized care may be available at no charge through a VA hospital, while the same care might be unavailable or beyond a veteran's means in the world of private medicine.

Medicare and VA Medical Treatment

Many veterans who are eligible for VA medical treatment are also covered by Medicare. The general rule is that for any specific medical treatment, you can choose either of the benefits, but not both. This means that if you are charged copayments for treatment at a VA facility, Medicare cannot pay for them. However, if you are treated by a private doctor or facility and the VA pays most but not all of the cost, Medicare may be able to pay some of the unpaid amount. If you are treated by a private doctor or facility and Medicare covers the bills, you cannot submit any unpaid portion to the VA.

There is a significant exception to this rule, which kicks in where the VA covers services that Medicare doesn't. For example, if the VA authorizes you to receive treatment at a private facility but does not cover all the services you receive, Medicare can pay for any of those services if Medicare does cover them.

If you had active duty in the military and were discharged under conditions other than dishonorable, you may be eligible for VA health care benefits. If you enlisted after September 7, 1980 or entered active duty after October 16, 1981, you must have served for 24 uninterrupted months to be eligible for health care. This minimum service time may not apply if you were discharged due to a service-connected disability or for hardship. In a few pilot programs at VA medical centers, dependents and survivors of a veteran may also receive some care if they are unable to afford care in the private sector. (But this kind of care for dependents and survivors is rare in a VA medical system heavily stressed by Vietnam, Iraq, and Afghanistan war veterans.) The VA may also pay for long-term care in certain private facilities for some veterans with serious service-connected disabilities, if there is no space in a local VA facility.

Additional Veterans Programs Are Available

This chapter explains the major programs for which older veterans are usually eligible. However, the VA administers many more programs that a veteran may find useful.

The VA also provides financial support for education and vocational training, life insurance, home loans and other housing assistance, and a National Cemetery burial program.

Eligibility requirements vary for each of these programs, but either active duty or active duty for training are usual requirements. (See "Types of Military Service Required," above, for definitions.) For information about other services the VA offers veterans and their families, visit the VA's website at www.va.gov.

Even if you qualify for treatment at a VA medical facility, however, you may not always be able to get the care when you need it, or the treatment may be available only at a VA facility far from your home. The reason for these limits, even for eligible patients, is that while there are close to 100,000 beds in VA hospitals, many more than 100,000 veterans and dependents need medical care.

To meet the demand for medical care, and particularly for the limited number of hospital beds, the VA has established a priority system for deciding who gets treatment directly from VA hospitals, clinics, and doctors:

- **Priority Group 1:** Veterans with service-connected disabilities rated 50% or more disabling
- **Priority Group 2:** Veterans with service-connected disabilities rated 30% or 40% disabling

- **Priority Group 3:** Veterans who are former POWs, were discharged for a disability incurred or aggravated in the line of duty, have service-connected disabilities rated 10% or 20% disabling, or were disabled by treatment
- **Priority Group 4:** Veterans who are receiving aid and attendance or housebound benefits (see "Aid and Attendance," above)
- **Priority Group 5:** Veterans with a 0% disability rating whose income and assets are below certain dollar limits
- **Priority Group 6:** Gulf War veterans receiving care solely for Gulf War–related disorders not amounting to compensable disabilities, veterans with compensable 0% service-connected disabilities, and World War I veterans, and
- **Priority Group 7:** All other veterans. If accepted for treatment, this group must pay a copayment for services.

Getting Information and Applying for Benefits

The Veterans Administration maintains a website (www.va.gov) with much useful information about the programs discussed in this chapter. The website can be a little overwhelming, but if you're comfortable navigating on the Internet, you may find the site very useful. You might find it easiest to use the site's search engine (in the upper right-hand corner of the home page) by filling in just the specific subject you are interested in, such as disability benefits or Aid & Attendance.

The VA maintains large regional offices in major cities, and many smaller offices known as Vet Centers in cities both large and small. Although applications are processed and decisions made at the regional offices, the Vet Centers provide information about benefits and claims. The Vet Centers can also provide you with application forms for various benefits, assist you in filling them out, and help you with any appeal if you are denied a benefit.

To find either the regional office or the Vet Center nearest you, look in the government pages in your telephone directory under United States Government, Veterans Affairs Department. Or, call the VA's national benefits information line at 800-827-1000, or their health benefits line at 877-222-8387. Also check the VA website at www.va.gov.

When appearing in person at a Vet Center, the veteran should bring discharge papers, medical records if applying for disability benefits, and wage or tax records indicating current income if considering an application for wartime service pension benefits.

A surviving spouse should bring the veteran's discharge or other military papers, marriage certificate, recent wage or tax records, and birth certificates for any minor children, or for a surviving child up to age 22 who is disabled or a full-time student, plus evidence of their disability or student status.

Requests for medical treatment or admission to a VA medical facility, or VA coverage of medical treatment by a private facility, are usually handled at the admitting office of the VA medical facility or clinic itself. A veteran seeking medical attention at a VA hospital should (after calling to find out its appointment procedures) bring discharge papers, documents indicating that the veteran is receiving VA disability benefits and whether or not any medical condition is service connected, and documents indicating whether the veteran is receiving a VA pension. ●

Medicare

The high cost of medical care and medical insurance, coupled with the lack of a comprehensive health plan available to all, is not a credit to the United States. Yet whenever discussion of this monumental failure makes its way into the political arena, proposals for creating a decent health care system run into dual roadblocks. The first is mounted by heavily bankrolled corporate interests—pharmaceutical, medical technology, and hospital companies; the insurance industry; and most doctors' groups—who fight any limits on their profit making. The second is set up by politicians who refuse to take any steps that might be seen as opposing the interests of the moneyed portion of the population.

In 1965, however, over howls of protest by many in corporate boardrooms and government, the Medicare national health insurance system was introduced as a way of providing a certain amount of guaranteed coverage for older citizens. And for over 40 years now, Medicare has been carving an inroad into the mountain of consumer health care costs.

Medicare pays for most of the cost of hospitalization and much other medical care for older Americans (though for some, it still leaves almost half of all medical costs unpaid). Medicare now provides this coverage for over 58 million people, most of them age 65 and older.

Despite its broad reach, Medicare does not pay for many types of medical services, and it pays only a portion of most services it does cover. Although Medicare expanded its coverage in 2006 to include some of the cost of prescription drugs, it has done nothing to address the overall spiraling costs of those drugs.

And while the 2010 federal health care reform act expanded Medicare coverage of certain preventive screenings and examinations, and slightly improved prescription drug coverage, it did not otherwise broaden Medicare.

This chapter discusses the Medicare system, what it covers, and how much it pays. Chapter 13 shows you how to apply for Medicare and take full advantage of its benefits.

The chapters that follow present detailed information about how to fill the gaps in Medicare coverage. Medigap supplemental insurance is discussed in Chapter 14, and the various Medicare Advantage plans are sorted out in Chapter 15. If you have a low income and few assets, Chapter 16 explains the government Medicaid program, which provides free coverage in place of buying private insurance or a managed care plan.

If You Will Turn 65 Soon

If you are turning 65 soon (and are not already enrolled in Medicare through disability benefits eligibility), there are several things you need to do to prepare for Medicare.

Find out if your current health insurance will continue when you hit 65 and, if so, how it works in conjunction with Medicare.

See what Medicare supplement ("medigap") insurance policies (Chapter 14) and Medicare Advantage plans (Chapter 15) are available where you live.

Decide whether to enroll in traditional fee-for-service Medicare (this chapter), and whether to add a medigap policy (Chapter 14) to this, or instead to enroll in a Medicare Advantage plan (Chapter 15).

Look into whether you may be eligible for Medicaid (Medi-Cal in California) coverage, or for state assistance with your Medicare costs (Chapter 16).

Learn about Medicare prescription drug coverage and the insurance plans available in your state to deliver that coverage (this chapter).

Speak to your physician about scheduling an initial Medicare physical examination (within six months after first enrolling) and about preventive services covered by Medicare that are appropriate to your physical condition and health history.

The Medicare Maze

There are two different ways that someone eligible for Medicare can receive the program's benefits. The first way is called "traditional Medicare" or "original Medicare," which includes Part A (hospital insurance) and Part B (medical insurance). With this type of Medicare coverage, a beneficiary can receive care from any doctor, hospital, clinic, or other provider who accepts Medicare patients. Medicare pays the provider a fee for each specific service. For services for which Medicare does not fully pay, the patient has several choices. The patient can choose to:

- pay out of pocket
- buy a private supplemental insurance policy—commonly known as "medigap" insurance—that pays much of what Medicare does not (see Chapter 14)
- buy a separate Medicare Part D prescription drug coverage insurance plan, or
- apply for Medicaid coverage (Medi-Cal in California), which is a federal program for low-income people that pays almost all of the health care costs that Medicare does not pay. Even if you do not qualify for Medicaid, you can apply for subsidized coverage of prescription drugs through Medicare Part D.

The second way that people can receive Medicare benefits is through a "Part C" Medicare Advantage plan, offered by private insurance companies. These plans cover everything that traditional Medicare does, plus some services Medicare doesn't cover at all. Some Medicare Advantage plans also include outpatient prescription drug coverage. And, they eliminate some of the copayments and deductibles required by traditional Medicare.

Medicare Advantage plans are managed care plans similar to an HMO. They are generally a bit less expensive than a combination of traditional Medicare with a medigap supplemental insurance policy. However, Medicare Advantage plans limit the doctors and other health care providers a patient may use, control referrals to specialists, and otherwise sometimes place restrictions on care. Medicare Advantage plans also annually change the copayment amounts they charge enrollees and sometimes limit or eliminate specific coverage, and sometimes even eliminate coverage entirely in a particular geographic area. (For more information, see Chapter 15, "Medicare Part C: Medicare Advantage Plans.")

Because of these limitations, only about 33% of Medicare beneficiaries are enrolled in Medicare Advantage plans, and many of those are required to enroll because of their dual status as enrollees in both Medicare and Medicaid (see Chapter 16).

Medicare Prescription Drug Coverage

Medicare now includes Part D, which provides some coverage for outpatient prescription drug costs. Unfortunately, Medicare Part D prescription drug coverage leaves many drug costs uncovered. And it does nothing about the soaring overall costs of prescription drugs. In fact, the law specifically bars the Medicare program from negotiating with drug companies for lower prices on behalf of Medicare patients. This restriction, which received almost no media attention, is a staggering giveaway to the pharmaceutical industry. It ensures that in the years to come, drug prices will continue to increase at rates far above the cost of living, which will, in turn, place enormous economic pressure on seniors and the Medicare program alike. Also, the law enacting the new program handed the drug plans over to private insurance companies—whose inefficient overhead and enormous profits will likely add to the cost of prescription drugs under the new program.

Nonetheless, the Medicare Part D program does provide some prescription drug coverage not previously available to many Medicare beneficiaries. (Medicare Part D's coverage is explained at the end of this chapter.)

Medicare and Medicaid: A Comparison

People are sometimes confused about the differences between Medicare and Medicaid. Medicare was created to deal with the high medical costs that older citizens face relative to the rest of the population—especially troublesome given their reduced earning power. However, eligibility for Medicare is not tied to individual need. Rather, it is an entitlement program; you are entitled to it because you or your spouse paid for it through Social Security and Medicare taxes.

Medicaid, on the other hand, is for low-income, financially needy people, set up by the federal government, and administered differently in each state.

Although you may qualify for and receive coverage from both Medicare and Medicaid, you must meet separate eligibility requirements for each program; being eligible for one program does not necessarily mean you are eligible for the other. If you qualify for both, Medicaid will pay for most Medicare Part A and B premiums, deductibles, and copayments or will offer you enrollment in a managed care plan that provides a combination of Medicare and Medicaid coverage.

Chapter 16 explains Medicaid and the chart below describes the basic differences between the two programs.

A Comparison of Medicare and Medicaid

Medicare	Medicaid
Who Is Eligible	
Medicare is for almost everyone 65 or older, rich or poor; people on Social Security disability; and for some people with permanent kidney failure.	Medicaid is for low-income and financially needy people, including those older than 65 who are also on Medicare.
Medicare is an entitlement program; people are entitled to Medicare based on their own or their spouse's Social Security contributions, and on payment of premiums.	Medicaid is an assistance program only for the needy.
Who Administers the Program	
Medicare is a federal program. Medicare rules are the same all over the country.	Medicaid rules differ in each state.
Medicare information is available at your Social Security office or through the Centers for Medicare & Medicaid Services.	Medicaid information is available at your local county social services, welfare, or department of human services office.

A Comparison of Medicare and Medicaid (continued)

Medicare	Medicaid
Coverage Provided	
Medicare hospital insurance (Part A) provides basic coverage for hospital stays and post hospital nursing facility and home health care.	Medicaid provides comprehensive inpatient and outpatient health care coverage, including many services and costs Medicare does not cover, most notably, prescription drugs, some diagnostic and preventive care, and eyeglasses. The amount of coverage, however, varies from state to state.
Medicare medical insurance (Part B) pays most of basic doctor and laboratory costs, and some other outpatient medical services, including medical equipment and supplies, home health care, and physical therapy. It covers some of the cost of prescription drugs for those who sign up for supplemental drug coverage (Part D).	Medicaid can pay Medicare deductibles and the 20% portion of charges not paid by Medicare. Medicaid can also pay the Medicare premium.
Costs to Consumer	
You must pay a yearly deductible for both Medicare Part A and Part B. You must also pay hefty copayments for extended hospital stays.	In some states, Medicaid charges consumers small amounts for certain services.
Under Part B, you must pay the 20% of doctors' bills Medicare does not pay, and sometimes up to 15% more. Part B also charges a monthly premium. Under Part D, you must pay a monthly premium, a deductible, copayments, and all of your prescription drug costs over a certain yearly amount and up to a ceiling amount, unless you qualify for a low-income subsidy.	

Medicare: The Basics

Medicare is a federal government program that assists older and some disabled people with paying their medical costs. Part A is called hospital insurance, and covers most of the costs of a stay in the hospital, as well as some follow-up costs afterward. Part B, medical insurance, pays some of the costs of doctors and outpatient medical care. And Part D pays some prescription drug costs. Medicare Part C refers to separate Medicare Advantage plans, which can replace Parts A and B (see Chapter 15).

Medicare is operated by the Centers for Medicare & Medicaid Services (CMS), part of the Department of Health and Human Services, in cooperation with the Social Security Administration. The Medicare program's daily business, however, is run by private companies, called carriers or intermediaries, operating under contract with the federal government.

Most of a patient's direct contact with Medicare happens with the company—Blue Cross, Blue Shield, or another large insurance company—that administers Medicare in his or her state or that runs the patient's Medicare Part D prescription drug plan.

One of the outrages of the current Medicare political storm is that giving Medicare administrative monopolies to these private insurance companies drives up the cost to the public.

Special Medicare Eligibility for End-Stage Renal Disease (ESRD)

While Medicare coverage is generally reserved for people age 65 or older and people with long-term disabilities, a special Medicare provision provides full Medicare coverage to most people suffering from permanent kidney failure, known as end-stage renal disease (ESRD), regardless of their age. The rules regarding eligibility for this coverage and the extent of this coverage are discussed fully later in this chapter.

Health Coverage If You Stop Working Before Age 65

Medicare and Medicare supplemental insurance and Medicare Advantage plans are available to most people age 65 and older. But what if you stop working before age 65—either because you choose to retire, are laid off, or lose your business? Chances are you'll lose your health insurance at the same time. Then the issue becomes finding affordable medical coverage, and a plan that will cover preexisting conditions, to fill the gap until you turn 65.

Here are some ways to try to stretch your medical coverage without turning to the open market for an individual health insurance policy:

- **Take advantage of continued health insurance from your employer.** If you are entitled to retirement benefits from your employer, these may include continued health care coverage. Be aware, however, that your employer is permitted to drop that retiree health coverage once you turn 65 and are eligible for Medicare. If you aren't automatically eligible for retiree health coverage, you may be able to negotiate continued health coverage with your employer as part of your severance package, or with the purchaser of your business as part of its sale price.

- **Convert to individual coverage under an employer-sponsored plan.** Some employer-sponsored insurance plans permit employees to convert their group coverage to individual coverage upon leaving their employment. If your plan allows this, you will probably have to pay all the premiums—and they may well be higher than when you were part of a group policy. Even if such individual coverage is available to you through your employer, you may want to compare its coverage and cost with individual insurance available through the new federal or state health insurance exchanges (see below).

- **Continue coverage under COBRA.** The U.S. Congress passed the Consolidated Budget Reconciliation Act (COBRA) in 1985. It mandates a period of continued health coverage for people who lose or leave their jobs (unless they're fired for gross misconduct) and their spouses and children. It also applies to employees whose hours are reduced below the number that qualifies them for health benefits. If you qualify, you are entitled to buy 18 months of health insurance from the same company following the end of your employer-sponsored coverage. However, the extent of your coverage may be reduced, and you'll have to pay the full premiums—which will probably be higher than what your employer paid for you. (For more information, see *The Essential Guide to Federal Employment Laws*, by Lisa Guerin and Sachi Barreiro (Nolo), or search "COBRA" on the Department of Labor website at www.dol.gov.) Also, check with the agency in your state dealing with labor and employment—most states have passed their own laws expanding on COBRA's coverage.

- **Find individual health insurance through your state's insurance exchange or the federal insurance marketplace.** Any individual can buy a health insurance policy regardless of his or her prior medical history. These policies are sold through what is called a health insurance exchange, or marketplace, established by the Affordable Care Act (also known as Obamacare). The cost of the health insurance policies depends on your age, the level of coverage you seek, and your income. Twenty-three states and the District of Columbia have established their own state health insurance exchanges, while residents of the other states are eligible to use the federal marketplace. To find out what's available where you live, go online to the government site www. healthcare.gov.

- **Claim early Medicare based on disability.** If you stop working because of a disability and you qualify for Social Security disability benefits, you will qualify for full Medicare coverage once you have been entitled to disability benefits for 24 months. (See Chapter 3 for a full discussion of Social Security disability benefits.)

Working After Age 65

If you have current health care coverage through your employer when you turn 65, you may want to continue with it and not sign up for Medicare Part B. (Medicare Part A is free for almost everyone, so there's little reason not to enroll in it after you turn 65, even if you keep your employer-based insurance. See Chapter 13 for more on enrolling for Part A.)

Many people who continue full-time employment after age 65 are enrolled in health insurance through their employer (often along with their spouse). If it's a large employer (with more than 20 employees), the employee with health coverage (and the Medicare-eligible spouse) can choose to keep that health insurance or drop it (and its premium costs) and enroll instead in Medicare Part B. A person in this situation gets to choose between employer-based coverage and Medicare Part B because the employer-based health insurance for a current employee and spouse will remain in full force (known as "primary coverage") when the employee becomes eligible for Medicare. (This may also be true for some small employers—those with fewer than 20 employees—who make special arrangements with their health insurance carrier; check with your employer to see if this is the case for you.)

As a rule, however, this primary coverage by employer-based health insurance does *not* apply to most employer-based health insurance for current employees of small employers with fewer than 20 employees or to retiree health insurance. For smaller company employees and for retirees, employer-based coverage automatically becomes "secondary" to Medicare when they turn 65 and will only help pay for costs that Medicare does not pay (such as deductibles and copayments). So, these employees and retirees need to enroll in Medicare Part B, or a Part C Medicare Advantage plan (see Chapter 15), as soon as they turn 65.

If you have the choice to remain enrolled in employer-based health insurance based on your or your spouse's current employment or to drop that insurance and enroll in Medicare Part B, how do you decide? As with most health insurance decisions, compare the costs. Look at the monthly premium, plus the deductibles and copayments, for your employer-sponsored coverage. Then compare that against the monthly cost for Medicare Part B (about $125 to $134 per month in 2018; more if you have income over $85,000), plus the cost of a medigap supplemental plan (average of $175 to $200 per month for the most common plan—see Chapter 14), and a Part D drug coverage plan (usually another $30–40 per month). Alternatively, you could enroll in a Part C Medicare Advantage plan, which provides the full coverage of Medicare Part B, a medigap supplement, and Part D drug coverage, for the lower cost of just the Medicare Part B premium plus another $30 per month (on average). Some Part C plans have no monthly premium.

Cost, however, is not the only consideration. Be aware that not all doctors accept patients who are covered by Medicare as their primary insurance. So, even if Medicare Part B plus supplementary insurance or a Medicare Advantage plan would be cheaper for you than keeping your employer-based coverage, before switching to Medicare you need to check whether the doctors you regularly use accept Medicare patients. Many doctors will continue to see existing patients who switch to Medicare even if those doctors do not accept new Medicare patients. But if one or more of your regular doctors would no longer see you as a patient if you switch to Medicare as your primary coverage, you have to consider whether being forced to switch to another doctor is worth the money you would save by switching to Medicare Part B.

Employer-Based Health Coverage for Retirees

Once you're Medicare eligible, your retirement health coverage may be cut off. About 12 million Medicare beneficiaries receive some kind of retirement health benefits from their former employers. These benefits often dovetail with Medicare coverage, paying its deductibles and copayments, and covering services Medicare does not, including prescription drugs. However, under a rule issued by the federal Equal Employment Opportunity Commission, employers are free to reduce that health coverage or eliminate it entirely for retirees age 65 or older—even if they maintain the coverage for younger retirees. If this happens to you, you'll have to fill in the gaps in Medicare coverage some other way, as described in Chapters 14 through 16.

Part A Hospital Insurance

Medicare is divided into several parts. Hospital insurance, referred to as Part A, covers most of the cost of care when you are at a hospital as an inpatient. Your remaining medical costs are covered, at least in part, by Medicare Part B. And Medicare Part D covers part of your prescription drug costs. If you are enrolled in a Medicare Part C Medicare Advantage plan (see Chapter 15), your hospital insurance is provided by that plan rather than by Medicare Part A.

Who Is Eligible

There are two types of eligibility for Medicare Part A hospital insurance: free and paid. Most people age 65 and older are eligible for free coverage, based on their work records or on their spouse's work records. People older than 65 who are not eligible for free Medicare Part A coverage can nevertheless enroll in it and pay a monthly fee. (See Chapter 13 for enrollment procedures.)

Free Coverage

Most people age 65 and older are automatically eligible for Medicare Part A hospital insurance. They do not have to pay any monthly premium for it; the coverage is free.

The two largest categories of people automatically eligible are:

- people age 65 or older who are eligible for Social Security retirement benefits, or have civil service retirement work credits equal to an amount that would make them eligible for Social Security retirement. (See Chapters 2 and 10 regarding eligibility for these two programs.) You are automatically eligible for Medicare coverage even if you do not actually begin collecting your retirement benefits at 65, as long as you could have started collecting them. If you wait to claim retirement benefits until after 65, you may still begin Medicare coverage at 65. However, if you begin collecting retirement benefits before age 65, you must wait until age 65 to get Medicare coverage.

- people age 65 or older who are eligible for Social Security dependents or survivors benefits. This includes same-sex spouses who are eligible for either of these Social Security benefits. Note that people who are age 65 or older and eligible for dependents benefits when a spouse turns 62 are entitled to Medicare coverage whether or not the spouse actually claims retirement benefits.

Some additional categories of people who may also be eligible for free coverage include:

- people of any age who have been entitled to Social Security disability benefits for 24 months
- people with amyotrophic lateral sclerosis (ALS) who have been approved for Social Security disability benefits (no waiting period), and
- anyone who has permanent kidney failure (ESRD) requiring either a kidney transplant or maintenance dialysis, if the person or spouse has worked a certain amount at jobs covered by Social Security. (There is a full discussion of this special ESRD-based Medicare eligibility later in this chapter.)

Paid Coverage

If you are age 65 or older but not automatically eligible for free Part A hospital insurance coverage, you can still enroll in the Medicare hospital insurance program by paying a monthly premium. The amount of your premium depends on how many Social Security work credits you or your spouse have earned, and on how long after your 65th birthday you apply for coverage.

If you are not eligible for free Part A coverage based on your or your spouse's work record, you can purchase the coverage by paying a monthly premium of $422 (in 2018); if you or your spouse has 30 to 39 work credits, your monthly premium will be $232. Also, if you enroll in Part A coverage more than a year after you turn 65, your premium will be 10% higher than these monthly figures (unless you fit under an exception, such as having health coverage through an employer).

CAUTION

Make sure to compare costs. If you are considering enrolling in and paying for Medicare Part A hospital insurance, it may be cheaper for you to do so through an HMO or a health plan. The cost of such coverage will be part of the broader coverage and cost for full participation in the HMO or health plan, which will vary among different plans. Before purchasing Medicare Part A coverage as an individual, compare premiums and benefits of various group plans.

If you enroll in paid Part A hospital insurance, you must also enroll in Part B medical insurance, for which you pay an additional monthly premium. However, you may enroll in Part B without Part A.

Types of Care Covered

Part A hospital insurance pays much of the cost you incur directly from a hospital as part of inpatient care. Under some circumstances, it also covers some of the cost of inpatient treatment in a skilled nursing facility and by a home health care agency. Doctors' bills are not included in Part A coverage; they are covered under Medicare Part B.

A few basic rules apply to all claims under Part A hospital insurance coverage, whether for inpatient care at a hospital or nursing facility or for home health care.

Doctor-Prescribed Care

The care and treatment you receive must be prescribed by a licensed physician.

Reasonable and Necessary Care

The inpatient care you receive must be medically reasonable and necessary—that is, the type of care that can be provided only at a hospital or nursing facility. If you could receive the particular treatment just as well and safely as a hospital outpatient, at the doctor's office, or at your home, Part A will not cover you if you receive that treatment as an inpatient. Also, Part A will not normally cover the cost of hospitalization for elective or cosmetic surgery—

except for reconstructive surgery after an accident or a disfiguring illness—because these are not considered medically necessary.

 CAUTION

"Held for observation" is not the same as "admitted."
Medicare Part A hospital insurance covers someone only if and when he or she is actually admitted to the hospital as an inpatient. Many times a patient is held and treated at the hospital—in a bed, in a room for more than 24 hours—but not formally admitted to the hospital. This is known as being "held for observation" and does not trigger coverage by Medicare Part A. Instead, Medicare Part B medical insurance (see later in this chapter) would be available to cover the care provided by the hospital and the doctors, and Medicare Part D prescription drug coverage could cover any medications provided.

The problem is that the copayments and deductibles a patient has to pay under Medicare Part B and Part D are generally much higher than under Part A. Also, being held for observation—rather than being actually admitted to the hospital—does not trigger eligibility for Part A coverage of follow-up skilled nursing facility or rehabilitation care (see the following section), which is quite common after hospital treatment. This can mean the entire very expensive cost of the nursing or rehab facility care must be paid out of the patient's pocket.

If you or a loved one are taken to the hospital and treated there for more than 24 hours, ask your doctor to have you or the loved one formally admitted to the hospital, rather than merely being held for observation, so that Medicare Part A coverage will be available to cover the stay and any following skilled nursing or rehabilitation facility inpatient care. Be aware that doctors and hospitals usually use Medicare's "Two Midnight" guideline in determining whether a patient is to be formally admitted as an inpatient. This refers to an expectation by the treating physician that the patient will need to remain in the hospital for at least two consecutive overnights ("two midnights"). However, this is only a guideline, not a hard-and-fast rule, and a doctor can admit a patient as an inpatient even if the doctor is not certain the patient will need to remain past two midnights, if in the doctor's reasonable opinion an inpatient admission is medically required. Medicare, however, reserves the right to challenge the reasonableness of that decision.

CAUTION

Custodial care isn't covered. Part A hospital insurance covers only skilled medical treatment of an illness or injury. It does not pay for a stay in a hospital or nursing facility, or for care from a home health agency, when the services you receive are primarily to make life more comfortable—to help with dressing, eating, bathing, or moving around. In reality, distinctions between medical treatment and custodial care sometimes blur, which can result in disputes between Medicare administration and patients.

Medicare-Approved Facility or Agency

Medicare issues licenses to hospitals, nursing facilities, and health care agencies certifying that they meet its standards for quality of care and staffing. Medicare will cover only care that is provided by facilities it approves.

Find out in advance if the facility to which you plan to be admitted, or the home health care agency you intend to hire, is approved by Medicare and accepts Medicare payment. Check with the facility's admissions services or administrator's office, or with the administrator of the home health care agency.

Nowadays it is rare to find a hospital or skilled nursing facility that is not Medicare approved. Some home health care agencies, however, are not Medicare approved. That does not necessarily mean that the agency is not reputable. Under most circumstances, Medicare Part A pays for very little home care, anyway. So if Medicare is not going to cover much of your costs, you may want to switch to an agency that is good and less expensive, but not Medicare approved, as soon as your Medicare coverage ends.

Facility Review Panel Approval

Each hospital and nursing facility has a panel of doctors and administrators that reviews your doctor's decision to treat you as a hospital inpatient or at a nursing facility. The panel usually agrees with your doctor's initial decision. And the panel and your doctor usually agree on how long you should remain in the facility. Sometimes, though, the panel decides you do not need to be an inpatient to receive certain treatment. Or it decides that you could be discharged from the facility earlier than your doctor recommended. The panel and your doctor will then consult with one another. Usually, they reach an agreement.

If, however, your doctor and the review panel do not agree that you require inpatient care, or they differ as to your discharge date, the question of whether Medicare Part A will pay for your inpatient care will be referred to a Peer Review Organization (PRO). (See Chapter 13 for more on the review process.)

> CAUTION
> **Psychiatric stays are limited.** Medicare Part A covers inpatient psychiatric hospital care, but the total number of days covered is limited. (See the "Psychiatric Hospitals" section, below, for details.)

Foreign Hospital Stays

In almost all situations, Medicare does not cover hospital stays outside the United States, Puerto Rico, the Virgin Islands, Guam, American Samoa, and the Northern Mariana Islands, even in an emergency. There are, however, three exceptions to this rule:

- If you are in the United States when an emergency occurs and a Canadian or Mexican hospital is closer than any U.S. hospital with emergency services, Medicare will help pay for your emergency care at that foreign hospital.
- If you live in the United States and a Mexican or Canadian hospital is closer to your home than the nearest U.S. hospital, Medicare can cover your care there even if there is no emergency.
- If you are in Canada while traveling directly to Alaska from one of the other states, or from Alaska to one of the other states, and an emergency arises, you may be covered for your care at a Canadian hospital. However, Medicare will not cover you if you are vacationing in Canada.

Many medigap supplemental insurance policies and Medicare Advantage plans provide coverage for foreign travel emergencies.

CAUTION

Consider buying travel insurance. Because there is no Medicare protection for you while you are traveling outside the United States, and if you have no other medical insurance that would cover you while traveling, it might be wise to look into traveler's insurance. These short-term policies are available for a one-time-only premium. A travel agent should be able to give you details. If you have a Medigap or Medicare Advantage plan, you may not need extra travel insurance.

Skilled Nursing Facilities

A growing number of patients recovering from surgery or a major illness are referred by their doctors to skilled nursing facilities (sometimes also called rehabilitative care centers). These provide an important, less expensive alternative to hospitalization. Medicare may cover some of your costs of staying in a skilled nursing facility, but strictly limits how much it will pay. (See "How Much Medicare Part A Pays," below, for details.)

You'll need to make sure your stay will be covered at all. You must meet two requirements before Medicare will pay for any nursing facility care. You must have recently stayed in a hospital, and your doctor must verify that you require daily skilled nursing care.

Prior Hospital Stay

Your stay in a skilled nursing facility must begin after you have spent at least three consecutive days, not counting the day of discharge, in the hospital as a formally admitted inpatient—and within 30 days of being discharged. If you leave the nursing facility after coverage begins, but are readmitted within 30 days, that second period in the nursing facility will also be covered by Medicare. (For details, see "Benefit Period or Spell of Illness," below.) **Note:** If you are enrolled in a Medicare Advantage (Medicare Part C) plan, the rules for skilled nursing facility coverage may be slightly less strict; see Chapter 15.

As of October 2016, hospitals are supposed to provide a written notice to patients who are at the hospital "under observation" for at least 24 hours, explaining whether the patient's stay at the hospital is officially an inpatient stay or an outpatient stay. If the stay was at least partly as an inpatient, the notice should indicate whether the inpatient status was for the three days (not counting the day of discharge) required for Medicare Part A to cover a following stay in a skilled nursing facility. If the stay was strictly an outpatient stay, the notice must also explain why the patient was not admitted as an inpatient.

When a patient seeks admission to a skilled nursing facility following a hospital stay that included a period of "under observation" outpatient status, the skilled nursing facility must give the patient a Skilled Nursing Facility Advance Beneficiary Notice of Non-Coverage (SNFABN) warning that care may not be covered by Medicare Part A.

Requiring Daily Skilled Nursing Care

Your doctor must certify that you require daily skilled nursing care or skilled rehabilitative services. This care includes rehabilitative services by professional therapists and skilled nursing treatment, such as giving injections, changing dressings, monitoring vital signs, or administering medicines or treatments, which cannot be performed by untrained personnel. This daily care must be related to the condition for which you were hospitalized.

If you are in a nursing facility only because you are unable to feed, clothe, bathe, or move yourself, even though these restrictions are the result of your medical condition, this will not be covered by Part A.

This is because you do not require skilled nursing care as defined by Medicare rules. However, if you require occasional part-time nursing care, you may be eligible for home health care coverage (described below) through Part A.

Inpatient Care Generally Covered by Part A

The following list gives you an idea of what Medicare Part A does, and does not, pay for during your stay in a participating hospital or skilled nursing facility. Remember, though, even when Part A covers a cost, there are significant financial limitations on its coverage. (See "How Much Medicare Part A Pays," below, for the dollar figures.)

Medicare Part A hospital insurance covers:

- a semiprivate room (two to four beds per room); a private room if medically necessary
- all meals, including special, medically required diets
- regular nursing services
- special care units, such as intensive care and coronary care
- drugs, medical supplies, and appliances furnished by the facility, such as casts, splints, wheelchair; also, outpatient drugs and medical supplies if they permit you to leave the hospital or nursing facility sooner
- hospital lab tests, X-rays, and radiation treatment billed by the hospital
- operating and recovery room costs
- blood transfusions; you pay for the first three pints of blood, unless you arrange to have them replaced by an outside donation of blood to the hospital, and
- rehabilitation services, such as physical therapy, occupational therapy, and speech language pathology services (speech therapy) provided while you are in the hospital or nursing facility.

Medicare Part A hospital insurance does not cover:

- personal convenience items, such as television, radio, or telephone
- private duty nurses, or
- a private room, when not medically necessary.

Levels of Nursing Facility Care

Most nursing facilities provide what is called custodial care—primarily personal, nonmedical care for people who are no longer able to fully care for themselves. Custodial care often lasts months or years, and is not covered at all by Medicare. For the most part, custodial care amounts to assistance with the tasks of daily life: eating, dressing, bathing, moving around, and some recreation. It usually involves some health-related matters: monitoring and assisting with medication and providing some exercise or physical therapy. But it is ordinarily provided mostly by personnel who are not highly trained health professionals, and does not involve any significant treatment for illness or physical condition.

A different, short-term kind of care known as skilled nursing facility care is covered by Medicare, although there are severe limits. (See "How Much Medicare Part A Pays," below, regarding these limits.) Skilled nursing facility care, which takes place in a hospital's extended care wing or in a separate nursing facility, provides high levels of medical and nursing care, 24-hour monitoring, and intensive rehabilitation. It is intended to follow acute hospital care due to serious illness, injury, or surgery—and usually lasts only a matter of days or weeks.

The nursing facility care and services covered by Medicare are similar to what is covered for hospital care. They include:

- a semiprivate room (two to four beds per room); a private room if medically necessary
- all meals, including special, medically required diets
- regular nursing services
- special care units, such as coronary care
- drugs, medical supplies, treatments, and appliances provided by the facility, such as casts, splints, wheelchair, and
- rehabilitation services, such as physical therapy, occupational therapy, and speech therapy, provided while you are in the nursing facility.

Medicare coverage for a skilled nursing facility does not include:
- personal convenience items, such as television, radio, or telephone
- private duty nurses, or
- a private room when not medically necessary.

Home Health Care

Progressive health care professionals often encourage people to get out of hospitals and nursing facilities and into their own or family members' homes while recovering from injury or illness. With less honorable motives, insurance companies also pressure hospitals to release patients earlier so that if they continue to receive care, it will be a less costly variety at home.

In response to both these movements, the use of home health care (including part-time nursing care and physical and other therapies), and home health care agencies to provide the care, has increased enormously over the past two decades. The following sections explain Medicare's substantial coverage of home health care. You can also read Medicare's online publication *Medicare and Home Health Care* at www.medicare.gov/pubs/pdf/10969.pdf.

RESOURCE
Learn more about home health care. For a complete discussion of long-term care, particularly for older people, and how to finance it, see *Long-Term Care: How to Plan & Pay for It,* by Joseph L. Matthews (Nolo). For ordering information, visit www.nolo.com.

Coverage Provided

Part A home health care coverage requires a prior three-day hospital stay. Home care without a prior hospital stay may be covered by Part B. If you qualify for home care coverage, Medicare pays for the following services provided by a participating home health care agency:
- part-time skilled nursing care—usually two to three visits per week as part of a plan certified by a physician, and

- physical therapy, occupational therapy, and speech therapy.

If you are receiving part-time skilled nursing care, physical therapy, occupational therapy, or speech therapy, Medicare can also pay for:

- part-time home health aides
- medical social services, and
- medical supplies and equipment provided by the agency, such as a hospital bed, a walker, or respiratory equipment.

However, Medicare will not pay for a number of services sometimes provided as part of home health care, including:

- full-time nursing care
- drugs and biologicals administered at home
- meals delivered to your home, or
- housekeeping services.

Restrictions on Coverage

Despite the obvious financial as well as recovery advantages of home health care, Medicare coverage for it is severely restricted to the following:

- The agency providing the care must participate in Medicare— meaning it must be approved by Medicare and must accept Medicare payment. Many agencies do not participate in Medicare, so find out before making arrangements.
- You must be confined to your home by an injury, illness, or other medical condition. If you need nursing care or other medical services but you are physically able to leave home to receive it, you might not be eligible for Medicare home health care coverage.
- You must initially require part-time skilled nursing care or physical or speech therapy. After your home health care coverage begins, Medicare can continue to cover your home care even if you need only occupational therapy—which helps you regain physical skills needed for daily living that you may have lost because of the illness or injury. Occupational therapy alone, however, cannot justify home health care coverage in the first place.

- Your doctor must determine that you need home health care and must help set up a care plan in cooperation with the home health care agency. If your doctor has not mentioned home care to you but you feel it would be a good idea, make your wishes known. Most doctors will prescribe home care, can give you a referral to a Medicare-approved agency, and will cooperate with the home health care agency.

Skilled Nursing Home and Home Health Care Even If No "Improvement"

Medicare Part A coverage for inpatient skilled nursing facility care or for home health care is intended for a period of recovery following a hospital stay for an illness, an injury, or surgery. But there is some dispute as to whether Medicare coverage ends when patients reach a "plateau" of recovery and their condition is stable with no likelihood of improving. Medicare takes the position that once there is no more improvement, Part A coverage ends. Several federal courts, though, have said that coverage should continue if only skilled care can help keep the patient's condition from deteriorating.

The question of whether a person's condition continues to require Medicare Part A–covered skilled nursing care, either in a nursing facility or at home, or instead only requires nonskilled custodial care, which Medicare Part A does not cover, is tricky. If you or a loved one are in a situation in which Medicare is threatening to cut off skilled nursing care, your best allies in keeping coverage are your doctor and the facility or agency providing the care. They need to make it clear to Medicare that skilled nursing care is still needed in order to maintain the patient at a functioning level, even if the patient's underlying condition is not likely to improve.

Hospice Care

Hospice care is home health care provided to a terminally ill patient who is in the last six months or so of life (as certified by his or her physician). Hospice care focuses not on treating the illness or fostering recovery, but on making the patient as comfortable as possible. Good hospice care may combine the efforts of family, doctors, nurses, social workers, dietitians, and clergy, as well as physical therapists and other trained caregivers.

Medicare does not provide 24-hour hospice care, but it does cover visits by health care workers to the patient's home on a regular basis—daily if necessary—including a hospice nurse on 24-hour call. Significantly, and unlike other nonhospital Medicare coverage, Medicare also pays for any medication prescribed by a physician for symptom management and hospice patient comfort.

Medicare may also cover up to five days of inpatient care in a hospital or skilled nursing facility to give the family or other primary caregivers a respite from their duties. If approved by the hospice, this five-day respite care period may be repeated during a patient's care.

The following sections explain how Medicare coverage of hospice works. Medicare's website also provides information about its hospice coverage in the booklet *Medicare Hospice Benefits*, which you can find at www.medicare.gov/Pubs/pdf/02154.pdf.

Coverage Provided

Medicare Part A can cover nearly the full cost of hospice care. Hospice care covered by Medicare includes:

- physician services provided by a physician connected with the hospice—Medicare Part B will continue to cover services provided by the patient's personal doctor
- nursing care
- medical supplies and appliances
- drugs for management of pain and other symptoms
- health aide and homemaker services
- physical and speech therapy, and
- medical social services, counseling, and dietary assistance.

Restrictions on Coverage

Care must be provided by a Medicare-approved hospice, under a plan developed by the hospice and the patient's attending physician. The patient's doctor and the hospice's medical director must certify that the patient is terminally ill, with a life expectancy of six months or less. And the patient must sign a statement choosing hospice care instead of standard Medicare Part A benefits.

Right to Return to Regular Medicare Coverage

Some people do not take advantage of hospice care, out of a misunderstanding about how it impacts their Medicare coverage. They may mistakenly fear that they'll permanently lose their regular Medicare coverage, won't be covered by Medicare for hospitalizations, or will outlive their six-month diagnosis and be stuck without Medicare coverage. The fact is, however, that a Medicare patient may disenroll from hospice care and return to regular Medicare coverage at any time. If the patient's doctor certifies that the six-month life expectancy no longer applies, the patient can "graduate" from hospice and return to regular Medicare.

This sometimes occurs with degenerative diseases, such as congestive heart failure or emphysema; the physician's best time estimate may be off by years. Most people who disenroll do so after the first or second 90-day evaluation period (discussed further in the next section).

How Much Medicare Part A Pays

To understand any Medicare decision about how much of your hospital, nursing facility, or home care bill it will pay, you have to know the basics of Part A payments. Those basics include benefit periods and deductible and coinsurance amounts.

Benefit Period or Spell of Illness

How much Medicare Part A pays depends on how many days of inpatient care you have during what is called a benefit period or spell of illness.

A benefit period or spell of illness refers to the time you are treated in a hospital or skilled nursing facility, or some combination of the two. The benefit period begins the day you enter the hospital or skilled nursing facility as an inpatient—and continues until you have been out for 60 consecutive days. If you are in and out of the hospital or nursing facility several times but have not stayed out completely for 60 consecutive days, all your inpatient bills for that time will be figured as part of the same benefit period (even if you are readmitted for a different illness or injury).

There is no limit to the number of benefit periods you can have over your lifetime, except for stays in psychiatric hospitals (see below).

Hospital Bills

Medicare Part A pays only certain amounts of a hospital bill for any one benefit period.

The Deductible Amount

For each benefit period, you must pay an initial amount before Medicare will pay anything. This is called the hospital insurance deductible. The deductible is increased every January 1. In 2018, the amount is $1,340.

First 60 Days Hospitalized

For the first 60 days you are an inpatient in a hospital during one benefit period, Part A hospital insurance pays all of the cost of covered services. You pay only your hospital insurance deductible. If you are in more than one hospital, you still pay only one deductible per benefit period—and Part A covers 100% of all your covered costs for each hospital. However, nonessentials, such as televisions and telephones, are not covered.

61 Through 90 Days

After your 60th day in the hospital during one spell of illness, and through your 90th day, each day you must pay what is called a "coinsurance amount" toward your covered hospital costs. Part A of Medicare pays the rest of covered costs. In 2018, this daily coinsurance amount is $335; it goes up every year.

Reserve Days

Reserve days are a last-resort coverage. They can help pay for your hospital bills if you are in the hospital more than 90 days in one benefit period. But the payment is quite limited. If you are in the hospital for more than 90 days in any one spell of illness, you can use up to 60 additional reserve days of coverage. During those days, you are responsible for a daily coinsurance payment. For 2018, the reserve days coinsurance amount is $670 per day. Medicare pays the rest of covered costs.

Two Benefit Spells May Be Better Than One

You can get more total days of full Medicare coverage during two spells of illness than in just one. As a result, it can be in your financial interest to stretch your hospital or nursing facility stays into two benefit periods, if possible. For example, using home health care may help you stay out of the hospital or nursing facility for 60 days before you must return as an inpatient for further treatment. If the timing of your inpatient treatment could be somewhat flexible, discuss that timing and its effect on Medicare coverage with your doctor.

EXAMPLE: Oscar is in the hospital with circulatory problems, being treated with medication. His doctor recommends surgery, operating on one leg at a time, monitoring the first leg before attending to the second. Oscar and his doctor plan the dates of surgery so that he will be released from the hospital and will convalesce at home, with the help of home health care services, for more than 60 days before he returns to have the second operation.

This way, Medicare will consider the time Oscar spends in the hospital after the second surgery to be part of a new spell of illness, even though it results from the same condition that made the first operation necessary. If there had not been a 60-day break between hospitalizations, Oscar would have been in the hospital a total of more than 60 days and would have had to pay a hefty coinsurance amount for every day after his 60th day in the hospital—up to his 90th day.

You do not have to use your reserve days in one spell of illness; you can split them up and use them over several benefit periods. But you have a total of only 60 reserve days in your lifetime. Whatever reserve days you use during one spell of illness are gone for good. In the next benefit period, you would have available only the number of reserve days you didn't use in previous spells of illness.

TIP

Try to save up your reserve days. Even if you are in the hospital for more than 90 days, you may want to save your reserve days for an even rainier day. For example, you may not want to use your reserve days if you currently have some private insurance, such as from an employer, that can help cover the costs of those extra days of hospitalization, but you may not have that insurance later in life.

EXAMPLE: Bert had a serious stroke, followed by several complications involving kidney failure and pneumonia. For six months, he was in and out of both a hospital and a skilled nursing facility (SNF), for a total of 130 days. Because Bert never spent 60 consecutive days out of the hospital or SNF, all his inpatient treatment was considered part of the same "benefit period." So when his time in the hospital reached 91 days, he had no choice but to begin using up his "reserve days" coverage. He used 20 reserve days during this benefit period, leaving him with only 40 reserve days for the remainder of his lifetime.

If Bert had remained out of the hospital and SNF for 60 consecutive days during any part of this stretch of treatment, he would not have had to use up any reserve days. Or, if his condition had permitted it, he might have been able to receive some care in an intermediate-level or custodial care nursing facility instead of in an SNF. However, this would have been a practical alternative only if he had some supplemental health coverage that would have paid for some or all of this level of care (Medicare doesn't cover it at all).

Or, if Bert's condition had permitted, he might have received some care at home from a Medicare-approved home health care agency. Medicare would have paid the full amount of this care. And it would not have affected his right to receive coverage when he needed to return to the hospital or SNF.

If you want to use your reserve days, you don't have to make a formal request or fill out any form. Medicare will automatically apply them to cover your hospital bills—minus the daily coinsurance you have to pay.

But if you do not want to use those reserve days, or want to use some but not all of them, you must notify the hospital administrator or billing office. Plan ahead: You must submit your notification before the reserve days come up.

Psychiatric Hospitals

Medicare Part A hospital insurance covers a total of 190 days in a lifetime for inpatient care in a specialty psychiatric hospital (meaning one that accepts patients only for mental health care, not just a general hospital).

If you are already an inpatient in a specialty psychiatric hospital when your Medicare coverage goes into effect, Medicare may retroactively cover you for up to 150 days of hospitalization before your coverage began. In all other ways, inpatient psychiatric care is governed by the same rules regarding coverage and copayments as regular hospital care.

There is no lifetime limit on coverage for inpatient mental health care in a general hospital. Medicare will pay for mental health care in a general hospital to the same extent as it will pay for other inpatient care.

EXAMPLE: During the five months before his 65th birthday, Horace spent 60 days in a psychiatric hospital. Those 60 days are subtracted from Horace's lifetime total of 190 days of Medicare coverage in a psychiatric hospital. It leaves him with only 130 days more coverage under Part A for psychiatric hospitalization.

Skilled Nursing Facilities

Despite the common misconception that nursing homes are covered by Medicare, the truth is that it covers only a limited amount of inpatient skilled nursing care.

For each benefit period, Medicare will cover only a total of 100 days of inpatient care in a skilled nursing facility. For the first 20 of these 100 days, Medicare will pay for all covered costs, which include all basic services but not television, telephone, or private room charges. For the next 80 days, the patient is personally responsible for a daily copayment; Medicare pays the rest of covered costs. In 2018, the copayment amount is $167.50; the amount goes up each year.

Reserve days, available for hospital coverage, do not apply to a stay in a nursing facility. After 100 days in any benefit period, you are on your own as far as Part A hospital insurance is concerned. However, if you later begin a new benefit period, your first 100 days in a skilled nursing facility will again be covered.

> EXAMPLE: Bettina was hospitalized for several weeks with a broken hip. Upon leaving the hospital, she was moved to a Medicare-approved SNF for rehabilitation and recovery. She remained in the SNF for 18 days, then went home. However, some setbacks in Bettina's healing forced her to return to the SNF a week later, where she stayed for another 12 days.
>
> Because Bettina's stays in the SNF were not separated by 60 days, they were considered to be within the same "benefit period." Therefore, of her total 30 days in the SNF, Medicare will pay the entire amount of her bills (minus Bettina's phone calls to her brother in New Zealand) for only the first 20 days. For the remaining ten days, Bettina will be responsible for a copayment of $167.50 per day, for a total of $1,675.
>
> If Bettina had had a medigap supplemental insurance policy (see Chapter 14) or a Medicare managed care plan (see Chapter 15) that covered Medicare nursing facility copayments, or had she been eligible for Medicaid (see Chapter 16), that insurance, care plan, or government program would have paid all or part of the $1,645. Having no such extra coverage, Bettina will have to pay out of her own pocket.

How Part A Payments Are Figured

To get a picture of how the overall Part A payment scheme works, an example of one person's hospital stay may be useful.

Annika was hospitalized for three weeks for a serious intestinal disorder, went home for a week, came back to the hospital for another ten days, was released again, and then had to return to the hospital for surgery. Annika spent two more weeks in the hospital recovering from the operation. Annika's hospital bill for all this treatment includes:

Semiprivate room, 45 days at $604 per day	$27,200
Surgery surcharge	1,675
Intensive care, 2 days at $1,820 per day	3,640
Laboratory	980
Medication	465
Whole blood (6 pints at $32 per pint)	192
Telephone	94
Television (6 weeks at $70 per week)	420
TOTAL DUE	$34,666

Medicare will pay all covered costs less the $1,340 deductible:

- 45 days in a semiprivate room ($27,200)

- surgery surcharge ($1,675)

- intensive care costs for two days ($3,640)

- the second three pints of blood ($96)

- laboratory work ($980), and

- medication ($465).

Medicare will not pay for:

- television or telephone costs ($514 must be paid by Annika), or

- the first three pints of blood; Annika must pay the $96.

So Medicare covers $34,056, minus the $1,340 deductible, which Annika must pay. Annika also remains responsible for the $610 in uncovered costs (phone, TV, and blood).

Remember, though, that Annika will still have to face her doctors' bills, whose coverage depends on her Medicare Part B medical insurance. (See "Part B Medical Insurance," below, for a discussion of Part B coverage.)

Home Health Care

Medicare Part A pays 100% of the cost of your covered home health care when provided by a Medicare-approved agency—and there is no limit on the number of visits to your home for which Medicare will pay.

Medicare will also pay for the initial evaluation by a home care agency, if prescribed by your physician, to determine whether you are a good candidate for home care.

However, if you require durable medical equipment, such as a special bed or wheelchair, as part of your home care, Medicare will pay only 80%.

Hospice Care

Medicare pays 100% of the charges for hospice care, with two exceptions. First, the hospice can charge the patient up to $5 for each prescription of outpatient drugs the hospice supplies for pain and other symptomatic relief. Second, the hospice can charge the patient 5% of the amount Medicare pays for inpatient care in a hospice, nursing facility, or the like every time a patient receives respite care.

There is no limit on the amount of hospice care you can receive. At the end of the first 90-day period of hospice care, your doctor will evaluate you to determine whether you still qualify for hospice— meaning your disease is still considered fatal and you are still estimated to have less than six months to live. A similar evaluation is made after the next 90-day period, and again every 60 days thereafter. If your doctor certifies that you are eligible for hospice care, Medicare will continue to pay for it even if it exceeds the original six-month diagnosis. And if your condition improves and you switch from hospice care back to regular Medicare coverage, you may return to hospice care whenever your condition warrants it.

> EXAMPLE: Ted is suffering from cancer. His doctors say it will be fatal within six months. Ted chooses to stop his chemotherapy treatment, stay at home, and receive hospice care there. After 90 days, however, Ted has not gotten any worse. His doctors determine that Ted's cancer has not progressed much and that Ted may live for another year or two. So Ted returns to traditional Medicare coverage.

After another nine months, however, Ted's cancer becomes much more aggressive. After Ted undergoes a short course of chemotherapy, his doctor estimates that Ted now has less than six months to live. Ted can now return to hospice care and stay on it for as long as his doctor still believes the cancer will be fatal within six months.

Part B Medical Insurance

The second part of Medicare coverage, Part B, is medical insurance. It is intended to help pay doctor bills for treatment either in or out of the hospital, as well as many of the other medical expenses you incur when you are not in the hospital.

Eligibility and Premiums

You are eligible for Medicare Part B medical insurance if you are age 65 or older and either a U.S. citizen or a legal resident of the United States who has been in the country lawfully for five consecutive years. This is true whether or not you are eligible for Medicare Part A. Anyone who wants Part B medical insurance must enroll in the program. (See Chapter 13 for details about enrollment.)

Everyone enrolled in Medicare Part B must pay a monthly premium; if you also are enrolled in a state Medicare Savings Program, administered by Medicaid (see Chapter 16), Medicaid pays your Part B premium.

The Medicare Part B premium is raised almost every year. For 2018, the amount of your premium depends on which of the following categories you fall into:

- **Lowest "hold harmless" premium.** If, at the end of 2017, you were collecting Social Security benefits *and* you were enrolled in Medicare Part B (with your Medicare premium being automatically deducted from your Social Security benefits), you will pay the lowest Part B premium in 2018. This is because a "hold harmless" Social Security rule caps the yearly raise in your Medicare Part B premium so that it's no greater than the yearly cost-of-living adjustment (COLA) to your Social Security benefits (see Chapter 2 regarding COLA). In 2013, this lowest category premium averages about $125 monthly—slightly more or less depending on your Social Security benefit amount.

- **Basic premium.** If you were not collecting Social Security benefits at the end of 2017, or you first enroll in Medicare Part B in 2018, you will pay a monthly Part B premium of $134.
- **Higher income-based premium.** If your adjusted gross income (based on your 2016 tax return) is at least $85,000 (or $170,000 for a couple filing jointly), your monthly Medicare Part B premium for 2018 will be higher than the basic premium, as shown on the chart below. (If, however, in the year since your 2016 tax return, you have become widowed or divorced or had a significant drop in income, you may contact Medicare and request an adjustment of this income-based premium.)

Yearly Income	Monthly Premium
Single $85,000–$107,000	$187.50
Married $170,001–$214,000	
Single $107,001–$133,500	$267.90
Married $214,001–$267,000	
Single $133,501–$160,000	$348.30
Married $267,001–$320,000	
Single more than $160,000	$428.60
Married more than $320,000	

Types of Services Covered

Part B medical insurance is intended to cover basic medical services provided by doctors, clinics, and laboratories. However, the lists of services specifically covered and not covered are long, and do not always make a lot of common sense.

Making the effort to learn what is and is not covered can be important, because you may get the most benefits by fitting your medical treatments into the covered categories whenever possible.

Doctor Bills

Part B medical insurance covers medically necessary doctors' services, including surgery, whether the services are provided at the hospital, at a doctor's office, or—if you can find such a doctor—at home. Part B also covers outpatient medical services provided by hospital and doctors' office staff who assist in providing care, such as nurses, nurse practitioners, surgical assistants, and laboratory or X-ray technicians.

TIP
Medicare pays for a second opinion before surgery. Before undergoing surgery, it is usually medically wise to get a second opinion from another doctor. Second opinions often lead to the decision not to have surgery. Recognizing this, and the savings involved, Medicare will cover your obtaining a second doctor's opinion before undergoing any kind of surgery. And if the second doctor's opinion conflicts with the original doctor's recommendation for surgery, Medicare will pay for an opinion by yet a third doctor.

Outpatient Care and Laboratory Testing

Medicare medical insurance covers outpatient hospital treatment, such as emergency room or clinic charges, X-rays, injections that are not self-administered, and laboratory work and diagnostic tests. Lab work and tests can be done at the hospital lab or at an independent laboratory facility, so long as that lab is approved by Medicare.

CAUTION
Beware of outpatient hospital charges. Medicare pays only a limited amount of outpatient hospital and clinic bills. And unlike most other kinds of outpatient services, Medicare places no limits on how much the hospital or clinic can charge over and above what Medicare pays. (See "Different Payment Structure for Hospital Outpatient Charges," below, for details.)

Ambulances

Part B medical insurance will cover the cost of transporting a patient by ambulance, if transport by any other means would not have been medically advisable. This may include not only emergencies, but also nonemergency trips following discharge from a hospital—for example, to the patient's home or to a nursing facility. Transporting residents of nursing facilities to see their doctors may also be covered. However, Medicare does not cover ambulance transport for regular visits from a person's home to a doctor's office, if the trip was arranged simply because the person needed some assistance.

If your doctor prescribes an ambulance for you for a trip from home to the doctor's office, Medicare may cover it but is not required to. Medicare will cover the ambulance trip only if the doctor's communication with Medicare convinces Medicare that the ambulance was medically necessary.

If Medicare covers an ambulance trip, the ambulance company must accept the Medicare-approved amount as full payment for its services. Medicare will pay 80% of the Medicare-approved amount. You, or your medigap insurer or managed care plan (see Chapters 14 and 15 for descriptions of these plans), are responsible for paying the remaining 20%. The ambulance company may not bill you for any amount over that 20%.

If you need help getting to and from doctor visits, but an ambulance is not considered medically necessary, look into free transportation for seniors in your community. Call your local senior center or the senior information line or elder care locator listed in the white pages of your telephone directory or look online for these kinds of resources.

Administered Drugs

Drugs or other medicines administered to you at the hospital or a doctor's office are covered by medical insurance. Medicare Part B does not cover drugs you take by yourself at home, including self-administered injections, even if they are prescribed by your doctor. Exceptions to this rule are self-administered oral cancer medication, antigens, and immunosuppressive drugs, which are covered by Medicare. Also, flu shots and pneumonia vaccines are covered by Medicare, even though other vaccinations are not; the flu shot you can obtain on your own, but the pneumonia vaccination requires a doctor's prescription.

Medical Equipment and Supplies

Splints, casts, prosthetic devices, body braces, heart pacemakers, corrective lenses after a cataract operation, therapeutic shoes for diabetics, and medical equipment such as ventilators, wheelchairs, and hospital beds—if prescribed by a doctor—are all covered by Part B medical insurance. This includes glucose monitoring equipment for people who have diabetes.

To learn more about the many types of medical equipment and supplies Medicare Part B covers, and how different equipment may be rented or purchased, see Medicare's online publication *Medicare Coverage of Durable Medical Equipment and Other Devices* at www.medicare.gov/pubs/pdf/11045-Medicare-Coverage-of-DME.pdf. To find a Medicare-certified supplier of medical equipment near you, go to the Medicare website home page at www.medicare.gov, and under the "Forms, Help, & Resources" tab, click "Find suppliers of medical equipment & supplies." This will take you to the "Medicare Supplier Directory."

Oral Surgery

Some types of surgery on the jaw or facial bones, or on the related nerves or blood vessels, can be covered by Part B medical insurance. However, surgery on teeth or gums, even when related to an injury or a disease that did not originate with the teeth, is usually considered to be dental work, and so is not covered by Medicare.

This is one of Medicare's somewhat nonsensical bureaucratic distinctions. Although normal dental care is not covered by Medicare, damage to teeth or gums connected to an injury or disease is a medical as much as a dental problem. However, there is one route to coverage: Even if the work is done by an oral surgeon rather than by a physician, Medicare may cover it if it is the kind of treatment that physicians also provide and if Medicare would have covered it if a physician had performed it. This may be determined by whether the treatment involves just the teeth and gums (not covered) or also the bones, inside mouth, blood vessels, or tongue (covered). If Medicare is to cover work performed by a nonphysician oral surgeon, that surgeon must participate in—that is, be certified by—Medicare. You should have your oral surgeon's office check with Medicare about coverage before undergoing any procedure.

Outpatient Physical Therapy and Speech Therapy

Part B of Medicare will cover some of the cost of outpatient physical and speech therapy—if it is prescribed and regularly reviewed by a doctor and provided by a Medicare-approved facility or therapist. However, there are limits on how much Medicare will pay for these therapies.

Medicare covers therapy only that improves a patient's condition or that is needed to maintain, by preventing or slowing a decline in, a patient's condition. Successfully getting Medicare coverage for therapy under this second standard—maintaining an existing condition—is often difficult, with Medicare and the insurance companies that offer Medicare Advantage policies (see Chapter 15) more frequently denying such claims. In order to meet this standard, you may need not only a good written explanation of medical necessity from the therapist to Medicare but also support from your treating doctor.

There are also yearly dollar limits on the amounts Medicare Part B will pay for outpatient therapy. And the amount Medicare pays will be partially determined by who provides you with the therapy services. These limits are explained in "Payments for Outpatient Therapies," below.

Supervised Exercise Therapy for PAD Patients

Peripheral artery disease (PAD) is a condition in which arteries or other blood vessels in the legs become clogged. PAD is not only painful but also increases the risk of heart attack and stroke. Researchers have determined that exercise therapy, such as treadmill walking, can significantly reduce PAD without surgery. This exercise therapy is particularly useful if conducted under the supervision of a certified exercise therapist. Medicare Part B will pay for a limited amount of such supervised therapy if it is prescribed by a physician: three half-hour sessions per week for up to twelve weeks, at up to $53 per session. The patient must pay out of pocket, or through other medical insurance, for any charges per session above this amount, or for extra sessions.

Home Health Care

The same home health care coverage is available under Part B medical insurance as is provided by Part A hospital insurance. (See "How Much Medicare Part A Pays," above, for information about home health care coverage under Part A.)

If you have both Part A and Part B, Part A will cover your home health care following a hospital stay of at least three days; otherwise, Part B will cover it. There is no limit on the number of home health care visits that are covered, and you are not responsible for paying your Part B deductible for home health care. Only skilled nursing care or therapy while you are confined to your home is covered, however, and such care must be ordered by your doctor and provided by a Medicare-approved home health care agency.

Part B medical insurance, like Part A coverage, will pay 100% of the approved charges of a participating home health care agency.

Chiropractors

Part B may cover some care by a Medicare-certified chiropractor. Generally, Medicare will cover a limited number of visits to a chiropractor for manipulation of neck or back vertebrae that are out of place.

Medicare will not, however, cover general health maintenance visits to a chiropractor, nor will it usually cover therapeutic manipulation other than that of the vertebrae. And Medicare generally will not cover X-rays or other diagnostic tests done by the chiropractor. Instead, your physician normally must order these tests.

If you go to a chiropractor and hope to have Medicare pay its share of the bill, have the chiropractor's office check with Medicare ahead of time about the treatment being proposed. And even if Medicare initially covers the treatment, it may not do so indefinitely. So, if you continue with the treatments, have the chiropractor's office regularly check with Medicare to find out how long it will keep paying.

Preventive Screening Exams

Medicare covers the following examinations to screen for a number of serious illnesses:

- a one-time routine physical exam (sometimes called an "initial wellness exam") within six months of the date a person first enrolls in Part B coverage
- an annual physical exam that includes a comprehensive risk assessment, which may lead to further Medicare-covered testing
- a Pap smear and pelvic exam every three years; every year for women at high risk of cervical or pelvic disease; Medicare covers this exam even if you have not yet met your annual Part B deductible
- colorectal cancer screening, as your physician deems necessary (sometimes without meeting your deductible)
- bone density tests for women at high risk of developing osteoporosis or for anyone receiving long-term steroid therapy, who has primary hyperparathyroidism, or who has certain vertebrate abnormalities
- blood glucose testing supplies—if prescribed by a physician—for patients with diabetes
- annual prostate cancer screenings for men over 55
- annual flu shot, with no deductible and no coinsurance amount
- positron emission tomography (PET) scans, a diagnostic test for certain cancers
- annual eye screening for glaucoma
- blood screening for early detection of cardiovascular disease, if your doctor says you have risk factors

- screening test for diabetes, if your doctor says you're at risk for the disease, and
- PET brain scans for patients with unusual Alzheimer's-like symptoms, if your doctor believes the source may be a different type of brain disease known as "frontotemporal dementia."

Mammography

Part B covers a yearly mammogram, even if you have not yet met your annual deductible. The mammogram must be performed by a doctor or facility certified by Medicare to perform mammograms.

Podiatrists

Medicare covers podiatrist services only when they consist of treatment for injuries or diseases of the foot. This does not include routine foot care or treatment of corns or calluses.

Eye Care and Eyeglasses

Medicare does not cover routine eye examinations, glasses, or contact lenses. The only exception is for people who have undergone cataract or other eye surgery. For them, Medicare covers glasses, contact lenses, or intraocular lenses, as well as the cost of an examination by a Medicare-certified optometrist. Medicare Part B does cover medical care from an ophthalmologist (an eye doctor with an M.D., not an optometrist) or other medical doctor for illness or injury to your eyes.

Clinical Psychologists or Social Workers

When a doctor or hospital prescribes it in conjunction with medical treatment, Medicare Part B can cover limited counseling by a clinical psychologist or clinical social worker. The practitioner must be Medicare approved. If your doctor suggests a clinical psychologist or social worker to help in your recovery from surgery, injury, or illness, contact the practitioner in advance to find out whether the services will be approved by Medicare.

Day Care Mental Health Treatment

Medicare Part B can, in some cases, cover mental health care, in the form of day treatment—also called partial hospitalization—at a hospital outpatient department or community mental health center. The facility must be Medicare approved and the particular day program certified for Part B coverage by Medicare.

Alzheimer's-Related Treatments

Until recently, Medicare did not cover various kinds of physical, speech, and occupational therapy, or psychotherapy and other mental health services, for people who had been diagnosed with Alzheimer's disease. Medicare's reasoning was that patients with Alzheimer's were incapable of medically improving, and that the treatment was therefore not "medically necessary."

Medicare has now reversed its backward stance. A patient can no longer be denied Medicare coverage for physician-prescribed therapies or treatments solely because the patient has been diagnosed with Alzheimer's. So, if you or a loved one has Alzheimer's and a physician prescribes a form of therapy or other treatment to counter the effects of the disease, make sure the treatment provider submits its bills to Medicare for payment.

Obesity

Medicare will cover various scientifically proven and medically approved weight-loss therapies and treatments for obesity, if properly prescribed by a physician. These range from stomach surgeries to diet programs to psychological and behavior modification counseling.

Not all treatments are covered, and not all patients will be eligible for all covered treatments. But if you are undergoing care from a physician for obesity, the physician can recommend a specific treatment for you and submit it to Medicare for coverage approval.

Services Not Covered by Medicare Part B

When you look at the list of what Medicare medical insurance does not cover, it's easy to understand why people with traditional Medicare still wind up personally responsible for half of their medical bills. It also underlines the need for you to consider additional medical insurance, either through private supplemental plans, an HMO or other Medicare Advantage plan, or Medicaid or Qualified Medicare Beneficiary coverage. (See Chapters 14, 15, and 16 for more on these alternatives.)

The categories of medical treatment and services listed below are not covered by Medicare.

However, the noncovered services listed below do not necessarily apply to HMO or other Medicare Advantage plan coverage. Many Medicare Advantage plans include some coverage for these medical services even though Medicare itself does not cover them.

Treatment That Is Not Medically Necessary

Medicare will not pay for medical care that it does not consider medically necessary. This includes some elective and most cosmetic surgery, plus virtually all alternative forms of medical care such as acupuncture, acupressure, and homeopathy—with the one exception of limited use of chiropractors. This is despite the fact that many people find these therapies more beneficial than traditional forms of medical care.

Vaccinations and Immunizations

Medicare Part B covers a yearly flu shot and pneumonia vaccination. Otherwise, it does not cover vaccinations and immunizations, such as those taken for travel abroad. An exception is for emergencies in which a vaccination is required because of risk of infection or exposure to communicable disease. Medicare Part B does not cover the shingles vaccine, though a Part D prescription drug plan might (see "Part D Prescription Drug Coverage," later in this chapter).

Medicare Medical Insurance Is Never Enough

Part B Medicare medical insurance is intended to pay for a portion of doctor bills, outpatient hospital and clinic charges. laboratory work, some home health care, physical and speech therapy, and a very few drugs and medical supplies. But there are heavy restrictions on what is covered and on how much is paid.

Private Medicare supplement insurance—referred to as medigap insurance—may help you make up the difference. Instead, some people fill in the gaps in Medicare by joining a Medicare Part C Medicare Advantage health plan, often in the form of a managed care plan, that combines basic Medicare-level coverage with supplemental benefits. (See Chapter 14 for a discussion of medigap insurance, and Chapter 15 to learn more about Medicare Advantage plans.) If you cannot afford private supplement insurance, you may be eligible for Medicaid—a public program for people with low income and few assets. (See Chapter 16 regarding the Medicaid program.)

Prescription Drugs You Take at Home

Medicare Part A covers drugs administered while you are in the hospital or in a skilled nursing facility. Part B medical insurance covers drugs that cannot be self-administered and that you receive as an outpatient at a hospital, a clinic, or at the doctor's office. (There are a few exceptions for self-administered drugs; see "Types of Care Covered," above.) Potential coverage for all other prescription drugs falls under Medicare Part D, which you must enroll in and pay for separately from Parts A and B. (See "Part D Prescription Drug Coverage," below.)

Nonprescription Drugs

Medicare Part B does not cover any of the cost of nonprescription ("over-the-counter") medicines, vitamins, or supplements, regardless of whether they provide help with a medical condition, even if they have been recommended by a doctor.

Hearing Exams and Hearing Aids

Medicare Part B does not cover routine hearing examinations or hearing aids. However, if your ears or hearing are affected by a specific illness or injury, examination and treatment by a physician are covered.

General Dental Work

Medicare does not cover work performed by a dentist or an oral surgeon, unless the same work would be covered if performed by a physician. In other words, if the treatment is considered medical rather than dental, Medicare may cover it. Generally, Medicare will not cover treatment unless the problem is unrelated to normal tooth decay or gum disease, and involves either the blood vessels, nerves, or interior of the mouth, or the bones of the mouth or jaw.

Long-Term Care

Medicare Part B covers some home health care, as described in the previous section. But that care is always relatively short-term, limited to a period of recovery from an acute illness, injury, or condition. Medicare does not provide the kind of long-term care, either at home or in a facility, that many older people need because of frailty or other inability to perform, without help, the activities of daily life. Medicaid and long-term care insurance does cover certain nursing home costs. For a complete discussion of coverage for nursing home costs, see *Long-Term Care: How to Plan & Pay for It*, by Joseph L. Matthews (Nolo).

How Much Medicare Part B Pays

When all your medical bills are added up, you'll see that Medicare generally pays for only about half the total. Medicare gets away with this in three major ways.

First, Medicare does not cover all major medical expenses—for example, it doesn't cover routine physical examinations, some medication, glasses, hearing aids, dentures, and some other costly medical services.

Second, Medicare pays only a portion of what it decides is the proper amount—called the approved charges—for medical services. In addition, when Medicare decides that a particular service is covered and determines the approved charges for it, Part B medical insurance usually pays only 80% of those approved charges; you are responsible for the remaining 20%.

Third, the approved amount may seem reasonable to Medicare, but it is often considerably less than what the doctor actually charges. If your doctor or other medical provider does not accept assignment of the Medicare charges, you are personally responsible for the difference.

Now that you know the worst, you can deal with the details of how much Medicare Part B pays. The rules are not hard to understand—just hard to swallow.

Deductible Amounts

Before Medicare pays anything under Part B medical insurance, you must pay a deductible amount of your covered medical bills for the year. The Part B deductible amount is currently $183 per year.

Medicare keeps track of how much of the deductible you have paid in a given year. It generally does a good job of keeping track, but it is always a good idea to keep your own records and double-check the accounting.

80% of Approved Charges

Part B medical insurance pays only 80% of what Medicare decides is the approved charge for a particular service or treatment. You are responsible for paying the other 20% of the approved charge, called your coinsurance amount. And unless your doctor or other medical provider accepts assignment (see "Assignment of Medicare-Approved Amount," below), you are also responsible for the difference between the Medicare-approved charge and the amount the doctor or another provider actually charges.

TIP

Low-income seniors may receive state help. Under programs known as Qualified Medicare Beneficiary (QMB), Specified Low-Income Medicare Beneficiary (SLMB), and Qualifying Individual (QI), Medicare recipients who have low incomes and few assets can receive considerable help with their basic Medicare expenses.

If you qualify as a QMB, your state will pay all Medicare premiums, deductibles, and coinsurance amounts. If you qualify as an SLMB, your state will pay the monthly Medicare Part B premiums, though not deductibles or coinsurance amounts. If you meet the standards as a QI, your state will pay all or part of your monthly Medicare Part B premium, but not any deductible or coinsurance. (See Chapter 16 for a full discussion of options for low-income persons.)

100% of Approved Charges for Some Services

There are several types of treatments and medical providers for which Medicare Part B pays 100% of the approved charges rather than the usual 80%, and to which the yearly deductible does not apply. In these categories, you are not required to pay the regular 20% coinsurance amount. In most of them, the provider accepts assignment of the approved charges as the full amount, so you actually pay nothing at all.

Home Health Care

Whether you receive home health care under Part A or Part B, Medicare pays 100% of the charges, and you are not responsible for your yearly deductible. However, if you receive medical equipment—a wheelchair, chair lift, or special bed—from the home health care agency, you must pay the 20% coinsurance amount.

Clinical Laboratory Services

Medicare pays 100% of its approved amount for such laboratory services as blood tests, urinalyses, and biopsies. And the laboratory must accept assignment, except in Maryland where a hospital lab can bill you, as an outpatient, for a 20% coinsurance amount.

Preventive Care Screenings

Medicare Part B will pay 100% of the Medicare-approved amount for any covered preventive screening examination appropriately prescribed by a physician (see "Types of Care Covered," above).

Flu and Pneumonia Vaccines

Medicare pays the full 100% of its approved charges for these vaccinations, and the yearly deductible does not apply. However, the provider is not required to accept assignment, so there may be up to an additional 15% charge on top of the amount Medicare approves.

Payments for Outpatient Therapies

How much Medicare pays for outpatient physical therapy (PT), speech-language pathology (SLP), and occupational therapy (OT) depends on where you receive the therapy.

Therapy received in a doctor's or therapist's office, a rehabilitation facility, or a skilled nursing facility while you're an inpatient. Medicare will pay 80% of the Medicare-approved amount. You or your supplemental insurance or managed care plan remain responsible for the other 20%. There is a cap on the total amount Medicare will pay for therapy in these settings. Medicare will pay up to $2,010 per year for outpatient physical therapy and speech-language pathology (combined). There is a separate cap of $2,010 for occupational therapy. These amounts may be increased if your therapist tells Medicare that more care is medically necessary and Medicare approves. This may require a written explanation from your therapist to Medicare, and sometimes supporting evidence from your treating physician as well.

Therapy received at home. If you receive therapy at home from a Medicare-certified home health care agency as part of a comprehensive Medicare-covered home health care program, Medicare will pay 100% of the cost. If you receive therapy at home that is not part of a Medicare-covered comprehensive home health care plan, Medicare will pay 80% of approved charges up to the yearly cap of $2,010 described immediately above.

Therapy received at a hospital outpatient department. There are financial advantages and disadvantages to receiving Medicare-covered therapy at a hospital outpatient department instead of in a doctor's or therapist's office, or at home. One advantage is that Medicare Part B pays the full Medicare-approved amount for the therapy, except for a patient copayment for each visit. This copayment is usually less than the 20% of the Medicare-approved amount a patient would be responsible for if therapy were provided in a doctor's or therapist's office, or at home.

The disadvantage is that a hospital outpatient department may charge an unlimited amount above the Medicare-approved amount for the therapy—an amount you would be personally responsible for. Before you begin therapy at a hospital outpatient department, find out whether they will accept "assignment" of the Medicare-approved amount as the total amount of the bill. (For a full explanation see "Legal Limit on Amounts Charged" and "Assignment of Medicare-Approved Amount," below.) If not, find out in advance how much more than the Medicare-approved amount they will charge. If it is more than you can comfortably afford, you might want to consider getting your therapy somewhere else.

Outpatient mental health treatment. For mental health services provided on an outpatient basis, Part B pays only 80% of approved charges. This is true whether the services are provided by a physician, clinical psychologist, or clinical social worker at a hospital, nursing facility, mental health center, or rehabilitation facility. The patient is responsible for the yearly deductible, for the unpaid 20% of the Medicare-approved amount, and, if the provider does not accept assignment, for the rest of the bill above the regular Medicare-approved amount, up to an additional 15%.

Legal Limit on Amounts Charged

By law, a doctor or another medical provider can bill you no more than what is called the "limiting charge," even if he or she doesn't accept assignment from Medicare. The limiting charge is set at 15%

more than the amount Medicare decides is the approved charge for a treatment or service. That means you may be personally responsible—either out of pocket or through supplemental insurance—for the 20% of the approved charges Medicare does not pay, plus any amount the doctor charges up to the 15% limiting charge. Regardless of how much the doctor or other medical provider charges non-Medicare patients for the same service, you can be charged no more than 15% over the amount Medicare approves.

Assignment of Medicare-Approved Amount

In most instances, Medicare pays 80% of the approved amount of doctor bills; you or your private insurance pay the remaining 20%. However, you can avoid having to pay anything above the Medicare-approved amount if your doctor accepts assignment of that amount as the full amount of your bill.

Over 99% of all doctors who treat Medicare patients accept assignment of the Medicare-approved amount. That is because almost all doctors have signed up with Medicare in advance, agreeing to accept assignment, and so have become what are called "participating doctors." They do this because they get paid by Medicare at a slightly higher rate.

There are still a few doctors, mostly specialists, who do not accept assignment. When deciding whether to see a new doctor you have been referred to, check to see whether the doctor accepts Medicare assignment.

TIP

Treating doctors must accept assignment for Medicaid and QMB patients. If you receive Medicaid assistance (called Medi-Cal in California) as well as Medicare, or are a Qualified Medicare Beneficiary (QMB), federal law requires that a doctor who agrees to treat you must also accept assignment. (See Chapter 16 for more on the Medicaid and QMB programs.)

Different Payment Structure for Hospital Outpatient Charges

Medicare pays hospital outpatient departments differently from how it pays doctors and other providers. Sometimes, the difference can mean savings for you, but other times it can leave you with a large unpaid bill. Unlike charges for doctors or other providers, Medicare Part B pays 100% of the Medicare-approved amount for services provided by a hospital outpatient department, except that for each service the patient may be responsible for a copayment that varies with the type of service provided. These copayments are usually smaller than the 20% coinsurance amount you would pay if you received the same service at a doctor's office or clinic. (Note, however, that if a doctor who is not employed by the hospital outpatient department provides services to you at the hospital, that doctor will bill you separately and Medicare will pay only 80% of the Medicare-approved amount for that bill.)

But there is also some payment risk if you receive care from a hospital outpatient department. As with individual doctors, the hospital does not have to accept "assignment" of the Medicare-approved amount as the full charge for a particular service. Unlike doctors who don't accept Medicare assignment, however, a hospital outpatient department is not restricted to charging only 9.25% more than the Medicare-approved amount. Their charges can go as high as they want, and you would be personally responsible for everything above the Medicare-approved amount.

 COMPUTER

The Medicare website at www.medicare.gov has two helpful links for information on keeping down your medical costs. The first, called the Health Care Provider Directory, will tell you which doctors and other health care providers in your area will accept assignment on Medicare-covered services. You'll find this directory at www.medicare.gov/physiciancompare/search.html.

The Medicare website also offers a list, sorted by geography, of Medicare-certified suppliers of medical equipment and supplies. These suppliers accept Medicare's approved amount as the limit of what they can charge. To use this directory, go to the Medicare website home page at www.medicare.gov, and under the "Forms, Help, & Resources" tab, click "Find suppliers of medical equipment & supplies." This will take you to Medicare's supplier directory.

There are several ways to respond to the high prices charged by hospital outpatient departments. First, before you receive any care at a hospital outpatient department, ask their financial office whether they accept assignment of the Medicare-approved amount as payment in full (except for your copayment). If so, find out what the copayment is. You'll then know the total amount—that is, the per-service copayment—that you'll have to pay each time you receive the service.

If the hospital outpatient department does not accept assignment of the Medicare-approved amount, find out how much more than that amount they will charge. If it's just a little bit higher, you might want to receive your treatment there anyway, if the care is recommended by your doctor and the facility is convenient for you.

Beware of Huge Outpatient Hospital Bills

There is no limit to the amount a hospital outpatient department can charge a Medicare enrollee above the Medicare-approved amount for a particular service. Because of this loophole in Medicare rules, Medicare patients wind up paying on average almost 40% of the total charges for hospital outpatient department charges. For outpatient surgery, and for outpatient radiology and other diagnostic services, patients end up paying about 50% of total hospital charges. Because of these high costs, you should be wary of receiving medical care at a hospital outpatient department. Be sure to find out the charges *before* beginning treatment.

If the hospital's charges will be considerably higher than the Medicare-approved amount, explain the situation to your doctor and ask whether the service could be performed just as well in a doctor's office or at an independent clinic or laboratory. If not, ask whether there is another hospital outpatient department where the service could be performed. If so, find out what that hospital's charges would be.

Private Fee-for-Service Plans Outside Medicare

Some businesses, unions, and other organizations offer general health insurance plans—either during employment or after retirement—that accept people eligible for Medicare. A private health insurance plan that accepts Medicare enrollees must offer at least as much coverage as basic Medicare would provide, and most of these plans provide more than that.

If you choose to join or remain with such a health plan once you become eligible for Medicare, the plan—and not Medicare— will make all decisions about coverage for specific services and the amount of payment.

You may be responsible for plan premiums and copayments, as well as the difference between what the plan pays the provider and what the provider actually charges. Unlike regular Medicare, there is no legal limit on the amount a provider may charge you above what the insurance pays.

Part D Prescription Drug Coverage

In 2006, Medicare began covering some of the costs of prescription medications you take at home. This Medicare Part D benefit is administered through private insurance companies that offer Medicare-approved prescription drug plans (PDPs), and through Medicare Advantage managed care plans that include a Part D drug benefit (MA-PDs). The federal health care reform act of 2010 began a gradual expansion of the Medicare Part D coverage for people with high annual drug costs.

The Part D program replaces drug coverage that was offered through medigap plans (see Chapter 14), many Medicare Advantage plans (see Chapter 15), Medicare drug discount cards, and most Medicaid coverage (see Chapter 16). It does not replace employer-sponsored prescription drug coverage for Medicare beneficiaries if that coverage is at least equal to the coverage offered by a basic Medicare Part D plan. And, some state-sponsored pharmacy assistance programs continue to help fill some of the drug coverage gaps in the Medicare program.

For many people, Medicare Part D reduces their out-of-pocket costs for prescription drugs. And people with very high annual drug expenses can see a substantial reduction in their out-of-pocket costs. For some people with low incomes, however, the new Medicare program may cost them *more* than they previously paid under state Medicaid programs.

The Politics of Part D Administration

Even for people who save money in the short run under Part D, those savings will likely be swallowed up in the long run by the program's little-discussed giveaway to two of the country's biggest industries: insurance and pharmaceuticals.

The enormous Medicare hospital and medical programs (Parts A and B) are operated by Medicare's own extremely low-overhead bureaucracy, with only certain administrative tasks run by insurers. Nonetheless, in enacting Part D, Congress handed over almost the entire prescription drug program to private insurance companies. That means the program has to support their notoriously inefficient overhead, plus their profits.

Also, a provision in the Part D law actually prohibits Medicare from negotiating with pharmaceutical companies for lower drug prices for Medicare beneficiaries. As a huge market, Medicare could utilize its buying power to get price reductions; the Veterans Administration, for example, has done this for many years and its drug prices are half as much as those through most Part D plans. The law's prohibition on such negotiations amounts to a massive pork barrel for the pharmaceutical industry, ensuring that overall drug costs for everyone on Medicare will climb steeply in the years to come.

Medicare Part D Drug Coverage: The Basics

Medicare Part D provides some coverage for the cost of prescription drugs for people enrolled in Medicare. Before you plunge into the details offered in this section, you may want to familiarize yourself with the overall operation of the program by reading through this summary.

Who is eligible? If you are entitled to Medicare Part A or are enrolled in Medicare Part B, you may join a Medicare Part D prescription drug plan. Participation is voluntary for most people. But, if you receive benefits through Medicaid (Medi-Cal in California) you are automatically enrolled in a Part D plan in order to continue receiving drug coverage.

Who runs the program? Medicare operates the overall program, but you must choose one of the specific Part D prescription drug plans offered by private insurance companies in your state. You enroll directly with that insurance company.

What does it cost to participate? Most people pay a monthly premium to the insurance company. The premium can range from $0 to $50 per month—the cost varies depending on the plans available in your town, and on the particular plan you choose.

What does it cover? All plans cover some, but not all, prescription drugs in every category of medication. Each plan has a list, known as a formulary, of the specific drugs it covers. The plan will pay its share only for drugs listed on its formulary and purchased from a pharmacy or another distributor that participates in that plan.

How much does the plan pay? For basic Part D coverage, there are four payment stages (these figures are for 2018):

- **Deductible.** You pay for the first $405 per year of the total cost of your drugs. Some plans waive or reduce this deductible.

- **Partial coverage.** Once your total yearly drug expense reaches $405 (and before it reaches $3,750), the plan pays roughly 75% and you pay 25% of your drug costs. Your portion comes in the form of a copayment for each prescription. Your copayment may be higher for brand-name drugs and less for generics, depending on your plan.

Medicare Part D Drug Coverage: The Basics (continued)

- **Coverage gap (the "doughnut hole").** Once your total yearly drug expense reaches $3,750 (and until your total out-of-pocket costs reach $5,000), you must pay the entire amount of your drug costs. Your plan generally pays no part of your prescription drug costs within this doughnut hole, although a few high-premium plans may pay some portion of your costs. However, in 2018, brand-name prescription drugs must be sold at a 65% discount to anyone who reaches the coverage gap and generic drugs are sold at a 56% discount.

- **Catastrophic coverage.** If your total out-of-pocket costs for drugs in one year reach $5,000, the Part D plan plus Medicare will pay 95% of all further costs; you pay the remaining 5% or up to $3.35 for a generic multisource drug and up to $8.35 for all other drugs.

How do I choose the right plan? Not all plans are alike, and choosing the best plan for you involves several steps. You must get the widest possible coverage of the drugs you take, with the fewest restrictions on the drugs' availability to you. And you must do so with the lowest overall out-of-pocket cost to you. That doesn't necessarily mean the lowest premium, but instead takes into account premium, deductible, copayments, availability of generic drugs, and coverage in the "doughnut hole" coverage gap. (See "Deciding on a Part D Plan," below, for a step-by-step discussion of choosing the right plan.)

Can I switch plans if I'm not happy with my plan? Anyone can switch Part D plans. People who receive both Medicaid and Medicare benefits, and people who live in long-term care facilties, can switch at any time. Most people, however, can switch only during an open enrollment period from October 15 to December 7 of each year. The rules and procedures for switching plans are explained in Chapter 13.

People With VA, TRICARE, or FEHB Medical Coverage Need Not Join a Part D Drug Plan

If you receive medical coverage through the Department of Veterans Affairs (VA), the Defense Department's TRICARE program, or the Federal Employee Health Benefits Program (FEHB), you do *not* need to join a Medicare Part D plan when you become eligible for it at age 65. You will continue to receive prescription drugs through your existing program (which provides essentially the same coverage as Part D, but at less cost to you). If for any reason you lose coverage under any of these programs, you have 63 days to join a Medicare Part D plan without a penalty for late enrollment.

Eligibility

Anyone who is entitled to Medicare Part A coverage (whether actually enrolled in it or not) or who is currently enrolled in Medicare Part B may join a Medicare Part D plan. This is true regardless of whether a person's Medicare eligibility is based on age or disability. Except for people who also receive benefits from the Medicaid program (Medi-Cal in California), enrollment in Part D is voluntary. (The enrollment process is explained in Chapter 13.)

If you qualify for Medicaid (see Chapter 16) as well as Medicare, you must enroll in a Medicare Part D plan in order to receive any prescription drug coverage. Medicaid no longer covers any drugs for people who are also eligible for Medicare if those drugs are covered by an available Part D plan. In some states, however, Medicaid continues to cover a few drugs that are not available under Part D. If you receive Medicaid benefits as well as Medicare, you may enroll in certain, but not all, Medicare Part D plans—but if you do not enroll yourself, Medicare will automatically enroll you in a plan.

Part D May Not Be Right for Everyone

If you have prescription drug coverage through a Medicare Advantage plan (see Chapter 15) or through employer-based coverage from your or your spouse's current work, you do not also need a Medicare Part D plan. Even if you're not otherwise covered for prescription drugs, enrollment in a Part D plan is voluntary. But program rules (for instance, a penalty on the premium you eventually pay if you later enroll in a plan after not enrolling when you turn 65) put some pressure on you to enroll even if you don't yet need the coverage. To decide whether enrolling is a good idea for you, and when, see "Deciding on a Part D Plan," below.

Premiums, Deductibles, Copayments, and Coverage Gaps

The cost structure of Medicare Part D is complicated. Except for those who qualify for a low-income subsidy, most beneficiaries pay monthly premiums, a yearly deductible, and a copayment for each prescription filled. And there is a coverage gap that affects most beneficiaries, making them personally responsible for all drug costs that are above a certain amount but below a "catastrophic" level. For those who qualify for the low-income subsidy, Part D costs are significantly less.

Premiums

Premiums are the monthly amounts you pay directly to your prescription drug plan or managed care plan to enroll you in Part D coverage. These amounts cover only your membership in the plan and do not pay the cost of any drugs, nor do they count toward your deductible or other cost-sharing amounts.

Standard enrollment. Most people must pay a monthly premium for Part D coverage, either for a stand-alone prescription drug plan or as part of the larger premium they pay if they are enrolled in a managed care plan. Monthly premium amounts for basic benefits vary from plan to plan and by geographic region.

CAUTION
Lowest premiums are not always the best. Finding a plan with a low monthly premium is important, but it is not the only factor to consider in choosing a plan. A low premium does you little good if the plan doesn't cover some of your medications, or if it covers them but requires much higher copayments than other plans. Also, you may want to pay a higher premium for a plan that offers you first-dollar coverage (no deductible) or some payments within the "doughnut hole" coverage gap. (See "Deciding on a Part D Plan," below, for more information.)

Medicare's "Extra Help" low-income subsidy. People with low incomes who enroll in Part D and qualify for Extra Help Categories One, Two, or Three (discussed below) pay no premium at all if they join a plan that charges below the average premium for their state. Unfortunately, plans with these lower premiums tend to have the most coverage restrictions. Beneficiaries who qualify for Category Four pay between 25% and 75% of a plan's full premium, depending on their actual income.

Apply for Medicare Part D's Extra Help Program Before, and Separately From, Enrolling in a Part D Plan

If you think you are anywhere close to qualifying for a Part D Extra Help low-income subsidy (discussed immediately below), you should apply for it. You apply for an Extra Help low-income subsidy separately from applying for Part D coverage, and applying for an Extra Help low-income subsidy does not commit you to join any Medicare Part D plan. If you are accepted for an Extra Help low-income subsidy, your Part D plan premium will be much less expensive regardless of which plan you choose. To learn about applying for an Extra Help low-income subsidy, see Chapter 13.

Medicare's Extra Help Program to Lower the Cost of Part D

There are four categories of people who qualify for an Extra Help low-income subsidy (LIS) to help pay costs associated with a Part D prescription drug plan. (Signing up for Extra Help assistance is explained in Chapter 13.)

The categories are defined by the beneficiary's income in relation to the Federal Poverty Guideline (FPG). In 2018, the FPG for a single person was an annual income of less than $12,060 ($13,860 in Hawaii, $15,060 in Alaska). For larger family units (people related by blood, marriage, or adoption and living together), the figure goes up by about $4,000 per person (about $5,000 per person in Hawaii and Alaska). FPG amounts go up slightly each year.

The amount of Part D low-income subsidy a beneficiary receives varies with the category:

- **Category One.** This category includes individuals eligible for Medicaid (see Chapter 16) whose incomes are under the FPG. They pay no premium or deductible, have no gap in coverage, and have reduced per-prescription copayments.

- **Category Two.** This category includes individuals eligible for Medicaid but with incomes above the FPG. They pay no premium or deductible and have no coverage gaps, but pay a higher per-prescription copayment than other Medicaid recipients.

- **Category Three.** This category includes individuals not eligible for Medicaid but with incomes less than 135% of the FPG and assets (not including their homes) of less than about $10,000 (about $15,000 for married couples living together). They pay no premium or deductible, have no gap in coverage, and have reduced per-prescription copayments.

- **Category Four.** This category includes individuals with incomes of 136% to 149% of the FPG and assets less than about $15,000 (about $30,000 for married couples). They pay a reduced premium and deductible and have reduced per-prescription copayments.

Medicare's Extra Help Program to Lower the Cost of Part D (continued)

Throughout this section, explanations of Part D payments and coverage for people eligible for Medicare's Extra Help program will refer to the above category numbers. These category numbers are only for the convenience of readers of this book; official Medicare publications do not usually assign any reference numbers to the categories.

Deductibles

The deductible is the amount you must pay out of pocket for covered medications before your Part D plan begins paying your covered prescription drug costs.

Standard enrollment. With most plans, a Part D enrollee must pay out of pocket for the first $405 (in 2018) of costs each year for prescription drugs that are covered by the enrollee's particular plan. But some plans offer "first dollar" (no-deductible) coverage, meaning they begin paying their share of covered drugs for an enrollee's first prescription of the year (see below).

With low-income subsidy. Part D beneficiaries in LIS Categories One, Two, and Three do not pay any deductible amount. Beneficiaries in Category Four pay a deductible amount of $83 per year.

Waiver of deductible. Some plans offer what is called "first dollar" coverage, which means you do not pay any deductible and the plan begins paying its share of drug costs with your first prescription. These no-deductible plans tend to have higher premiums. The amount you save, if any, will depend on the plan's premium and other cost features. (See "Deciding on a Part D Plan," below, for more information.)

Initial Copayments

After you have reached your deductible amount in out-of-pocket costs for covered prescription drugs, your plan pays most of the cost of a covered drug and you are personally responsible for the remainder, known as a copayment. This arrangement continues until you and your Part D plan combined reach a specific yearly total of expenditures—the beginning of the "coverage gap"—on drugs covered by your Part D plan.

Standard enrollment. After you pay your $405 deductible for covered drugs, your Part D plan pays 75% of the cost for covered drugs (and you pay the remaining 25% out of pocket) until your total covered expenditures have reached the beginning of the year's coverage gap. For 2018, the coverage gap begins at $3,750 in total costs for covered drugs.

With low-income subsidy. Category One beneficiaries pay $1.25 per prescription for generic covered drugs and $3.70 per prescription for brand-name covered drugs—the Part D plan pays the rest. Categories Two and Three beneficiaries pay $3.35 per prescription for generic covered drugs and $8.35 for brand-name covered drugs. Category Four enrollees pay 15% of the cost of drugs, after paying their $83 deductibles.

What Counts as an Out-of-Pocket Cost?

Many of the rules concerning deductibles, copayments, and catastrophic limits revolve around the amount you pay out of pocket for your medications. In calculating these amounts, Medicare considers only what it determines to be a "true out-of-pocket" cost, or "TrOOP."

In order for a prescription drug payment to qualify as a TrOOP, the prescription drug must be:

- a drug prescribed by a physician and covered by the specific plan's formulary, or covered for a particular enrollee through an exception to the formulary, and
- paid for by the beneficiary, a relative, a charity, church, or service organization, or the like, but not by another insurance plan.

It's important to remember that what you pay for your premium is *not* considered an out-of-pocket cost.

You Pay the Full Cost of Any Drugs That Your Particular Plan Doesn't Cover

It is important to understand that your plan will pay its portion of the costs only for those drugs specifically included on its formulary (a list of the drugs your plan covers), unless you obtain an exception from the plan. Similarly, amounts you personally pay for drugs count toward your deductible and the coverage gap limits only if the drugs are specifically covered by your plan's formulary, or are covered by your plan after you obtain an exception for that drug from your plan. (See "Restrictions on Coverage," below, for a discussion of plan formularies and other plan payment restrictions.)

Actual copayments may vary. Your actual copayments for each prescription can vary:

- The total cost of a drug can vary from plan to plan. This is because each plan individually negotiates prices with pharmaceutical companies. So, if your copayment is a percentage of the drug's total cost, what you pay will also vary. For example, if 30 doses of a medicine cost a total of $80 with Plan 1 and $100 with Plan 2, a 25% copayment would be $20 per prescription with Plan 1, but $25 with Plan 2.
- A plan is permitted to set up a different copayment system—such as tiered copayments for generic drugs and brand-name drugs, or higher copayments for certain drugs but none at all for other drugs—from the standard copayments described above. Plans may change their copayment structure as long as the average copayments for all covered drugs work out to be the same as with the standard copayment schedule. For this reason, before choosing a plan you must find out in advance what the actual copayment is for your specific drugs.

Coverage Gap (the "Doughnut Hole")

One of the notorious parts of the Part D program is the gap in coverage, or "doughnut hole," within which most Medicare beneficiaries must personally pay all of the cost of their prescription drugs. And if they want to keep their Part D coverage, they must continue to pay their plan's monthly premium even though the plan is not paying for any drugs because the gap has been reached.

Under Obamacare, Drugs Cost Less in the Coverage Gap

As a result of the federal health care reform act of 2010, the coverage gap will shrink over time until it is completely eliminated by 2020. In addition, during those years there are restrictions on the price pharmaceutical companies may charge to Medicare Part D enrollees. In 2018, brand-name drugs must be sold at a 65% discount, and generic drugs at a 56% discount, to anyone with a Medicare Part D plan whose annual covered drug costs have reached the coverage gap.

Finding a Plan That Offers Coverage in the Gap

If you have high drug costs, you may find a plan with some coverage in the doughnut hole coverage gap. A few plans pay some of a patient's drug costs within the gap—some of these plans pay a smaller than normal share within the gap while others reduce the extent of the gap (meaning they pay their share for a larger portion of a patient's total drug costs than a standard plan does). The premiums for these plans tend to be quite a bit higher than for more standard plans. But the higher premium may be worth it if you expect that your yearly drug costs will extend well into the coverage gap. About 5% of Medicare beneficiaries signed up with such plans in Part D's first year of operation.

Standard enrollment. Once you and your plan together have paid for a certain amount of prescription drugs that are covered by your Part D plan, your plan will pay nothing more that year until you reach what is called a "catastrophic coverage" level of spending. In 2018, your Part D plan will stop paying its portion of your covered medications when your total covered drug costs reach $3,750. Your premiums do not count toward this amount. The plan will begin to pay again when total expenditures for covered drugs reach the catastrophic coverage amount (see below). A few plans continue to pay for drugs during the gap; many plans that provide gap coverage do so only for generics. These plans are considerably more expensive than plans that have no gap coverage. (See "Finding a Plan That Offers Coverage in the Gap," above.)

With low-income subsidy. There is no coverage gap for those qualifying for any category of low-income subsidy.

Reducing costs within the doughnut hole. You may reach the coverage gap but still have months to go before getting to either the catastrophic coverage limit or the end of the year. If so, you may want to consider using one or more of these seven strategies for lowering the total cost of your medications, and thus the amount you pay out of pocket, within the gap. For more on finding the programs that might work for you, see "Finding discount programs," below.

Some Discount Drug Purchases May Not Count as Out-of-Pocket Costs

If your out-of-pocket cost for prescription drugs reaches more than $5,000 for the year (in 2018), you will probably pass the coverage gap and reach Part D's catastrophic coverage. Once you reach that coverage, your Part D plan will begin to pay 95% of your drug costs until the end of the year.

But not all of the money you spend out of your own pocket for prescription drugs during the coverage gap will necessarily "count" toward reaching the catastrophic coverage threshold. If you buy discounted prescription drugs through a state or local government-assisted drug program, the amounts you spend out-of-pocket for those drugs might not count. That's because government funding is already supporting the purchase of these low-cost drugs. If you use one of these programs, check with the program staff about whether your out-of-pocket costs for drugs they supply will count toward reaching catastrophic coverage under Plan D.

The seven strategies are:

- **State and community assistance programs.** Some states have programs to help older patients pay for prescription medicines that are not otherwise covered by Medicare or Medicaid. Some of these programs offer across-the-board discounts on all drugs while others provide only limited discounts on certain drugs. Some programs offer special tax credits for prescription drug costs and others limit their prescription drug assistance to lower-income seniors. Local community-based programs also sometimes provide free or discounted drugs to seniors. To find out about state and community-based prescription drug assistance programs near you, call the Eldercare Locator at 800-677-1116 or go to the official Medicare website listing of state pharmaceutical assistance programs at www.medicare.gov/pharmaceutical-assistance-program/state-programs.aspx. You can also contact the local office of your State Health Insurance Assistance Program (SHIP), discussed at the end of Chapter 13.

- **Veterans benefits.** If you are a veteran, you may be eligible for free or low-cost medical treatment by Veterans Affairs health providers. If so, this can include free (for disabled or low-income veterans) or low-cost prescription drugs, if prescribed by a VA doctor. Even if you normally see a civilian doctor and use Medicare to cover your care, you might want to see a VA doctor to get a prescription for long-term medication that would be expensive if you had to pay for it out of pocket. (For a discussion of medical benefits for veterans see Chapter 11.)

- **Physician samples.** In an effort to push their particular brands of drugs, pharmaceutical companies give free samples to doctors. The doctors, in turn, distribute those drugs free to patients. Doctors do not normally have enough samples to fill a long-term need for a medication. But your doctor may have enough free samples of your drugs to help lower your out-of-pocket costs while you are within the Part D coverage gap.

- **Switching to generic.** If you have been taking a brand-name medication, you may find that you can obtain the same results at a lower price with its generic equivalent, if one is available, or with a lower-cost drug that treats the same condition. (In 2018, however, under new rules provided by the health care reform act, you can buy brand-name drugs at a 65% discount once you have reached the coverage gap. In some cases that may make the brand-name drugs cheaper than the generic equivalent.) Check with your doctor to see if a generic or another drug is available and whether the doctor believes that it would provide you with the same results. If so, you might want to try it. If you are satisfied with the less-expensive drug, you might save considerable money by continuing to use it. And you may even want to continue using it year-round, particularly if your drug plan offers it at a lower copayment than with the brand-name equivalent you originally used.

- **Pharmaceutical company discount programs.** Under pressure from consumer groups, some pharmaceutical companies have created programs to provide certain specific medicines at reduced prices for Medicare patients. Most of these programs are available only for seniors with limited incomes. The programs do not necessarily include every drug manufactured by the company. And the discounts are not usually very generous. Nonetheless, even a small discount on an expensive drug can amount to significant savings over time. In order to participate in one of these programs, you have to register with the pharmaceutical company. The doctor who prescribes the medication for you may have to fill out enrollment papers for you, too. Some of these programs provide free or discounted drugs only to doctors, who then distribute them to patients. To learn about specific pharmaceutical company programs that might help with the costs of drugs you take, see the official Medicare website's Pharmaceutical Assistance Programs page at www.medicare.gov/pharmaceutical-assistance-program.

- **Nonprofit and retail discount programs.** Several nonprofit and retail organizations, including large chain pharmacies, have set up programs—some through the use of discount "cards"—to provide discounted prescription drug medications, particularly for seniors. These organizations use their large membership's purchasing power to leverage drug companies into offering discounts on certain drugs, passing those savings on to their members. There is usually a membership fee and a copayment or processing fee for each medicine you order. Savings from these programs average less than 10%. For an expensive drug, however, that can still amount to a substantial amount.

- **Medications from Canada.** The exact same prescription drugs for which we pay exorbitant prices in the United States are available for far less—often 50% to 80% less—in Canada. That is because the Canadian public health system limits what pharmaceutical companies can charge for drugs there. (Even at these much-reduced prices, the drug companies profitably continue to sell their wares in Canada.) Because of the huge price differences, many people in this country have been taking the trouble to buy their prescription medications from Canadian pharmacies.

    The U.S. Food and Drug Administration, acting to protect American pharmaceutical companies at the expense of consumers, has made it illegal to import American-made drugs from Canada. But individuals have not been prosecuted for importing legitimate drugs from Canada. And the U.S. Customs service does not seize any mail-order drugs imported from Canada. As a result, many people use mail-order and online prescription drug outlets to buy drugs from Canada, while others physically travel across the border to obtain their drugs at Canadian health clinics.

    If you choose to explore this option, you may be able to find services providing medicines from Canadian pharmacies by searching on the Internet under "prescription drugs Canada." But before using any mail-order or online Canadian drug outlet, ask people you know, or your local senior center, or a SHIP counselor (see Chapter 13) if they know anything about the particular program and the reliability of its services.

Finding discount programs. There are several ways to find out about government, pharmaceutical company, and nonprofit organization discount drug programs available where you live—starting with the four options below. Once you locate a program for which you might be eligible, you or your doctor must contact the program directly in order to enroll.

- **Information from Medicare.** Medicare itself can direct you both to your state assistance program and to pharmaceutical company programs for a particular drug. It can also alert you to local programs in your area, and can refer you to nonprofit and retail organizations that offer drug discount cards and other plans.

  Medicare's information is on its website at www.medicare. gov. Under the "Forms, Help, & Resources" tab, click "Find health & drug plans." This will take you to a page called "Medicare Plan Finder." This link asks you for some personal information—which is strictly confidential—in order to determine which programs you might be eligible for. It then directs you to your state's prescription drug assistance program and to any community-based programs in your area. And it directs you to some pharmaceutical company discounts that may be available for that drug. Finally, the Medicare website lists contact information for some of the nonprofit and retail organizations that offer drug discount cards and similar plans, and explains their basic benefits and eligibility rules.

  You may also get this same information by calling Medicare's toll-free telephone line at 800-MEDICARE and asking about prescription drug assistance programs.

- **State Health Insurance Assistance Program (SHIP) and Health Insurance Counseling and Advocacy Program (HICAP).** Every state has a program to provide free counseling and assistance regarding Medicare, Medicaid, health insurance, and related problems. This program is called the State Health Insurance Assistance Program (SHIP) or the Health Insurance Counseling and Advocacy Program (HICAP). The program maintains local offices with trained counselors who can help you learn about your state's prescription drug assistance program and other drug discount programs that may be available to you. They can also help you with the enrollment process. For more about SHIP and HICAP, see Chapter 13.

Waiver or Reduction of Copayments

Under certain circumstances, you may not have to pay the normal copayment for a covered drug. For example:

- If you reside for more than 90 days in a long-term care nursing facility and are enrolled in both Medicare Part D and Medicaid, you do not have to make any copayments for covered drugs.

- Some plans waive or reduce copayments for certain drugs, particularly generic versions, mostly to coax people to join their particular plans. Waiving or reducing the copayment for a particular drug during a period of time, however, does not obligate the plan to continue doing so, nor must it continue to waive or reduce copayments on any comparable drug. The plan can change its copayment rules at any time.

- Pharmacies may waive copayments for any enrollee with a low-income subsidy, for any drug. There are no Medicare rules about when pharmacies may do this, except that they are not supposed to advertise a policy of waivers. So, you may not know in advance whether your pharmacy will waive a copayment for you. If you are a Part D enrollee who receives a low-income subsidy, you should always ask the pharmacy to waive your copayment. You may be pleased to find out that the pharmacy is willing to do so.

- **Area Agency on Aging.** The Area Agency on Aging is a federal government clearinghouse for information about issues relating to seniors. Your agency can provide you with information about your state's assistance program and about community-based drug assistance programs. To find the Area Agency on Aging office nearest you, call their toll-free line at 800-677-1116 or visit www.eldercare.gov.

- **Drug discount information clearinghouses.** Through several clearinghouses, most of which provide their information on the Internet, you can find out about numerous drug assistance and drug discount card and similar programs. Here are some of these clearinghouses and the information they offer:

- Partnership for Prescription Assistance (www.pparx.org; 888-477-2669) helps patients identify programs that can provide them with free or low-cost medications.

- The Medicine Program (www.themedicineprogram.com; 573-996-7300) identifies the programs for which a patient might be eligible, and provides information to help patients apply for free medication.

- RxAssist Patient Assistance Program Center (www.rxassist.org) maintains a website that provides both a direct link to pharmaceutical company drug assistance programs and information about other sites and organizations that can help you apply for assistance, as well as links to nonprofit and retail drug discount cards and similar programs.

Catastrophic Coverage

Once your total expenditures for medications covered by your plan reach a certain level, the plan will provide "catastrophic coverage" that pays almost the entire cost of covered drugs. Your total expenditures are amounts paid by you and your plan combined during any year.

Standard enrollment. After the catastrophic limit for the year is reached, you pay 5% of the cost, or $3.35 per prescription for generic drugs and $8.35 per prescription for brand-name medications, whichever is greater. Your plan pays the rest, with no limit on the total amount. In 2018, catastrophic coverage begins at $5,000 in your out-of-pocket costs.

With low-income subsidy. After the catastrophic limit for the year is reached, Categories One, Two, and Three beneficiaries have no copayments for medications covered by their plans. Category Four beneficiaries pay $3.35 per prescription for generic drugs and $8.35 per prescription for brand-name drugs.

Restrictions on Coverage

Medicare gives the private insurance and Medicare Advantage companies that operate Part D plans a lot of leeway in imposing limits on the coverage they offer. There are a number of different ways the plans may limit coverage, including restricting the specific drugs covered, providing different levels of payment for different drugs, requiring drug regimens such as step therapy, or requiring prior approval before covering certain drugs.

Certain Drugs Excluded by Law

The Medicare program specifically prohibits Part D plans from covering most medications within certain categories of drugs, even if these medications were lawfully prescribed by your physician. These categories include:

- barbiturates (certain sedatives and sleeping pills)
- benzodiazepines (certain tranquilizers)
- drugs used for weight loss or weight gain, and
- over-the-counter medications.

Many of these drugs, which the Part D plans are required to exclude, would have been covered by Medicaid (Medi-Cal in California) for those people who qualify for that program. But "dual eligible" beneficiaries—those who are eligible for both Medicare Part D and Medicaid (including many nursing facility residents)—are required to get their drug coverage through a Part D plan. Dual eligible beneficiaries in some states, however, may still get coverage for some of these drugs if the Medicaid programs in their states will allow it. Certain state Medicaid programs continue to allow coverage for these excluded drugs for those individuals who are also enrolled in a Medicare Part D plan. (See Chapter 16 for more information on Medicaid.)

Formularies

Every Part D plan issues a list, called a formulary, of the specific drugs it covers. Medicare requires each plan to include in its formulary at least two drugs in each "therapeutic class"—meaning a group of drugs used to treat a specific illness or condition. Some plans offer more than two drugs in certain categories. But the availability of coverage for these "extra" drugs may depend on plan member's paying a higher premium or copayment, or having to get prior authorization or another exception from the plan before using the drug.

Formulary Changes May Force You to Change Plans

A Part D plan may also change its formulary whenever it wants, by providing 60 days' notice to Medicare and plan members. Such changes may include dropping a drug entirely from its formulary, dropping the coverage of a brand-name drug and substituting its generic equivalent, or increasing a patient's copayment for a drug. If your plan changes coverage for one of your drugs, you have some protection, as follows:

- If the plan entirely drops a drug it has been covering for you, it must continue to cover it for you until the end of the calendar year.
- If the plan raises the copayment it charges for a drug, the plan must continue providing it to you at the former copayment level until the end of the calendar year.

However, if the plan switches from covering a brand-name drug to a generic equivalent, it may immediately require you to use the generic or else lose all coverage for that drug.

If you don't want to continue with a plan after it changes its coverage, you can explore switching to a different plan. If you are eligible for both Medicare and Medicaid, or are a resident of a long-term care facility, you may switch plans at any time. If not, you may switch plans only during the annual open enrollment period (starting October each year).

If you do not want to change plans, or can't find a plan with better coverage, consider asking your physician to switch you from your previous drug to a different, equivalent drug that your plan covers.

Under Part D rules, if a drug is not on your plan's formulary, the plan will not pay any portion of the cost of that drug, even if a physician has lawfully prescribed it for you (unless you ask for and receive an exception, discussed below). Also, the money you spend on that nonformulary drug will not count toward your Part D deductible or the coverage gap and catastrophic coverage limits.

Tiered Copayments

Medicare allows the insurance companies that operate Part D plans to charge different copayment amounts for different drugs within the same class, even if the drugs are "therapeutically equivalent" (meaning they are used in a similar way to treat the same illness or condition). Part D plans may structure their copayments in a number of ways: They may have lower copayments for generic drugs than for brand-name equivalents; there may be no copayments at all for certain generic drugs; or there may be different copayments for different brands within the same class.

Exceptions to Drug Restrictions

Plan formularies and other cost containment restrictions are not necessarily the last word on coverage for a drug you use or want to use. Every plan is required to have two systems in place to allow you to challenge that plan's listing or decision regarding coverage of your drug.

The first system allows you to file a request for an "exception" to the plan's listing or decision. This means that you ask the plan to provide coverage that differs from its standard formulary. This type of exception usually requires that you and your doctor show some kind of "medical necessity," meaning that the particular drug you want works better for you or has fewer or milder side effects than other drugs in the class.

The second system permits you to appeal a plan's decision. Each plan has its own appeal process, but every plan allows you to ask for an internal review by the plan itself. If an internal review is unsuccessful, you may seek independent review and ultimately take the plan to court, if necessary.

Plans' exceptions and appeals processes are discussed in Chapter 13.

Drug Substitution

The Medicare Part D program allows plans to substitute a generic or another therapeutically equivalent drug instead of the drug you request. That means that although your doctor prescribes a specific drug for you, the plan can have the pharmacy dispense to you a different but equivalent drug. Of course, "equivalence" does not mean "exactly the same." You may have better results or fewer side effects with the drug your physician prescribes you. But under these drug substitution rules, a plan may overrule you and your physician and pay only for the substituted drug. In order to overcome such a drug substitution, you must request an exception to the plan's substitution policy. (See Chapter 13 for more information about exceptions and appeals.)

Prior Authorization

A Part D plan may place certain drugs on a restricted list that requires the plan's prior authorization before it will cover the drug. This means that if you and your physician decide you should take any drugs on this restricted list, you must obtain the plan's approval or else the plan will not cover it. The plan may offer less expensive drugs that it considers to be "equivalent," in which case your doctor may need to give a medical reason why you need this particular drug. Or, perhaps the drug you want to use is prescribed only in special situations, in which case your doctor may need to show the plan that yours is such a special case.

Step Therapy

Step therapy refers to a treatment structure in which a patient must try a certain drug—one that is less expensive for the insurance company—before the plan will cover a different drug in the same class. If a Medicare Part D plan offers more than two drugs within a drug class, the plan may impose a step therapy requirement for certain drugs in that class. If that happens to you, your doctor must certify that you have tried the lower-tier drug and that it did not work well for you. Then, the plan will allow you to "step" up your therapy to the next-higher-tier drug.

Supply Limits

You will pay a copayment for each prescription you fill. So, one way to keep copayment costs down might be to have the doctor prescribe a large supply of a certain medicine so that it will take fewer prescriptions to get the same number of doses. Plans may block this tactic by imposing a supply limit that restricts the number of doses of a drug that may be filled per prescription.

Broader Coverage, But Difficult Access, for Certain Drugs

Medicare requires each Part D plan to cover at least two drugs for each therapeutic category. And for the following six specific categories of drugs, Medicare plans must provide coverage for "all or substantially all" available drugs:

- antidepressants
- antipsychotics
- anticonvulsants (treatment of seizures)
- antiretrovirals (treatment of certain viruses, including HIV)
- immunosuppressants (cancer treatment), and
- antineoplastics (chemotherapy).

Although Part D plans must extend coverage to all drugs in these categories, the plans may restrict access to these drugs (except antiretrovirals) in other ways. Plans are permitted to make obtaining these drugs more difficult or expensive through "management" devices, such as tiered copayments, prior authorization, and step therapy requirements.

Pharmacy Restrictions

Each Part D plan contracts with certain pharmacies to deliver prescription medications. To receive full coverage from your plan, you must get your drugs from a participating pharmacy, which includes large chains, independent drugstores, HMO pharmacies, or mail-order pharmacies. If you fill your prescription at a pharmacy that does not contract with your plan (an "out-of-network" pharmacy), you may have a larger copayment, or you might not receive any coverage at all (depending on the drug and on your plan's rules).

Deciding on a Part D Plan

If you are eligible for Medicare and are also enrolled in the Medicaid program (Medi-Cal in California), Medicare will automatically sign you up for a Part D drug plan. If you are not enrolled in Medicaid, your participation in Medicare Part D is voluntary. Deciding whether to join a Part D plan, and if so what plan to choose, depends on several factors:

- whether you have other health insurance coverage (through your or your spouse's employer or union) that includes drug coverage
- whether you enroll in a Medicare Advantage (Medicare Part C) managed care plan that includes prescription drug coverage
- whether you are eligible for a low-income subsidy
- your age and health
- the total cost of the drugs you use
- whether your drugs are covered by a particular plan
- how much the plan charges in premiums and copayments, and
- the plan's restrictions on access to drugs.

Should You Participate in Part D?

Medicare Part D is mandatory for people who are also enrolled in Medicaid. For those who qualify for a low-income subsidy, Part D is an attractive low-cost option. And for most other people, Part D is still better than no coverage at all. But for a few people, deciding whether to join a Part D plan is a bit more complicated.

In an effort to encourage everyone to join a Part D plan as soon as they are eligible, Medicare has created a financial penalty for those who delay enrolling. The penalty takes the form of a rise in premiums of 1% per month—if and when you do eventually enroll in a plan— for every month you delay enrolling after you first become eligible.

And that rise is permanent. So, for example, if you wait to join a Part D plan for two years after you are first eligible for Part D coverage, you will always pay 24% (1% per month for 24 months) more in premiums for any plan you join.

No Penalty for Delayed Enrollment If Covered by Equivalent Employer-Sponsored Health Insurance

As explained above, Medicare imposes a financial penalty on people who delay enrolling in Part D coverage. But this penalty does *not* apply if you are covered by an employer- or union-sponsored health plan (for either current employees or retirees) that provides what is called "creditable prescription drug coverage," meaning coverage that is as extensive as a basic Part D plan. When you first become eligible for Medicare, your employer- or union-sponsored plan will notify you whether that plan qualifies as creditable coverage. If your employer-sponsored plan does offer creditable coverage, you may remain in that plan as long as you can and want to, and incur no penalty if you later join a Medicare Part D plan.

If you subsequently lose coverage by a creditable plan, or the plan's drug coverage falls below what qualifies as creditable, then you may enroll without penalty in a Part D plan. You will pay no higher premium than a person who is first eligible for Medicare as long as you enroll in a Part D plan within 63 days from the date you lose creditable coverage.

If your health plan does not qualify as providing creditable coverage, you must join a Part D plan when you first become eligible or else pay the 1% per month premium penalty when you do finally enroll. Even if you join a separate Part D plan, you may want to keep your employer-sponsored coverage instead of relying entirely on Medicare coverage. If your employer-sponsored coverage provides less expensive and/or more complete general health coverage than Medicare Parts A and B do, you may want to retain that coverage even though you also join a Part D plan.

This penalty for late enrollment offers a strong incentive for most people to join a Part D plan as soon as they are eligible. This is true even if you do not presently have many out-of-pocket prescription drug costs and:

- do not regularly take any prescription drugs, or
- take only one relatively low-cost drug.

If you are not enrolled in an employer-sponsored insurance plan with drug coverage or a Medicare Advantage plan with drug coverage, and you have no or very low regular prescription drug costs, you have the following two options.

Option 1: Not enrolling. You can choose not to enroll in any drug plan for as long as you do not have any significant out-of-pocket drug costs. This means you will incur the 1% per month penalty on the premium cost of any plan in which you eventually enroll. But that penalty will be partially or fully offset by the fact that you will not be paying any monthly premium for the years you are not enrolled.

The risk with this approach is that after a few years your drug needs may change and you may then want to enroll in a particular plan that has a high monthly premium. If so, the 1% per month of delay penalty might add up to more than you have saved by not enrolling early. For example, if you delay 36 months before enrolling, then enroll in a plan that has an initial premium of $50 per month, you will be penalized $18 per month in premiums. And these monthly premium amounts go up each year.

Option 2: Enrolling in a low-premium plan. For many people in the categories above, a better option than not enrolling at all in a plan is to enroll as soon as eligible in a low-premium plan. Several insurance companies offer plans with no monthly premium, or a premium under $10. These plans tend to have poorer coverage than plans with higher premiums. But if such a plan is available where you live, it may allow you to enroll in Part D for little or no money as soon as you are eligible, thus avoiding the late enrollment penalty. If and when your drug costs go up and you need better coverage, you can then switch to a more comprehensive plan with a higher premium. (For an explanation of switching plans, see Chapter 13.)

Stand-Alone Drug Plan or Managed Care Plan

Part D drug coverage is available either through a separate, stand-alone prescription drug plan (PDP) or as the prescription drug component (MA-PD) of full health coverage under a Medicare Advantage plan (see Chapter 15). Each type of plan offers a generally equivalent range of available coverage, though each specific plan is slightly different and costs vary.

If you belong to a Medicare Advantage plan that does not offer MA-PD drug coverage and you want drug coverage, you must leave your plan and enroll in a stand-alone PDP, which also means returning to regular Medicare coverage (also referred to as Medicare fee-for-service) as described in earlier sections of this chapter. Or, you may join a Medicare Advantage plan that offers MA-PD drug coverage. (Making this choice is discussed in Chapter 15.)

Finding Out About Available Part D Plans

You may enroll only in a plan that operates in the state where you live. There are several ways to find out about the specific Part D plans available to you.

Medicare. The Centers for Medicare & Medicaid Services (CMS) is the federal agency that administers the Medicare program, including Part D prescription drug coverage. It provides personalized help in locating Part D plans. CMS can tell you not only what plans are available where you live, but can also narrow your choice for you according to the medications you regularly take. You can contact CMS by phone at 800-MEDICARE (800-633-4227). Or, you can visit its website at www.medicare.gov and find information tailored to your specific geographic location and medication regimen.

SHIP or HICAP. Every state has a certified program that provides free advice to consumers about Medicare, Medicaid, and other health insurance matters. It's called the State Health Insurance Assistance Program (SHIP), or sometimes the Health Insurance Counseling and Advocacy Program (HICAP). These programs maintain local offices in most urban areas as well as some central rural locations.

Trained counselors in these offices can tell you about all the Part D plans available in your state, and can identify the plans that cover the drugs you regularly use. Once you have investigated several plans, the counselors can meet with you in person to help you make a final decision. To find your SHIP or HICAP office, see the contact information at the end of Chapter 13.

State department of insurance. Every state has a government agency that oversees insurance matters. You can contact your state department of insurance for the names, addresses, and phone numbers of every company offering a Part D plan in your state. See the end of Chapter 14 for a website that lists all of the state departments of insurance.

Have Your Information Handy When You Contact Part D Assistance

In figuring out which Part D plan is best for you, you'll want to consider the medications you regularly use and the pharmacy where you prefer to get your drugs. Before you contact any agency or counselor for assistance in choosing a plan, have the following information handy:

- a list of the specific drugs you regularly use, including the brand (or generic) name, the dose size and frequency, and the current monthly cost
- the name and address of your pharmacy
- whether you currently receive Medicaid benefits, and
- whether you are, or think you might be, eligible for a Part D low-income subsidy.

CAUTION

Get complete information from the plan itself. You can get very helpful information about Part D plans from several sources. But the most thorough information about a specific plan comes from the plan itself. So, before you make a final choice, contact any plan that interests you and ask them to send you a complete description of the plan, including all the matters discussed in this section. You can get the phone number and address of any plan from Medicare itself, or from the other sources discussed above. Make sure to get any important information from the plan in writing. Unfortunately, the insurance companies' telephone information centers tend to be somewhat unreliable. Also, you have no way of forcing the insurance company to abide by what someone tells you on the phone.

Choosing a Part D Drug Plan

Once you decide to enroll in Part D and you find out what plans are available where you live, you must consider several factors in deciding which plan to choose. (When you're ready to join a particular plan, you enroll directly with that plan. The mechanics of enrollment are discussed in Chapter 13.) Here is a step-by-step guide to choosing the plan that's right for you (you can also use the Medicare Plan Finder at Medicare.gov).

Step 1: List your regular medications and their costs. The first step in deciding on a specific plan is to list the medicines you regularly take, including:

- the brand name and generic name (if there is one) of each drug; (if you take the generic version and don't know the brand name, ask your doctor what it's called)
- the dosage you take
- how many doses are in each prescription you fill, and
- how often you fill the prescription.

Step 2: See which plans include your medications in their formularies. The single most important thing to consider in choosing a plan is whether all the drugs you regularly take are included in the plan's formulary. Eliminate from consideration any plan that does not include either the brand-name or the generic version of your drugs. Some plans may cover only the generic version of a drug you take, while others may cover both the brand-name and the generic versions. Under any plan that covers a brand-name drug, copayments for the brand-name will be higher than for the generic version.

Free One-on-One Help in Choosing a Part D Plan

If you have any doubts or questions about choosing a Part D plan, it may be a very good idea to get free personal advice from an expert counselor with SHIP or HICAP near you. These trained counselors are familiar with all the plans offered in your geographic area. They will sit down with you and help you match your needs, preferences, and finances with the available plans. To find your local SHIP or HICAP office, see the contact information at the end of Chapter 13.

Step 3: Check with the different plans to see what the total monthly cost of your drugs would be, as well as your initial copayments. For each plan that includes all your drugs on its formulary, ask the sponsoring company to provide you with an estimate (in writing) of the total monthly cost of each of your prescriptions—taking into account your normal dosage and number of doses. (Total costs differ among insurance companies because each one negotiates different drug prices with the pharmaceutical companies.) Also ask the plans to tell you what your copayments would be for each prescription during the initial coverage period (prior to the "doughnut hole" coverage gap).

Step 4: See whether the plan provides "first dollar" coverage. The standard Part D benefit requires each person to pay out of pocket a $405 (in 2018) per year deductible before the plan begins providing any coverage. Some plans, however, provide what is called "first dollar" coverage, meaning that they waive this deductible and begin paying their share from the first dollar you spend on covered medicines. These plans are generally more expensive, but may be worth it if your prescription costs are high.

Step 5: Ask whether the plan offers any coverage within the "doughnut hole" coverage gap. A few plans offer some coverage within each year's "doughnut hole" coverage gap, during which most people must pay the entire amount of the cost of their drugs. If the total cost of your drugs will put you into the coverage gap, this added coverage may be very important. You can determine whether the cost of your drugs will enter into the coverage gap by calculating the total monthly cost of each of your drugs under each plan, multiplying each by 12 (months), then adding them all together.

Step 6: Total the various costs, including the monthly premium. Eliminate those plans that don't cover your particular medications on their formulary. For the remaining plans, use the information you've gathered to determine how much money you would spend each year under each plan you are considering. For each plan, add up:

- the plan's yearly premiums
- your yearly deductible amount (if the plan does not provide "first dollar" coverage)
- your copayments for all your drugs during the initial coverage period, and
- how much you would pay out of pocket during the coverage gap (this requires you to figure out how quickly—meaning, with how many monthly prescriptions—you would reach the coverage gap; you do this by adding up the total monthly cost of your drugs under each plan).

Once you've added up all of these items for each plan, you'll be able to compare the annual cost of each plan side by side. Before you make your final decision, though, there's one more step.

Step 7: Look into access restrictions. Though the cost of drugs is important, you should also consider ease of access to your drugs when choosing among plans. This is particularly true if your costs would be nearly the same for two or more plans. Plans restrict access in two different ways. They may place restrictions on coverage—for example, they may require or have drug substitution, prior authorization, step therapy, and supply limits—and they may require you to purchase your drugs from selected pharmacies and other sources. If a plan places a difficult or cumbersome restriction on your access to the drugs you need, you may want to consider a different plan with fewer restrictions at a somewhat higher cost.

TIP

Switching from one plan to another. Enrolling in a particular Part D plan is not necessarily forever. If you pick a plan that doesn't suit your needs and you can find a better one, you may switch plans. When and how often you may switch plans depends upon whether you are also eligible for Medicaid, you receive a Part D low-income subsidy, or you reside in a long-term care facility. The options for switching plans are explained in Chapter 13.

Medicare Coverage for People with End-Stage Renal Disease (ESRD)

Most people qualify for Medicare only when they reach age 65 or after they have received Social Security disability benefits for two years. But you may be eligible for a special category of Medicare coverage, regardless of your age or ability to work, if you suffer from long-term kidney failure, known as end-stage renal disease (ESRD).

Eligibility for ESRD Medicare Coverage

To be eligible for ESRD-based Medicare coverage, you have to meet two conditions. One is medical—you must be diagnosed with ESRD, as defined by Medicare. The other has to do with the amount of Social Security work credits that have been earned by you, your spouse, or (if you are a minor) your parent.

Qualifying Medical Condition

To qualify for Medicare's special coverage for people with serious kidney disease, your treating physician (usually a nephrologist or other kidney specialist) must diagnose you as having ESRD. Under Medicare's definition, ESRD means that your kidneys have permanently stopped functioning, so that in order to stay alive, you require either long-term dialysis or a kidney transplant. The required dialysis may be either at a medical facility or at home.

Earned Work Credits

Depending on your age, you or your spouse (or one of your parents, if you are a minor) must have earned a certain number of Social Security work credits, also referred to as quarters of coverage (QCs), in order to be eligible for ESRD-based Medicare coverage. Workers can accumulate up to four QCs each year, based on their salary or wages and other earned income; the way Social Security calculates these work credits is explained in Chapter 1, "Social Security: The Basics."

Overall work record. To qualify for ESRD-based Medicare coverage, you must have earned at least one QC for each year after the year you turned age 21, up to the year you were diagnosed with ESRD. Or, you may qualify instead based on your spouse's (or parent's, if you're a minor) work record, if he or she earned at least one QC for each year after turning 21, up to the year you were diagnosed with ESRD (or, up to the year your spouse reached age 62 or died). If you or your spouse were collecting Social Security disability benefits during any year, that year does not count in calculating the QCs needed. Regardless of your age, a minimum of 6 QCs by you or your spouse is required for you to be eligible for ESRD-based Medicare coverage.

Recent work record. Even if the overall number of QCs earned by you or your spouse does not meet the standard described above, you may still qualify for ESRD-based Medicare coverage if you or your spouse earned at least 6 QCs over the 13 calendar quarters immediately prior to the onset of your ESRD condition (or prior to the death of your spouse).

TIP

Go to Social Security's website. You can find out how many quarters of work credit you or your spouse have earned by going to the Social Security website www.ssa.gov/myaccount and creating a personal account.

Medical Care Covered by ESRD Medicare

If you qualify for this special Medicare eligibility for ESRD, Medicare will cover not only costs related to your treatment for ESRD but also for *all other medical care normally covered by Medicare.* That means you will be fully eligible, on the same terms as anyone else, to:

- enroll in coverage for inpatient care under Medicare Part A, outpatient care under Medicare Part B, and outpatient prescription drugs under a Medicare Part D insurance plan (Parts A, B and D are explained in this chapter)
- purchase a "medigap" supplemental private insurance policy to pay some of the costs Medicare doesn't pay (see Chapter 14), or
- enroll in a Part C Medicare Advantage plan, which puts all these coverages into one package (see Chapter 15).

Like anyone else eligible for Medicare, you will need to choose which parts of the program to enroll in, and will have to pay each part's premiums, deductibles, and copayments, as well as the 20% of most charges that Medicare Part B does not pay. The deductibles, copayments, and unpaid Medicare Part B 20% underline the importance of purchasing a medigap supplemental insurance policy, joining a Medicare Advantage plan, maintaining employer-sponsored health coverage, or (if you have low income and few assets other than your home), determining if you are eligible to enroll in your state's Medicaid program (see Chapter 16).

To receive maximum Medicare coverage for costs specifically related to your ESRD care, you must enroll in both Medicare Part A and Medicare Part B (which charges a monthly premium), or enroll in a Part C Medicare Advantage plan (these plans combine Part A and Part B coverage). Once you are enrolled in Part A and Part B, or in Part C, Medicare will cover:

- dialysis and related services, including the daily room cost if you receive your dialysis while an inpatient in a Medicare-participating hospital
- dialysis and related services if you receive dialysis as an outpatient at a Medicare-approved dialysis facility

- training for self-dialysis, for both you and a person you designate to help you at home with your self-dialysis, if you request self-dialysis and your treating physician approves
- self-dialysis equipment and supplies for use at home, including certain drugs that your doctor may prescribe, or
- services from your physician(s), as well as laboratory and other tests.

> CAUTION
>
> **Medicare doesn't pay for dialysis assistants at home.** While Medicare will pay for the training of a person to assist you with self-dialysis at home, Medicare will not pay for the person's actual services, nor for a professional dialysis aide to help you at home.

Coordination of Medicare with Group Health Insurance Coverage

At the time you become eligible for ESRD-based Medicare, you might already have health care coverage through an employer group health plan, based on your or your spouse's current employment or through a retirement plan. If so, and if you enroll in ESRD-based Medicare, the private insurance will be the primary payer for your health care costs during a "coordination of benefits" (COB) period of 30 months, with Medicare as the secondary payer. This means that for this initial period, Medicare will contribute to payment of costs that your health plan does not pay (which can include deductibles, copayments, and sometimes a yearly cap on payments for renal services). The COB begins the first month that you become eligible for ESRD-based Medicare, whether or not you actually enroll at that time. At the end of the 30-month period, the roles are reversed, with Medicare becoming the primary payer and your employer group health plan becoming the secondary payer.

When ESRD Medicare Coverage Begins

ESRD-based Medicare coverage becomes effective at different times, depending on the nature of your treatment.

Hemodialysis provided at a facility. If you receive hemodialysis at a dialysis center or clinic, your Medicare coverage becomes effective on the first day of your fourth month of treatment. If, however, you are resuming dialysis after your ESRD-based Medicare coverage ended (due to recovery of kidney function following a transplant or dialysis—more on this below), your Medicare coverage can begin again without the three-month waiting period described above.

Home (self) dialysis. If you and your physician decide that you want and are able to perform self-dialysis at home, Medicare coverage becomes effective as soon as you begin treatment—even if you begin treatment at a facility, before switching to home—if you complete a self-dialysis training program at a Medicare-certified facility and then perform self-dialysis at home.

Kidney transplant. If you are to receive a kidney transplant, your Medicare coverage begins the month you are admitted to the hospital for the transplant or for medical care preparing you for the transplant. The coverage can extend up to two months prior to the transplant if you're in the hospital that long prior to the surgery.

When ESRD Medicare Coverage Ends

ESRD-based Medicare coverage ends 12 months after you stop dialysis. If you've had a transplant, ESRD-based Medicare coverage stops 36 months after the date of the surgery (unless you are then still on dialysis).

Applying for ESRD Medicare Coverage

You apply for ESRD-based Medicare coverage through the Social Security system. You can begin this process online at Social Security's website www.ssa.gov or by phoning Social Security at 800-772-1213.

(If you phone, there's usually quite a long wait, but the Social Security phone system allows you to leave your name and number and get a return call instead of waiting on the line; this call-back service works well.)

Special Length-of-Coverage Rules for Immunosuppressive Drugs

Very expensive drugs used to stop the body from rejecting a transplanted kidney are often used by transplant patients for months or years following the surgery. Medicare will pay 80% of the cost of those drugs for three years or indefinitely, depending on how you qualify for Medicare:

- If your Medicare coverage is based on ESRD-based eligibility alone, Medicare will cover the drugs for 36 months.

- If, before you got ESRD, you were eligible for Medicare because you were age 65 or older or had received Social Security disability benefits for at least 24 months, Medicare will cover the drugs indefinitely.

- If, after you had a transplant that was covered by Medicare, you qualify for Medicare because you're age 65 or older or have been receiving Social Security disability benefits for at least 24 months, Medicare will cover the drugs indefinitely.

Your specialist physician's office can provide initial help and ongoing support for the medical information you'll need to supply with your Medicare application. If you have problems with eligibility, you can also get help from the National Kidney Foundation at 800-622-9010 or online at www.kidney.org. ●

Medicare Procedures:
Enrollment, Claims, and Appeals

Chapter 12 described the eligibility rules for Medicare. As you'll remember, most people are eligible for Part A hospital insurance free of charge; if you are not, you may enroll by paying a monthly premium. Part B medical insurance coverage is available to most people age 65 and older, and everyone covered pays a monthly premium for it. And Part D—which covers some of the cost of prescription drugs you take at home—is available to everyone who is eligible for Part A or B. Everyone who enrolls in Part D pays a monthly premium for prescription drug coverage except those who are also eligible for Medicaid or who receive a special Part D low-income subsidy.

This chapter explains:

- how to enroll in Medicare Part A and Part B
- how to get Medicare to pay its share of your medical bills once you are enrolled
- what portion of the bill you must pay yourself
- how to read the notice Medicare sends you
- how to appeal a Medicare decision regarding your claim, and
- the separate procedures for enrolling in a Part D plan, switching Part D plans, requesting an exception to a Part D plan's formulary or another access restriction, and appealing a Part D plan's decision.

Enrolling in Part A Hospital Insurance

Medicare Part A, also called hospital insurance, covers most of the cost of inpatient care in a hospital or skilled nursing facility, and also the costs of home health care. Most people age 65 or older are eligible for Part A coverage. Some will receive it automatically and free of charge, along with their Social Security benefits. Others will need to enroll and possibly pay a monthly fee.

Those Who Receive Social Security Benefits

If you are under age 65 and already receive Social Security retirement, dependents, or survivors benefits or Railroad Retirement benefits, you don't need to do any paperwork to enroll in Medicare Part A hospital insurance. Social Security will automatically enroll you, and coverage will take effect on your 65th birthday. About three months before your 65th birthday, Medicare will mail you a Medicare card and information sheet.

Since Medicare Part A is free for people age 65 or over who receive Social Security benefits, automatic enrollment provides excellent supplemental coverage even if you have other health care coverage. The only downside is that once you are automatically enrolled in Medicare, you can no longer contribute to a health savings account (HSA), although you remain free to use any money already in the account. Also, Medicare does not allow you to "disenroll" from Part A once you begin collecting Social Security benefits.

CAUTION

No new contributions to health savings accounts. Once you are enrolled in Medicare (Parts A and B, or Part A alone), which you receive automatically once you claim Social Security benefits at age 65 or older, you are no longer allowed to make new pretax contributions to your health savings account (HSA). You can continue to use the funds already in your HSA account, however. This is true even for employees with HSA health plans who continue to work.

If you receive Social Security disability benefits for two years, regardless of your age, you will be automatically enrolled in Medicare Part A, effective 24 months from the date Social Security declared that your disability began. The Medicare card you receive in the mail will indicate that you are enrolled in both Part A and Part B. If you do not want to be enrolled in, and pay the monthly premium for, Part B, there is a form for you to sign and return to Medicare. If you do want to be enrolled in both Parts A and B, you don't have to do anything. Just sign your card and keep it handy.

Managed Care Plans Handle Medicare Paperwork

Many people who are about to qualify for Medicare have an HMO or another managed care insurance plan that they intend to keep when they become eligible for Medicare. Other people decide to join an HMO or another managed care plan when they first become eligible for Medicare.

If you intend to remain with your current insurance plan when you become eligible, it can sign you up for Medicare and switch you to the plan's Medicare coverage. Begin this process two to three months before you become eligible for Medicare.

Similarly, if you decide to join a managed care plan for the first time when you become eligible for Medicare, you can sign up for Medicare at the same time you sign up for the plan. Try to get the paperwork started at least two months before your Medicare eligibility begins. Medicare managed care plans are discussed in Chapter 15.

If you are receiving Social Security benefits but do not receive your Medicare card in the mail within a month of your 65th birthday, or within a month of your 24th month of disability benefits, contact your local Social Security office or call the national Social Security office at 800-772-1213.

Those Who Do Not Receive Social Security Benefits

If you are soon to turn 65 but you are not receiving Social Security retirement, dependents, or survivors benefits, Railroad Retirement benefits, or federal civil service retirement benefits, you must apply either online on the official Social Security Administration website at www.ssa.gov/medicare, or at your local Social Security office, to enroll in Medicare Part A. If you are going to apply for retirement or other Social Security benefits to begin on your 65th birthday, you can apply for Medicare at the same time, at your local Social Security office.

Your Medicare Card

When you are enrolled in Medicare, you will be sent a Medicare card that states:

- your name
- whether you have both Part A and Part B coverage or just Part A
- the effective date of your Medicare coverage, and
- your health insurance claim number—also called your Medicare number.

Important: New cards are coming. Beginning in April 2018 and running through April 2019, Medicare will be replacing all Medicare cards. Sometime during that period you will receive your new card in the mail. It will have a new Medicare number on it, which (for security reasons) will not include your Social Security number. When you receive your new card, notify all your medical providers of your new Medicare number. If you haven't received your new card by May 2019, contact Medicare at 800-633-4227.

Always carry your Medicare card with you. You will be asked to present it when you seek medical treatment at a hospital, a doctor's office, or another health care provider.

Also, you must include your Medicare number on all payments of Medicare premiums or correspondence about Medicare.

If you lose your Medicare card, you can have it replaced by applying in person at your local Social Security office or by calling the toll-free information line at 800-MEDICARE, or Social Security's main office at 800-772-1213. Alternatively, you can apply for a new card online at www.medicare.gov.

Who Is Eligible

If you are eligible for Social Security benefits, you can receive free Medicare Part A coverage at age 65 whether or not you actually claim your Social Security benefits.

For example, many people who continue working after reaching age 65 do not claim retirement benefits until later. Still, they can receive free Part A Medicare coverage by applying for it at their local Social Security office.

Also, if you are not automatically eligible for free Part A coverage, you may be able to purchase it for a monthly premium. The amount of the premium depends on how many work credits you or your spouse have earned. (See "Part A Hospital Insurance" in Chapter 12 for details.)

When to Apply

Whether you wish to claim Social Security benefits and Medicare, or just Medicare, apply well before you turn 65. You can apply as early as three months before your 65th birthday.

Signing up early is important for two reasons: First, it will ensure that your coverage begins as soon as you are eligible, on your 65th birthday. Second, if you wait more than three months after your 65th birthday to enroll, you will not be allowed to enroll in Part B until the following January 1, and your eligibility will not begin until July 1 of that year. (See "Enrolling in Part B Medical Insurance," below, regarding delayed enrollment.)

CAUTION
Avoid delays in Part B coverage. If you do not enroll in both Parts A and B during your initial enrollment period, your enrollment in Part B will not only be delayed, but you will also have to pay a higher monthly premium for it. (See "Enrolling in Part B Medical Insurance," below, for details.)

When Benefits Begin

If you apply for Part A of Medicare within six months after you turn 65, your coverage will date back to your 65th birthday. But if you apply after that, your coverage will date back only up to six months before the month in which you applied. If your Medicare eligibility is based on disability, however, your coverage will date back up to one year before the date on which you apply.

Appealing Denial of Coverage

Eligibility for coverage by Part A of Medicare depends solely on your age and on the number of Social Security work credits you or your spouse have acquired. (See "Part A Hospital Insurance" in Chapter 12 for a review of the eligibility requirements.) You can be denied coverage by Medicare Part A only if there is a dispute about whether you have reached 65, about the number of your or your spouse's work credits, or about the validity of your marriage.

Decisions about these matters are handled not by Medicare but by Social Security. And, like any other decision of the Social Security Administration, a decision denying eligibility for Medicare Part A hospital insurance coverage can be appealed. The appeal process is discussed later in this chapter.

Enrolling in Part B Medical Insurance

Medicare Part B, referred to as medical insurance, covers doctors' services plus laboratory, clinic, home therapy, and other medical services you receive other than when you are a patient in a hospital or skilled nursing facility. Most people age 65 are eligible for Part B.

Everyone must pay a monthly premium to enroll, although some people may pay for Part B fees in the premiums they pay to HMOs or other Medicare Advantage plans (see Chapter 15).

This section explains who is automatically enrolled in Part B, who must take steps to enroll, and when to do so.

Those Who Receive Social Security Benefits

If you are younger than 65 and already receiving Social Security retirement, Railroad Retirement, dependents, or survivors benefits, you will be automatically enrolled in both Medicare Part A and Part B within three months of turning 65. Your coverage will become effective on your 65th birthday. Near that time, you will be sent your Medicare card through the mail, along with an information packet. The monthly premium for Part B coverage will be deducted automatically from your Social Security check, beginning with the first month after your 65th birthday.

If you do not want Medicare Part B coverage—perhaps because you are still working and are covered by an employment-related health plan—notify Social Security of that fact on the form that comes with your Medicare card. If you reject Part B coverage when you are first eligible for it, you can enroll in Part B later on, although only during the first three months of any year. And if you enroll later, your premiums may be higher.

Those Who Do Not Receive Social Security Benefits

If you are turning 65 but are not eligible for Social Security benefits, or are not yet going to claim benefits to which you are entitled, you may still enroll in Part B medical insurance either online on the official Social Security website at www.ssa.gov/medicare, or at your local Social Security office.

You can enroll during an initial period of seven months, which begins three months before the month you turn 65 and ends three months after the end of the month you turn 65. For example, if you turn 65 in July, your initial enrollment period starts April 1 and ends October 31. However, the earlier you enroll during this initial period, the better. If you enroll during the three months before you turn 65, your coverage will begin on your 65th birthday. If you enroll during the remaining four months of your initial enrollment period, your coverage may be delayed from one to three months after you sign up, depending on how long it takes to process your application.

Delayed Enrollment

If you do not enroll in Part B medical insurance during the seven-month period just before and after you turn 65, but later decide you want the coverage, you can sign up during any general enrollment period. These are held January 1 through March 31 every year. If you sign up any time during one of these general enrollment periods, your coverage will begin on July 1 of the year you enroll.

Your monthly premium will be higher if you wait to enroll during one of the general enrollment periods instead of when you turn 65. For each year you were eligible for Part B coverage but did not enroll, your premium will be 10% higher than the basic premium.

Free Late Enrollment If Covered by Current Employment Health Plan

If you are covered by a group health plan based on your own or your spouse's current employment, you can enroll in Part B coverage after your 65th birthday without having to wait for the open enrollment period and without any penalty. This exception refers only to a group health plan based on current employment, not to one based on retirement benefits from employment.

If you have delayed signing up for Medicare Part B because you have been covered by a health plan based on current employment, you can sign up for Part B coverage at any time while you are still covered, or within seven months of the date you or your spouse end that employment, or the date the health coverage ends, whichever comes first.

If you sign up while you are still covered by a group health plan based on current employment, or during the first full month that you no longer have this coverage, your Part B coverage will begin the first day of the month you sign up. You can also choose, instead, to have your coverage begin with any of the following three months. If you sign up during any of the remaining seven months of your special enrollment period, your Part B coverage will begin the month after you sign up.

To enroll in Part B after age 65 (when you already have Part A), you can fill out an *Application for Enrollment in Medicare Part B* (Form CMS40B) and bring it or mail it to a Social Security office. If for any reason you are not already enrolled in Medicare Part A, you can sign up for both Part A and Part B online at https://secure.ssa.gov/iClaim/rib (you cannot sign up online for Part B only).

Medicare's Payment of Your Medical Bills

Medicare does not handle day-to-day paperwork and payments with patients and doctors or other health care providers. It contracts out this work to what are called Medicare carriers or intermediaries. These are huge private corporations, such as Blue Cross or other large insurance companies, each of which handles claims for an entire state, and sometimes for more than one state.

The Medicare intermediary in your state receives, reviews, and pays claims. It sends notices that tell you and the medical provider of the amount of benefits paid, the amount of your medical bill that has not been paid, and the amount the health care provider is legally permitted to charge. (See "Your *Medicare Summary Notice,*" below, for more on these notices.) And it is with the intermediary that you will initially correspond if you want to appeal a decision about Medicare coverage of health care charges. (See "Appealing the Denial of a Claim," below, for appeal procedures.)

Medicare intermediaries handle billing for inpatient charges covered under Part A differently from outpatient charges covered under Part B. This section explains the differences in the billing process.

 TIP

HMOs and Medicare Advantage plans do their own paperwork. If you belong to an HMO or another Medicare Advantage plan, the billing office there handles all the Medicare-related paperwork. In fact, Medicare pays Medicare Advantage plans a flat amount for each enrolled patient, rather than a separate payment for each treatment. All you have to do is pay your plan's own monthly premiums and copayments and deal with its paperwork. You don't have to directly handle any Medicare forms and you won't receive any *Medicare Summary Notices.*

Inpatient and Home Care Bills

Medicare Part A covers inpatient care in a hospital or skilled nursing facility, as well as some home health care. (See "How Much Medicare Part A Pays" in Chapter 12 for a review of Medicare Part A coverage.)

Medicare Billed Directly by Facility

When you first check into a hospital or skilled nursing facility, you present your Medicare card to the admissions office and it takes care of the rest. Similarly, when you and your doctor make arrangements for a Medicare-approved home care agency to provide your care, you give the agency your Medicare number and it takes care of all the paperwork. The provider—the hospital, skilled nursing facility, or home health care agency—sends its bills directly to Medicare. The patient should not have to do a thing to get Medicare to pay its part of the bill.

The hospital, nursing facility, or home care agency accepts as payment in full the amount the Medicare intermediary decides is the approved charge for those of your inpatient services that are covered by Medicare (but see Chapter 12 for a reminder of what costs are covered). Unlike doctors' bills—in which you may be personally responsible for the difference between Medicare's approved charges and the actual amount of a bill—a hospital, nursing facility, or home care agency is not permitted to bill you for any covered inpatient charges over the amounts paid by Medicare.

The Medicare carrier will also send you a copy of the bills so that you will know how much has been paid and how much you must cover on your own.

Patient Billed for Some Charges

The hospital, nursing facility, or home care agency will bill you, and your private Medicare supplement insurance company (if you have such insurance), for:

- any unpaid portion of your deductible
- any coinsurance payments—for example, for hospital inpatient stays of more than 60 days, and

- charges not covered at all by Medicare, such as for a private room you requested that was not medically necessary, or for television and telephone charges.

The Medicare carrier will send you a form called a *Medicare Summary Notice* that will show what hospital services were paid for and the portion of your deductible for which you are responsible. The hospital or other facility will bill you directly for the unpaid portion of your deductible and for those amounts not covered by Medicare or by Medicare supplemental insurance. (See Chapter 14 regarding supplemental insurance.)

Outpatient and Doctor Bills

How much of your covered doctor and outpatient medical bills Medicare Part B will pay depends on whether your doctor or other medical provider accepts assignment of the Medicare-approved amount as the full amount of the bill. (For more information, see "How Much Medicare Part B Pays" in Chapter 12.)

If the doctor accepts assignment, you—perhaps assisted by private medigap insurance or Medicaid—are responsible only for your yearly Part B deductible, plus the 20% of the approved charges Medicare does not pay.

If the doctor or other provider does not accept assignment, then you and your additional insurance may also be responsible for all amounts of the bill up to 15% more than the Medicare-approved amount.

Assignment Method of Payment

If your doctor or other health care provider accepts assignment of your Medicare claim, you are personally responsible for your yearly medical insurance deductible, and then only the 20% of the Medicare-approved amount of the bill that Medicare does not pay. By accepting assignment, the doctor or other provider agrees not to charge you a higher amount than what Medicare approves for the treatment or other covered service you have received.

Catching Overbilling

Medicare has been doing a better job in recent years of cracking down on billing errors and fraud by health care providers. But you must still check your bill carefully to determine whether the facility or other provider has billed you for services you did not receive or services that Medicare has paid, or has charged more than once for the same service.

The Medicare intermediary may look closely at the portion of the bill Medicare is supposed to pay, and if you have medigap supplemental insurance, the insurance company will also check the bill. But neither one will carefully examine the amounts for which you are personally responsible.

Check all medical bills to make sure there are no charges for services you did not receive. Then, place the bill from the facility or other provider next to the statement from the Medicare carrier and from your medigap insurance company. Compare them to see whether any amount the facility or other provider has billed you directly has been paid by Medicare or by your medigap insurer.

If so, you must contact the billing office at the facility or other provider, sending a copy of your statement from the Medicare carrier or medigap insurer that shows that the charges have been paid. If the problem is billing for a service you do not believe you received, ask the facility's or provider's billing office to send you a copy of your medical record where the service was recorded.

For more information about how to deal with what you believe are billing errors, go to the Medicare website at www.medicare.gov and look under the tab "Claims & Appeals," then click on "File a complaint."

After you and the health care provider are informed by a *Medicare Summary Notice* form from Medicare how much the Medicare-approved charges are, the provider's office will either bill you directly for the remaining 20% of approved charges or bill your medigap supplemental insurance carrier if you have one.

EXAMPLE: Franco was examined for a painful knee by his regular doctor, who then decided to refer him to an orthopedist. Franco asked his doctor to refer him to someone who accepted Medicare assignment. The orthopedist examined Franco, took X-rays, and prescribed exercises and some medication. Franco's own doctor charged $100 for Franco's original examination. The orthopedist charged $150. Both doctors accepted assignment.

Medicare's approved amount for Franco's regular doctor was $75 and, for the orthopedist, $120. Because Franco had already paid his yearly deductible for Part B, Medicare paid 80% of the approved amount of each doctor's bill: $60 to Franco's regular doctor (80% of $75 = $60) and $96 to the orthopedist (80% of $120 = $96). Medicare sent these amounts directly to the doctors. Franco had to pay only the remaining 20% of the approved amounts.

The following chart shows who paid what amount of Franco's bills in this example.

Payment of Doctor Bills—Assignment Accepted

	Initial exam	Orthopedic exam	Total
Doctors' normal charges	$100	$150	$250
Amount approved by Medicare	$75	$120	$195
Amount paid by Medicare (80%)	$60	$96	$156
Amount patient paid (20%)	$15	$24	$39

Payment When No Assignment

If your doctor or other health care provider does not accept assignment of the Medicare-approved charges as the full amount of the bill, you —or you and your medigap supplemental insurance—will owe the difference between what Medicare pays and the full amount of the doctor's bill, up to 15% more than the Medicare-approved amount. But Medicare pays a bit less than 80% of the approved amount on these claims. And you end up having to pay one-third (33.25%) of the Medicare-approved amount, rather than one-fifth (20%) of the approved amount.

Medicare has a complicated way of calculating this. For nonparticipating doctors, Medicare lowers the approved fee to 95% of what it would be for participating doctors. But it allows nonparticipating doctors to charge 15% of this lowered fee to patients, in addition to their 20% copayment.

EXAMPLE: In the example above, Franco's own doctor normally charged $100 for an examination and the orthopedist charged $150. If neither doctor accepted assignment, but stuck to their normal fees, the payment amounts would be as follows.

Medicare's approved amount for Franco's regular doctor was $75 and, for the orthopedist, $120. But Medicare will allow only 95% of this fee as the approved fee since the doctor doesn't accept assignment. The doctor can charge 115% of this lowered fee (which works out to an additional 9.25% of the regular approved fee). Medicare will pay 80% of the lowered fee.

The following chart summarizes who paid what amount of Franco's bills in this example. You'll see that his payment is one-third of the regular approved amount.

Payment of Doctor Bills—Assignment Accepted

	Initial exam	Orthopedic exam	Total
Doctors' normal charges	$100.00	$150.00	$250.00
Amount approved for nonparticipating doctors (95% of approved fee)	$71.25	$114.00	$185.25
Total amount doctor allowed to charge (115% of lowered fee)	$81.94	$131.10	$213.04
Amount paid by Medicare (80% of lowered fee)	$57.00	$91.20	$148.20
Amount paid by patient (20% of lowered fee)	$14.25	$22.80	$37.05
Additional amount doctor can charge (15% of lowered fee)	$10.69	$17.10	$27.79
Total amount paid by patient (20% of lowered fee + additional amount)	$24.94	$39.90	$64.84

TIP

Handling Medicare billing paperwork is free. Even a doctor or another health care provider who does not accept assignment must fill in the Medicare paperwork and send it to Medicare for payment—and you cannot be charged for processing this Medicare paperwork.

Paying Your Share of the Bill

Doctors and other health care providers must wait to find out how much the Medicare-approved charges are before asking you to pay your share. Until they know what the Medicare-approved amount is, they cannot know the legal limit—15% over those approved charges—on how much they can require you to pay.

Following your treatment or other service, the doctor's or other provider's office will submit their bills for payment to Medicare. You do not have to submit the paperwork yourself.

If you have private medigap supplemental insurance that pays your deductible and the 20% coinsurance amount that Medicare does not pay, the doctor's office will send its paperwork to the insurance company as well as to Medicare. The doctor will receive payment directly from both Medicare and the supplemental insurance, after Medicare has determined the approved amount for the care you received.

Every three months you will receive a form called a *Medicare Summary Notice*, or *MSN*, that includes the following information about every Medicare-billed service you received during the previous three-month period:

- how much of each bill is Medicare approved
- how much Medicare will pay the provider
- how much of your deductible has been met, and
- how much must be paid by you or your private medigap insurance.

Your *Medicare Summary Notice*

A form called a *Medicare Summary Notice* (MSN) is sent to you to explain what Medicare Part B is covering of your recent medical services and how much Medicare is paying for those services. You receive such a notice every three months; if you did not have any medical services during those three months, you won't receive an MSN for that period.

Don't Let a Doctor Take More Than the Law Allows

Medicare rules are clear—and every doctor and other health care provider knows them. You can be charged only an extra 9.25% above what Medicare decides is the approved amount for a specific medical service (which is actually an extra 15% of the approved amount for unassigned claims). And the *Medicare Summary Notice* form does the arithmetic for you, stating the amount of the maximum charge.

If a doctor or another provider does not accept assignment and bills you more than the allowable amount, send the doctor's office a copy of your *Medicare Summary Notice* form, underlining the spot where the maximum bill is stated—and keep a copy for yourself. If you already paid the bill, and the amount you paid was more than the allowable Medicare-approved amount plus 15%, you are entitled to a refund.

Again, contact the doctor's or other provider's billing office and request your refund, letting them know the date you paid the bill, the amount you paid, and the Medicare-approved amount. If they will not refund the overpayment, contact the Medicare carrier, which will then contact the doctor or other health care provider directly.

The MSN is not a bill. It simply allows you to check the information Medicare has received from your medical providers and to see how much Medicare will pay and how much is left over to be paid by your supplemental insurance carrier or by you out of pocket. Every time you get an MSN form, you should check it carefully to see that the information is correct and that you agree with

Medicare's decisions. For an example of an MSN, information about what you need to look at closely on the form, and how to challenge any errors you find, go to the special Medicare web page explaining the latest version of the MSN form: www.medicare.gov/pubs/pdf/SummaryNoticeB.pdf.

You can also receive your MSNs electronically rather than on paper through the mail. If you sign up for electronic MSNs, you'll get a monthly MSN rather than one every three months. You can sign up for that service by going to www.medicare.gov/forms-help-and-resources/e-delivery.html.

Appealing the Denial of a Claim

Unfortunately, not every request for Medicare payment runs a smooth course. Occasionally, a Medicare hospital or nursing facility review committee may decide your inpatient stay need not last as long as you and your doctor think, and will recommend ending Medicare Part A coverage. Or, more commonly, the Medicare carrier will deny Part B coverage for what you believe is a covered medical service. Or sometimes it will cover only some but not all of a treatment that you believe should be covered.

You may appeal any of these decisions. This section explains the procedures you must follow.

Decisions About Inpatient Care (Medicare Part A)

Occasionally, disputes arise about whether treatment as an inpatient in a hospital or skilled nursing facility continues to be medically necessary. These disputes often pit the patient and doctor on one side, and the facility's Medicare review committee on the other. The review committee may believe that the patient can be moved from the hospital to home or to a nursing facility sooner than the doctor advises, or moved from the skilled nursing facility to a nonskilled facility or to home care. If this happens to you, there are several steps you can take to convince Medicare to pay for your continued inpatient care.

Help From the State Health Insurance Assistance Program (SHIP) and Medicare Rights Center

Every state has a program to provide free assistance to any person with questions or problems regarding Medicare, medigap supplemental insurance, Medicare managed care, Medicaid, and long-term care. For example, people often have questions about enrollment, paying bills, and filing appeals. The overall program is called the State Health Insurance Assistance Program (SHIP), though in your state the program may go by one of several different names—Health Insurance Counseling and Advocacy Program (HICAP), Senior Health Insurance Benefits Advisors (SHIBA), or something similar. Whatever the name, the program provides free counseling by professional staff plus trained volunteers. The offices are often connected to legal service agencies that can provide free or low-cost legal advice if the matter involves an interpretation of a law or rule, or a legal battle.

SHIP offices are staffed by dedicated people who are not only knowledgeable and trained to give helpful advice but are also willing to fight for your rights. They sit down with you in person, review your story and papers until they understand your situation, and help you handle the paperwork and telephoning sometimes necessary to make your enrollment or appeal work.

To find the SHIP office nearest you, see the contact information at the end of this chapter.

Help with all sorts of Medicare questions and problems is also available from the nonprofit Medicare Rights Center. Its website, www.medicarerights.org, provides the answers to many common questions about Medicare. And you can call the center toll free at 800-333-4114 to speak, at no cost to you, with a knowledgeable counselor.

Coverage Decisions

Initial Medicare approval of whether your treatment must be as an inpatient is made by the facility's Utilization Review Committee (URC), a group of doctors and hospital administrators. The committee makes this determination before you are admitted, or within one day of your emergency admission. The URC also periodically reviews your condition and progress in the facility, and can decide—after checking your medical records and consulting with your doctor—that you no longer require inpatient care at that facility.

Such a decision does not mean that you will be kicked out of the facility, but it may mean that the URC will recommend to Medicare that your inpatient stay at the facility no longer be covered by Part A insurance. If you and your doctor believe you should remain in the hospital, there are procedures to follow that may reverse the URC's decision. And even if the decision is not reversed, the process of appealing can give you a bit more time in the facility without being personally responsible for the huge inpatient bills.

Notice of Noncoverage. If the URC decides that your condition no longer requires inpatient care, it will consult with your doctor. If your doctor agrees, the URC will give you a written Notice of Noncoverage stating that your Medicare hospitalization coverage will end on a certain day. If you do not feel that you should be discharged from the hospital at that point, first express your wishes to your doctor. Ask that the doctor request from the URC that a longer period of inpatient care be approved.

If your doctor is unavailable, ask to speak with the hospital ombudsman. Many hospitals have an ombudsman who is an independent volunteer whose job is to help mediate disputes between the patient and the hospital.

If the doctor or ombudsman cannot change or delay the URC's decision, or your doctor will not oppose the decision, but you still feel that you should not be discharged, you will have to file an appeal to protect your right to have Medicare Part A cover your inpatient care.

If your doctor disagrees with the URC opinion that you should be discharged, the URC will either back off its decision and not contest your Medicare coverage—in which case you will hear nothing about it—or it will ask for an opinion from the state's Peer Review Organization (PRO). The PRO is a group of doctors who are paid by Medicare to review the medical necessity and appropriateness of inpatient care. This is a bit like the foxes guarding the chickens, but the PROs are also medical professionals who respect the opinions of treating physicians. The PRO will review your medical records, the URC's recommendation, and your doctor's position.

If the PRO agrees that your continued stay at the hospital is medically necessary, you will hear nothing more about the matter and Medicare will continue to cover your inpatient care. However, if the PRO decides that your inpatient care is no longer medically necessary, you will receive a Notice of Noncoverage stating that your coverage for hospitalization will end as of a certain day.

Immediate Review

If you receive a Notice of Noncoverage, it will contain important information, including when the URC intends to end your Medicare coverage and whether your doctor or the state PRO has agreed with the decision. How you'll obtain immediate review—the first step in appealing the decision—differs slightly depending on whether your doctor agreed with the URC or the decision was made by the PRO over your doctor's objection.

Immediate review of joint URC and doctor decision. If the Notice of Noncoverage states that your doctor agreed with the URC that coverage for your inpatient care should end, you must take some action to get the process moving.

If you are in the hospital, chances are you may have physical difficulty making phone calls and having conversations to get your immediate review started. You may have a friend or relative act on your behalf by making the necessary call requesting review of your case. You may also ask your doctor to initiate the review, even though he or she initially agreed with the URC's recommendation that Medicare inpatient coverage should end on the specified date. You can ask to speak with the hospital ombudsman, who can then make your request for immediate review.

Once the PRO has been notified that you are requesting immediate review, it will contact you in order to discuss the matter.

Request an immediate review by the PRO by noon of the first workday after you receive the Notice of Noncoverage. Contact may be made by phone or in writing at the number and address of the PRO given on the notice.

A representative of the PRO will speak with you directly about why you believe you still require inpatient care—and with the doctor who had you admitted to the hospital, or with the physician overseeing your care.

Your Doctor Can Be Your Best Ally

The most important element in winning an appeal, particularly for coverage of inpatient care, is gaining your doctor's cooperation. The decision on a Medicare appeal often depends on what the doctor notes in your medical records about your condition and the treatment involved—and on how much assistance you can get from the doctor in providing clarification to the people doing your Medicare review.

The problem is that many doctors view their responsibility to the patient as including only the technical treatment of a medical condition: your body and how it works. Many doctors are not particularly concerned with how you pay the bill, as long as you pay it. And if it's someone else's bill—the hospital's, for example—the doctor may not care if it's paid at all.

If you are fortunate, your doctor will give some attention to your Medicare needs, calling the Medicare appeal personnel and writing a letter, if necessary. If so, you'll find the Medicare appeal process fairly simple. But if your doctor won't take the time to listen to your Medicare problem and help you with the appeal, you may have a frustrating time, which cannot help your recovery process. It may also prompt you to consider changing doctors.

TIP

Try again with your doctor. Help from your doctor is the best hope you have of convincing the PRO to approve your continued coverage. Speak with the doctor again and try to change his or her mind. Sometimes a doctor agrees with the URC decision on care without consulting the patient, or based on an expectation of the patient's improvement that has not occurred. Also, there may be more than one doctor treating you. If so, try to enlist the help of your other doctors. Ask them to speak with your admitting physician to convince him or her that you need more inpatient care.

The PRO will review your case and, within a matter of days, inform you directly of its decision—either by phone or in writing. If the PRO agrees with the facility that your coverage should end, coverage will continue only until noon of the day after you receive notice of the PRO's decision. After that, the facility will bill you for all inpatient costs.

TIP

Your coverage will continue during the review. If you have requested an immediate review of a joint URC and doctor decision, Medicare will continue to cover your inpatient care until the PRO makes a decision.

Immediate review of a URC decision your doctor opposes. If your doctor believes that you need to remain in the hospital but the URC disagrees, the URC will have taken your case to the PRO before you receive a Notice of Noncoverage. And the notice will tell you that the PRO has already agreed with the URC.

You must still ask the PRO for immediate review. But unless you and your doctor can present some strong reasons why the decision should be changed, it will likely remain in effect.

The review process should then proceed as follows:

- Contact the PRO at once by phone or in writing to explain why you believe your continued inpatient care is necessary.
- Ask your doctor—or several doctors if more than one is treating you—to immediately call the PRO to give reasons why your inpatient care continues to be medically necessary. If doctors who are treating you have not previously been in contact with the PRO regarding your case, they can help immensely now by backing up what your admitting physician has said about your continuing need for inpatient care.
- Within three working days of your request for review, the PRO will notify you in writing of its decision.
- Medicare Part A coverage will end the third day after you receive the Notice of Noncoverage, even if the PRO has not yet decided. If the PRO takes the full three days to decide on your coverage and then agrees with the Notice of Noncoverage, you will be personally responsible for the full cost of one full day of hospital costs—the day after coverage stops but on which the PRO has not yet decided.

If the PRO upholds the decision that your inpatient coverage should end, that is not the last word on your Medicare coverage. Similarly, if you did not request immediate review, you can still appeal the decision of noncoverage. Several stages of appeal are open to you, as described below.

Have Your Bill Submitted to Medicare

Whether or not you asked for immediate review, you must ask that the hospital or other facility billing office submit the bill to the Medicare intermediary for payment. If you can get strong backing from your doctors, the intermediary might reverse the decision of the URC. Without such support, however, the intermediary will probably uphold the decision of the URC. Either way, if you want to pursue an appeal of the decision, you must have the hospital submit the bill to Medicare. Only by getting a Medicare carrier's decision can you move your appeal to the next stage.

Unfortunately, while the intermediary is deciding on your claim, the hospital or nursing facility may bill you for the uncovered part of your inpatient stay. If you pay the bill and later win your appeal, Medicare will reimburse you.

Reconsideration of Carrier's Decision

If the Medicare intermediary denies the claim for payment of part of your inpatient bill, you have 60 days from the date you receive the denial notice to submit a request for reconsideration. You'll find the address for sending this request on the notice denying your claim.

This reconsideration will be made by what Medicare calls a Qualified Independent Contractor (QIC). The QIC was not involved in the original determination of your appeal.

This request for reconsideration can be made by filing a special *Medicare Reconsideration Request* form. You can find this form online on Medicare's official website at www.cms.gov/Medicare/CMS-Forms/CMS-Forms/downloads/cms20033.pdf. Or, this request can be made in the form of a simple letter explaining why your stay in the facility continues to be necessary. Once again, however, it is not so much what you say in your letter as whether you have the support of one or more of your doctors. Ask every doctor who supports your position to send a letter to the intermediary stating his or her medical opinion, and also to give you a copy. Attach a copy of each doctor's letter to your request for reconsideration, and always keep an extra copy for yourself.

It is sometimes difficult to get a doctor to write a letter on your behalf, even if the doctor supports your position. Sometimes it is simply a matter of the doctor being too busy, or not concerned enough with your financial problem, to speak with you in person before you must send in your request for reconsideration. Other doctors charge a fee for writing any letter that does not involve consultation about treatment— as opposed to payment of bills—and the fee may be too high for you.

If you have not obtained a letter from a doctor who supports your position, at least list his or her name and phone number in your request to the QIC. Ask that the QIC contact the doctor before completing its reconsideration.

The QIC will give you a written decision on its reconsideration. If it again denies coverage, you have 60 days to begin the next step in the appeal process.

TIP
Put everything in writing and keep copies. Keep copies of all correspondence and other papers concerning Medicare claims and appeals. Also, keep notes on all conversations you have with your doctor, representatives from the hospital, the PRO, and the intermediary. Write down the date of the conversation, the name of the person with whom you talked, and what information was given or taken.

Request an Administrative Hearing

If, upon reconsideration, your appeal is denied by the QIC, you have 60 days from the date on the QIC's written decision to request a hearing by an administrative law judge (ALJ). The hearing is held before an ALJ who is attached to a local office of the Office of Medicare Hearings and Appeals (OMHA). You may ask that an actual hearing be held, which the ALJ will conduct either in person or by telephone. Or you may ask that the ALJ decide your appeal without a hearing, just by reviewing written materials. You can request a decision by an ALJ only if the amount you're contesting is $140 or more.

The form for requesting this administrative hearing is provided online by Medicare at www.cms.gov/Medicare/CMS-Forms/CMS-Forms/downloads/cms20034ab.pdf. For more information about how the hearing process works, you can go directly to the website of the Office of Medicare Hearings and Appeals at www.hhs.gov/omha.

As with every other stage of a Medicare appeal, your doctors' cooperation is the single most important element. Your doctor could appear personally at the hearing and testify on your behalf in front of the judge, but most doctors would charge an arm and a leg to do this. Instead, ask your doctor—or several of your doctors, if possible—to write an explanation of why your medical condition required inpatient treatment. You can then present the written explanation to the judge. Be aware that many doctors charge for writing such a letter, and Medicare laws permit them to do so.

Appeals Council and Federal Lawsuit

If the decision of the administrative law judge goes against you, you can file an appeal to the Social Security Appeals Council. And if that appeal goes against you, you can file an action in federal court challenging the Medicare decision. (See Chapter 9 for more information.)

You can file such a lawsuit only if the amount you are contesting is $1,400 or more. Because of the time and expense involved, it is likely you would file such a lawsuit only if the amount is quite a bit higher than that anyway. If you are considering such a lawsuit at this stage, consult with an experienced attorney. You may be able to get a referral to such an attorney from a SHIP office (see contact information at the end of this chapter).

Payment of Doctor and Other Medical Bills (Part B)

During the course of one or more of your Medicare Part B medical insurance claims, you may disagree with the carrier's decision about whether a particular treatment or service is covered by Medicare. If you find that the Medicare carrier has denied coverage for a certain bill, you have a right to appeal. However, the Medicare Part B appeal process is quite limited, and most people have more success informally contacting the carrier than they do with formal appeals.

Read the Medicare Summary Notice

The place to start with a question or complaint about your Medicare Part B coverage of a particular treatment or service is the *Medicare Summary Notice* (MSN) you receive from the carrier. (See "How to Read a *Medicare Summary Notice*," above, for a discussion of the MSN.) It not only shows whether a health care service is covered but also gives a description of the service, a Medicare code number—called a procedure code—for the service, and an explanation of why a particular service was not covered.

Certain services are covered if they are described one way by your doctor's office in the Medicare forms they submit, but not covered if described differently. These problems are sometimes caused simply by a wrongly placed checkmark—for example, indicating a routine physical exam (not covered) instead of indicating physical examination for a particular patient complaint (covered). Such a mistake could be made by any number of people involved in handling your claim: your doctor, someone in your doctor's office, or someone in the Medicare carrier's vast paperwork machinery.

The MSN may also indicate that you were denied coverage for a particular service because you had the service performed too frequently during a given time. For example, you may have had two mammograms in one year when Medicare normally only covers one per year. However, if the treatment was determined to be medically necessary by your doctor—because, for example, you have a family history of breast cancer, or prior exams have disclosed potential problems—Medicare can and should cover the second mammogram.

In either situation, the next step is to contact your doctor's office to get a letter supporting the medical necessity for the treatment provided.

Check With Your Doctor's Office

If you believe that the MSN incorrectly describes the service or treatment you had, call your doctor's office and ask whether the claim form sent to Medicare had the same information as shown on your MSN. If either the claim form or the MSN had incorrect information, ask that the doctor's office contact the carrier with the correct information.

If coverage was denied because Medicare claims the treatment was not medically necessary or that you received the treatment too often, ask the doctor to write a letter explaining why the treatment was medically necessary. Also, ask that doctor to make a copy of any of your medical records that support this conclusion—and to send the letter and records to you so that you can then deal with the Medicare carrier.

Contact the Medicare Carrier

Most mistakes in billing and coverage are corrected informally, by phone and letter. The Medicare carriers know that mistakes are often made, and they would rather correct them quickly and inexpensively than go through a lengthy and more costly appeal process.

The number to call to reach your carrier is printed in the "Customer Service Information" box in the upper right-hand corner of the first page of your MSN. When you reach your Medicare carrier, give your name, your Medicare number, and the date of the MSN, explaining that you want to discuss coverage of a particular item. Then explain why you believe a mistake was made and describe your doctor's response to the problem. If you have a letter or any medical records from the doctor that explain matters, tell the Medicare carrier what you have. The carrier will either contact your doctor's office or ask you to send in a copy of your doctor's letter, or both.

If this informal contact results in a change in decision by the Medicare carrier, it will send you a revised MSN explaining what the new Medicare payments are and how much you owe. If it does not change the coverage decision based on this informal contact, your next step would be to push on to a more formal written appeal.

Write a Request for Redetermination

If you have not been able to resolve the coverage question informally, you have 120 days from the date you receive the MSN within which to file a written request for redetermination of the carrier's decision—also called a request for review. The bottom of the second page of your MSN provides information and a short form to help you appeal the decision.

Make a copy of the MSN, circle the items you want to challenge, sign the back of the copy, and send it to the carrier listed on the front of the form. Although the MSN says you may write your appeal on the form itself, it is better to send along a separate, signed letter with the MSN, stating your reasons for appealing. There is very little space allowed for your statement on the appeal form, usually not enough to explain your reasoning adequately. Or, you can file your request for redetermination on a form provided by Medicare online at www.cms.gov/cmsforms/downloads/CMS20027.pdf, but this form, too, has only limited space to explain your reasons for requesting a change in Medicare's decision.

The letter should include your full name as it appears on the MSN, your Medicare number, the date of the MSN, the date of the disputed medical service, and a brief explanation of why you believe the treatment or other service should be covered. Include any letter or other records from your doctor that support your position.

TIP
Hold on to the documents. Keep copies of all letters and documents you send to or receive from the Medicare carrier and from your doctor. Also, keep notes of every conversation you have with anyone at the Medicare carrier, including the date of conversation, the name of the person with whom you spoke, and any action decided upon in the phone call—such as, you will send them a letter, they will contact your doctor, or they will call you back within a week.

Time to Seek Assistance

If you are considering a request for a review of your medical bills, or you have completed the written review and are considering a request for a hearing, it may be time for you to get some assistance from a local State Health Insurance Assistance Program (SHIP) office (see contact information at the end of this chapter). This is particularly true if the amount you are contesting would put a sizable hole in your budget.

If you are considering an appeal to an administrative law judge for a hearing, you may want to consider not only help from SHIP but also the assistance of an experienced Medicare lawyer. (See Chapter 9 for tips on finding legal help.) SHIP can also help refer you to such lawyers.

On the following pages are samples of request for redetermination letters to a Medicare carrier. There are no magic words you must include in such a letter, but these examples demonstrate the kind of simple information required. A letter should include several key points, each of which should be described as briefly and clearly as possible. Keep in mind that the letter is meant merely to point out how and where the error was made and where proof of the error can be found, not to serve as proof itself. Only your medical records and the opinion of your doctors can actually prove anything.

First, you should briefly describe the treatment you received.

Second, you should point out the specific reasons why the intermediary's decision not to cover the treatment was incorrect—for example, you did not have merely a routine physical exam but an exam to determine the cause of a specific problem, or you did not have a dental exam but an examination by an oral surgeon of the nerves in your jaw.

Third, refer to the doctor's letter or other medical records that support your claim.

Notice that at the bottom left of each letter is the notation "cc:" and next to it the name of the doctor. This indicates to the Medicare carrier that you have sent a copy of this letter to your doctor—an action you should take so that the letter goes into your medical file. Sending a copy of the letter to the doctor will help prepare the doctor if the Medicare carrier contacts him or her, and it may remind the doctor to do a better job of explaining the medical necessity of your care the next time you have treatment.

When the carrier reconsiders your claim, it will review your file, check the documents on which the original decision was made, and investigate any new information you have presented or the carrier has obtained by contacting your doctor. You do not have an opportunity at this stage to appear in person and explain things.

If a mistake was made because incorrect or incomplete information had originally been provided to the carrier or someone made a simple clerical error, the carrier is likely to reverse its decision and provide you with coverage. You will then receive a written notice of its review determination and a new MSN.

Request for Redetermination Letter: Sample #1

Betty Patient
222 Public Street
Consumer, USA 12345
Telephone: 123-123-1234

March 1, 20xx

Transprofit Insurance Company
P.O. Box 123
Moneyville, USA 12345

Re: Request for Review and Redetermination
Medicare Part B
Medicare Number xx-xxx-xxxxA
MSN Notice dated January 2, 20xx

To Whom It Concerns:

This letter is a request for review and redetermination of a decision made by Transprofit denying coverage of medical treatment I received on November 1, 20xx. A copy of the MSN notice of January 2, 20xx, denying coverage, is enclosed.

I believe that Transprofit denied coverage of the mammogram I received on November 1, 20xx, from Dr. Alice Well because I had previously had a mammogram in January 20xx, which Medicare covered, and Medicare does not normally cover more than one mammogram per year. However, this second mammogram was medically necessary because I have a family history of breast cancer and because my previous mammogram in January showed some spots of potentially cancerous tissue.

Apparently the original Medicare claim from my doctor's office did not include this background information. However, I am enclosing a copy of a letter from Dr. Well and a copy of the medical records from my January mammogram to indicate why the second mammogram was medically necessary.

Based on this information, please reconsider the original decision denying Medicare coverage of the November 1, 20xx treatment.

Yours truly,

Betty Patient

cc: Dr. Alice Well

Request for Redetermination Letter: Sample #2

Andy Q. Everyone
18B Main Street
Anytown, USA 12345
Telephone: 222-222-2222

June 1, 20xx

Ourworld Insurance Inc.
P.O. Box 567
Big Money, USA 12345

Re: Request for Review and Redetermination
Medicare Part B
Medicare Number xx-xxx-xxxxB
MSN Notice dated March 1, 20xx

To Whom It Concerns:

This letter is a request for review and redetermination of a decision made by Ourworld Insurance denying coverage of medical treatment I received on January 10, 20xx. A copy of the MSN notice of March 1, 20xx, denying coverage, is enclosed.

I believe that Ourworld Insurance denied coverage of the eye exam I received on January 10, 20xx, from Dr. Barry Eyesore, because Dr. Eyesore's office mistakenly noted on the Medicare claim form that I underwent a routine eye examination refraction on that date, marking on the form Procedure Code 92015.

This was a mistake. In fact, I had a specific examination and treatment for blurred vision and eye pain that I had been suffering. Dr. Eyesore's records indicate that this was a medically necessary examination for a medical condition, for which he prescribed medication, rather than a routine eye examination. Enclosed is a copy of my medical record from Dr. Eyesore indicating the nature of the exam on that date.

Based on this additional information, please reconsider the original decision denying Medicare coverage of the January 10, 20xx examination and treatment of my eyes.

Yours truly,

Andy Q. Everyone

cc: Dr. Barry Eyesore

If there is a dispute about whether a certain treatment truly was medically necessary, the carrier may well reverse itself at this stage, but it does so less often than in cases of simple clerical errors or missing documentation from the doctor.

Once the Medicare carrier has received your request for redetermination and your supporting documents, someone within the company who was not involved in making the original decision will decide on your request. You will receive a written response from the carrier, called a Medicare Redetermination Notice, about 60 days after you file your request and supporting papers. It will contain information about a further appeal if you are not satisfied with the decision.

Request for Reconsideration by Qualified Independent Contractor (QIC)

If the carrier reviews your file and still refuses to cover your treatment, you can continue your appeal by requesting a reconsideration.

You have 180 days from the date you receive the written notice of determination to request a reconsideration by what's called a Qualified Independent Contractor (QIC). A QIC is a company separate from the Medicare carrier itself. The address to which to send your request is printed on the carrier's written notice of determination.

You can file your Request for Reconsideration on a form provided by Medicare online at www.cms.gov/cmsforms/downloads/CMS20033. pdf. However, space on the form is limited, and you may prefer to write a letter request instead, an example of which is shown below (see "Letter Requesting Reconsideration by QIC"). The letter requesting a reconsideration is similar to the letter requesting redetermination, except that you should refer to the date of the carrier's written notice of determination following your request for redetermination in addition to the original MSN.

In separate paragraphs, make the following points:

- Describe the treatment you received and the dates on which you received it. This description should be brief, since the carrier will get its full explanation from your medical records.

- State the specific reasons why the intermediary's initial decision not to cover the treatment was incorrect.
- Refer, by name and date, to your doctor's letter and to the specific medical records that support your claim.

Attach to your request for a reconsideration copies of letters from your doctors and of your medical records, if you have them. Also, call your doctors' offices to request that they send copies of your records to the address you have been given on the notice.

You will get a written decision, called a Medicare Reconsideration Notice, from the QIC within about 60 days after you file your request for reconsideration. If you are not satisfied with this decision, you have 60 days from the date you receive the notice to request a hearing before an administrative law judge.

Hearing Before Administrative Law Judge

If your claim for doctor bill coverage is once again denied after the reconsideration by the QIC, you can request a hearing before an administrative law judge if the amount you are contesting is $150 or more. If the amount in dispute is less than $150, the hearing before the carrier's hearing officer is the end of the line.

You must request a hearing before an administrative law judge within 60 days of the date you receive written notice of the decision by the carrier's hearing officer. (See Chapter 9 for a full discussion of the administrative hearing process.) Medicare provides an online form to request this hearing at www.cms.gov/cmsforms/downloads/CMS20034AB.pdf.

Medicare Appeals Council Review

If you do not receive a favorable ruling from the administrative law judge, you may appeal the decision to the Medicare Appeals Council. In Medicare Part B claims, the written appeal must be filed within 60 days of the date of the administrative law judge's written decision.

Letter Requesting Reconsideration by QIC

Rosa Albertez
3456 Broadway Anytown, USA 45678
Telephone: 333-333-3333

June 1, 20xx

Your Money Insurance Co.
P.O. Box 1234
Greentown, USA 12345

Re: Request for Reconsideration by QIC, Medicare Part B
Medicare Number xx-xxx-xxxxC
Notice of Determination After Review Dated May 1, 20xx

To Whom It Concerns:

This letter is a request for a reconsideration by QIC following a determination made on May 1, 20xx. That determination upheld a decision made by Your Money denying coverage of a medical service I received on February 1, 20xx, and laboratory work performed on February 5, 20xx. A copy of the MSN notice of March 15, 20xx, denying coverage, is enclosed. Also enclosed is a copy of the written determination after review, dated May 1, 20xx.

I believe that Your Money denied coverage of the physical examination I received from Dr. Walter Thorough and of laboratory work ordered by Dr. Thorough because Dr. Thorough failed to give certain information to the carrier. The physical and the laboratory tests were not routine examinations but were a response to severe muscle fasciculation and cramping that I had been suffering over the previous several weeks. Dr. Thorough's records indicate that the examination and laboratory tests were medically necessary to diagnose and treat my condition.

I have enclosed a copy of my medical records from Dr. Thorough, as well as a letter from Dr. Thorough, both of which make clear that the examination and laboratory tests were medically necessary and should be covered by Medicare.

Yours truly,

Rosa Albertez

cc: Dr. Walter Thorough

Federal Court Case

It is highly unlikely that a Medicare Part B decision will involve enough money that it would be economically sensible for you, and a lawyer representing you, to file a lawsuit in federal court to challenge a negative decision by the Medicare Appeals Council. However, if your claim is for $1,500 or more, you do have such a right. You must file the lawsuit within 60 days of the written decision by the Appeals Council.

Medicare Part D: Enrollment, Exceptions, and Appeals

How you enroll in a Part D plan will depend on several factors, including whether you:

- receive Medicaid benefits
- live in a long-term care facility
- have had employer-sponsored health coverage that included drug coverage, and
- qualify for a Part D low-income subsidy.

Note that if you believe you might be eligible for the Part D low-income subsidy, you must file two separate applications—one for Part D coverage, and one for the low-income subsidy.

Once you are enrolled in a Part D plan, your plan's decisions about coverage and costs are not necessarily final. The plan may exclude one of your drugs from coverage, may require you to jump through hoops to get coverage for a particular drug, or may charge you a higher copayment for your drug than for a generic equivalent. In any of these situations, you have the right to request an exception. And you have the right to appeal the plan's decision.

Enrollment

How and when you enroll in a Part D plan depends on whether you are a Medicaid beneficiary or have been accepted for a Part D low-income subsidy. Regardless of the plan you enroll in or how you are enrolled, your coverage will not begin until the first of the month following the completion of your enrollment.

Applying for Extra Help Paying for Medicare Part D

Medicare's Extra Help program offers different levels of assistance (also called a low-income subsidy) to help pay for the cost of prescription drugs above and beyond what a standard Part D plan pays. (See Chapter 12.) But you apply for Extra Help by sending an application to the Social Security Administration (SSA) rather than to Medicare or to a Part D plan. Contact the SSA to get an Extra Help application and instructions. You can reach the SSA toll free at 800-772-1213, or visit the special Social Security website page called "Extra Help with Medicare Prescription Drug Plan Costs," at www.ssa.gov/medicare/prescriptionhelp, to file an application online. In person, you can apply at a Social Security office near you. Or, you can also apply for Extra Help at a local county Social Services office or another local government office in your state that processes Medicaid applications.

Free one-on-one help is available at your local SHIP or HICAP office. These programs have trained counselors on staff to help you with your application. To find the office nearest you, contact the SHIP or HICAP program in your state (for details, see the end of this chapter).

If your application for Extra Help is approved, the benefits will be retroactive to the date you first applied. Once approved, your participation in Extra Help will remain in effect for one year. Within the first year of your Extra Help, the Social Security Administration will review your finances to see if you remain eligible. If so, your participation in Extra Help will be automatically renewed. After the first year, SSA will periodically review your Extra Help eligibility.

Enrolling in a Part D Plan

Most people will follow the standard enrollment procedures described below. If you are a Medicaid beneficiary or are qualified for a Part D low-income subsidy, your enrollment procedures will differ slightly (see below).

Standard enrollment. If you are not a Medicaid beneficiary and have not qualified for a Part D low-income subsidy, you enroll in Part D by signing up directly with the plan you want to join. Private insurance companies administer each Part D plan using their own enrollment forms and procedures. Some plans may permit you to enroll online, while others may require written forms. You must contact the plan directly to find out the details of their coverage and costs, and to enroll in the plan.

Your Part D plan will cover the cost of your medications only after you have completed enrollment in the plan and your Medicare Part A or B coverage has begun. This means that any drugs you buy while your application is pending will not be covered. It is therefore a good idea to decide on a plan and submit an application in the months before you become eligible for Medicare, so that coverage will begin as soon as you are eligible.

If you do not enroll in a Part D plan when you are first eligible for it, your premiums will be higher when you do finally enroll. Medicare charges an additional 1% for each month you delay enrolling. So, if you intend to enroll in a Part D plan as soon as you are eligible for Medicare, you should do the paperwork ahead of time. This will ensure not only that your coverage begins immediately, but also that you will not have to pay a higher premium because of a simple paperwork delay.

Medicaid beneficiary. If you are a Medicare beneficiary who is also eligible for Medicaid assistance (Medi-Cal in California), you may enroll in any Part D plan. But in order to get the full benefit of your low-income subsidy, you must enroll in a plan whose premium is at or below your state's average. If you enroll in a plan with a premium higher than the state average, you will be responsible for the extra premium cost out of your own pocket.

If you don't enroll in a Part D plan on your own, the Medicare program will automatically enroll you in a plan with a premium below the state's average. And if that plan doesn't fit your needs for drug coverage, you may switch plans at any time (see "Switching Part D Plans," below).

Low-income subsidized enrollment. If you are eligible for one of the Part D low-income subsidies but are not a Medicaid beneficiary, you may enroll in a Part D plan at any time, directly with the plan of your choice. If at any later time your plan no longer offers you the best coverage, you may switch to another plan (see "Switching Part D Plans," below).

Exceptions

Part D plans use a variety of methods to restrict or control the use of medications by their enrollees, thereby reducing their own costs. (See "Part D Prescription Drug Coverage" in Chapter 12.) These restrictions include excluding drugs from coverage, setting higher costs for certain drugs within the same class, substituting one drug for another, imposing a drug supply limit, and requiring you to try a series of other drugs before the plan will cover the one you want.

Medicare gives plans very broad discretion to create and change coverage restrictions. This means that you may begin coverage with a plan whose restrictions do not seriously affect you, only to find the plan changes its rules later on. You may then find yourself with a restriction on one of your drugs that is financially burdensome, physically discomfiting, or even medically dangerous. For example, your plan may drop one of your drugs from its formulary and replace it with a drug that the plan considers "equivalent," but this drug may not provide you with the same quality of relief or may have more side effects. Or, your plan may increase the copayment for your drug, costing you more money per prescription.

Eventually, you may be able to switch to a plan with fewer restrictions on your drugs. But until you are able to do so, or if there is no other plan available at the same cost with fewer restrictions, you have a chance to get your plan to lift its restriction in your individual case. You do this by requesting an "exception" from your plan's rules, based on "medical necessity." You make this request to the plan itself, not to Medicare. Each plan has its own rules for handling exception requests, and Medicare requires only that a plan have a formal procedure and make a decision, called a "Coverage Determination," within 72 hours after you file an exception request.

Medical necessity. Your doctor's support is the key to success with any exception request. To convince your plan that you need easier access to your drug, you must show that you have a medical necessity to take that particular drug rather than another drug that the plan considers equivalent. Medical necessity does not necessarily mean that you will have very serious or dangerous medical consequences if you take the equivalent drug. But it does mean that there will be some change in your physical condition—for example, less effective treatment or more severe side effects—if you take the so-called equivalent drug instead of the one you usually take.

Help With Exceptions and Appeals

As discussed in these sections about exceptions and appeals, it's crucial to have your doctor's help in explaining the medical necessity of a particular drug. But your doctor can only do so much—he or she is not going to help you fill out request and appeal forms, or write your letters to the insurance company explaining your situation. To get help with the exception or appeal process itself, you may want to contact the counselors at your local SHIP or HICAP office, whose expert advice is free. You can find the local office of these counseling organizations by calling the central office for your state; for contact information, see the end of this chapter.

You can also get free expert counseling from the Medicare Rights Center; contact them through www.medicarerights.org.

If your appeal reaches the later stages, and particularly if you intend to take it to federal court, you will likely need the assistance of a lawyer experienced in Medicare appeals. (For a discussion of when a lawyer may be needed, and how to find one, see Chapter 9.)

Your chance of convincing the plan of your medical need for a particular drug almost certainly requires an explanation from your doctor. The plan may request a letter from your doctor, or a copy of your medical records demonstrating your complaints to the doctor about the substituted medicine, or simply a phone conversation with your doctor. Whatever form the contact will take, it is important that you prepare your doctor to explain your problem. Meet with or talk to your doctor by phone about the problem and about your exception request. This will allow you to make certain that the doctor understands the full extent of your difficulty with the substituted drug, and gives the doctor advance warning that the plan will be requesting information.

If the plan denies your request for an exception, you may file an appeal. Appeals are discussed below. And if your appeal is denied, or if you simply do not want to bother going through the appeal process, you can switch to another plan that offers better coverage of your drug (if you can find one) as soon as you are permitted to switch by Part D enrollment rules (see "Switching Part D Plans," below).

Appeals

Part D plans regularly make decisions and change rules about their drug coverage. But these decisions and rules are not necessarily the final word about coverage. You can appeal a plan's rule or decision if you find that it forces you to give up, or pay a higher copay for, a drug you and your doctor believe is medically necessary. Appeals initially go to the plan itself. At later stages, an appeal may be considered by independent reviewers outside the plan.

If at any stage of the process an enrollee wins a change in the plan's decision, its effect will be retroactive back to the time the enrollee first challenged the plan's coverage decision. This retroactivity works well when the issue is the amount of money an enrollee has to pay out of pocket. Retroactivity is only cold comfort, however, if the enrollee has been forced to make do with a substitute drug during the time spent on the appeal.

In almost every case, success with an appeal depends on your doctor's presenting a convincing argument that the drug in question is "medically necessary" to you (see "Exceptions," above).

Types of Decisions That Can Be Appealed

Part D enrollees may appeal several types of plan decisions, including a plan's:

- denial of an exception request
- decision not to cover a drug, or to cover it only at a higher copay because it is not on the plan's formulary or because of some other access restriction (such as step therapy or therapeutic substitution)
- decision not to cover a drug for a particular enrollee because it is not "medically necessary"
- decision not to cover a drug because it is excluded from the Medicare Part D program, and
- decision not to cover a drug, or to cover it at a higher copay, because it was provided by a pharmacy that did not have a contract with the plan (called an out-of-network pharmacy).

Appeal Procedure

Each plan determines the details of its appeal procedure. But all plans must follow certain basic rules.

Coverage determination. When a plan makes a decision about coverage or an exception request, it issues a written letter called a "coverage determination." The plan must issue the coverage determination within 72 hours of the enrollee's filling of a prescription, denial of a prescription, or request for an exception.

Redetermination. Once an enrollee receives an unfavorable written coverage determination from the plan, the enrollee has 60 days to request what is called a "redetermination." This second-round decision will also be made by the plan itself, though it may be made by someone within the plan bureaucracy other than the person who made the original coverage determination. From the date the plan receives a written request for redetermination, it has seven days within which to issue its redetermination decision.

Reconsideration. If an enrollee's request for redetermination still does not result in a favorable decision, the enrollee may file a written request for reconsideration by an Independent Review Entity (IRE). This is where an independent arbitrator reviews and considers both the enrollee's request and the plan's reasons for denying the request. An enrollee must file a request for reconsideration by an IRE within 60 days following receipt of the redetermination decision. Your plan will provide contact information for the IRE that will hear your request. Once the IRE receives your written request for reconsideration, it has seven days to make a decision.

Administrative hearing. If the IRE turns down the enrollee's request, the enrollee has 60 days within which to file a request for a hearing before an administrative law judge (ALJ). To have an administrative hearing with an ALJ, the amount in controversy must be at least $150. But unless the drug coverage question for an enrollee involves only a one-time prescription, the ongoing cost of the drug to the enrollee will almost always exceed $150. The ALJ must issue a decision within 90 days from the date of receiving the request.

Medicare Appeals Council. If the enrollee gets a negative decision from the ALJ, the enrollee has 60 days to file an appeal to the next highest level, called the Medicare Appeals Council (MAC). The MAC has 90 days to issue its decision.

Federal court. If the MAC denies an enrollee's appeal, and the amount in controversy concerning the drug is at least $1,500, the enrollee may file a claim in federal court. The enrollee has 60 days from the MAC's decision to file the claim in federal court. If your coverage issue involves continuing expensive medication and you believe that appealing your decision to federal court may be worth the time and expense, you almost certainly will want to consult with an attorney who specializes in Medicare appeals. For more information on hiring an attorney, see Chapter 9.

Switching Part D Plans

The fact that you have enrolled in a particular Part D prescription drug plan does not mean that you are forever stuck with that plan, or with the insurance company that issued the plan. There are several good reasons why you might want to switch from one plan to another. You may want to switch plans in the following cases:

- You begin taking a new medication, and your old plan does not cover that drug or covers it at a higher copayment than offered by another plan.
- Your current plan drops one of your drugs from its list of covered medications.
- Your current plan raises its premiums, or changes its terms of coverage, making a different plan a better fit for you.
- A new plan is offered, or you learn about another plan, which would give you better coverage or lower costs than your current plan.

Whatever your reason, you may switch plans—to a different plan offered by the same insurance company or to a plan with a different company—at least once every year. And some people may switch as often as every month.

When You May Switch Plans

Monthly switch. People in two different categories may switch from one Part D plan to another as often as every month, with the new plan's coverage beginning on the first of the month following enrollment. Dual eligibles—people enrolled in both Medicare and Medicaid (Medi-Cal in California)—may switch plans as often as monthly. And a person who lives in a long-term care nursing facility (if the facility is certified by Medicare or Medicaid) may also switch plans monthly.

Once-yearly switch. Low-income subsidy beneficiaries and standard enrollees (people who do not receive Medicaid coverage and who do not reside in a long-term care facility) may switch plans once a year, but the switch must happen during an open enrollment period (from October 15 to December 7 each year).

Plans You May Switch To

If you want to switch from one Part D drug plan to another, you may switch to any Medicare-approved plan currently offered in your state by any company. If you are switching during the open enrollment period from October 15 to December 7 of each year, you may enroll in any plan being offered for the following calendar year, to begin coverage on January 1.

If you are a dual-eligible beneficiary (Medicare and Medicaid or Medi-Cal), the full cost of your Part D premium is paid by Medicare, as long as your plan's premium is less than your state's average for all Part D plans. If you want to continue receiving that full premium payment, you may only switch to a new plan with a premium lower than your state's average premium. If you switch to a plan with a premium above your state average, you must pay the difference between the new premium and the state average.

How to Switch From One Plan to Another

Switching from one plan to another is not difficult, but it does involve several steps.

Step 1: Find a plan in your area. Find out what plans are offered in your geographic area and select a plan that's right for you, using the selection methods explained in "Part D Prescription Drug Coverage" in Chapter 12.

Step 2: Enroll in the new plan. Once you've found a plan you like, contact the insurance company directly to make sure you are eligible for the plan. If you are eligible, follow the insurance company's directions to enroll in the plan.

Step 3: Cancel your old plan. Once you receive written confirmation from your new insurance company that you are enrolled in your new plan, it's time to cancel your old plan. Notify your old plan—in writing —that you are canceling your policy. Do this even if the new insurance company has told you that it will notify the old company. Make sure that your cancellation is effective after your new plan is in effect.

CAUTION
Don't cancel your old plan too soon. You may be signing up for a new plan to begin the following month, or changing plans during the yearly open enrollment period to begin coverage on January 1. In either case, do not cancel enrollment in your current plan until you have written notification of enrollment in your new plan. And make sure you check the date that the new coverage begins, so that you do not cancel your old plan before the new one goes into effect. As with any bureaucratic institution, delays and mistakes do occur. You want to avoid having any gaps in your insurance coverage.

Step 4: Don't double-pay. Make sure your old and new insurance policies don't overlap. If you pay for your Part D plan by sending the insurance company a check, this is easy—you simply do not send in any payment to the old company once your new coverage begins. But many people have their Part D premium amount automatically paid (for example, withheld from their Social Security benefit or transferred directly from their bank). If you pay your old Part D plan automatically, you must stop the automatic payment as of whatever date you begin your new plan.

Step 5: Notify your pharmacist. After you receive confirmation of enrollment in the new plan, notify the pharmacists you use about your new plan. This will make things go more smoothly when you fill your prescriptions.

State Health Insurance Assistance Programs (SHIPs)

Every state has a nonprofit organization for consumer counseling about Medicare, medigap, Medicare Advantage plans, and related matters. The organization operates under the general name State Health Insurance Assistance Program (SHIP) or Health Insurance Counseling and Advocacy Program (HICAP), though in some states it has a similar but slightly different name. These central offices can direct you to a local counseling office near you. You can find the phone number and website for your state's SHIP/HICAP office on the SHIP-Talk organization website at www.shiptalk.org. You can also find the website for your state's SHIP/HICAP office by going to Medicare's website at www.medicare.gov/Contacts.

Medigap Insurance

Even for people who have coverage from both Medicare Part A and Part B, a serious illness or injury can cause financial havoc because of the bills Medicare leaves unpaid. Well over half of all Medicare recipients age 65 and older respond to this risk by buying a private supplemental health insurance policy known as medigap or med-sup insurance.

The term medigap comes from the fact that these insurance policies are designed to cover the gaps in Medicare payments. Unfortunately, most medigap coverage is not nearly as complete as its advertising would lead you to believe.

The alternatives, managed care and other Medicare Advantage plans, typically provide broader coverage at slightly lower cost than most medigap insurance policies. However, Medicare Advantage plans restrict the doctors and other providers available to you. And in recent years, some Medicare Advantage plans have been raising enrollee costs, reducing coverage, and dropping coverage entirely in many areas, adding an element of risk to the Medicare Advantage option.

Before choosing one type of coverage or another, compare benefits and approaches and measure your preferences against the price you would have to pay for each.

This chapter gives you guidance about the gaps in Medicare that need to be filled, and the types of medigap insurance policies that exist to partially fill them. Chapter 15 covers the various types of Medicare Advantage plans available as alternatives to medigap supplements. Before selecting either a medigap policy or a Medicare Advantage plan, review the advantages and disadvantages discussed in Chapter 15, and use the charts at the end of that chapter to compare the costs of and coverage provided by individual policies and plans.

As with other decisions about Medicare and related insurance coverage, you can get excellent, free counseling regarding medigap insurance from your local office of the State Health Insurance Assistance Program (SHIP), also known in some states as the Health Insurance Counseling and Advocacy Program (HICAP).

Insurance From Continuing or Former Employment

Many people who become eligible for Medicare at age 65 continue to work and have health insurance through their employers. Many others have health insurance through a spouse's employer.

And many other people keep their job-related health insurance after they retire, as part of their retirement benefits packages, although they usually have to pay much more than current employees.

Most employment-based health plans require you to sign up for Medicare Part A when you turn 65, but cover your hospitalization in conjunction with Medicare. Most plans based on current employment do not, however, require you to sign up (and pay for) Medicare Part B, but many retiree plans do require you to enroll in Medicare Part B. The health benefits or human resources office at your work or union can explain the details of coordinating coverage.

The fact that you are eligible for a work-related health plan, however, does not mean that you have to continue with it. Work-related health insurance has become more expensive and less comprehensive for employees—particularly retired employees. You may find that Medicare plus a medigap policy, or Medicare through a Medicare Advantage managed care plan, provides you with as good or better coverage at a better price than your employer-based medical insurance does.

Even if you decide not to participate in the regular health plan offered in your workplace, your employer's insurance company may offer you a different policy with limited coverage for some services Medicare does not cover at all, such as prescription drugs, dental care, or hearing aids. Compare such a policy with the medigap policies and managed care plans discussed in this chapter to see which one offers you the best coverage for your money.

Gaps in Medicare

When considering the kinds of supplemental coverage available, keep in mind the specific gaps in Medicare payments that you are trying to fill. Medicare coverage is explained in detail in Chapter 12, but some of the most significant things it does not cover, or covers but only partially pays for, are listed below.

Gaps in Part A Hospital Insurance

Medicare Part A covers almost all the cost of most hospital stays. Its most common gap is the deductible, which everyone must pay before Medicare pays any part of a hospital bill. A much less frequent but much more frightening gap is the daily coinsurance amount for hospital stays of more than 60 days. All of the gaps are listed below.

Hospital Bills

Medicare Part A hospital insurance does not pay the following costs during a hospital stay:
- a deductible for each benefit period—$1,340 in 2018
- a daily coinsurance amount ($335 in 2018) for each day you are hospitalized more than 60 days and up to 90 days for any one benefit period
- a daily coinsurance amount ($670 in 2018) for each day you are hospitalized more than 90 days and up to 150 days for any one benefit period
- anything past a hospitalization of 150 days
- first three pints of blood, unless replaced, or
- anything during foreign travel.

Skilled Nursing Facility Bills

Medicare Part A does not pay the following costs during a stay in a skilled nursing facility:

- a coinsurance amount of $167.50 per day for each day you are in the facility more than 20 days and up to 100 days for any one benefit period, and
- anything for a stay of more than 100 days.

Home Health Care

Medicare Part A does not pay the following costs for home health care:
- 20% of the approved cost of durable medical equipment or approved nonskilled care, and
- anything for nonmedical personal care services.

Gaps in Part B Medical Insurance

Medicare Part B leaves some very large gaps in the amounts it pays doctors, depending on whether the doctors accept assignment. Everyone faces the 20% of the Medicare-approved amount that Medicare does not pay. And if your doctor does not accept assignment, you are also responsible for up to 15% more than the amount Medicare approves.

Medicare Part B does not pay the following costs for doctors, clinics, laboratories, therapies, medical supplies, or equipment:

- a yearly deductible ($183 in 2018)

- 20% of the Medicare-approved amount

- 15% above the Medicare-approved amount if the provider does not accept assignment, or

- 20% of the total charges for some outpatient hospital services.

Standard Medigap Benefit Plans

The federal government regulates Medicare supplement (medigap) insurance policies—and insurance companies may not offer medigap policies that duplicate Medicare's own coverage. You may choose among the nine currently available standard medigap plans. The standard policies are specifically tailored to Medicare coverage, each one filling a certain number of Medicare's gaps.

Important Changing Landscape for Medigap Policies

First, in 2006, the Medicare Part D prescription drug program went into effect. The Part D program replaced the drug coverage that had been provided in medigap policies under standard plans H, I, and J.

On June 1, 2010, the medigap landscape changed again. New medigap policies in plans E, H, I, and J are no longer sold, though people with existing policies under those plans may continue them. People who continue with these policies should be aware, though, that their premiums are likely to rise more steeply over the coming years because there will be increasingly fewer people enrolled in these plans.

Beginning June 1, 2010, policies began to be issued under two new plans, M and N. Also, the little-used at-home recovery benefit is no longer part of any new policies, and a hospice copayment benefit has been added to new policies under all plans.

For more information on these changes and the coverage provided under each plan type, see "Descriptions of the Standard Medigap Plans," below.

CAUTION

Delay may limit your choices. Insurance companies would be happiest if they could sell coverage only to healthy people. When you're shopping for a medigap policy, you may find it hard to buy a policy if you're already ill. (The Affordable Care Act eliminated preexisting condition limitations for regular private insurance, but not medigap.)

The federal government has, however, established some protections for people buying medigap policies. Being able to take advantage of these protections depends on when and under what circumstances you apply. You'll receive the most coverage options if you apply within the first six months after you begin your Medicare Part B coverage. In a few other circumstances, you may also have options to purchase some, though not all, medigap policies without fear of being turned down because of your preexisting condition. If you wait too long to apply for a policy, however, the insurance companies are allowed to review your medical records and reject you if they consider you a bad profit risk. (To understand the rules regarding your right to purchase a medigap policy, see "Terms and Conditions of Medigap Policies," below.)

Medigap Does Not Cover Long-Term Care

Many older people fear the possibility of living out the final years of life in a nursing home. The prospect of nursing home life itself provokes distress for many, as does the financial ruin that can be brought about by the cost of long-term care. Unfortunately, neither Medicare nor medigap supplemental insurance nor managed care health plans protect against this potentially enormous cost. Medicare covers only a limited period of skilled nursing facility care and covers nothing of long-term custodial, or nonmedical, care in a nursing home. Medigap policies and HMOs similarly fail to cover long-term nursing home care.

Long-term care at home is increasingly an option for people who in years past would have been forced to enter a nursing home. More services are available at home, and more agencies and providers offer home care. However, neither Medicare nor medigap policies cover long-term home health care.

There is a type of private insurance that can cover some of the cost of long-term nursing home or at-home care. Referred to as long-term care insurance, it is available in a variety of benefit packages but comes with numerous restrictions and exclusions. The cost of these policies varies greatly, depending on the extent of coverage and the age of the person covered. Medicaid also covers long-term care costs.

For a complete discussion of these policies, the kinds of care they cover, and Medicaid coverage for nursing homes, see *Long-Term Care: How to Plan & Pay for It*, by Joseph L. Matthews (Nolo). (Visit Nolo's website at www.nolo.com for ordering information.)

Not every company offers every plan. And only the benefits included in the plans are standardized. Other important aspects— premium increases and preexisting illness exclusions—vary from policy to policy and require careful comparison shopping.

When you consider medigap policies, your task is to see how many of the gaps in Medicare payments you can fill within the constraints of your budget. The broader the coverage in a medigap policy, the higher the cost.

And although the benefits are standardized, the cost of a standard policy varies widely from company to company. So you must determine not only which benefit plan best suits your needs, but which company offers which plan at the best price. Then examine the other elements of each policy, such as premium increases and preexisting illness exclusions, before making your choice.

Basic Benefits Included in All Medigap Plans

The benefits included in the standard medigap plans and a chart comparing their coverage follow.

All standard medigap policies begin by offering the same basic benefits, including coverage of:

- hospital coinsurance amounts under Medicare Part A (but not necessarily the deductible)
- 365 days of hospital coverage after Medicare coverage ends
- some or all of the cost of covered blood transfusions
- some or all of the Medicare Part B coinsurance amount (the 20% of Medicare-approved amounts that Medicare Part B does not pay), and
- some or all of the out-of-pocket cost for hospice care (for all policies issued on or after June 1, 2010).

Notice that these basic benefits really are meant to close gaps in Medicare coverage, not to provide separate medical insurance. If a hospitalization or medical treatment is not covered at all by Medicare, a medigap policy will not cover any of it, either. The exception to this is those medigap policies that cover foreign travel.

Inpatient Hospital Costs

For every benefit period, every medigap plan pays all your Medicare Part A coinsurance amounts through your first 90 days as an inpatient, plus your coinsurance amount for any reserve days. After your reserve days are used up, every plan pays for the entire Medicare-approved amount of hospital charges for an additional 365 days. All plans pay some amount for the first three pints of blood you receive (Plans A through J pay the full amount; K pays 50%; L pays 75%). All plans except Plan A pay the yearly Part A hospital inpatient deductible (but Plans K and M pay only 50%, Plan L pays only 75%).

Medigap: It Pays to Shop Around

The federal government decides what benefits must be included in standard medigap policies. But it does not control prices, which vary widely. Prices vary for different ages and change from state to state, reflecting regional health care costs and level of competition for customers.

But the price for the same policy may vary tremendously even within the same state. Even the most basic Plan A policy can vary in cost by hundreds or even thousands of dollars per year in some states. And the more extensive the plan, the greater the cost disparity among policies from different insurance companies.

Most of the time, there is no basis for the price disparities other than "name" recognition. Don't fall for the first policy that comes along. Even when you've decided what standard policy you want, comparison shop for the best price from several different insurance companies.

Medical Expenses

Every plan pays some of the 20% coinsurance amount that Medicare Part B does not pay (except for preventive care copayments, which are covered separately). Plans A through J and Plan M pay the full Part B coinsurance amounts; Plan K pays 50% and Plan L 75% of the Plan B coinsurance amounts (up to those plans' yearly caps, after which they pay 100%). And Plan N pays the full Part B coinsurance amount except for a $20 copayment for office visits and a $50 copayment for emergency room visits (which the patient must pay out of pocket).

Only Plans C, F, and J pay the yearly Medicare Part B deductible. And only Plans F, G, I, and J pay the 15% "excess charges" above the Medicare-approved amount that a doctor is allowed to charge a patient if the doctor does not accept "assignment." (See "How Much Medicare Part B Pays" in Chapter 12 for more on Part B payments.)

CAUTION
Make sure there are limits on premium raises. It is always important to check the terms under which an insurance company may raise the amount of your premium. But it is particularly important when the initial premium already stretches your budget. Pay particular heed to the rules regarding hikes in medigap insurance premiums. (See "Terms and Conditions of Medigap Policies," below.)

Descriptions of the Standard Medigap Plans

Medigap policies are standardized. That means every policy in each lettered plan category must offer the same minimum coverage regardless of which insurance company offers it (though extra coverage may be added, and premiums vary). These standard plans changed as of June 1, 2010. After that date, no new policies are sold in Plans E, H, I, and J. People who are already enrolled in one of those plans' policies will be allowed to continue with it. Also, two new policy categories—Plans M and N—became available as of June 1, 2010.

Special Rules for Massachusetts, Minnesota, and Wisconsin

If you live in Massachusetts, Minnesota, or Wisconsin, the standard medigap policies are somewhat different from the standard policies offered elsewhere. Each of these three states has a basic plan plus options. You pay extra for any of the options you choose. The basic benefits in Massachusetts and Wisconsin include some things that the ten standard medigap policies do not. For information on the details of medigap policies in any of these states, call your state's department of insurance. You'll find its phone number and contact information for its website at the end of this chapter.

Standard Medigap Insurance Policies

All plans include these basic benefits:

- Hospitalization: Medicare Part A coinsurance plus 365 days of coverage after Medicare ends.
- Medical costs for outpatients: Some or all of the Medicare Part B coinsurance (the 20% of Medicare approved costs that Medicare Part B does not pay).
- Blood transfusions: All plans cover some or all of the first three pints of blood each year.
- Hospice: All plans issued June 1, 2010 or later cover hospice copayments (Plan K 50%, Plan L 75%); for policies issued before June 1, 2010, only Plans K and L provided this coverage.

A bullet below means that the plan covers the item 100%.

	A	B	C	D	E[1]	F[6]	G	H[1]	I[1]	J[1]	K	L	M[4]	N[4]
Medicare Part A Deductible		•	•	•	•	•	•	•	•	•	50%	75%	50%	•
Medicare Part B Deductible			•			•				•				
Part B Coinsurance	•	•	•	•	•	•	•	•	•	•	50%	75%	•	$20
Skilled Nursing Coinsurance			•	•	•	•	•	•	•	•	50%	75%	•	•
At-Home Recovery [2]				•			•		•	•				
Blood Transfusion Coinsurance (first three pints of blood)	•	•	•	•	•	•	•	•	•	•	50% of first 3 pints	75% of first 3 pints	•	•
Foreign Travel			•	•	•	•	•	•	•	•			•	•
Preventive Care Coinsurance [2]	•	•	•	•	•	•	•	•	•	•	•	•	•	•
Medicare Part B Excess Charges						•	•[5]		•	•				
Prescription Medicine	No plan offers prescription drug coverage—you'll need to sign up for Medicare Part D to cover your medications (see "Part D Prescription Drug Coverage" in Chapter 12).													
Cap on out-of-pocket expenses [3]											$5,240 per year (in 2018)	$2,620 per year (in 2018)		

[1] As of June 1, 2010, no new Plan E, H, I, or J policies will be sold. Existing policies may be continued.

[2] Coverage for preventive care (that is not covered by Medicare Part B) continues for Plans E and J issued before June 1, 2010.

[3] After the cap on out-of-pocket expenses is reached, the policy will pay 100% of all covered Part A and Part B costs.

[4] Available as of June 1, 2010.

[5] 80% for policies issued before June 1, 2010; 100% for all Plan G policies issued June 1, 2010 or later.

[6] There are also high-deductible Plan F policies in which the insured pays the first $2,000 out of pocket before the policy pays anything.

The standard plans are summarized in the "Standard Medigap Insurance Policies" chart, above, and are discussed more fully in the subsections that follow, with separate sections on rules for policies issued before and after June 1, 2010.

Medigap Plan A

Policies Issued Pre-June 2010

Plan A medigap policies include only the basic benefits discussed earlier. (See "Basic Benefits Included in All Medigap Plans," above.) Because of their limited benefits, Plan A policies are the least expensive.

Plan A policies are most useful if the doctors who regularly treat you accept assignment of Medicare-approved amounts, and you can afford to pay for the uncovered costs of doctors who do not accept assignment but by whom you might have to be treated. (See "How Much Medicare Part B Pays" in Chapter 12 regarding assignment practices.) Also, you must be able to afford the Part A hospital insurance deductible, bearing in mind that because there is a separate deductible for each separate hospital stay, you may have to pay it more than once in a year. (See "How Much Medicare Part A Pays" in Chapter 12 regarding Part A coverage.)

If these potential expenses plus the cost of a Plan A policy would put a severe strain on your finances, consider the alternative of an HMO, which may provide broader coverage for less money. (See Chapter 15 for a full discussion of the HMO option.)

Policies Issued June 1, 2010 or Later

Plan A policies issued June 1, 2010 or later also include coverage for hospice copayments.

Medigap Plan B

Policies Issued Pre-June 1, 2010

In addition to the basic benefits, a Plan B policy also pays your Medicare Part A deductible.

If your doctors all accept assignment but your budget would be severely strained by paying more than one hospital deductible in a year, Plan B may be marginally better for you than Plan A.

However, if you have to pay more than a few dollars a month more for Plan B than for Plan A, it may be a bad bargain.

Measure the yearly cost of a Plan B against the cost of a Plan A policy. If you are reasonably healthy—meaning you do not expect frequent hospitalizations—and the difference in premiums is more than 25% of the Part A Medicare deductible ($1,340 in 2018), it is probably not worth the extra premium, and you should stick to a Plan A policy.

Policies Issued June 1, 2010 or Later

Plan B policies issued June 1, 2010 or later also include coverage for hospice copayments.

Medigap Plan C

Policies Issued Pre-June 1, 2010

Plan C adds three benefits beyond the basic and other benefits offered in Plan B. First, it pays your yearly Medicare Part B deductible of $183. (But because this policy will probably cost you more than $183 per year over Plan A or B, that alone isn't a good reason to purchase it.)

Second, Plan C policies cover the Medicare coinsurance amount for skilled nursing care. Remember that under Medicare skilled nursing coverage, you are personally responsible for a coinsurance amount ($167.50 per day in 2018) for stays of 21 to 90 days in a skilled nursing facility. This can add up to a considerable amount of money, but it applies only if you are covered by Medicare for short-term skilled nursing care in a nursing facility. (See "Part A Hospital Insurance" in Chapter 12 regarding Medicare skilled nursing coverage.) If you have a medical condition that puts you in and out of the hospital, this can be a valuable addition to your policy. But the odds are low that most people will be in a skilled nursing facility for more than 20 days more than once or twice in a lifetime.

Finally, Plan C offers some coverage for medical care while traveling outside the United States. For people who travel abroad frequently, this can be a valuable benefit. After you pay a $250 deductible, Plan C pays for 80% of emergency medical costs you incur abroad. For purposes of these policies, emergency means any unplanned medical costs; it is not restricted to "emergency room" treatment (as it's called in the United States).

However, there are some restrictions on the coverage. Your emergency medical care must begin within the first 60 days of each trip abroad; if you take long trips, this policy will not protect you after the first two months. And there is a $50,000 lifetime maximum on these foreign travel medical benefits. If you spend a good portion of each year abroad, you may need a separate—that is, nonmedigap—health insurance policy to cover you fully for treatment received outside the United States.

Remember that your overseas medical care must be emergency care; if you regularly spend time abroad and simply want to be able to see a doctor for ongoing medical problems, this policy will not cover such visits.

The cost for Plan C policies is considerably higher than for Plan A or B but runs about the same as for Plans D and E.

Policies Issued June 1, 2010 or Later
Plan C policies issued June 1, 2010 or later also include coverage for hospice copayments.

Medicare SELECT Medigap Policies

In addition to regular fee-for-service medigap policies, there is a category of supplemental insurance that is partly fee for service and partly managed care. It is called Medicare SELECT. A SELECT policy must provide the same benefits as any of the standard medigap policies, but it has a two-tiered payment system.

If you use hospitals—and under some policies, doctors—who are members of the policy's network, the policy pays full benefits. If you use a provider outside the network, the policy pays reduced benefits. In this way, a Medicare SELECT medigap policy works like a preferred provider organization or an HMO with a point-of-service option, except that those managed care plans usually cover more services than most medigap policies. Because of the provider restrictions, Medicare SELECT policies are somewhat less expensive than regular medigap policies.

Medigap Plan D

Policies Issued Pre-June 1, 2010

Plan D is the same as Plan C, except it does not pay the yearly Medicare Part B deductible and it does pay for at-home recovery (home health aide services).

Policies Issued June 1, 2010 or Later

Plan D policies issued June 1, 2010 or later also include coverage for hospice copayments, but do not include at-home recovery.

Medigap Plan E

CAUTION

Plan E has been discontinued. No new Plan E policies have been sold since May 31, 2010. If you already had a Plan E policy as of that date, you may continue it.

Plan E adds minimal coverage of some preventive care but eliminates Plan D's coverage of at-home recovery. Plan E pays for only $120 per year of such preventive health care and screening, so it's not much of a benefit.

Medigap Plan F

Policies Issued Pre-June 1, 2010

Plan F offers the most significant added benefit beyond Plans B, C, D, and E: payment of 100% of what a doctor actually charges you above the Medicare-approved amount. (Remember, doctors who do not accept assignment are permitted to charge a patient up to 15% more than the Medicare-approved amount for any covered service, as discussed in "How Much Medicare Part B Pays" in Chapter 12.) If you receive extensive medical care from doctors who do not accept assignment, that extra 15% mounts up quickly.

Because the extra 15% of medical bills can amount to a lot of money, insurance companies charge higher premiums for Plan F than for the plans discussed previously. If you are in generally good health and the few doctors you see all accept assignment, this higher premium may not be worth the extra coverage. If, on the other hand, you require frequent or extensive medical care and you receive it from doctors who do not all accept assignment, Plan F may be worth the higher premiums.

If you like the coverage offered by Plan F but find the higher premiums too much for your budget, many companies that offer Plan F also offer a high-deductible version of this plan for a much lower premium. These high-deductible plans provide coverage only when your out-of-pocket costs for covered services exceed a certain amount for the year.

Policies Issued June 1, 2010 or Later

Plan F policies issued June 1, 2010 or later also include coverage for hospice copayments.

Medigap Plan G

Policies Issued Pre-June 1, 2010

Plan G is similar to Plan F. However, unlike Plan F, Plan G does not cover the Medicare medical insurance deductible. Plan G policies issued before June 1, 2010 cover only 80% of the excess charges some doctors and other providers charge under Medicare Part B.

Policies Issued June 1, 2010 or Later

Plan G policies issued June 1, 2010 or later provide 100% coverage for doctors' excess charges under Medicare Part B, and also include coverage for hospice copayments.

Medigap Plan H

CAUTION

Plan H has been discontinued. No new Plan H policies have been sold since May 31, 2010. If you already had a Plan H policy as of that date, you may continue it.

Plan H policies (without the drug coverage provided before January 1, 2006) cover the Part A deductible, Part A skilled nursing facility coinsurance amounts, and some coverage for emergency care while traveling outside the United States. Without their previous drug coverage, Plan H policies provide the same coverage as a Plan C policy except for the yearly Part B deductible that a Plan C policy covers. If you are considering keeping a Plan H policy, comparison shop with available Plan C policies.

Medigap Plan I

> ⚠ **CAUTION**
>
> **Plan I has been discontinued.** No new Plan I policies have been sold since May 31, 2010. If you already had a Plan I policy as of that date, you may continue it.

Plan I policies (without the drug coverage provided before January 1, 2006) cover 100% of doctors' excess charges under Part B, which can be a significant amount if you regularly see a number of doctors or have major treatment in any particular year. It also includes coverage of at-home recovery, in addition to the more commonly covered Part A deductible, skilled nursing facility coinsurance amounts, and emergency care during foreign travel. It is comparable to a Plan F policy, except that Plan F pays the Part B deductible instead of covering at-home recovery. If you can find a Plan F policy for a considerably lower premium than your Plan I policy, it may be worth it to switch.

Medigap Plan J

> ⚠ **CAUTION**
>
> **Plan J has been discontinued.** No new Plan J policies have been sold since May 31, 2010. If you already had a Plan J policy as of that date, you may continue it.

Plan J policies (without the drug coverage provided before January 1, 2006) are the luxury model of medigap policies, and also the most expensive. They cover 100% of doctors' excess charges and the Part B deductible, as well as all the other costs covered by any other plan policy.

Medigap Plan K

Policies Issued Pre-June 1, 2010

Plan K policies cover many Medicare gaps but pay only 50% of certain covered costs. Plan K compensates for this partial coverage by providing a cap on an insured person's out-of-pocket expenses. In addition to the standard Part A hospital coinsurance and extra lifetime hospital inpatient coverage offered under all medigap plans, Plan K policies cover 100% of the coinsurance amounts for Part B preventive care, and 50% of the Part A inpatient deductible, Part A coinsurance amounts for blood transfusions, skilled nursing facility stays and hospice care, and Part B coinsurance amounts. Plan K policies also place a $5,240 per year limit (in 2018) on a policyholder's out-of-pocket costs for covered medical expenses. After the policyholder reaches that amount, the policy pays 100% of all covered Part A and B costs.

Policies Issued June 1, 2010 or Later

There are no changes to Plan K policies issued June 1, 2010 or later.

Medigap Plan L

Policies Issued Pre-June 1, 2010

Plan L policies provide the same coverage as Plan K policies, and have the same kind of yearly cap on a policyholder's out-of-pocket expenses. But Plan L policies cover 75% of the Part A inpatient deductible, Part A coinsurance amounts for blood transfusions, skilled nursing facility stays and hospice care, and Part B coinsurance amounts. And Plan L's yearly cap on out-of-pocket expenses is $2,620 (in 2018). Because of this better coverage, Plan L policies are more expensive than Plan K policies.

Policies Issued June 1, 2010 or Later

There are no changes to Plan L policies issued June 1, 2010 or later.

Medigap Plan M

Beginning June 1, 2010, this new type of medigap policy is being sold. Plan M policies offer the same coverage as Plan D, but pay only 50% of the Medicare Part A deductible.

Medigap Plan N

Beginning June 1, 2010, this new type of medigap policy is being sold. Plan N policies offer the same coverage as Plan D, but you must pay a $20 copayment for each health care provider visit under Medicare Part B and a $50 copayment for an emergency room visit.

Terms and Conditions of Medigap Policies

In addition to comparing the services covered, the amount of benefits, and the monthly cost of different medigap insurance policies, there are several other things to consider before making a final decision.

Look first at how high the company says it may raise its premiums in the years to come—and therefore whether you will still be able to afford the policy when you may need it most. Also important are policy terms that determine whether you are covered for a particular illness during a certain time period after you purchase the policy.

Premium Increases

It is one thing to find insurance coverage you can afford today. It may be quite another to find a policy that you can continue to pay for in the future when your income and assets have decreased and the policy premium has increased. In choosing a medigap policy, consider what the contract says about how much the policy premiums will rise over time. If the current premium will already be a significant strain on your financial resources, consider a less expensive policy, because any policy is sure to get more expensive in the future.

There are several ways insurance companies set up premium increases in medigap policies. Choosing the best premium increase terms—what the insurance companies call "rating" methods—is something for you to consider along with other terms of the policy.

Level Premiums

The best method for the consumer is one called "level premiums." This means that premiums do not go up on your policy as you reach a certain age, but only when the insurance company raises premiums on all medigap policies of the type you have. Of course, the premiums will go up regularly, but the amount they go up will be at least partially controlled by market forces and by your state's insurance commission.

Attained Age

"Attained age" policies base your premium entirely upon your age. The company charges the same premium to everyone of the same age who has the same policy. As you get older, the premiums rise in lockstep, by a set amount. Some policies mandate that your premiums go up yearly, others hike the premiums when you reach a certain age plateau, such as 70, 75, or 80. Attained age policies tend to be cheaper at age 65 than comparable policies. However, once you reach 70 or 75, attained age policies tend to become, and stay, more expensive than other types.

When considering a policy with attained age premium increases, ask to see not only how much it would cost you at your present age, but also the current premium costs at each of the next age levels. That will give you a sense of how high the rates jump for that policy. Figure that your premiums will rise by at least the same percentages, and calculate how much your policy is likely to cost at your next two age levels. Only then will you have a realistic picture of how much this policy will cost.

 COMPUTER

Medigap information from Medicare's website. Medicare's official website at www.medicare.gov offers a link that can provide you with the names and contact information of insurance companies that offer specific medigap policies available where you live. On the medicare.gov home page, click the "Supplements & Other Insurance" tab, then click "Find a Medigap policy." Enter the requested information about your location. It will then provide you with information about specific medigap policies being sold where you live, including what the policies cover and which companies offer each type of policy, with contact information for those companies.

Issue Age

The initial premium for an "issue age" policy is determined by your age when you first purchase it. From then on, as long as you keep the same policy, you pay the same premium as someone else who buys the policy at the same age at which you bought it.

For example, if you buy an issue age medigap policy at age 65, in five years you will pay the same as a person who first buys the policy at that time at age 65. Your premium will steadily rise, but the increases may be controlled by the insurance company's need to keep the premium competitive to continue signing up new policyholders.

No Age Rating

A few insurance companies sell policies that charge the same amount regardless of age. They base their premiums entirely on the cost of medical care in the geographic area in which you live. (For this reason, these are sometimes referred to as "community-rated policies.") These policies tend to be a bit more expensive than others for people ages 65 to 75 and a bit less expensive for people age 75 and older.

Eligibility and Enrollment

Your ability to purchase the medigap policy of your choice depends on when and under what circumstances you apply for it. We discuss applying during open enrollment periods, applying during limited guaranteed enrollment periods, and applying outside these enrollment periods on your own, below.

Applying During Open Enrollment

You are guaranteed the right to buy any medigap policy sold in your state, without any medical screening or limits on coverage, if you:

- are within your first six months of Medicare Part B, or
- leave a Medicare Advantage plan within a year of age 65.

Your First Six Months With Medicare Part B

During the six months after you first enroll in Medicare Part B (see "Enrolling in Part B Medical Insurance" in Chapter 13 for enrollment procedures), you may buy any medigap insurance policy sold in the state where you live. During this initial enrollment period, federal law prohibits an insurance company from requiring medical underwriting—that is, prior screening of your health condition—before issuing a policy. Nor may the insurance company delay coverage because of preexisting health conditions. Companies are also prohibited from charging higher premiums based solely on your age or area of residence.

Most people enroll in Medicare Part B as soon as they turn 65. Your six-month open enrollment period for medigap begins on the first of the month during which you reach age 65 and are enrolled in Part B.

If you did not enroll for Medicare Part B on your 65th birthday but enroll during a yearly Medicare general enrollment period (January through March), your six-month open enrollment period for any medigap policy begins on July 1 of the same year. If you did not enroll in Medicare Part B on your 65th birthday because you were still covered by an employer-sponsored health plan, you have a six-month open enrollment period for any medigap policy beginning whenever you enroll in Medicare Part B.

You Leave a Medicare Advantage Plan Within a Year of Age 65

If you joined a Medicare Advantage plan (see Chapter 15) at age 65 when you first became eligible for Medicare, but you leave the plan within a year, you have a guaranteed right to buy any medigap plan sold in your state. This is true whether your Medicare Advantage plan dropped you—perhaps because it stopped doing business in your county of residence, or because you moved out of its business area—or because you left the plan voluntarily.

However, to protect this guaranteed right, you must apply for a medigap policy within 63 days of the date your Medicare Advantage plan coverage ends. If you are still in the six-month period immediately following your enrollment in Medicare Part B, you have whatever is left of that six-month period within which to apply for a medigap policy, or 63 days from the end of your Medicare Advantage coverage, whichever is greater.

Medigap Coverage If You Move

What happens if you buy a medigap policy while living in one place, then move elsewhere? Because all medigap policies are "guaranteed renewable," your insurance company can't cancel your policy. This is true even if you move to an area where the company doesn't normally sell similar policies. However, the insurance company has a right to increase your premium if you've moved to an area where the costs of medical care are higher. The rates must be approved by the department of insurance in the state to which you have moved.

Applying With Limited Guaranteed Enrollment

You have the guaranteed right to buy a medigap policy if, under certain circumstances, you:

- lose your Medicare coverage, or
- drop medigap, join a Medicare Advantage plan, then leave the Medicare Advantage plan.

You can use this right for any of several standard medigap plans, though not for all plans (see below). For those plans to which you have no guaranteed right, however, you may still purchase a policy if the issuing insurance company approves your application.

You Lose Coverage by a Medicare Advantage Plan or an Employer-Sponsored Policy

With alarming frequency, insurance companies all over the United States are dropping their Medicare Advantage plans in counties in which the companies are unhappy with their profit margins. (See Chapter 15 for details.)

If you have been dropped from a Medicare Advantage plan because the plan is leaving Medicare altogether, or is leaving the county in which you live, you have a guaranteed right to purchase any standard medigap Plan A, B, C, or F policy sold in your state. (In Massachusetts, Minnesota, and Wisconsin, you have a right to purchase a medigap policy with provisions similar to these four standard medigap plans.) You have the same guarantee if you are losing your Medicare Advantage coverage because you are moving out of the plan's service area.

These rules also apply if you lose employer-sponsored insurance which had operated like a medigap policy, meaning that it paid for some costs your Medicare coverage did not.

If you had a medigap Plan D, E, or G before dropping it to join a Medicare Advantage plan that has now dropped you, you also have a guaranteed right to again purchase that same plan from the same insurance company, if the company still sells the plan in your state.

To take advantage of any of these guaranteed rights, you must apply for a medigap plan within 63 days from the end of your Medicare Advantage or employer-sponsored coverage.

Some States Offer Extra Protection

Some states' laws offer even more protection around your right to purchase a medigap policy than the federal guarantee described in this chapter. These state laws typically give you more medigap plans from which to choose. To find out what extra protection your state might offer, call your state's department of insurance (see contact information at the end of this chapter) or your local SHIP office (see contact information at the end of Chapter 13).

You Dropped a Medigap Policy to Join a Medicare Advantage Plan or a Medicare SELECT Policy, Then Left the New Plan Within a Year

If you once had a medigap policy but dropped it to join a Medicare Advantage plan or to purchase a Medicare SELECT policy (see "Medicare SELECT Medigap Policies," above), you may have a guaranteed right to drop the Medicare plan and repurchase a medigap plan. However, you must meet two conditions:

- The Medicare Advantage plan or Medicare SELECT policy you drop must be the only one in which you have been enrolled.
- You must leave the Medicare Advantage plan or drop the Medicare SELECT policy within a year of when you joined.

If you meet these two conditions, you may either buy your original medigap policy from the same company (if it is still sold in your state), or buy any medigap Plan A, B, C, or F sold in your state. There is a time limit on applying for the new medigap policy, however. Your guaranteed right to purchase lasts only 63 days from the end of your previous coverage.

Applying Without Guaranteed Enrollment

If you want to buy a medigap policy but have none of the guaranteed rights described above, an insurance company can freely choose whether or not to sell you a policy. Even if the company does offer you coverage, it may attach whatever terms, conditions, and premiums it chooses, as long as the coverage matches one of the standard plans.

In such circumstances, the insurance company is likely to demand that you undergo medical underwriting (screening)—particularly before they'll sell you one of their more desirable policies. The screening will involve a detailed examination of your medical history.

If your history shows a likelihood of extensive or expensive medical treatment in the foreseeable future, the company might refuse to sell you the policy. Or, they might offer to sell it to you at a high premium, perhaps also with limitations on when coverage begins.

Preexisting Illness Exclusion

Most medigap policies contain a provision excluding coverage, for a set time immediately after you purchase a policy, of any illness or medical conditions for which you received treatment within a given period before your coverage began. Six months is a typical exclusion period. Many policies provide no coverage for six months after you buy the policy for illnesses you were treated for within six months before the policy started. Usually, the shorter the exclusion period, the higher the premium.

If you have a serious medical condition that may require costly medical treatment at any time, and you have been treated for that condition within the recent past, consider a policy with a short exclusion period or none at all.

Discounts for the "Healthy"

Some insurance companies offer extra discounts on medigap policies for people they consider to be better risks than others. For example, women may be offered lower premiums than men because women tend to remain healthier longer, meaning the insurance company collects more premiums before having to pay out on claims. For the same reason, nonsmokers are also frequently offered discounts.

You may also be able to reduce your premiums if you have been free of any serious illness or condition and are willing to prove it by undergoing what is called medical underwriting—a screening process during which the insurance company examines your medical history to see whether you are likely to cost them a lot of money in the near future. If the screening shows that you have had no serious illnesses or medical conditions over the previous ten years, you may be able to purchase the policy at a significantly lower premium than if you had bought it without first being medically screened. Ask the insurance company whether they offer this sort of discount.

Finding the Best Medicare Supplement

Shopping for a medigap policy can be difficult, not only because of the differences in policy terms among the ten standard policies, but because of the wide spectrum of prices among insurance companies. Near the end of Chapter 15 is a chart to help you do a side-by-side comparison among different medigap and Medicare Advantage plans.

Fortunately, your first step, namely finding out what medigap insurance policies are available in your state, is fairly simple. Your state department of insurance can give you a complete list of available policies (see the contact information at the end of this chapter). Be warned, however, that their lists are often a bit stale, so you'll need to follow up with the insurance companies or insurance agents for the latest facts and figures. Many people also use insurance agents to find policies, although you should first read the cautions in "Using an Insurance Agent," below. In addition, some seniors' organizations offer discounts on certain medigap policies.

Medicare.gov also has a useful medigap policy finder that lists and compares policies in your area.

Using an Insurance Agent

If you use an insurance agent to present you with a choice of medigap policies, make sure the agent is experienced with the provisions of several different policies. Insurance agents tend to work with policies from certain companies and may not know of less expensive or less restrictive policies from other companies. So you may want to consult more than one agent.

Even if you arrange to get your insurance through an agent, keep your own ears and eyes open for policies that might fit your needs. Friends, relatives, and organizations to which you belong may all be resources to find out about available plans. And senior organizations can be a good source of information. A good insurance agent should be willing to find out the details of a policy you have located yourself. If the agent cannot or will not check on such a policy, it is probably time to find a new agent. Likewise, if an insurance agent is unwilling to sit down with you and compare the coverage and costs of different policies, then you ought to comparison shop for a new insurance agent.

Senior Associations

A number of organizations of seniors or retired people advertise medigap policies. These organizations do not actually act as insurers. Instead, they negotiate deals with insurance companies to offer medigap policies to their members, sometimes at reduced rates.

But some senior organizations act almost as fronts for insurance companies. These organizations may appear to exist for the benefit of older people, offering a number of programs or services for seniors. But many of these alleged benefits are nearly worthless. In truth, these organizations exist to sell themselves through membership dues and products (including overpriced insurance) behind a facade of supposedly protecting senior citizens.

Help With Decisions About Medigap and Medicare Advantage Plans

Each state has a program to assist people with Medicare, medigap supplemental insurance, and Medicare Advantage plans. It is called the State Health Insurance Assistance Program (SHIP), although in some states it may have another, similar name.

SHIP has professional staff and volunteers who are knowledgeable not only about the rules pertaining to Medicare and medigap insurance but also about what policies are available in your state and what HMOs and other Medicare Advantage plans are available in your local area. SHIP staff can look over particular insurance policies and managed care plans and help you see the strengths and weaknesses of each.

In larger states there are many SHIP offices, and you can reach the office nearest you by calling the state's general toll-free number. In smaller states there may be fewer offices, and you will be referred to a SHIP program at a local senior center or another nonprofit organization. (See the end of Chapter 13 for contact information.)

The best way to tell whether the policies a particular organization offers are good or bad is to compare their specific terms and prices with those of other policies offered by different insurance companies or health plans. In the final analysis, it is the terms of the policy, not an organization's good intentions or friendly advertising, that determine the quality of your coverage. The insurance company, not the senior organization, determines your coverage and pays your claims.

Beware of Mail-Order and Limited-Offer Policies

Beware of medigap policy offers you receive unsolicited in the mail. Their flashy promises often far outstrip their coverage. If you do become aware of a policy through the mail, and its provisions seem good to you after comparing it with other policies, check the reputation of the company offering the policy. You can get information on the company from your state's insurance department or commission, or from your state or local consumer protection agency.

Also be wary of policies that are offered with short-time enrollment periods. You have likely heard or seen advertisements for insurance that holler: "Limited offer! One month only! Buy now, the greatest offer in years! Once the offer is over, you'll never get another chance at an opportunity like this again! Once-in-a-lifetime offer!"

This is nonsense.

If it's a reputable company with a legitimate policy to offer you, the same or similar terms will be available any time—although you must keep in mind your own six-month open enrollment period after you sign up for Medicare Part B. These advertising slogans are just another way insurance companies have of pressuring you into buying a policy without first carefully considering and comparing its terms.

Most companies permit you to look over your policy and carefully examine its terms for ten days before you are obligated to keep it. If you decide you don't want the policy—for any reason—you can return it within ten days to the company or to the insurance agent you bought it from. You'll be owed a refund of all the money you have paid up to that point. And if you are buying a new medigap policy to replace one you already have, you are legally entitled to 30 days to review the new policy to decide whether you want to keep it. You can cancel it without penalty at any time during those 30 days.

Only One Medigap Policy Required

You need only one policy to supplement your Medicare coverage—and it is illegal for an insurance company to sell you a health insurance policy that duplicates coverage you already have with a medigap policy.

When you apply for a medigap policy, you will be asked to provide information concerning any health insurance policies you have. This gives written notice to the seller of your policy—insurance agent, broker, or company representative—about your existing insurance so that you will not be held responsible for paying for duplicate coverage if the insurer mistakenly sells it to you.

If you already have medigap insurance but want to replace it with a new policy, some rules help protect you while you make the change.

Replacement Policies

If you are considering replacing your existing policy with a new one, there are a number of things to keep in mind.

First, even if your new policy would ultimately provide better coverage, it may have a preexisting condition exclusion that would deny you coverage for up to six months after you switched policies. If you have been treated in the previous six months for any serious medical condition that might require further treatment in the near future, don't cancel a basically good policy for one that is only slightly better.

Second, unless you are signing up within the first six months following your enrollment in Medicare Part B, the new insurance company from which you applied for coverage might reject you if you have had serious medical problems in the recent past. Don't cancel your old policy until you have been given written notice from the new insurance company—not just from the agent or broker who sold you the policy—that your new policy is in effect.

When you apply for a replacement policy, you must sign a statement agreeing that you will drop your old policy when the new one takes effect. The law gives you a review period within which to decide between the old and new policies. Once you have received written notice of your acceptance in the new insurance plan, and you have been given a written copy of the new policy, you have 30 days to cancel either the new policy or the old one.

Dread Disease Policies: A Dreadful Idea

A few insurance companies offer policies that do not provide medigap supplemental coverage but provide particularized health coverage that may overlap some with medigap policies and even Medicare coverage itself. Most of these policies cover treatment for a specific disease and are known as indemnity or "dread disease" policies. They are often solicited over the phone or by direct mail and are offered at low monthly premiums.

One of these policies may initially sound promising if it covers a particular disease—for example, a specific type of cancer—for which you have a high risk. However, close examination of these policies usually shows them to be a waste of money. They pay only a small, set amount of money for each day you are hospitalized or for each medical treatment for the specific disease, usually far less than the Medicare deductible or coinsurance that a medigap policy would pay.

And because they pay only when you are treated for the specific disease, you wind up needing to carry a medigap policy anyway to cover all medical bills not related to this particular disease. Or if you don't carry a medigap policy, you will be responsible for paying out of pocket for all medical bills not covered by this specific-disease policy. Either way, these policies are a bad investment.

Department of Insurance

You can contact your state's department of insurance to ask for information about medigap insurance policies being sold in your state. To find contact information for your state, see the official Medicare website listing of state departments of insurance at www.medicare.gov/Contacts.

Medicare Part C:
Medicare Advantage Plans

Medicare Part C health plans, referred to as Medicare Advantage plans, fill gaps in basic Medicare, as do medigap policies. But the two systems operate differently. As explained in Chapter 14, medigap policies work alongside Medicare: Medical bills are sent both to Medicare and to a medigap insurer, and each pays a portion of the approved charges. With a Medicare Advantage plan, on the other hand, enrollees no longer deal with Medicare directly, although enrollees still have to pay their monthly premium for Medicare Part B (see Chapter 12). A Medicare Advantage plan provides all basic Medicare coverage and often offers some extended coverage in addition to basic Medicare. The extent of coverage beyond basic Medicare, the size of premiums and copayments, and decisions about whether a particular treatment should be covered, are all controlled by the Medicare Advantage plan, not by Medicare. (See "Comparing Medigap and Medicare Advantage Plans," toward the end of this chapter, to help compare specific policies.)

Medicare Advantage plans come in two basic forms: managed care plans and fee-for-service plans:

- **Managed care plans.** In return for coverage beyond basic Medicare, Medicare Advantage managed care plans charge a low monthly premium—or none at all—and small copayments. But they limit the doctors and other providers from which you can receive care. They restrict doctors as well—placing limits on treatments and the length of hospital stays for managed care patients.

- **Fee-for-service plans.** With these plans, you may receive care from any doctor or other provider who participates in Medicare. But for each service or treatment, the doctor or other provider must accept the Medicare Advantage plan's restrictions and amount of payment. If a doctor or another provider will not accept the plan's restrictions or payment level for a particular medical service, the plan will not cover the patient's care by that provider. In that case, the patient must either personally pay the provider or seek care from a different provider who will accept the plan's terms.

Medicare Part D Means New Decisions About Medicare Advantage Plans

Deciding whether to remain in or join a Medicare Advantage plan has become trickier since the introduction of prescription drug coverage under the Medicare Part D program. Before Part D, many Medicare Advantage plans offered some prescription drug coverage. Now, some Medicare Advantage plans offer drug coverage, but others have none.

If a Medicare Advantage plan includes drug coverage, enrolling in that plan means that you do not also enroll in a Part D plan. But enrolling in a plan with drug coverage is a good idea only if that plan covers the drugs you regularly take, and offers them at a reasonable copayment without serious access restrictions. (Coverage restrictions are discussed in more detail in Chapter 12. See "Part D Prescription Drug Coverage.")

If a Medicare Advantage plan does not offer Plan D coverage, you may still want to keep or join that plan if you like its other coverage features and costs. But if you also want prescription drug coverage, you will have to enroll in a separate, stand-alone Part D prescription drug plan.

If your current Medicare Advantage plan offers Plan D drug coverage but does not cover your drugs, or does so with high copayments or access restrictions, consider joining a different Medicare Advantage plan that better meets your needs. Or, leave the managed care system altogether and return to original Medicare coverage under Parts A and B, and separately enroll in a stand-alone Part D prescription drug plan that does a good job of covering your drugs. (See Chapter 12.) If you leave Medicare Advantage altogether, you may also want to take out a medigap supplemental insurance policy to fill some of the gaps in Medicare coverage that your Medicare Advantage plan used to cover. (See Chapter 14.)

If you are considering a Medicare Advantage plan, you must decide whether any of the plans available in your area offer adequate care at an affordable cost. You should evaluate not only the cost of premiums and copayments but also how the plan limits the particular doctors and other providers you can get care from. Despite the lower monthly cost for Medicare Advantage plans, their limitations have resulted in only about 30% of Medicare beneficiaries enrolling in these plans.

When considering a Medicare Advantage plan, you'll also need to assess the risks of yearly changes—including the chance that a particular plan may drop out of an entire geographic region—associated with these types of plans. Just because many of them are sponsored by big insurance companies does not make them stable. In the past several years, the number of plans people have to choose from has steadily declined. Many seniors have been dropped from Medicare Advantage plans that stopped serving the areas where they lived and have been forced to find another plan or return to original Medicare coverage. And millions of people have found their premiums shooting up, copayments rising, and coverage shrinking for those services not legally required by Medicare.

Not only do you risk your plan's disappearing or becoming far more expensive, but if you choose to return to regular Medicare, your chance to buy a medigap insurance policy (as discussed in Chapter 14) may be much more limited.

To learn what Medicare Advantage plans are available in the area where you live, you can visit the Medicare website at www. medicare.gov. To find out the recent history of a particular Medicare Advantage plan—whether it has dropped patients or hiked costs, for example—call your local SHIP or HICAP counseling office (see the end of Chapter 13 for contact information) or your state department of insurance (see Chapter 14 for contact information). If you are dropped from a Medicare Advantage plan, your alternatives and when you must exercise them are explained in "Your Rights When Joining, Leaving, or Losing a Medicare Advantage Plan," below.

Joining a Medicare Advantage Plan Means Leaving Direct Medicare Protection

If you join a Medicare Advantage plan, in effect you leave the Medicare program. The insurance company that runs the Medicare Advantage plan gets a monthly payment from Medicare on your behalf, but the plan itself then decides what health care providers you can use, and approves or denies medical coverage for all of your specific medical care. (When the plan denies coverage, the plan itself handles the first level of your request for reconsideration. But if your request for reconsideration is still denied, then you are entitled to independent review, just as in an appeal under original Medicare (covered in Chapter 13). For more information, see Nolo's website article on "Appealing a Denial of Medicare Part C.")

If you leave a Medicare Advantage plan, you are permitted to rejoin traditional Medicare. But if you return to Medicare after the first year following your initial Medicare eligibility, you may find that not all medigap supplemental insurance policies will accept you. And you may be able to join another Medicare Advantage plan only during open enrollment.

Medicare Advantage Managed Care Plans

Many Medicare Advantage plans are structured as managed care plans. In these plans, a patient's care is managed by the insurance company that issues the plan. The basic premise of managed care is that the member-patient agrees to receive care only from specific doctors, hospitals, and others—called a network—in exchange for reduced overall health care costs. The patient also agrees that the plan, rather than Medicare itself, will decide whether a particular medical service is covered.

There are several varieties of Medicare Advantage managed care plans. Some have severe restrictions on consulting with specialists or seeing providers from outside the network. Others give members more freedom to choose when they see doctors and which doctors they may consult for treatment. Generally, more choice translates into higher cost.

Health Maintenance Organization (HMO)

The HMO is the least expensive and most restrictive Medicare Advantage managed care plan. It is also the most common type of Medicare managed care plan. There are four main restrictions.

Care Within the Network Only

Each HMO maintains a list—called a network—of doctors and other health care providers. The HMO member must receive care only from a provider in the network, except in emergencies.

If the plan member uses a provider from outside the network, the plan pays nothing toward the bill. And because a Medicare Advantage plan member has withdrawn from traditional Medicare coverage, Medicare itself picks up none of the tab, either. The plan member must pay the entire bill out of pocket.

Because of this restriction, it is very important to find out whether the doctors and other providers you use are included in the HMO's network. This is particularly true for your primary care physician, who will not only handle routine medical problems but will also decide whether you should be referred for treatment or to a specialist. It is also important to make sure that the hospital in your vicinity, or a hospital you and your doctor prefer to use, is in the network. If all of your doctors and your preferred hospital are in the HMO's network, the restriction may not be as important to you.

However, most HMOs and other managed care plans (except for integrated HMOs like Kaiser Permanente) do sometimes drop doctors and hospitals. And doctors' groups and hospitals leave HMOs that become too stingy in reimbursing for medical care or authorizing services for their patients. If the plan or one of your providers decides to cut ties, you won't be able to continue seeing that provider. So, even if you begin a managed care plan with all the right doctors and hospital, you may later find yourself traveling long distances to get to a new hospital and searching for new doctors, or searching for a new managed care plan or medigap policy.

This instability of many managed care plans makes it important for you to discuss with your doctors any particular HMO you are considering. Ask whether your doctor has experienced problems with the plan, particularly with approval of treatments, referrals to specialists, or early release from inpatient hospital care.

Some doctors are uncomfortable speaking with patients about insurance companies. But responsible physicians will at least tell you if their offices have had regular, serious problems getting a plan's coverage for their patients, and certainly should tell you if they are considering dropping their contract with a particular plan.

Emergency and Urgent Care Anywhere

Federal law requires that all Medicare Advantage plans cover emergency services nationwide, regardless of restrictions they place on the use of doctors and hospitals for routine care. The law also requires that these plans pay for covered services you receive from a non-plan provider if the treatment was urgently needed while you were temporarily outside the plan's geographic service area. Urgently needed care means care for an unforeseen illness or injury for which a reasonable person would not wait until they could return home to seek medical help.

This required emergency coverage does not apply to most foreign travel. However, some plans offer such coverage on their own. If you travel or live any part of the year outside the United States but are not covered while abroad, it may be a good idea to buy a temporary travel medical policy covering you for the time you are out of the country.

All Care Through Primary Care Physician

An HMO member must select a primary care physician from the plan's network. This is the doctor the member must usually see first for medical needs. In most HMOs, a member may not see other doctors or providers—even from within the plan's network—or obtain other medical services without a referral by the primary care physician. Even if you regularly see a variety of specialists, your primary care physician must refer you to those doctors. You may not usually make an appointment to see them on your own.

This system encourages the primary care physician—who is paid less than a specialist by the plan—to take care of medical problems that don't absolutely require a specialist. Because of the hassle of the extra step, it also discourages the plan member from seeking specialist care.

This restriction is a significant reason that managed care is cheaper for insurance companies than traditional fee-for-service policies. Since many seniors require specialist care, this restriction is also a reason that many of them reject HMO coverage in favor of medigap insurance or less restrictive types of managed care.

Prior HMO Approval of Some Services

HMOs require that your primary care physician or other network physician obtain prior approval from the plan for certain medical services the doctor may want to prescribe. If plan administrators do not believe a service is medically necessary, or believe service from a nonspecialist or other less expensive treatment would do just as well, they may deny coverage for that prescribed service.

HMO With Point-of-Service (POS) Option

A few Medicare Advantage HMOs have a significant wrinkle that makes them more attractive—and more expensive—than standard HMO plans. These plans offer what is called a point-of-service option. This option allows a member to see physicians and other providers who are not in the HMO's network, and to receive services from specialists without first going through a primary care physician.

However, if a member does go outside the network or sees a specialist directly, the plan pays a smaller part of the bill than if the member had followed regular HMO procedures. The member pays a higher premium for this option than for a standard HMO plan, and a higher copayment each time the option is used.

Special Needs Plans for Certain Chronic Conditions

In some states, a particular kind of Medicare Advantage plan, called a Special Needs Plan, may be offered to people with a specific serious chronic or disabling medical condition. Like all other Medicare Advantage plans, these C-SNPs (meaning Chronic-Special Needs Plans) offer both inpatient and outpatient care at least as broad as Medicare Part A and Part B, plus prescription drugs. Unlike other Medicare Advantage plans, though, a C-SNP is tailored to a specific condition, providing a network of doctors and other providers who specialize in the treatment of that condition, a broad selection of the drugs used to treat that condition, and usually a "care coordinator" who monitors a patient's health status and helps ensure that the patient follows proper care procedures at home.

C-SNPs are offered in only about half of all states with a total enrollment of only about 0.5% of all Medicare beneficiaries. And almost all C-SNPs (more than 95% of all C-SNPs offered) cover one or more of only three sets of conditions. If your doctor certifies that you have one of these three sets of conditions, you might qualify for a C-SNP that specifically covers your condition and actually find such a policy offered where you live:

- cardiovascular disorders, including chronic or congestive heart failure
- diabetes mellitus, or
- chronic lung failure.

If you have one of the following conditions, technically you might also qualify for a C-SNP, but insurance companies have offered such C-SNPs in only a very few places in the country:

- cancer
- stroke
- alcohol/drug dependence
- Alzheimer's or dementia
- disabling mental health disease
- neurological disorders
- HIV/AIDS
- autoimmune disorders
- end-stage liver or kidney disease, or
- severe hematological disorders.

Special Needs Plans for Certain Chronic Conditions (continued)

In addition to the difficulty of finding a C-SNP for your condition where you live, there is the issue of whether the plan would actually be better for you than other Medicare Advantage plans. In theory, concentrating providers around a single condition and coordinating care should improve care. However, the government's own Medicare Payment Advisory Committee has found that on average C-SNPs do not perform as well as regular Medicare Advantage plans do, as judged by certain "quality measures." Of course, that's on average, and specific plans might do quite well on those measures.

If you are interested in exploring whether a C-SNP might be right for you, you can find out what plans are available in your area by going online to the government's Medicare Plan Finder, www.medicare.gov/find-a-plan/questions/home.aspx. If you find a plan that interests you, be sure to compare it to what's offered by other Medicare Advantage plans in your area, including asking the insurance company what the plan's "quality measures" ratings are. For help in choosing a plan, you can get free counseling from a local office of the State Health Insurance Assistance Program (SHIP). (See information about SHIP at the end of Chapter 13.) More information is also available from Medicare's online pamphlet *Your Guide to Medicare Special Needs Plans (SNPs)* at www.medicare.gov/Pubs/pdf/11302.pdf.

If you decide that you want to try a C-SNP offered where you live, you may enroll (with your doctor's certification that you have a qualifying condition) or disenroll under the same terms as you could with any Medicare Advantage plan (see "Your Rights When Joining, Leaving, or Losing a Medicare Advantage Plan," below). In addition, you can enroll in a C-SNP anytime you are newly diagnosed with the condition that qualifies you for the plan.

Preferred Provider Organization (PPO)

Although it has a different name, the PPO works the same as an HMO with a point-of-service (POS) option (discussed above). If a member receives a service from the PPO's network of providers, the cost to the member is lower than if the member sees a provider outside the network.

PPOs tend to be more expensive than standard HMOs, charging both a monthly premium and a higher copayment for nonnetwork services. However, many people find that the extra flexibility in choosing doctors is an important comfort to them, and therefore worth the extra money.

Provider Sponsored Organization (PSO)

The PSO is a group of medical providers—doctors, clinics, and a hospital—that skips the insurance company middleman and contracts directly with patients. As with an HMO, the member pays a premium, as well as a copayment each time a service is used.

PSOs are rare, and you're unlikely to find one where you live. However, if a PSO operates in your area, you may want to consider it as an alternative to other types of Medicare Advantage Plans.

Medicare Advantage Fee-for-Service Plans

In recent years, insurance companies have been offering a new type of Medicare Advantage plan, called "private fee-for-service," that they tout as offering greater enrollee "freedom" in choice of doctors and other providers. Unfortunately, for reasons described below, many people discover that this freedom is an illusion. Nonetheless, in some places—particularly in rural areas—these fee-for-service plans are a viable alternative if there are few or no other Medicare Advantage plans available.

How Most Medicare Advantage Fee-for-Service Plans Work

Unlike managed care plans, most Medicare Advantage private fee-for-service plans do not maintain a membership network of doctors, hospitals, and other health care providers from which a plan enrollee must receive health care services. Instead, a private fee-for-service plan may cover care provided by any health care provider that accepts Medicare patients. Also, many of these plans have a cap on the total out-of-pocket payments an enrollee will pay each year for care that is covered by the plan.

Fee-for-Service Plans With Tiered Payment

A few fee-for-service plans maintain provider networks, just like a managed care plan. With these plans, you may receive medical services from any doctor or other provider who accepts the terms of the plan. But if you receive medical services from a provider within the plan's network, your out-of-pocket costs are lower than if you receive services from a provider who is not in the plan's network.

Disadvantages of Medicare Advantage Fee-for-Service Plans

Fee-for-service plans impose several significant restrictions that may severely limit a patient's choice of doctors and other providers, making such a plan a poor option if other types of Medicare Advantage plans are available. These restrictions are:

- **Strict rules for providers.** For any specific medical treatment or service, a doctor or another provider must accept the terms offered by the fee-for-service plan. These terms include the nature and extent of care the insurance company will approve and what the provider will be paid. If the doctor or other provider is not willing to accept the plan's terms, the plan will not cover the particular care with that provider. In that case, the patient must either personally pay for the care or seek treatment from a different provider.

- **Lack of predictable care.** The fact that a doctor or another provider previously accepted a plan's terms does not mean the provider will accept the terms the next time the patient wants care, either for the same or a different medical service. In other words, if you enroll in one of these plans, you won't know whether care from a particular doctor or other provider will be covered by the plan until the time comes when you need it.
- **Few additional services.** Fee-for-service plans usually don't cover as many extra services (meaning services not covered by original Medicare Part A and Part B) as do other types of Medicare Advantage plans.
- **Extra costs.** In some plans, you may have to pay the doctor or other provider out of your pocket—up to 15% more than the amount the plan pays the provider.

If you are considering a private fee-for-service plan, be sure to carefully evaluate your choices by following the suggestions offered in the rest of this chapter.

Choosing a Medicare Advantage Plan

To evaluate a Medicare Advantage plan of any type, it is important to get a complete written explanation of its coverage, costs, and procedures. These are usually contained in a printed brochure called a summary of benefits, available from each plan. Also, ask each plan for a chart showing premiums and copayments. Compare that written information with each important category discussed in this chapter.

If you do not understand exactly what the coverage, costs, and procedures are, ask a plan representative to tell you where they are explained in the written information. If you can't get an important piece of information in writing, don't join the plan.

Choice of Doctors and Other Providers

For many people, the most important factor in choosing a Medicare Advantage plan is whether the doctors, hospitals, and other providers they already use and trust are in the plan's network of providers or, in the case of fee-for-service plans, whether those providers regularly accept the plan's terms.

Tracking Membership Satisfaction

Your state department of insurance or department of corporations is charged with monitoring Medicare Advantage plans. And it pays to see whether many members complain about crucial services. Most complaints are based on a plan's having:

- rejected referrals to specialists
- ordered early discharge for hospital inpatients
- dropped coverage in certain geographic areas
- dropped doctors and hospitals from its network
- raised copayments
- switched drugs on the plan's formulary, or
- dropped extra coverage.

An excellent and free source of information about Medicare Advantage plans is the State Health Insurance Assistance Program (SHIP), in some places called the Health Insurance Counseling and Advocacy Program (HICAP). To find your local office, contact the SHIP or HICAP office in your state (for contact information, see the end of Chapter 13).

Managed care plans. If the people and places you prefer for care are in a managed care plan's network, the tight restrictions of HMOs may not have much effect on you, at least for the foreseeable future. But if they're not, you will have to find new doctors, which is rarely an easy or comfortable process. And you might have to use a hospital that is more distant from your home, leaving you a little less secure.

The problem is not quite as great with PPOs or HMOs with a point-of-service option. These plans permit you to use providers who are not in a plan's network. So, if you want to continue with a particular doctor or provider who is not in the network, you may do so, but with a higher copayment each time you use the nonnetwork provider. If you are frequently treated by nonnetwork doctors, the extra payments may cancel out the cost advantage of managed care.

Private fee-for-service plans. With Medicare Advantage private fee-for-service plans, the decision is more difficult. With most of these plans, there is no network, so there is no simple automatic way to know that the doctors and other providers you use will accept the plan for any particular treatment or service. Before joining one of these plans, it is important to talk directly with your primary care doctor and any other doctor or other provider you regularly receive care from. Ask them whether they have experience with the plan you are considering and if so, whether they often refuse to accept the plan's terms. If your regular providers have little experience with the plan, or regularly refuse the plan's offered terms, joining that plan is probably not a good idea if you want to continue being treated by the same providers.

Help With Medicare Advantage Choices

People finding their way through the Medicare Advantage maze can get help from the State Health Insurance Assistance Program (SHIP), also frequently called the Health Insurance Counseling and Advocacy Program (HICAP). SHIP is funded by a combination of government grants and private donations and has no connection to the health care or insurance industries. SHIP provides free counseling about Medicare Advantage plans and medigap policies. Local staff can help you compare plans and policies. They can also tell you about other people's recent experiences with specific plans and policies.

To find the SHIP or HICAP office nearest you, contact your state's central SHIP or HICAP office (see the end of Chapter 13 for contact information).

 COMPUTER

Compare plans on Medicare's website. Medicare's official website at www.medicare.gov offers a link that can give you the names and contact information for insurance companies offering Medicare Advantage plans available where you live. On the medicare.gov home page click on "Forms, Help, & Resources," where there is a box titled "Find health & drug plans"; clicking on that box takes you to a page called the "Medicare Plan Finder," which asks for your zip code and some personal information (optional). This page can then take you to information about specific Medicare Advantage plans being sold where you live, including basic information about what the policies cover and how to contact the insurance companies offering those plans.

In addition, it offers patient satisfaction ratings and statistics on how many people left each plan. Be aware, though, that the information on this page is only intended to give you basic information about these health plans. To get the detailed information you need—about costs, networks, and coverage—and to make a decision, you must contact the plans themselves. Also, you should always double-check such information with your local SHIP or HICAP office, because some of it may be out of date, and it may not include how many people have been dropped by the plan.

Access to Specialists and Preventive Care

The requirement that you must visit your primary care physician to obtain most specialist referrals is one of the main customer objections to managed care plans. If you are considering a Medicare Advantage managed care plan, try to learn how difficult it is to get referrals to specialists, using the suggestions in this section.

Coverage for Referrals

Your primary care physician refers you for testing, laboratory work, and treatment by most specialists. Speak with your primary care doctor and other providers you see regularly about their experiences with a particular plan. Does the plan often overrule the doctor's recommendation? Has the plan set guidelines for the doctors that might affect their ability to send you for treatment?

Access to Specialists

Medicare rules require managed care plans to develop a specific treatment plan for patients with a complex or serious condition, such as heart disease, cancer, or kidney failure. The treatment plan must outline what specialists you require, and it must allow you to see them without a referral from your primary care doctor. If you have a condition that requires care by specialists, find out from the plan whether your condition is considered sufficiently serious or complex to permit direct access to your specialists.

Preventive Care Options

Under Medicare rules, a managed care plan must permit members to obtain routine preventive women's health care screening from a gynecologist without first seeing a primary care physician. It must also permit a member to obtain Medicare-mandated mammograms without a referral. Find out from a managed care plan what other preventive care services—such as annual physical exams, prostate screening for men, cholesterol testing, or hearing exams—the plan permits members to schedule on their own.

Now You Get Coverage, Now You Don't

The government does not regulate Medicare Advantage plan coverage except to insist that the plans offer at least basic Medicare benefits. Nor is there any regulation of premiums and copayments. What this means is that Medicare Advantage plans are free to change coverage and charges at any time.

To compete with other insurance plans, your plan might expand coverage. In recent years, for example, short-term custodial care and overseas travel coverage have been added to many plans, although most charge an added premium for these "extras."

But plans will just as often cut back on coverage. In some plans, benefits are shifted from no-premium plans to deluxe plans with a premium. Raising copayments for specific services—particularly prescription drugs—is also common, as is restricting access to certain medications.

Prescription Drug Coverage

Since January 1, 2006, Medicare has offered prescription drug coverage through its Part D program. Many people enroll in Part D coverage through separate, stand-alone prescription drug plans. But many other people get prescription drug coverage through their Medicare Advantage plan, putting all their Medicare and supplemental coverage under one umbrella.

If you are thinking about joining a Medicare Advantage plan with prescription drug coverage, it's very important that you examine that coverage closely. When you are considering plans that include drug coverage, be sure to review that coverage just as you would when considering a stand-alone prescription drug plan. (See "Part D Prescription Drug Coverage" in Chapter 12.) In particular, you must determine whether the plan:

- includes on its formulary (its list of covered drugs) the drugs you regularly take
- charges reasonably low copayments for those drugs, and
- imposes no significant access restrictions to those drugs.

Once you have determined how well various Medicare Advantage plans cover the particular prescription drugs you take, you must weigh that information along with the other aspects of the plans discussed in this chapter. If you use many costly prescription drugs, how well a particular plan covers your drugs should be a major part of your decision. If you use few prescription drugs, then the other aspects of a plan may influence your decision more strongly.

Before you choose any Medicare Advantage plan, be sure to investigate the stand-alone Part D prescription drug plans that are available to you. Then, add the costs of the Part D stand-alone drug plan that best covers your drugs to the costs of a Medicare Advantage plan without drug coverage. It is this combination of costs and stand-alone Part D drug coverage benefits that you should consider when comparing these plans to other Medicare Advantage plans that include drug coverage.

Consider Total Costs, Not Just Premiums

Many Medicare Advantage plans, particularly managed care plans, charge relatively small premiums, often much lower than the combined premiums of a medigap policy plus a Part D drug plan. But premiums do not tell the whole story of what your supplemental Medicare coverage will actually cost you. This is because a Medicare Advantage plan's medical coverage and its prescription drug coverage will both require you to make copayments.

Most Medicare Advantage managed care plans charge a copayment for doctor visits (usually $5 to $20), and many older people frequently consult several doctors. Drug coverage is offered only for drugs on a plan's formulary (see "Part D Prescription Drug Coverage" in Chapter 12), and copayments vary depending on the type of medication and whether it is a brand name or generic drug. Within these parameters, Medicare Advantage drug copayments can run up to 25% of the drug's actual retail cost.

Only by comparing the copayments and premiums of various plans can you fully understand how much each plan is likely to cost you.

Extent of Service Area

Consider the extent of a plan's service area, particularly if you live in a rural or spread-out suburban area. If the service area is not broad enough to include a good selection of specialists, you may find your future care choices limited.

Also, find out whether the plan has what are called extended service areas. Some plans permit you to arrange medical care far from your home if you travel frequently or spend a regular part of the year away from its primary service area. This allows you to take care of nonurgent medical needs even if you are not at your primary residence.

Appealing a Plan's Decision About Your Care

About 30% of Medicare Advantage plan patients report having been denied coverage for medical care or services their plan deemed to be medically unnecessary or otherwise not covered. This phenomenon of having an insurance company overruling your doctor can be upsetting, and if it involves a serious condition, the plan's rejection can be devastating.

There is a standard process for you to appeal such a denial of coverage. Unfortunately, the first step in the review process is handled by the plan's insurance company itself. The plan will provide you with a written decision denying the coverage, which will also include instructions for filing the initial step in your appeal. This first step is a written request for reconsideration of their decision; you must do so within 60 days of receiving the notice from the plan denying coverage. The plan must then make a reconsideration decision within a set time limit: 30 days for a decision regarding coverage of a service you want to have performed; 60 days regarding payment for a service you've already had.

If the plan does not provide the coverage you want after this initial reconsideration, your next step is to appeal to an independent review entity (IRE), that does not work for the plan insurance company. At this point, your appeal will follow the same procedures as if you were in traditional Medicare, as explained in Chapter 13.

Other Plan Features

In addition to the key features of Medicare Advantage plans, many plans offer a variety of other features beyond basic Medicare coverage. The following extra benefits are either minor services some plans provide or major medical expenses for which some plans pay a small portion. If you are likely to use any of these benefits, a plan that offers them may be more attractive to you.

Short-Term Custodial Care

Following an injury, surgery, or a serious illness, you may not be strong enough to take care of yourself, but may not require skilled nursing care. Instead, you might need custodial care—help with dressing, bathing, eating, and other regular activities of daily living.

Custodial care is not covered at all by Medicare, unless you are already receiving skilled nursing care or therapy. But some Medicare Advantage plans do offer coverage for short-term custodial care, either at home from a certified home health care agency or in a certified nursing facility.

Such plans usually limit the number of home care visits or days you can spend in a nursing facility and charge copayments as well as a separate premium for the coverage. Despite these limitations, this can be valuable added coverage, because almost every senior can use this kind of care at some point.

Medical Equipment

By way of reminder, Medicare pays 80% of the amount it approves for most doctor-prescribed medical equipment, such as wheelchairs, hospital beds, ventilators, and prosthetic devices. But the recipient is responsible for 20% of the approved amount, plus anything above that amount if the equipment company does not accept Medicare assignment. Some Medicare Advantage plans pay the full cost of prescribed medical equipment, although it must be purchased or rented from a provider in the plan's network or, if you choose a private fee-for-service plan, from one that accepts the plan's term and payment level.

Chiropractic Care, Acupuncture, and Acupressure

Medicare pays for a very limited amount of chiropractic care and pays nothing at all for acupuncture or acupressure treatment. Some Medicare Advantage plans cover a greater amount of chiropractic care. And a few recognize the value of acupuncture and acupressure and pay for some of the cost.

Treatments must be received from providers in the plan's network or those who accept the plan's terms, and a copayment is almost always charged for each visit. However, if you regularly use one of these treatments and your practitioner happens to be in the plan's network or regularly accepts your fee-for-service plan's terms, this coverage can be a good money saver.

Foreign Travel Coverage

Many people travel abroad to visit family; others hope to do some foreign traveling during retirement. Medicare provides no coverage for medical costs incurred outside the United States, nor do most Medicare Advantage plans. But a few Medicare Advantage plans offer coverage for emergency care while abroad. And some also offer free or low-cost immunizations for foreign travel. If you plan on traveling abroad frequently or for long stays, this coverage can be valuable.

Eye Examinations and Glasses

Medicare covers only eye examinations and optometry services that are necessary because of an eye disease or other medical conditions. It does not pay for any part of regular vision testing or for eyeglasses or contact lenses, except after cataract surgery. A number of Medicare Advantage plans offer some kind of bonus vision coverage, although none of them pays the full cost of glasses.

Some plans cover an eye examination every two years and offer a set annual amount—usually $50 to $100—toward prescription lenses. Instead of a set amount, other plans offer discount examinations, lenses, frames, and contacts. The managed care plans include only network optometrists; they often simply hook you up to an existing chain of optometry clinics and provide you with a discount.

Hearing Tests and Hearing Aids

Some Medicare Advantage plans offer a free regular hearing exam, plus discounts on hearing aids. As with other Medicare Advantage coverage, the care must be obtained from a hearing center that is connected to the plan's network or that accepts the plan's terms and payment amounts.

Dental Work

A few Medicare Advantage plans offer discounts on dental work. The discounts usually include a low copayment for cleaning and examination and up to a 35% reduction in the cost of other services. The networks of dentists are usually quite limited, however. Finding a dentist who participates in the plan, and with whom you are comfortable, is the key to making this extra coverage worthwhile.

After-Hours Advice and Treatment

People don't always become ill during regular office hours. But visiting an emergency room can be a miserable—and often unnecessary—experience. Some Medicare Advantage managed care plans maintain 24-hour phone lines staffed by experienced nurses who can help you stay out of the ER. Other plans—usually provider-sponsored organizations or individual groups of doctors within larger HMOs—maintain evening and weekend clinics. There, you can consult a doctor for a lower copayment and less stress than a visit to an emergency room.

Chronic Disease Management and Wellness Programs

The managed care industry does better than original Medicare in recognizing how much money it saves by monitoring and managing chronic conditions and offering programs to improve general health. As a result, many managed care plans offer free or low-cost educational and monitoring programs to help people with chronic illness keep their conditions under control. Some programs include blood pressure and cholesterol education for heart patients, diabetic classes to control blood sugar levels, and classes for Parkinson's patients to reduce their risk of falls. Some plans offer programs to help people lead healthier lives, such as nutrition and exercise programs to improve flexibility and cardiac health, to help lose weight, and to quit smoking.

Comparing Medigap and Medicare Advantage Plans

After you've found several medigap (see Chapter 14) and Medicare Advantage plans that seem to fit your needs and budget, the best way to compare them is to view their costs and coverage side by side. Refer to the "Comparing Medigap to Managed Care" chart below for a comparison of the major benefits of medigap and Medicare Advantage plans. Then, use the next chart to help you compare the actual plans you are considering.

Your Rights When Joining, Leaving, or Losing a Medicare Advantage Plan

Insurance companies offering Medicare Advantage plans are free to charge whatever they want in premiums and copayments. They alone decide what types of medical care to cover, although they must provide at least the same basic services that Medicare does. Moreover, they may offer a Medicare Advantage plan one year and withdraw it the next—leaving its beneficiaries without coverage. Some Medicare Advantage plans do this region by region around the nation, deciding which spots are profitable enough for them and dropping plans—and the people in them—in places that don't measure up.

Despite this general corporate freedom for Medicare Advantage insurance companies, they must follow a few rules concerning people's rights to join or to leave their plans.

Joining When First Eligible for Medicare at Age 65

When you approach age 65, you have an initial seven-month window in which to sign up for a Medicare Advantage plan (if you are otherwise eligible for Medicare and you sign up for Parts A and B). This seven-month period begins three months before the month you turn 65 and ends three months after the month in which you turn 65. During this period, you may join any Medicare Advantage plan that operates in the county of your primary residence. The plan must

Comparing Medigap to Managed Care

	Medigap Plans	Managed Care Plans
Choice of Doctor and Providers	As long as doctor or other provider accepts Medicare, a medigap policy will cover whatever Medicare does.	Choice restricted to doctors and providers in the network. PPO and some HMO options allow nonnetwork providers at higher cost. Fee-for-service plans cover care only from providers who accept a plan's terms.
Access to Specialists	As long as specialist accepts Medicare, a medigap policy will cover whatever Medicare does.	Must get referral from primary care doctor to specialist also in plan's network. Limited direct access available for some serious conditions. In fee-for-service plans, specialist must accept plan's terms.
Premiums	Varies widely, with higher cost for plans with more services. Plan A: $50–$400/month. Plans B–G: $100–$400/month. Plans H–J: $75–$500/month ($150–$500/month for continuing plans with drug coverage). Plan K: $50–$150/month. Plan L: $75–$200/month.	Usually no or low premium for basic HMO that only provides coverage equal to traditional Medicare Part A and Part B. Member must pay Medicare Part B premium. Broader coverage or more provider choices may cost between $25–$200/month.
Copayments	No copayments for services except under Plan N policies, which charge a $20 copayment for each doctor's office visit and $50 for each emergency room visit.	Require copayment for most services, generally $5–$25 per visit. In fee-for-service plans, may be responsible for up to 15% more than what plan pays.
Treatment Approval	Automatic if service is covered by Medicare.	Coverage denied if plan decides that treatment is medically unnecessary (perhaps if a different, cheaper treatment is available) or experimental.
Geographic Mobility	Most plans may be used wherever you obtain Medicare-covered services in the United States.	With managed care plans, non-emergency coverage limited to specific geographical area. Some plans offer care away from home. All plans must cover emergency care anywhere in the U.S.

Comparing Medigap to Managed Care (continued)

	Medigap Plans	Managed Care Plans
Emergency Care Overseas	Covered by Plans C–J, M, and N.	Some plans cover, but may charge a higher premium.
At-Home Recovery	Covered by Plans D, G, I, and J, but only if also receiving skilled nursing care at home (only if issued before June 1, 2010).	Some plans cover, but for a higher premium and copayment.
Eye Exams and Glasses	No, unless connected to illness or injury.	Most offer limited discounts on exams and lenses.
Hearing Exams and Aids	No, unless connected to illness or injury.	Most offer discounts on exams and hearing aids.
Dental Discounts	No.	Some offer discounts.
Wellness Programs	No.	Many offer a variety of low-cost or free wellness programs, including heart-healthy education, weight loss, quitting smoking, and cholesterol management.
Chiropractic Care	Only if covered by Medicare.	Some offer broader coverage than Medicare.
Prescription Drugs	No coverage (except for some people who had a Plan H, I, or J prior to January 1, 2006 and who keep that plan). Requires purchase of a separate stand-alone Medicare prescription drug plan. Must add the premium cost of the Medicare drug plan to the cost of the medigap policy when comparing costs with a managed care plan. Must also compare the drug copayments of the drug plan against the copayments of the managed care plan.	Some plans offer coverage, with copayments of $0–$25 per prescription. Amount of copay depends on whether you use generic or brand-name medication and your specific plan's formulary list (which may have separate copayment levels for different medications).

Comparing Medigap Policies and Managed Care Plans

		Plan Name	Plan Name	Plan Name	Plan Name	Plan Name
Cost (monthly premium)						
Copayments (amount I must pay per visit)						
Other Medicare gaps left unfilled						
Is there coverage outside the plan?	Yes					
	No					
Cost of care outside the plan						
Dental care covered	Yes					
	No					
Choice of dentists	Yes					
	No					
Short-term custodial care	Yes					
	No					
Eyeglasses	Copayments					
	Visits per year					
Other services:						
Hearing exam	Yes					
	No					
Chiropractic	Yes					
	No					
Foreign travel	Yes					
	No					
Exercise program	Yes					
	No					
Other	Yes					
	No					
Prescription drug coverage (compare Part D drug plans and managed care plans)	Copayments					
	Annual limit					

accept you, on the same terms and conditions as anyone else of your age, without any medical screening and regardless of your medical history or physical condition (unless you have ESRD and are not already getting health benefits through the same organization that offers the Medicare Advantage plan you want to join). If you don't sign up during this initial period, you may join later during a plan's open enrollment period (see below).

Joining During a Plan's Open Enrollment Period

Every Medicare Advantage plan must have at least one month every year of what is called "open enrollment"—meaning that during that time anyone eligible for Medicare may join the plan regardless of their medical history or condition. Open enrollment is October 15 to December 7 each year, with coverage to begin the following January 1. But some plans also have more open enrollment during other months of the year.

Leaving a Medicare Advantage Plan

When you can leave an Advantage plan depends on how long you ago you joined. If you first join a Medicare Advantage plan during your Initial Enrollment Period, you can drop the plan anytime during the first 12 months. But you can only switch to a new Medicare Advantage plan during an Open Enrollment Period, which runs October 15 to December 7 each year (except for five-star plans, which you can switch to at any time).

In later years (or in your first year if you joined an Advantage plan during a general Enrollment or Special Enrollment period), you can switch back to traditional Medicare only during the Medicare Advantage Disenrollment Period that runs from January 1 to February 14 each year. If you want to switch from one Medicare Advantage plan to another, you can do so only during the Open Enrollment Period, which runs October 15 to December 7 each year. (Once you select a new plan to enroll in, you'll be automatically disenrolled from your old plan when your new plan begins.) But again, you can switch to a five-star rated plan anytime (once per year).

Joining When Dropped From Another Medicare Advantage Plan

If you have been enrolled in a Medicare Advantage plan and that plan notifies you—by October 1—that at the end of the year it is dropping the plan in the county where you live, you have several options. You may return to original Medicare Part A and Part B coverage, and you are guaranteed the right to supplement that coverage by purchasing one of several medigap insurance policies. (See "Finding the Best Medicare Supplement" in Chapter 14 for a discussion of choosing a medigap policy.)

Or, you may enroll in any other Medicare Advantage plan being sold in your county, if the plan has not reached its membership limit for the year. You have this right to join a new Medicare Advantage plan during a special enrollment period from December 8 through the last day of February.

Joining When Moving to a New Geographic Area

Each Medicare Advantage plan serves only a specific geographic area, often a single county. If you move from the plan's service area, you lose the right to continued coverage with that Medicare Advantage plan.

If you move out of a plan's service area and want a Medicare Advantage plan, you must apply to a plan that serves your new community. If you notify your current plan before you actually move, you have the right to enroll in a new plan (that operates in your new area) beginning the month before the month during which you move, and continuing for two full months after you move. If you don't notify your existing plan until after you move, you have a right to switch plans beginning the month you notify your plan, plus two more full months thereafter. You also have the right to join a new Medicare Advantage plan (one that operates in your new area) during that plan's open enrollment period, which runs from October 15 through December 7, and sometimes longer, each year. ●

Medicaid and State Supplements to Medicare

When all types of medical expenses for older Americans are added up, Medicare pays for only about half of them. This leaves most people with considerable worry about how they will cover the rest. One approach is to buy private Medicare supplement insurance; another is to enroll in a Medicare Advantage plan. But many people cannot afford such insurance or health plans. For a number of low-income people, fortunately, there are some alternatives.

If you have a low income and few assets other than your home, you may qualify for assistance from your state's Medicaid program. Medicaid pays not only Medicare premiums, deductibles, and copayments, it also covers some services Medicare does not.

If you have too high an income or too many assets to be eligible for Medicaid, you may still qualify for one of several Medicaid-administered programs to help you meet medical costs: Qualified Medicare Beneficiary (QMB), Specified Low-Income Medicare Beneficiary (SLMB), or Qualifying Individual (QI). (For a discussion of these programs, see "Other State Assistance," below.)

Medicaid Defined

Medicaid's purpose is to help pay medical costs for financially needy people. The program was established by the federal government and is administered by the individual states. Medicaid operates in addition to Medicare to pay for some of the medical costs Medicare doesn't cover.

The basic difference between Medicare and Medicaid is simple: Medicare is available to most everyone age 65 or older, regardless of income or assets, while Medicaid is available to people over 65 or disabled, and to families with minor children, and in some states, to individuals of any age, who are financially needy. Just how "needy" you must be in order to get Medicaid is up to the state in which you live.

There are currently more than 30 million adults who receive some form of Medicaid assistance; about one-fourth of them are also on Medicare. (For a fuller comparison of the programs, see "Medicare: The Basics" in Chapter 12.)

There are federal guidelines for Medicaid, but they are fairly broad. Each state is permitted to make its own rules regarding eligibility, coverage, and benefits. This chapter explains the basic eligibility and coverage rules of Medicaid, and indicates where eligibility standards may be higher or lower than the basic levels.

Who Is Eligible

Generally, states use one of two ways to determine who is eligible for Medicaid. One way is to base eligibility on income and assets alone ("categorically needy"). The other is to base eligibility on income and assets plus medical costs ("medically needy").

Medicaid Eligibility Expanded to People Under 65 in Some States

Under Medicaid rules that have been in effect since the program's beginnings, eligibility has been limited to people age 65 or older, disabled, or with minor children, if they also met the financial standards discussed in the following sections. However, under the health care reform law passed in 2010, individual states may expand Medicaid eligibility to financially needy people of any age. Under a Supreme Court ruling upholding the law, states were given the option to expand the age of eligibility or not. As of early 2014, about half of the states had decided to expand Medicaid under the Affordable Care Act.

Categorically Needy

To qualify for Medicaid as categorically needy, your income and assets must be at or below certain dollar amounts Some states use the same income and asset limits set by the federal Supplemental Security Income, or SSI, program. Other states establish their own Medicaid limits.

430 | SOCIAL SECURITY, MEDICARE & GOVERNMENT PENSIONS

SSI-Based Standards

In most states you can automatically receive Medicaid if you are eligible for SSI assistance. To be eligible for SSI, you can't earn more than about $1,000 to $1,400 per month, or about $1,400 to $2,200 for a couple, depending on your state. Also, you can't possess cash and other assets of more than $2,000 for an individual and $3,000 for a couple.

Fortunately, a number of important assets are not counted in the SSI eligibility calculation. You may own your own home of any value; a car in some states only up to a certain market value; engagement and wedding rings; household goods; life insurance; and a burial fund. (For details of SSI eligibility rules, see Chapter 7.)

State Standards

States have gone in all directions when establishing their own Medicaid standards. In a few states, the standards are slightly less difficult to meet than SSI standards. In some others, the standards are stricter, including a dollar limit on the value of your home and lower limits on the values of your automobile and other property.

To find out your state's standards, contact your local county department of social services or department of welfare. You can also find the basic Medicaid eligibility requirements in your state by visiting the website of your state's Medicaid program. To find that website, go to medicaid.gov, to the "Medicaid" tab, and then click on "By State."

If you are anywhere close to the eligibility limits in your state, consider applying for Medicaid or a state Medicare supplement (described in "Other State Assistance," below) as well.

Medically Needy

What if your income and assets are higher than your state Medicaid limit under categorically needy, but your medical expenses cancel much of this out? You may be what's called "medically needy," and eligible for Medicaid coverage in some states. Medically needy means your income and assets are over the Medicaid eligibility levels for your state but your current or expected medical expenses will reduce your income or assets to eligible levels.

This process of subtracting actual medical bills from income and assets is called "spending down," in Medicaid slang. This is because medical bills would force you to spend your extra money down to the point that you would meet eligibility levels.

The following states offer Medicaid coverage to medically needy people:

Arizona	Minnesota
Arkansas	Montana
California	Nebraska
Connecticut	New Hampshire
District of Columbia	New Jersey
Florida	New York
Georgia	North Carolina
Hawaii	North Dakota
Illinois	Pennsylvania
Iowa	Rhode Island
Kansas	Tennessee
Kentucky	Utah
Louisiana	Vermont
Maine	Virginia
Maryland	Washington
Massachusetts	West Virginia
Michigan	Wisconsin

EXAMPLE: Roberta's income is low, but her savings are $2,000 more than what is allowed to qualify for Medicaid as categorically needy by the rules in her state. However, surgery, home nursing care, physical therapy, and medication have left Roberta with medical bills of almost $3,000 (not paid for by Medicare). Roberta's state offers Medicaid coverage to the medically needy. If she paid her $3,000 medical bills, she would be spending her savings down to a level that would meet the Medicaid standards. Instead of forcing her to spend that money and be reduced to Medicaid savings levels, Roberta qualifies immediately for Medicaid, which will pay the bills.

Medicaid When One Spouse Is in a Nursing Home

The Medicaid rules get a bit tricky when one spouse is in a nursing home while the other spouse remains at home. Most states look only at income in the nursing home resident's name, but some states consider the joint income of both. A monthly allowance is permitted for at-home spouses, who are also allowed to keep their homes and to retain between about $25,000 and $121,000 in other assets, depending on the state. These figures go up periodically, usually on January 1 or July 1 of each year.

However, Medicaid may also place a lien on the home or on other assets in an amount equal to the entire amount Medicaid spends on nursing home care for the spouse. When the at-home spouse dies or sells the house, Medicaid will enforce the lien, taking money that the at-home spouse would otherwise be able to spend or leave to survivors.

To take best advantage of Medicaid coverage for long-term care, it is important to understand these rules and also the alternatives to nursing homes that can serve your needs while preserving as much of your savings as possible.

Long-term care and how it is paid for, including a comprehensive discussion of Medicaid nursing home rules, is covered fully in *Long-Term Care: How to Plan & Pay for It*, by Joseph L. Matthews (Nolo).

TIP
If your income and assets are a little too high for Medicaid, the government may help through other programs. If your income and assets are low but slightly too high for you to be eligible for Medicaid in your state, you may still be eligible for state Qualified Medicare Beneficiary (QMB), Specified Low-Income Medicare Beneficiary (SLMB), or Qualifying Individual (QI) benefits. These programs help meet medical costs not paid for by Medicare. You may also qualify for a low-income subsidy to help pay the costs that come with Medicare Part D prescription drug coverage. (See "Other State Assistance," below, for details.)

Determining Couples' Income and Assets

In determining your eligibility, Medicaid generally considers your income and assets plus those of your spouse, if you live together. If you are divorced or separated and living apart, your spouse's income and assets are not counted, except to the extent that your spouse is actually contributing to your support.

This rule of considering a spouse's income in determining Medicaid eligibility has had the unfortunate effect of keeping many older couples from marrying. They fear that if they marry, a serious illness could bankrupt both of them before they would become eligible for Medicaid assistance.

If both become eligible for Medicare, however, this loss of Medicaid may not be as serious. And if they marry, each becomes eligible at age 62 for Social Security dependents benefits based on the other's work record. If one person has earned considerably higher Social Security or civil service benefits than the other, this ability to get dependents benefits may make a considerable difference. (See Chapter 4 regarding dependents and Chapter 10 regarding civil service benefits.) The same is true of Social Security or civil service survivors benefits. Marriage would allow one spouse to claim these benefits when the other dies, and to collect them for life (see Chapters 5 and 10 for details).

Financial Help From Friends or Family

The income or assets of your children, other relatives, or friends, even if you live with them, are not considered in deciding your Medicaid eligibility. However, if you receive regular financial support from a relative or friend—cash or help with rent—Medicaid can consider that assistance as part of your income.

Also, if you are living rent free with children or other relatives and they give you all of your food and clothing, Medicaid could figure out a dollar amount for that support and count it as part of your income. This does not happen frequently. But it is possible that during the application process, the person reviewing your eligibility could visit your home and determine whether you are receiving substantial, regular income in the form of noncash support.

Medical Costs Covered by Medicaid

Medicaid covers the same kinds of services as Medicare and, in most states, also covers a number of medical services Medicare does not. One of its best features is that it covers most long-term care, both at home and in nursing facilities. This includes not only long-term skilled nursing care, but also nonmedical personal care—such as adult day care and at-home assistance with the activities of daily living (ADLs). These are the very needs that force many people into nursing homes and keep them there for years.

Medicaid also pays many of the amounts Medicare does not pay in hospital and doctor bills. Specifically, this means Medicaid pays:

- the inpatient hospital insurance deductible and coinsurance amounts that Medicare does not pay
- the Medicare Part B medical insurance deductible
- the 20% of the Medicare-approved doctors' fees that Medicare medical insurance does not pay, and
- the monthly premium charged for Medicare Part B medical insurance.

Services Covered in Every State

In every state, Medicaid completely covers certain medical services, paying whatever Medicare does not. It has to do so—it's a matter of federal law.

These services include:

- inpatient hospital or skilled nursing facility care
- nursing home care in approved facilities
- outpatient hospital or clinic treatment
- laboratory and X-ray services
- physicians' services
- home health care, and
- transportation—by ambulance, if necessary—to and from the place you receive medical services.

Most Prescription Drug Coverage Comes From a Separate Drug Plan Under Medicare Part D

For people who are eligible for both Medicare and Medicaid (known as "dual eligibles"), Medicaid does not provide much prescription drug coverage. Instead, a dually eligible person must receive most drug coverage through a Medicare Part D prescription drug plan. This may be with a Medicaid/Medicare managed care plan, or through a separate stand-alone Part D prescription plan.

People who become dually eligible will be automatically signed up for a Part D prescription drug plan. But a dual eligible who does not like the coverage or access to drugs offered by the automatic-enrollment plan may switch plans at any time. Automatic enrollment for dual eligibles and their right to switch plans is explained in the sections that discuss Part D prescription drug coverage in Chapters 12 and 13.

Medicare Part D provides coverage for most categories of drugs but not all. To fill these gaps, many state Medicaid programs cover some of the drugs, both prescription and over the counter, that Medicare Part D plans do not.

Optional Services

In all states, Medicaid also covers many other types of medical services (over 30 types, if you add them up). However, state Medicaid programs are not required to cover these optional services, and in some states they may charge a nominal fee for them. (See "Cost of Medicaid Coverage," below.)

Most states provide the following optional medical services commonly used by older people:

- **Prescription drugs.** All states provide Medicaid coverage for prescription drugs, though there may be a small copayment for each prescription filled. For people eligible for Medicare as well as Medicaid (known as "dual eligibles"), however, Medicaid no longer covers most drugs. Instead, dual eligibles receive their drug coverage through a separate Medicare Part D plan. In some states, though, Medicaid covers the cost of some prescription and over-the-counter drugs for dual eligibles that Medicare Part D plans do not cover.

- **Eye care.** Standard eyesight exams (every one to two years), plus the cost of eyeglasses.
- **Dental care.** Routine dental care, though the list of dentists whom you're allowed to see may be quite limited; most states also cover the cost of dentures.
- **Transportation.** Nonemergency transport to and from medical care, usually with some sort of van service under contract to the county.
- **Physical therapy.** Most states provide some amount of physical therapy beyond the very limited amount covered by Medicare.
- **Prosthetic devices.** All states cover the costs of medically necessary prosthetics beyond what is paid for by Medicare.

The types and amount of coverage for other optional services vary widely from state to state. However, these other optional services often include chiropractic care, podiatry, speech and occupational therapy, private-duty nursing, personal care services, personal care and case management services as part of home care, adult day care, hospice care, various preventive, screening, and rehabilitative services, and inpatient psychiatric care for those 65 and older.

CAUTION

Coverage changes frequently. Medicaid coverage for optional services changes frequently, with states adding some services and dropping others. Check with your local social services or social welfare office for the latest. You must also find out the terms on which such optional services are offered. Sometimes you can obtain such services only if the care is provided by county or other local health clinics, rather than from a private doctor or clinic of your choice.

Medicaid Through Managed Care

People who qualify for both Medicaid and Medicare are known as "dual eligibles." Increasingly, Medicaid and Medicare coverage is offered to dual eligibles through managed care (an HMO or similar plan). In some cases, these managed care plans are optional—a dual eligible can choose to receive traditional Medicare Part A and Part B and enroll in a Medicare Part D prescription drug plan, with Medicaid paying for the Medicare premiums and also providing some additional coverage (which varies from state to state). In many geographic regions, though, dual eligibles who want Medicaid coverage are required to enroll in a Medicaid managed care plan.

These Medicaid managed care plans operate like Medicare Advantage plans, explained in Chapter 15. Their advantage for the patient is that all medical care—inpatient and outpatient, and usually prescription drugs— is handled by a single program, instead of the patient having to negotiate both Medicare and Medicaid, and perhaps a private insurance company for drug coverage. However, these plans require that medical care be received only from certain doctors, hospitals, clinics, and other providers, and they control a patient's ability to see specialists.

Some of these managed care plans for dual eligibles are called "Special Needs Plans" (SNPs). This means that the plan is specially designed for older people, particularly those with chronic conditions. The major difference between an SNP for dual eligibles and other Medicaid managed care plans is that an SNP has what's called a "care coordinator" or "interdisciplinary care team" that helps the patient deal with the several different medical providers that older people often see, and tries to help the patient follow all medical instructions and properly take medications. If you are interested in an SNP for dual eligibles, you may enroll in it at any time of the year.

Each participating Medicaid/Medicare managed care plan for dual eligibles operates differently. Your county department of social services (or other department that administers Medicaid in your state) can explain what Medicaid managed care options are available to you. To help compare such a managed care plan with standard Medicare and Medicaid coverage—if your Medicaid program gives you the choice— contact the SHIP office nearest you for free counseling (see contact information at the end of Chapter 13).

Requirements for Coverage

Even if a particular medical service or treatment—such as a prosthetic device—is generally covered by Medicaid, you must make sure that the care was prescribed by a doctor, administered by a provider who participates in Medicaid, and determined to be medically necessary.

Care Must Be Prescribed by Doctor

The medical service you receive must be prescribed by a doctor. For example, Medicaid will not pay for chiropractic services or physical therapy you seek on your own. And if it pays for certain prescription medications not covered by Medicare, it might not pay for an equivalent medicine you could buy over-the-counter.

For services in which a medical doctor is generally not involved—such as regular eye exams or dental care—Medicaid may place restrictions on how often you can obtain the service and who can authorize it. And Medicaid will cover some services for those who qualify as medically needy only if the care is provided by certain public health hospitals, clinics, or agencies.

Provider Must Be Participating in Medicaid

You must receive your treatment or other care from a doctor, a facility, or another medical provider participating in Medicaid. The provider must accept Medicaid payment—or Medicare plus Medicaid—as full payment. And if you see a nonphysician such as a physical therapist or chiropractor, or are visited by a home care agency, that provider must be approved by Medicaid.

Not all doctors and clinics accept Medicaid patients. You can get referrals from your local social welfare office. And before you sign up with any doctor or other provider, ask whether they accept Medicaid payment.

Treatment Must Be Medically Necessary

All care must be approved by Medicaid as medically necessary. For inpatient care, the approval process is similar to the one used for Medicare coverage. By requesting your admission to a hospital or another facility, your doctor sets the approval process in motion. You won't need to be involved. In fact, you won't even hear about it unless the facility decides you should be discharged before your doctor thinks you should. (See "What to Do If You Are Denied Coverage," below.)

You must get prior approval from a Medicaid consultant before you obtain certain medical services. The rules vary from state to state, requiring prior approval for such services as elective surgery, some major dental care, leasing of medical equipment, and nonemergency inpatient hospital or nursing facility care.

If a particular medical service requires prior Medicaid approval, your doctor or the facility will contact Medicaid directly. You may be asked to get an examination by another doctor before Medicaid will approve the care, but this does not happen often.

If you have questions about the approval process, discuss it with both your doctor and a Medicaid worker at your local social service or welfare office. Ask what Medicaid considers most important in making the decision about the medical care you are seeking. Relay that information to your doctor, so that the doctor can provide the necessary information to Medicaid.

Cost of Medicaid Coverage

Almost all Medicaid-covered care is free. And Medicaid also pays your Medicare premium, deductibles, and copayments if you are a dual eligible. However, there are a few circumstances in which you might have to pay small amounts for Medicaid-covered care.

No Payments to Medical Providers

Hospitals, doctors, and other medical care providers who accept Medicaid patients must accept Medicare's approved charges—or the amount approved directly by Medicaid if it is not covered by Medicare—as the total allowable charges. They must accept as payment in full the combination of payments from Medicare and Medicaid, or Medicaid alone; they cannot bill you for the 15% more than the Medicare-approved amount (which they could do if you were not on Medicaid).

Fees to State Medicaid Agency for Services

Federal law permits states to charge some small fees to people who qualify for Medicaid as medically needy. (See "Who Is Eligible," above, for the definition.) If you qualify as categorically needy, however, states can charge you a fee only for optional covered services. (See "Optional Services," above, for a description of these services.) State Medicaid charges will take one of three forms: an enrollment fee, a monthly premium, or copayments.

Enrollment Fee

Some states charge a small, one-time-only fee when medically needy people first enroll in Medicaid. This fee cannot be charged to people who are considered categorically needy.

Monthly Premium

States are permitted to charge a small monthly fee to people who qualify for Medicaid as medically needy. The premium may be charged whether or not Medicaid services are actually used that month. The amounts vary with income and assets, but usually come to no more than a few dollars.

Copayments

State Medicaid programs are permitted to charge a copayment for each Medicaid-covered service you receive. A copayment can be charged to the medically needy for any service, and to the categorically needy for optional services only. (See "Optional Services," above, for a description of these services.)

Medicaid and Private Health Insurance

Insurance companies are not permitted to sell you a medigap insurance policy if you are on Medicaid. However, you are permitted to have other private health insurance—such as that provided by a retirement program or a policy you purchase to protect against a specific illness—and still qualify for Medicaid.

Medicaid will deduct the amount of your private health insurance premiums from the calculation of your income when determining whether you are under the allowable income levels to qualify.

However, if you do have private health insurance, and a medical service is covered by both your insurance and by Medicaid, Medicaid will pay only the amount your insurance doesn't. If you receive a payment directly from your insurance company after Medicaid has paid that bill, you must return that insurance money to Medicaid.

Other State Assistance

Many people with low income and assets have trouble paying the portion of medical bills left unpaid by Medicare and cannot afford private medigap insurance, but do not qualify for Medicaid. If this is your situation, you may still get help paying Medicare premiums and portions of Medicare-covered costs that Medicare does not pay.

Three cost-reduction programs—called Qualified Medicare Beneficiary (QMB), Specified Low-Income Medicare Beneficiary (SLMB), and Qualifying Individual (QI)—are administered by each state's Medicaid program. They do not offer the extensive coverage beyond Medicare that Medicaid does, but the savings to you in Medicare-related medical costs can be substantial

You Also Qualify for Medicare Part D Prescription Drug Program Extra Help

If you qualify for any of the state assistance programs described in this section, you also qualify for a low-income subsidy called Extra Help to help pay the personal out-of-pocket costs that come with Medicare's Part D prescription drug coverage. The Medicare Part D program and Extra Help are explained in Chapter 12. You can apply for the Part D low-income subsidy when you apply for other state assistance programs (discussed below).

Qualified Medicare Beneficiary (QMB)

If you are eligible for Medicare and meet the income and asset eligibility requirements for the QMB program, your state will pay all of your Medicare Part A and Part B premiums, deductibles, and coinsurance. Depending on how much you use Medicare-covered services in a year, this could mean a savings of up to several thousand dollars.

Income Limits

To be eligible as a QMB, your income must be no more than slightly above the Federal Poverty Guidelines (FPG). This figure is established each year by the federal government; in 2018, the income level is about $12,000 per year for an individual; about $16,000 per year for a married couple. These figures are slightly higher in Alaska and Hawaii. Some states, however, allow residents to have higher income and still qualify as QMBs.

It's important to know, however, that certain amounts of income are not counted in determining QMB eligibility. Particularly if you are still working and most of your income comes from your earnings, you may be able to qualify as a QMB even if your total income is almost twice the FPG. QMB follows the SSI guidelines for countable income, described in Chapter 7. If, after applying these rules, the figure you arrive at is anywhere close to the QMB qualifying limits, it is worth applying for it.

Asset Limits

There is a limit on the value of the assets you can own and still qualify as a QMB—generally, no more than about $8,000 for an individual and about $12,000 for a married couple. However, many assets, such as your house, your car, and certain personal and household goods, are not part of the resources that are counted. (See "Who Is Eligible" in Chapter 7 for how SSI counts assets.)

Specified Low-Income Medicare Beneficiary (SLMB) and Qualifying Individual (QI)

If your income is slightly too high for you to qualify for QMB benefits, you may still be eligible for one of two other state medical assistance programs: Specified Low-Income Medicare Beneficiary (SLMB) or Qualifying Individual (QI). The resource limits for eligibility are the same as for a QMB, but the income limits are 20% to 80% higher, depending on the program.

If your counted monthly income—after the same adjustments made in calculating income for SSI purposes (see Chapter 7 for these calculations)—is under $1,500 for an individual, or $2,000 for a couple, you are likely to qualify for SLMB or QI support. (These figures go up slightly each year.)

Because the SLMB and QI programs are for people with higher incomes, they have fewer benefits than the QMB program. The SLMB and QI programs pay all or part of the Medicare Part B monthly premium, but do not pay any Medicare deductibles or coinsurance amounts. Nonetheless, this means potential savings of more than $500 per year.

Applying for Medicaid, QMB, SLMB, or QI

Before you can get coverage by the Medicaid, QMB, SLMB, or QI programs, you must file a written application separate from your Medicare application. An application for Medicaid also serves as an application for QMB, SLMB, or QI. If you are found ineligible for one program, you may still be found eligible for one of the others.

This section explains some of the things you will need to do and documents you will need to gather to file an application for Medicaid, QMB, SLMB, or QI.

Where to File

To qualify for Medicaid or the QMB, SLMB, or QI programs, you must file a written application with the agency that handles Medicaid in your state—usually your county's department of social services or social welfare department.

In many states, if you are applying for SSI benefits at your local Social Security office, that application will also serve as a Medicaid application. You will be notified of Medicaid eligibility at the same time as you receive notice regarding SSI. (See Chapter 7 for a full discussion of the SSI program.)

If you or your spouse is hospitalized when you apply for Medicaid, ask to see a medical social worker in the hospital. He or she will help you fill out the application.

Required Documents and Other Information

Because eligibility for Medicaid and the QMB, SLMB, or QI programs depends on your financial situation, many of the documents you must bring to the Medicaid office are those that will verify your income and assets.

Although a Medicaid eligibility worker might require additional specific information from you, you will at least be able to get the application process started if you bring:

- pay stubs, income tax returns, Social Security benefits information, and other evidence of your current income
- papers showing all your savings and other financial assets, such as bankbooks, insurance policies, and stock certificates
- automobile registration papers if you own a car
- your Social Security card or number
- information about your spouse's income and separate assets, if the two of you live together, and

- medical bills from the previous three months, as well as medical records or reports to confirm any medical condition that will require treatment in the near future. If you don't have copies of these bills, records, or reports, bring the names and addresses of the doctors, hospitals, or other medical providers who are treating you.

Even if you don't have all these papers, go to your local social services or social welfare department office and file your application for Medicaid as soon as you think you may qualify. The Medicaid eligibility workers will tell you what other documents you need—and sometimes can explain how to get necessary papers you don't have, or help get them for you.

Application Procedure

A Medicaid eligibility worker—or an SSI eligibility worker if you apply for SSI at a local Social Security office—will interview you and assist you in filling out your application. There may be lots of forms to fill out, and you may have to return to the office for several different interviews.

> **TIP**
>
> **Don't get discouraged.** Delays, repeated forms, and interviews do not mean you will not be approved. The state has created procedures that make it difficult for people to get through the qualification process, driving some people to give up on benefits to which they are entitled. Patience is not only a virtue, it is an absolute necessity.

Normally, you will receive a decision on your Medicaid application within a couple of weeks after you complete the forms and provide the necessary information. The law requires that a decision be made within 45 days. If you don't hear from Medicaid within a month after you apply, call the eligibility worker who interviewed you. Sometimes it takes a little polite pushing to get a decision out of an overworked social services agency.

Retroactive Benefits

If you are found to be eligible and have already incurred medical bills, Medicaid may cover some of them. This retroactive eligibility can go back to the beginning of the third month before the date you filed your application. Make sure to show your Medicaid eligibility worker any medical bills you have from this period.

If you are denied eligibility for Medicaid, QMB, SLMB, or QI, you have a right to appeal.

Review of Eligibility

How long your Medicaid coverage will last depends on your finances and your medical costs. Medicaid eligibility is reviewed periodically, usually every six months and at least once a year.

If, upon review, the Medicaid agency finds that your financial situation has changed to put you over the eligibility limits for your state's Medicaid program, your coverage may be discontinued. Until then, you will be continued on Medicaid or QMB, SLMB, or QI coverage, even if your income or assets put you over the limits some months before.

Likewise, if you became eligible for Medicaid as medically needy because of high medical costs, but those medical costs have ended, you may be dropped from Medicaid when your review is completed. Until the review, however, you will remain on Medicaid regardless.

If new medical costs arise after your coverage has been ended, you may apply again for Medicaid coverage.

What to Do If You Are Denied Coverage

If you are denied Medicaid, QMB, SLMB, or QI coverage for which you believe you are eligible, go immediately to the office where you applied. Ask about the procedure in your state for getting a hearing to appeal that decision. In some states, if you request a hearing in writing within ten days after receiving the notice saying that your coverage is going to end, your coverage can stay in effect until after the hearing officer makes a decision.

At an appeal hearing, you will be able to present any documents or other papers—proof of income, assets, medical bills—that you think support your claim. You will also be allowed to explain why the Medicaid decision was wrong. If expected medical bills, which you claim will qualify you as medically needy, are the main question concerning your eligibility, then a letter from your doctor explaining your condition and the expected cost of treatment would be important.

The hearing itself is usually held at or near the welfare or social service office. You are permitted to have a friend, relative, social worker, or lawyer, or another representative appear with you to help at the hearing.

Getting Assistance With Your Appeal

If you are denied Medicaid, QMB, SLMB, or QI, you may want to consult with someone experienced in the subject to help you prepare your appeal. The best place to find quality free assistance with these matters is the nearest office of the State Health Insurance Assistance Program (SHIP) (see the end of Chapter 13 for contact information).

If there is no SHIP office near you, you may be able to find other assistance through your local senior center or by calling the senior information line listed in the white pages of your telephone directory.

You can also hire a Medicaid lawyer or health care lawyer to help.

Although the exact procedure for obtaining this hearing, and the hearing itself, may be slightly different from state to state, they all resemble very closely the hearings given to applicants for Social Security benefits (covered in Chapter 9).

You should be notified of the decision on your appeal within 90 days after the hearing.

For more information, see Nolo's series of articles on Medicaid appeals at www.nolo.com/legal-encyclopedia/medicaid-law.

Index

SOCIAL SECURITY, MEDICARE & GOVERNMENT PENSIONS

Discrimination, disability-based, 53

Divorce

name changes due to, 18

Social Security dependents benefits eligibility and, 79–80, 112

Social Security disability benefits eligibility and, 55

Social Security planning for divorced people, 111–113

Social Security survivors benefits eligibility and, 93, 96, 112

veterans survivors benefits and, 215

See also Remarriage

Doctors

choice of providers, Medicare Advantage and medigap plans, 398, 400, 401–404, 407, 408, 409–411, 421

discussing HMOs with, 402–403

doctor-prescribed care rule (Medicare Part A), 238

and federal employee disability claims, 200, 201

home health care plans, 248

Medicaid acceptance and payments, 438, 440

Medicare acceptance, 235

Medicare assignment basics, 275, 328–331

and Medicare facility review panels, 240–241

and Medicare Part A appeals, 336–342

and Medicare Part B appeals, 344–347

Medicare Part D exception requests, 299, 300, 357–358

online Medicare doctor directory, 276

Peer Review Organizations (PROs), 241, 336–340

second opinions, 260

skilled nursing need certifications, 243, 248

and Social Security disability claims, 144, 145, 146–147, 159

specialist access, 403–404, 412–413, 421

terminal illness certifications/evaluations (hospice care coverage), 250, 257

See also Assignment; Doctors' bills

Doctors' bills

allowed excess charges if doctor does not accept assignment (Medicare), 230, 273, 274–275, 332–333, 379–380, 381, 382, 440

checking and correcting, 329

if you are overcharged, 333

Medicaid coverage, 230, 434

Medicare billing and payments, 230, 328–332

Medicare coverage basics, 230, 260, 271

medigap coverage basics, 373, 374, 375

paying your share of excess charges (Medicare), 332–333

See also Medicare Part B

Domestic workers, 20–21, 22

Doughnut hole (Medicare Part D coverage gap), 283

basics, 281, 287, 288–290

Extra Help program beneficiaries, 285, 287

nonformulary drugs and, 288, 299

plans offering coverage within, 281, 284, 308–309

reducing your costs, 290–296, 308–309

Dread disease insurance policies, 395

H

Health care benefits. *See* Medicaid; Medical benefits; Medicare *entries*; Medicare supplements; Private health insurance

Health Care Provider Directory (Medicare), 276

Health care reform. *See* Affordable Care Act

Health Insurance Counseling and Advocacy Program (HICAP), 294, 305–306, 335. *See also* SHIP

Health insurance exchanges, 233

Health insurance, individual/private. *See* Private health insurance

Health savings accounts (HSAs), 319

Hearings
    Medicaid and other state program denials, 446–447
    Medicare appeals, 342–343, 346, 351, 360
    Social Security appeals, 154, 155–156, 163–170, 172–173, 175

Hearing tests and hearing aids, 270, 418–419, 422

Hematological disorders, 405

HICAP (Health Insurance Counseling and Advocacy Program), 294, 305–306, 335. *See also* SHIP

Higher-income people
    Medicare Part B premium amounts, 259
    Social Security benefits and, 13

HIV/AIDS, 405

HMOs
    long-term care and, 371
    Medicare Advantage plans through, 402–404, 410

Medicare billing and enrollment paperwork, 326
    See also Managed care plans; Medicare Advantage plans

Home health care
    at-home recovery benefits, 370, 379, 381, 422
    ESRD patients, 310, 313
    hospice care, 249–250, 257–258
    if your condition does not improve, 248
    long-term care, 371
    Medicaid coverage, 434, 436
    Medicare Advantage plans, 417, 422
    Medicare billing and payments, 327–328
    Medicare coverage gaps, 369
    Medicare Part A coverage, 240, 246–248, 257, 272
    Medicare Part B coverage, 246, 264, 272, 273
    medigap coverage, 370, 379, 381, 422
    short-term custodial care, 240, 417

Home health care agencies, Medicare approval requirement, 240, 247, 264

Homeopathic care, 268

Hospice care
    Medicaid coverage, 436
    Medicare coverage, 249–250, 257–258
    medigap coverage, 370, 375, 376, 377, 378, 379, 380, 382

Hospital insurance and care
    "held for observation" care, 239, 243
    hospital outpatient services and charges, 260, 272, 274, 276–277
    inpatient care required before skilled nursing facility coverage begins, 242–243

eligibility, 71, 229, 429–433, 441

getting help, 430, 437, 447

long-term care coverage, 432, 434

managed care programs, 227, 229, 437

Medicare assignment requirement, 275

medigap insurance and, 441

optional coverage, 435–436, 440

prescription drug coverage basics, 435–436

private health insurance and, 441

protecting assets from, 71, 432

Social Security disability and, 70–71

SSI and, 118, 121, 127, 430, 444

statistics, 428

vs. Medicare, 228–230

See also Dual Medicaid/Medicare eligibles

Medi-Cal, 127. *See also* Medicaid

Medical benefits

if you retire before age 65, 232–233

veterans/military personnel, 217, 218–220, 221, 282, 291

See also Medicaid; Medicare Advantage plans; Medicare *entries*; Medigap insurance

Medical equipment and supplies

ESRD patients, 313

Medicare Advantage plan coverage, 417

Medicare Part A coverage, 244, 245, 247, 257, 272

Medicare Part B coverage, 262, 272

online supplier directory, 262, 276–277

prosthetic devices, 436

Medical examinations

federal employee disability claims, 201

initial exam after Medicare enrollment, 226, 265

Social Security disability claims, 144, 146–147, 160

See also Medical underwriting; Preventive care and screenings

Medical insurance. *See* Medicare Advantage plans; Medicare Part B; Outpatient care

Medically necessary standard

Medicaid, 439

Medicare Advantage plan decisions, 404, 416, 421

Medicare Part A, 238–239

Medicare Part B, 267, 268, 344

Medicare Part D exceptions, 299, 356–358

Medically needy eligibility (Medicaid), 430–431, 440–441, 446

Medical records

Medicare disputes and, 337, 338, 344–347, 350, 351, 357

medigap applications and, 370

Social Security disability claims, 57, 73

veterans' disability benefits, 210, 221

Medical social services, Medicare coverage, 247, 249

Medical tests. *See* Laboratory tests and services; Preventive care and screenings

Medical transportation, 261, 434, 436

Medical underwriting, 370, 386, 389, 390

Medicare, 223–364

alternatives for early retirees, 232–233

basics, 225–228, 231

compared to Medicaid, 228–230

coverage basics, 225, 230

dependent spouses' eligibility, 6, 83, 237

disability-based enrollment, 70, 75, 233, 237, 322

P

PAD (peripheral artery disease), 263–264

Parents

dependent, survivors benefits for, 95, 99, 138

See also Children; Social Security dependents benefits

PARS (Public Agency Retirement Systems), 19

Partial hospitalization (day care treatment), 267, 434, 436

Past-due benefits (Social Security), 178. *See also* Retroactive benefits

Payment of benefits

Social Security/SSI, 137, 149–150, 151–152

See also Medicare billing and payments

PDPs, 278, 305. *See also* Medicare Part D

Peace Corps service, 186

Peer Review Organizations (PROs), 241, 336–340

Pension benefits

foreign pensions, 28, 42–43

military personnel/veterans, 186, 189, 208, 214, 216–217

private, 3, 4, 6, 46, 89, 104

Social Security benefits offsets for, 42–43, 87–89, 103–104, 184

See also Federal civil service benefits

Peripheral artery disease (PAD), 263–264

Personal care services, 369, 434, 436. *See also* Custodial care

PERS (Public Employees Retirement System), 87

PET scans, 265, 266

Pharmaceutical companies

drug discount programs, 291, 292, 293–296

Medicare negotiation prohibition, 279

Pharmacy restrictions (Medicare Part D), 301–302

Physical therapy

Medicaid coverage, 436

Medicare Part A coverage, 244, 247, 249

Medicare Part B coverage, 263, 267, 273–274

See also Rehabilitation services

PIA (Primary Insurance Amount), 24, 26

Pneumonia vaccinations, 262, 268, 273

Podiatric care, 266, 436

Point-of-service options, HMOs with, 404, 410–411

Political asylees, 120

PPOs (preferred provider organizations), 407, 410–411

Preexisting illness exclusions, medigap policies, 370–371, 386, 390, 394–395

Preferred provider organizations (PPOs), 407, 410–411

Premiums

Medicaid, 440

Medicare Advantage plans, 235, 238, 398, 400, 404, 407, 413, 415, 421

medigap policies, 235, 370, 371, 373, 374, 383–385, 387, 421

for private insurance, Medicaid eligibility and, 441

See also Medicare premiums; *specific Medicare programs*

⚖ NOLO *Online Legal Forms*

Nolo offers a large library of legal solutions and forms, created by Nolo's in-house legal staff. These reliable documents can be prepared in minutes.

Create a Document

- **Incorporation.** Incorporate your business in any state.
- **LLC Formations.** Gain asset protection and pass-through tax status in any state.
- **Wills.** Nolo has helped people make over 2 million wills. Is it time to make or revise yours?
- **Living Trust (avoid probate).** Plan now to save your family the cost, delays, and hassle of probate.
- **Trademark.** Protect the name of your business or product.
- **Provisional Patent.** Preserve your rights under patent law and claim "patent pending" status.

Download a Legal Form

Nolo.com has hundreds of top quality legal forms available for download—bills of sale, promissory notes, nondisclosure agreements, LLC operating agreements, corporate minutes, commercial lease and sublease, motor vehicle bill of sale, consignment agreements and many, many more.

Review Your Documents

Many lawyers in Nolo's consumer-friendly lawyer directory will review Nolo documents for a very reasonable fee. Check their detailed profiles at **Nolo.com/lawyers**.

On Nolo.com you'll also find:

Books & Software

Nolo publishes hundreds of great books and software programs for consumers and business owners. Order a copy, or download an ebook version instantly, at Nolo.com.

Online Legal Documents

You can quickly and easily make a will or living trust, form an LLC or corporation, apply for a trademark or provisional patent, or make hundreds of other forms—online.

Free Legal Information

Thousands of articles answer common questions about everyday legal issues including wills, bankruptcy, small business formation, divorce, patents, employment, and much more.

Plain-English Legal Dictionary

Stumped by jargon? Look it up in America's most up-to-date source for definitions of legal terms, free at nolo.com.

Lawyer Directory

Nolo's consumer-friendly lawyer directory provides in-depth profiles of lawyers all over America. You'll find all the information you need to choose the right lawyer.

SOA23